The Greater Yellowstone Ecosystem

Robert B. Keiter

and Mark S. Boyce,

Editors

with a Foreword by

Luna B. Leopold

Yale University Press

New Haven and London

The Greater Yellowstone Ecosystem

Redefining America's

Wilderness Heritage

To my wife, Linda
Robert B. Keiter

To my children, Cody,
Jonathan, and Aaron
Mark S. Boyce

Designed by Nancy Ovedovitz and set in Times Roman type by Keystone Typesetting. Printed in the United States of America by Vail-Ballou Press, Binghamton, New York.

Library of Congress Cataloging-in-Publication Data

The Greater Yellowstone ecosystem : redefining America's wilderness heritage / edited by Robert B. Keiter and Mark S. Boyce ; with a foreword by Luna B. Leopold.
  p. cm.
Includes bibliographical references and index.
ISBN 0-300-04970-6 (cloth)
    0-300-05927-2 (pbk.)
1. Ecology—Yellowstone National Park Region—Congresses. 2. Environmental policy—Yellowstone National Park Region—Congresses. 3. Wildlife conservation—Yellowstone National Park Region—Congresses. 4. Fire ecology—Yellowstone National Park Region—Congresses. 5. Wildlife reintroduction—Yellowstone National Park Region—Congresses. I. Keiter, Robert B., 1946– . II. Boyce, Mark S.
QH105.w8G75 1991
333.95′09787′52—dc20   91-10623

The paper in this book meets the guidelines for permanence and durability of the Committee on Production Guidelines for Book Longevity of the Council on Library Resources.

10   9   8   7   6   5   4   3

Title page illustration: Woodcut showing first known image of fire in Yellowstone National Park by Thomas Moran, 1871 (from *The Aldine* 6(4):74, April 1873). View is to the east from West Thumb Geyser Basin, with smoke rising from Pumice Point. Fire history reconstruction by Romme and Despain (*BioScience* 39:695–699, 1989) has dated the last Pumice Point fire to 1867 (+/− 3 years). Moran may have seen the fire (though the report of the expedition does not mention it), or he may have seen the recent burn site and added smoke to his landscape for dramatic effect (courtesy of Paul Schullery).

Contents

PART II   FIRE POLICY AND MANAGEMENT

PART III   CONSERVATION BIOLOGY AND WILDLIFE ECOLOGY

Foreword

Words can assume quite different meanings as time passes, as context changes, or even as they are spoken by different people. In the field of resource management, the interpretation of a few key phrases has caused and continues to cause untold havoc in the formulation of policy, in the choices made among competing claims, and in understanding the implications of research results.

The words chosen by Congress to govern competition for water in the western states in the 1897 bill establishing the United States Forest Service illustrate these problems. Forest lands to be administered by the new Service were reserved for two purposes, the growth of timber and the maintenance of "favorable conditions of stream flow." The interpretation of those few words and the scientific information needed to maintain these "favorable conditions" are now being argued in several courts. This litigation will undoubtedly consume a decade or more and may eventually affect the landscape in many palpable ways. At stake is the ability of the U.S. Forest Service to prevent water diversions in the forest from drying up mountain streams.

Another example of such confusion stems from policy statements in the original Wilderness Bill that hamper development of management tools. I well remember receiving a phone call in 1964 from the office of Senator Clinton Anderson of New Mexico. At his office, I was received by his assistant, Luna Diamond, and ushered into an anteroom where there was a small group of conservationists, among them David Brower, Howard Zahnheiser, and Bernard Frank. We went in to the Senator's private office where he gave a short talk, paraphrased below.

Gentlemen, tomorrow we are going to pass a wilderness bill. But I want to tell you that I haven't been able to get everything you and I wanted. I've had to compromise. Probably the most serious shortcoming of the bill is the provision for exploration and mining to continue in designated wilderness areas for some years into the future.

The passage of time has demonstrated that this provision was far less important than feared. The major problem has been the popularity of wilderness with consequent growing pollution, overuse of some camp sites, and other intrusive uses that threaten the very concept of "untrammeled" wilderness.

The Yellowstone ecosystem is similarly beset with various and conflicting interpretations of the roles of diverse agencies, each of which has a major influence on the character and the viability of the regional landscape. There is a fragile consensus that the region, dominated by two national parks (Yellowstone and Grand Teton) and seven national forests (Shoshone, Bridger-Teton, Caribou, Targhee, Beaverhead, Gallatin, and Custer), should be managed as an integral unit at least in some respects. But so different are the basic laws, the history, and the viewpoints among the agencies and among competing interest groups that advances toward coordinated management are indeed slow.

That the basic purposes of national forests and national parks are so different is understandable. But it means that joint management, even of parts of the biota they share (such as big game), is difficult. Moreover, enactment of divergent policies among seven adjacent forests regarding allowable timber cutting, even in the same ecotype, is a situation the public finds difficult to accept. The Forest Service's proclaimed new management policy of "New Perspectives" forestry has been embraced by the Bridger-Teton Forest, but seems to have made little or no impression in several other forests in the area. That same forest, however, has opened 95 percent of its nonwilderness land to oil and gas leasing. How that can jibe with the "New Perspectives" policy is again puzzling. The administrative discretion allowed by law to most resource agencies is generally as wide as a barn door.

The Park Service is finding it difficult to follow the much-cherished recommendation of the Leopold report,* which states unequivocally that "above all other policies, the maintenance of naturalness should prevail." Overly generous agreements with concessionaires and the present unwillingness to curtail the flood of visitors often makes naturalness a rare commodity in Yellowstone and elsewhere in the national parks. And the problem is even worse on park-forest borders, where the two agencies (U.S. Forest Service and National Park Service) often pursue entirely different management policies.

*A. S. Leopold et al., "Study of Wildlife Problems in the National Parks," in *Report of the Special Advisory Board on Wildlife Management for the Secretary of the Interior.* Washington D.C.: Government Printing Office, 1963.

Some of these problems might eventually be mitigated by knowledge gained from research. In fact, the Leopold report made a strong plea for research "which must form the basis for all management programs." Though that report speaks especially of ecological research, I would stress what might be called management-oriented research, which is more closely allied with the social and behavioral sciences than with the biological sciences. An example from such research is the knowledge gained by the decision of the Park Service to allow only "catch and release" fishing on a reach of the Madison River in Yellowstone. To the Service's surprise, fishermen flocked there even though the usual take-home-the-bounty was not permitted. Such management studies and techniques are a form of research especially needed by resource agencies dealing with a diverse public.

Another example is the little-appreciated University of Wyoming–National Park Service Research Center that funds research projects and operates a field station. In 1989, forty-three projects were funded, involving scientists from thirty-one institutions. Ten projects in Yellowstone National Park included seven that dealt with effects of fire. Two projects dealt with a problem of immediate concern and considerable controversy, the relation of ungulate grazing and migration to available forage.

All improvement in understanding the biological and physical processes operating in the ecosystem will over time add to our ability to deal with the complex issues of policy and procedure. But there is, in my opinion, a class of investigation specifically aimed at evaluating alternative practices that should be pursued. Perhaps the Center could define a type of investigation that involves actual experimental comparison of management practices and could call attention to the need for such research.

Moreover, the research carried out by academics under the auspices of the Center does not take the place of an expanded research arm of the Park Service itself. The types of projects funded by a center must perforce be of limited duration, but there is also a need for a commitment to long-term monitoring. This includes following through time biomass production under fenced and under grazed conditions, bank erosion of stream channels, changes in some components of water quality, aggradation-degradation of channel beds, and changes in riparian vegetation, to name a few. It might be advantageous to plan a specific division of research objectives between the Center and the Research Division of the Park Service, the former concentrating on basic research, and the latter on management research and long-term monitoring.

The research arm of the U.S. Forest Service is not an example to follow in the program visualized here. The Forest Service has a large, dispersed, technically qualified staff that is amazingly independent of the operations on the national forests. In fact, the research arm does not deign to work on any immediate and practical problem of forest management and therefore contributes but little to the types of problems discussed in the present volume.

This volume is a much-needed survey of the many problems associated with process-based ecosystem management. The contributors present and discuss such issues as fire policy, the natural regulation hypothesis, wolf reintroduction, and the legal-policy implications of current ecosystem management initiatives. Particularly useful is the final chapter in the volume, written by the editors. I suggest, in fact, that a reader study this chapter as a useful prelude to understanding the many issues covered throughout the book.

LUNA B. LEOPOLD
JANUARY 1991

Preface

In April 1989 the University of Wyoming hosted a symposium on the Greater Yellowstone Ecosystem. More than five hundred people from throughout the United States and Canada gathered in Laramie to examine the ecology and administration of Greater Yellowstone, attesting to the public's enduring fascination with the world's first national park. At the time, the Yellowstone region was awash in controversy. Yellowstone National Park was under intense scrutiny in the aftermath of the 1988 summer fires and the winter wildlife "die-off" that was occurring at that very moment on its northern range. Federal interagency management policy coordination initiatives—unique in the history of the National Park Service and the U.S. Forest Service—were just getting under way and were neither well understood nor accepted. To the consternation of state officials and local ranchers, the Park Service was openly promoting the reintroduction of wolves as part of its natural-process management philosophy. The time was plainly ripe to convene an interdisciplinary gathering to assess Greater Yellowstone's future.

Since then, little has changed in Greater Yellowstone. The Park Service's natural-fire management policy is still under review; whether a natural-burn policy will be reinstituted remains unclear. The Park Service's wildlife management policies are still being attacked by local ranchers who view park wildlife as a threat to their domestic livestock and by critics who contend that herd levels remain unnaturally high and are damaging park vegetation. The federal interagency management initiatives are still being pursued, even though local politicians and industries have harshly criticized a draft proposal calling for an emphasis on the region's natural values. The wolf recovery controversy has now reached the halls of Congress. In the aftermath of a congressionally funded study concluding that wolves would not adversely affect park wildlife, Congress has established a committee to study reintroduction strategies, but wolf reintroduction still faces strident local opposition. These controversies are serving, quite obviously, as harbingers of greater changes in federal land and resource management policy—changes that will have national, and even international, ramifications for park and forest management during the next century.

Indeed, Yellowstone is the symbol of modern society's commitment to preserving the vestiges of its wilderness heritage. But keeping faith with nature while providing for human use and enjoyment presents truly vexing dilemmas for today's land and resource managers. Modern scientific knowledge, which is linked to the emerging discipline of conservation biology and the field of ecology, is expanding our understanding of the complex relationship between native wildlife populations and ecological processes, as well as the techniques and strategies necessary to ensure natural diversity. At the same time, the nation's growing population, which is accustomed to a standard of living based on fossil fuels and wood fiber, is increasing demands on the nation's scarce public lands and natural resources. With more leisure time and money, people are visiting places like Yellowstone in record numbers, but their presence is straining the human carrying capacity of a fragile wilderness environment. They are also demanding more services and amenities, which inevitably means further development and incursions on the natural landscape. Locally, communities that have long depended on extractive industries for their economic sustenance are confronting the likelihood that extensive commodity development activities may no longer be compatible with scenic values, recreational interests, or wildlife habitat requirements.

The challenge, therefore, is how to accommodate humans in this wildland environment and also ensure the ecological integrity to the underlying natural systems. In response to this challenge, federal land and resource management policies are undergoing an extraordinary transition in the Yellowstone region. The major factor influencing this transition is the concept of Greater Yellowstone as an ecosystem or ecological entity subject to vital natural processes that defy conventional political boundaries. Managers will have to devise policies that reflect a comprehensive understanding of Greater Yellowstone's ecological complexities and that also take account of political, economic, and social realities.

This book examines several—but by no means all—of the critical resource policy issues now confronting Greater Yellowstone. We first explore the emerging notion of ecosystem management, analyzing the scientific, legal, and economic dimensions of current management policies as well as recent regional coordination initiatives. We then assess the ecological impacts of the recent fires, as well as the scientific underpinnings and management implications of the natural-burn policy. Next, drawing upon the discipline of conservation biology, we reexamine the longstanding controversies surrounding wildlife management strategies for elk and bison. Finally, we delve into the realm of restoration ecology and explore the question of whether wolves, a natural predator that once roamed throughout the region, should be reintroduced into Yellowstone National Park.

As we suggest in the conclusion, each of these issues is linked to ecosystem dynamics as well as to regional economic concerns, which almost ensures a collision between the compelling logic of modern science and the stubborn force of local tradition. Although modern scientific knowledge is changing the shape of the public debate over Greater Yellowstone's future, it remains unclear exactly how ecosystem management will accommodate ecological imperatives with long-standing human interests. Indeed, the controversies are proving to be a test of strength between preservationists, who are now committed to science as the means for protecting the nation's wilderness heritage, and local development interests, who remain skeptical of any regime that gives nature priority over economic concerns. The resolution of this dilemma will test the depth of our nation's commitment to its wilderness heritage.

We are convinced that important developments are occurring in Greater Yellowstone, and that these developments are changing the way land and resource management agencies approach their trust obligations. We also believe that the topics addressed here reveal the depth and complexity of this change. The Park Service's ecological-process management policy represents one part of this change. The Forest Service's use of ecological considerations in its management planning, as well as its shifting multiple-use priorities, represents another. A perceptible shift in public values— reflecting advances in modern scientific knowledge, yet tempered by local tradition and economic reality—is clearly influencing these developments. In a region as rich and diverse as Greater Yellowstone, neither agency can divorce its resource management policies from the other or from state and local concerns. There simply is no alternative but to collaborate in defining an ecosystem-management ethic. We hope this book will clarify the choices and consequences involved.

ROBERT B. KEITER

MARK S. BOYCE

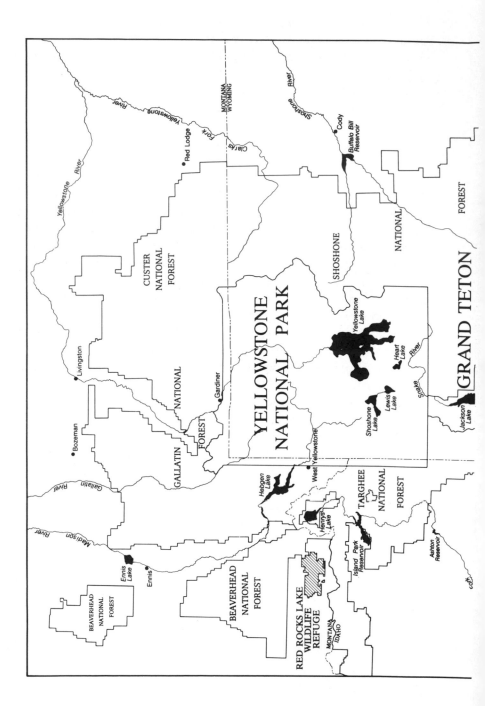

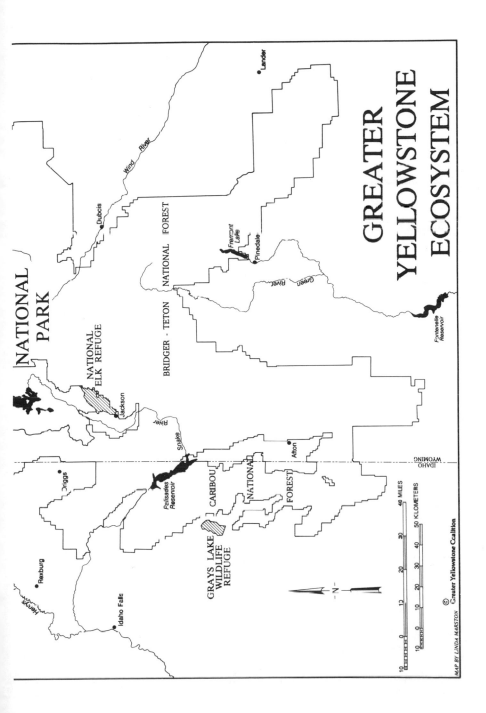

GREATER
YELLOWSTONE
ECOSYSTEM

NATIONAL
PARK

NATIONAL
ELK REFUGE

BRIDGER - TETON   NATIONAL   FOREST

Wind River

Dubois

Lander

Fremont
Lake

Pinedale

Green River

Fontenelle
Reservoir

Jackson

Snake River

Driggs

Rexburg

Idaho Falls

Henrys Fork

Palisades
Reservoir

CARIBOU

NATIONAL

FOREST

GRAYS LAKE
WILDLIFE REFUGE

Atton

IDAHO
WYOMING

N

10   0   10   20   30   40 MILES

10   0   10   20   30   40   50 KILOMETERS

MAP BY LINDA MARSTON   © Greater Yellowstone Coalition

PART I   **THE CHALLENGE OF
            MANAGING THE GREATER
            YELLOWSTONE ECOSYSTEM**

There is yet no ethic dealing with man's relation to land and to the animals and plants which grow upon it. . . . [A] land ethic changes the role of Homo sapiens *from conqueror of the land-community to plain member and citizen of it. It implies respect for his fellow members, and also respect for the community as such. . . . Examine each question in terms of what is ethically and aesthetically right, as well as what is economically expedient. A thing is right when it tends to preserve the integrity, stability, and beauty of the biotic community. It is wrong when it tends otherwise.*

Aldo Leopold, A Sand County Almanac. *Oxford: Oxford University Press, 1949. Reproduced by permission.*

Overleaf: *Northern entrance to Yellowstone National Park, Gardiner, Montana, circa 1900. Photo courtesy of the American Heritage Center, University of Wyoming, Laramie, Wyoming.*

CHAPTER 1   **An Introduction to**
             the Ecosystem
             Management Debate
             Robert B. Keiter

Ever since the year 1872, when Congress desig-
nated Yellowstone National Park as the world's first national park, the
name Yellowstone has been synonymous with lofty idealism and often
heated controversy. And since 1891, when President Benjamin Harrison
established this nation's first national forest reserve adjacent to Yellowstone
National Park, the entire Yellowstone region has been a principal battleground over federal land and resource management policy. Although the
passage of time has more than validated the wisdom of these early designations, debate over how these lands are to be managed has escalated into a
symbolic issue of national and international significance. Indeed, a controversy like the one surrounding the summer 1988 fires illustrates the scientific, philosophical, legal, and economic complexities confronting today's
land managers, who are responsible for maintaining the Yellowstone domain in the face of a growing population with increasingly diverse expectations and values.

At one level, the Yellowstone controversies are focused on the National
Park Service's management policies, particularly its commitment to letting
natural processes prevail on park lands.[1] This conflict is illustrated by the
current debate over the park's policy of permitting natural fires to burn and
its commitment to restoring wolves. At another level, the controversies
involve the appropriate level of development on the public and private
lands surrounding Yellowstone and Grand Teton national parks. In the
national forests, these controversies focus on such issues as wilderness

designation, oil and gas exploration, timber harvesting levels, and live-stock grazing allotments.[2] On the private lands, the controversies involve the level and intensity of development appropriate to the surrounding natural setting.

To regard these issues in isolation or as unrelated matters, however, would be a mistake. Park Service management decisions, whether involving resident wildlife or natural fire, have profound influences on surrounding communities and neighboring landowners. Similarly, the U.S. Forest Service's wilderness designation, mineral leasing, timber harvesting, and grazing policies have significant environmental consequences for wildlife and adjacent park lands, as well as economic repercussions within nearby communities. In fact, almost all of the Yellowstone region lands are ecologically interconnected in complex and dependent relationships, just as the local economies are directly connected to the surrounding public lands and resources. Because the same issues are surfacing across the nation's public domain, the resolution of Yellowstone controversies will have a pronounced influence on how similar problems are addressed elsewhere in the United States and throughout the world. In short, the Greater Yellowstone public lands represent a test case—or paradigm—for redefining mankind's role in wildland areas of ecological importance.

ECOLOGY AND ECONOMICS

The general public tends to regard the Yellowstone region as essentially one large national park, but the regional landownership and management pattern is actually quite complex. The National Park Service and the U.S. Forest Service are the principal landholders in what both agencies now refer to as the Greater Yellowstone Area. According to them, Greater Yellowstone encompasses more than 7.3 million hectares (18 million acres) of public and private lands located in the states of Wyoming, Montana, and Idaho.[3] It includes two national parks (Yellowstone and Grand Teton), portions of six national forests (the Bridger-Teton, Shoshone, Targhee, Gallatin, Custer, and Beaverhead), three national wildlife refuges (National Elk Refuge, Red Rock Lakes, and Grays Lake), Bureau of Land Management landholdings, and state and private lands. National park lands and Forest Service wilderness areas total approximately 2.5 million hectares (6 million acres) and account for nearly half of the federal land base. The Forest Service manages its wilderness lands under a preservationist mandate designed to minimize intrusive human activity,[4] whereas the Park Service is obligated both to preserve its lands and to provide for public enjoyment, a dual mandate that has historically found the agency wavering between its two obligations.[5] The nonwilderness national forest lands, which also total approximately 2.5 million hectares (6 million acres), are managed under a "multiple-use" mandate, which provides for logging, mining, grazing, and recreational activities as well as wildlife and watershed protection.[6] The region's remaining land is mostly in state or private ownership; it is generally not governed by federal law and is open to development.

Yellowstone and Grand Teton national parks are at the center of a vast complex of designated and de facto wilderness lands that constitutes one of the largest conglomerations of wildlands left in the United States. Environmental groups and most biologists regard this park-wilderness complex as the core of a regional ecosystem characterized by a rich diversity of wildlife and manifold natural wonders.[7] The largest elk herds in the world reside in Greater Yellowstone, as does one of the world's few remaining free-roaming bison herds. The region provides critical habitat for such rare or endangered species as the grizzly bear, whooping crane, bald eagle, peregrine falcon, and trumpeter swan.[8] The world's largest undisturbed geothermal region, which has dramatically shaped the Yellowstone landscape, is an integral part of the ecosystem. The Greater Yellowstone watershed includes the headwaters of three major river systems, the Snake-Columbia, the Green-Colorado, and the Yellowstone-Missouri. The region's vegetation is predominantly lodgepole pine and spruce forests, which blanket much of the high mountain plateau. As a relatively untouched wilderness environment, Greater Yellowstone provides scientists with an unparalleled opportunity to study and understand how natural systems operate.

This Greater Yellowstone ecosystem cannot be easily defined by boundary lines of any lasting significance. Neither the wildlife nor these natural features are confined to the national parks. Many species range well beyond park borders to meet their seasonal habitat needs, just as the geothermal aquifers, river systems, and forests extend far beyond the parks. Congress, when it initially established park boundaries, was preoccupied with preserving Yellowstone's geothermal curiosities; it lacked any knowledge or appreciation of ecological realities.[9] Now that ecological connections between the national parks and surrounding lands are better understood, environmental groups and others have begun calling for an ecosystem-based approach to public land management.[10] Noting that the 1988 summer fires ignored political boundaries, just as the elk and bison have perennially relied on seasonal habitat far beyond park boundaries, environmentalists argue that the Yellowstone region properly should be labeled the Greater

Yellowstone Ecosystem and managed as an integrated ecological entity. This type of management, they assert, should protect the region's world-renowned natural features and emphasize its amenity values, such as wildlife protection, recreational opportunities, and aesthetic vistas.[11]

Since the early settlers arrived more than a century ago, people have become a ubiquitous presence throughout the Yellowstone region. Some of the initial inhabitants carved ranches and farms out of the wilderness, others sought their fortune in mining, and still others logged the forests for their livelihood.[12] These early economic activities, which largely relied upon public domain resources, continue today, with oil and gas exploration joining hard-rock mining as an important mineral development activity.[13] In addition, tourism has become a major industry throughout the region, and recreational use of the public lands has increased dramatically.[14] During the summer months, several million visitors descend on the national parks, swelling the local population to more than ten times its normal size. And the tourist season is now extending through the winter months, with park visitors, skiers, and snowmobilers all seeking access to what had previously been an undisturbed winter landscape.

The surrounding states and local communities are heavily dependent on the region's public lands for their economic sustenance. Wyoming's Governor Michael Sullivan candidly acknowledges the Yellowstone region's "immense importance" to his state.[15] He undoubtedly also speaks for his counterparts in Idaho and Montana when he observes that "tourism, minerals, timber and agriculture-related businesses rely upon the resources in the Yellowstone area and local communities rely upon the revenues produced by those businesses."[16] The states derive significant tax revenues from natural-resource development activities and sales tax receipts; local communities benefit directly from revenues generated by timber harvesting and grazing. The state of Wyoming, for example, derives 70 percent of its tax base from mineral extraction, some of which occurs on the public lands in the Yellowstone region.[17] The Wyoming legislature, recognizing the state's strong interest in its public lands, recently adopted legislation establishing a federal lands coordinator position in the governor's office to ensure that the state's interests are represented before the federal land management agencies.[18]

The nonwilderness public lands in the Greater Yellowstone region are managed under the multiple-use principle and thus are available for resource extraction activities, such as mineral exploration and timber harvesting.[19] Geologists believe the Overthrust Belt, which extends into the Yellowstone region and contains significant oil and gas deposits, holds real promise for further discoveries. A productive natural-gas field has been developed in the southern portion of the Bridger-Teton National Forest, and exploration activity is contemplated throughout the Yellowstone region. Noting the continuing decline in the nation's petroleum supplies, oil company executives argue that the key to enhancing domestic production and guaranteeing the nation's energy security is further exploration on previously unexplored lands in the Yellowstone region and elsewhere.[20] Since park and wilderness lands are off limits for exploration, the oil companies have sought exploratory drilling rights on the remaining public lands. In response, the Forest Service has undertaken an extensive leasing program, while providing for pre-lease environmental review and by imposing some restraints on development.[21] The oil industry, however, has objected to some of these constraints, claiming a legal right to explore on leased lands.[22] Environmentalists have responded that broad-scale oil and gas activities are fundamentally incompatible with the natural setting and threaten important wildlife habitat and water quality.

Over the years, the timber industry has actively logged throughout the Yellowstone region national forests. Logging provides employment opportunities, usually at high-paying wages, in an often depressed local economy. Timber sales return some revenue to the federal treasury, generate important tax revenues to the local counties, and provide some degree of local economic diversification.[23] According to the Forest Service and timber company executives, timber harvesting is a useful resource management tool; it can minimize insect damage and disease in the forests, diminish the impact of fires, enhance wildlife habitat, and increase water yields. In addition, logging roads provide recreational access to the forests and enable fire fighters to reach potentially dangerous forest fires.[24] But environmentalists contend that extensive logging and the accompanying road construction threaten wildlife habitat, water quality, and the aesthetic appearance of the forests. They also note that revenues from timber sales usually do not offset the Forest Service's timber management costs.[25]

The livestock industry also depends on the Yellowstone region public lands for seasonal grazing. Cattle and sheep ranches are scattered throughout the region, and ranching remains a traditional way of life for many longtime residents. The grazing fees these ranchers pay for access to the public domain provide the Forest Service and local communities with some revenues, though critics complain that public grazing fees do not reflect the prevailing market price. The region's expansive ranchlands contribute to its bucolic and rural appearance. Dude ranching and horsepacking have become a tourist attraction and an additional source of income for some ranchers. But livestock do not mix easily with Greater Yellowstone's free-roaming wildlife, and intensive grazing has caused environmental harm on the public lands. Nearly 40 percent of occupied grizzly bear habitat on the public domain is leased for livestock grazing, and several of these areas have become mortality sinks for the bear.[26] Livestock and wildlife conflicts are intensifying on critical winter-range lands, where native wildlife are competing with cattle for scarce forage. Because bison and elk are known to carry brucellosis, a disease causing spontaneous abortion in cattle, ranchers are intent on keeping these animals away from their herds; they have pressured local politicians to sanction hunting both within and outside the national parks.[27] Unsupervised livestock grazing also has caused damage to riparian areas and eroded stream quality in the Greater Yellowstone forests. Moreover, recreational conflicts between people and livestock are growing as more backcountry users find their solitude disturbed by grazing cattle and sheep.

With employment opportunities in the local communities linked to the public domain, there is little consensus on how the Yellowstone region public lands should be managed. Some local residents, joined by groups such as the Wyoming Heritage Society and the Multiple-Use Land Alliance, believe that an emphasis on preservation could preclude important economic activity and cause severe dislocations. Acutely aware of the legal significance of current boundary lines, they have taken the position that commodity development activities should continue as usual in the Yellowstone region national forests and that management policies in the region's national parks should be directed toward promoting human use and enjoyment of these areas.[28] They note that the town of Dubois, Wyoming, lost more than 150 jobs when the Louisiana-Pacific lumber mill, the town's largest employer, was forced to close its operations because it was unable to purchase timber in the heavily logged northern section of the Bridger-Teton National Forest.[29] They also observe that jobs in the resource extraction industries—even though they tend to follow boom and bust cycles—usually pay high wages.[30] And they argue that state and local governments, as well as the federal treasury, derive important tax revenues from mineral development activity, timber harvesting, and livestock grazing fees.[31]

Other residents, joined by national and local environmental organizations, believe that federal land managers should give priority to the region's environmental and amenity values. Indeed, the communities and businesses that depend directly upon Greater Yellowstone's scenery, wilderness, and wildlife for economic sustenance view the public domain as a valuable resource in its undeveloped state. Becoming quite sensitive to the ecological connections vital to preserving the region's natural integrity, they have weighed into the current debate over wilderness designation in Idaho and Montana, supporting proposals to expand wilderness protection, and they have mounted intense opposition to the Forest Service's oil and gas leasing policies. They applauded the Forest Service's decision to stop logging in the northern Bridger-Teton National Forest, which was reached after the agency concluded that extensive logging was diminishing critical wildlife habitat and compromising important recreational values.[32] Pointing to recent data indicating that tourism and recreation account for substantially more jobs and income in the region than the resource development industries,[33] local officials in Teton County, Wyoming, argue that recreation and tourism can provide a permanent and stable foundation for the regional economy.[34] And they note that Teton County already has developed a comprehensive land-use plan limiting development on private lands (which constitute only 3 percent of the county's land base) to ensure environmental protection and scenic preservation.[35]

The formidable task confronting public land managers in Greater Yellowstone is how to protect the region's natural values while also accommodating human interests and economic activity. Answering this question raises difficult scientific, philosophical, legal, and economic issues. The scientific issues focus on the need to develop a comprehensive understanding of ecological relationships throughout the region as well as a better understanding of the cumulative impact that development activity has on the region's ecological systems. These issues are pushing scientists beyond the bounds of current knowledge, as illustrated by the unpredicted magnitude of the 1988 fires, the ongoing research into elk ecology on Yellowstone's northern range, the efforts to develop and refine computer models for evaluating grizzly bear habitat requirements, and the current studies seeking to predict the impact of a reintroduced wolf population.[36] The philosophical issue is whether public lands and resources should be managed to give priority to nature or exploited and developed for human benefit—a long-standing point of conflict between preservationist and utilitarian schools of thought.[37] The difficult legal question is how to reconcile fundamentally different legal mandates and policies when official decisions are likely to have adverse environmental or economic impacts on nearby resources, lands, and communities.[38] The economic issues are challenging public officials to devise resource management plans that will preserve the natural integrity of the region but also provide sufficient economic opportunities to sustain local economies and ensure a reasonable return to the federal treasury.[39]

THE VIEW FROM THE LAND MANAGEMENT AGENCIES

Initial answers to these dilemmas must come directly from the National Park Service and the Forest Service. From the Park Service's perspective, its policy goals are to protect the region's natural character and to maintain natural processes. It is committed to continuing its experimental management regime, which now focuses on the ecosystem as a whole rather than on single species that traditionally dominated management efforts.[40] Park Service officials believe that Yellowstone's uniqueness and its historical legacy compel them to test the natural-process management hypothesis as well as other management theories.[41] And, recognizing that public and private lands throughout the region are inextricably intertwined, the Park Service is convinced that Greater Yellowstone can best be managed by giving primacy to "protecting the integrity of the natural systems that are the area's single most important resource."[42] Although this "does not mean that other uses must be totally excluded" from the lands surrounding the parks, it does reflect the Park Service's belief that "a healthy Yellowstone ecosystem will benefit the regional economy most in the long run."[43] Yellowstone's superintendent recently framed the issue in these terms: "Are the immediate or short-term gains had by a relatively few people near the park worth the loss the world will feel if America loses the grizzly bear in Yellowstone or permits the park's geysers—some 60 percent of the world's geysers—to suffer irreparable harm?"[44] Fearing the gradual erosion of the region's natural integrity, the Park Service views Greater Yellowstone as an opportunity to design "an international model of far-sighted planning."[45]

Not surprisingly, Forest Service officials do not place the same emphasis on Greater Yellowstone's natural values. Instead, they emphasize that the regional conflicts reflect "intense competition for the unique and scarce products and experiences the area offers" and that the controversies can best be understood as a conflict between widely divergent "public values."[46] Rather than underscoring the region's natural attributes or ecological connections, they argue that Congress intentionally has given the Park Service and the Forest Service different mandates, and that "there is strength through diversity" in each agency's separate mission and philosophy.[47] The Forest Service thus takes the position that no one mandate or philosophy should prevail in setting the Greater Yellowstone management agenda, and that the agencies should view "coordination as a key to making diversity a strong concept."[48] Recognizing that "our society is changing rapidly," they believe that resource managers "must respond to public values" while staying "better tuned into the social-political realities of our dynamic society."[49]

In spite of these somewhat divergent positions, the Park Service and the Forest Service are actively seeking common ground in the Yellowstone region. Acting through the Greater Yellowstone Coordinating Committee, an administratively conceived group composed of the principal regional and local management officials,[50] the agencies have initiated a cooperative interagency effort to resolve their shared problems.[51] The GYCC character- izes these unprecedented coordination efforts as "the precursor of future land management throughout the country."[52] Thus far, the agencies have designed a unique "process" for addressing resource management conflicts and establishing coordination standards. The first phase of this process culminated with publication of "An Aggregation of National Park and National Forest Management Plans," which inventories resources and compares resource management provisions.[53] The second phase, which is the real heart of the coordination effort, involves drafting a "Vision for the Future" document. This document will identify important characteristics of the Yellowstone area, establish "a series of related goal statements," and then articulate "coordinating requirements, standards and guidelines, to support and implement each goal."[54] Utilizing this document, each agency will review and amend its regional guidelines and local management plans to ensure meaningful coordination. This process has been open to the public, and the GYCC plans to draw on public comments to frame its conception of future management goals and priorities.

The Greater Yellowstone land management agencies did not easily or willingly arrive at this point. A 1985 congressional oversight hearing on management in the Yellowstone region,[55] augmented by a highly critical report prepared by the Congressional Research Service,[56] raised troubling questions about current management directions and an apparent lack of communication and coordination among the agencies. The CRS report concluded that extensive commodity development activity and accompany- ing access roads cumulatively were causing adverse environmental impacts and threatening wildlife populations.[57] It also concluded that recreation was the most important economic activity in the region, but that it received inadequate attention from the agencies.[58] Moreover, the report reached the startling conclusion that the grizzly bear's survival was in jeopardy.[59] Facing the threat of congressional intervention, the agencies revitalized the GYCC and have begun addressing the coordination problem as well as their own management priorities.

Administratively, the Park Service and the Forest Service are moving toward the concept of ecosystem management for the Greater Yellowstone region. The GYCC's efforts in bringing its "Vision for the Future" document to fruition reflect an unprecedented level of cooperation between two agencies that historically have distrusted each other. The draft "Vision" document sets forth a clear commitment to preserving Greater Yellowstone's sense of naturalness and ecological processes, while contemplating future economic development that is consistent with this commitment to the region's natural values.[60] The draft document envisions "a landscape where natural processes are operating with little hindrance on a grand scale. . . . [T]he overriding mood of the GYA [Greater Yellowstone Area] will be one of naturalness, a combination of ecological processes operating with little restraint and humans moderating their activities so that they become a reasonable part of, rather than encumbrance upon, those processes."[61] In addition, the Forest Service, though reluctant to accept explicitly the notion of ecosystem management, is beginning to emphasize wildlife preservation, recreational opportunities, and other amenity values on individual forests within Greater Yellowstone.[62]

The GYCC's initial coordination efforts, however, have done little to satisfy its critics. Environmentalists, pointing to the lack of legally binding commitments, remain concerned that the region's natural values will ultimately be sacrificed to ensure access to minerals, timber, and forage on the national forest multiple-use lands.[63] Conversely, the timber industry, ranchers, and oil and mining companies fear that coordination will inevitably preclude access to the region's commercially valuable natural resources, generally limit human activity to protect natural features and wildlife species, and ultimately impose constraints on the use of private property.[64] Noting the potential for significant controversy and calling for prudence from the GYCC, Wyoming's Governor Sullivan observes that "Congress, in its ultimate wisdom and over much time, has found no single legislative panacea that will solve every management issue in the [Yellowstone] region."[65] Sullivan is concerned that the GYCC, with its commitment to revising management plans that are the product of much public input and political compromise, "must tread the very fine line between setting policy and implementing policy."[66]

A PREVIEW OF THE FUTURE

In one form or another, public land management disputes have mirrored the inherent tension between preservationist and utilitarian beliefs ever since Congress began establishing the nation's public land policies nearly a

century ago. Yet the controversies engulfing the Greater Yellowstone region are not being addressed in the same manner that earlier ones were.
Modern ecological knowledge has changed the terms of the debate, augur-
ing a fundamental reorientation in public land management policy. Indeed,
a revised preservationist ethic is displacing the ethic of consumption that
has historically determined public lands management policy, and it is now
rising to a dominant position on the Greater Yellowstone public domain.
This revised preservationist ethic is based on the principle of preserving
ecological components and processes on a system-wide or ecosystem scale.
Forty years ago, Aldo Leopold brilliantly laid the philosophical foundation
for this development in his *Sand County Almanac* essays, where he argued
that land management policy should be based on a "land ethic" designed
"to preserve the integrity, stability, and beauty of the biotic community."[67]
Today, in Greater Yellowstone, there is evidence that this notion of ecosystem-based management is being taken seriously and that traditional
management priorities are being rethought.[68]

The chapters that follow in this section are intended to provoke further
discussion and debate about these developments and the future of the
Greater Yellowstone region. They reflect the diverse views of scientists,
lawyers, and an economist who have studied the region. Collectively, the
authors ask and answer a plethora of provocative questions underlying the
complex policy issues now confronting the land management agencies.
Can Greater Yellowstone be regarded and defined as an ecosystem?[69] Is the
Park Service's natural-process management policy scientifically justified
and ecologically viable?[70] Can recreation compete with timber as an economically viable use of national forest land?[71] Is there a legal basis for
giving primacy to the Park Service's preservationist mandate?[72] Is the
GYCC, with its regionalism initiatives, operating within the bounds of
current law?[73] Can the legal system be revised to take account of natural
resource systems?[74]

Although definitive conclusions are elusive, it is clear that the Greater
Yellowstone region is in transition. Park and forest management policies
are being reconsidered in light of ecosystem realities, jurisdictional boundaries are fading in importance, and hard questions are being asked about
regional economic priorities. But it remains to be seen whether the agencies
can overcome local political realities as well as their own institutional
traditions to promulgate and implement meaningful ecosystem management policies. In the meantime, the current administrative initiatives have
legitimized Greater Yellowstone as an ecological unit as well as the concept
of ecosystem management as a natural resource management principle.

The beginnings of a new era in Greater Yellowstone are indeed becoming evident.

NOTES

1. A. Chase, *Playing God in Yellowstone: The Destruction of America's First National Park* (1986); F. Craighead, *Track of the Grizzly* (1979).
2. R. Bartlett, *Yellowstone: A Wilderness Besieged* (1985); R. Reese, *Greater Yellowstone: The National Park and Adjacent Wildlands* (1984); Keiter, Taking Account of the Ecosystem on the Public Domain: Law and Ecology in the Greater Yellowstone Region, 60 U. Colo. L. Rev. 923 (1989).
3. Greater Yellowstone Coordinating Committee, *The Greater Yellowstone Area: An Aggregation of National Park and National Forest Management Plans* 2-8 to 2-9 (1987) [hereinafter Aggregation Report]. *But see* Congressional Res. Serv., Library of Congress, 99th Cong., 2d Sess., Greater Yellowstone Ecosystem: An Analysis of Data Submitted by Federal and State Agencies 4-7 (Comm. Print 1986) [hereinafter CRS Ecosystem Report] (concluding that the Greater Yellowstone region encompasses approximately 14 million acres). This discrepancy reflects the difficulty in establishing or agreeing upon definitive boundaries of any permanence for such a dynamic, complex ecological area as Greater Yellowstone. *See* Patten chapter 2 in this volume.
4. Wilderness Act of 1964, 16 U.S.C. § 1131 (1982). The Wilderness Act, however, provides that preexisting activities, such as mining or livestock grazing, may continue after an area is designated as wilderness. *Id.* at § 1133(d).
5. National Park Service Organic Act, 16 U.S.C. § 1 (1982). *See generally* A. Runte, *National Parks: The American Experience* (2d ed. 1987); J. Sax, *Mountains Without Handrails: Reflections on the National Parks* (1980).
6. Multiple Use-Sustained Yield Act of 1960, 16 U.S.C. §§ 528-531 (1982); National Forest Management Act of 1976, 16 U.S.C. §§ 1600-1614 (1982). *See* Coggins, Of Succotash Syndromes and Vacuous Platitudes: The Meaning of "Multiple Use, Sustained Yield" for Public Land Management, 53 U. Colo. L. Rev. 229 (1981); Wilkinson & Anderson, Land and Resource Planning in the National Forests, 64 Or. L. Rev. 1 (1985).
7. R. Reese, *supra* note 2, at 36-63; Clark & Zaunbrecher, The Greater Yellowstone Ecosystem: The Ecosystem Concept in Natural Resource Policy and Management, Renewable Resources J., Summer 1987, at 8-16. *See also* Patten chapter 2 in this volume.
8. *See* Endangered Species Act, 16 U.S.C. § 1533 (1982); 50 C.F.R. § 17.11 at 74, 84 (1988).
9. A. Runte, *supra* note 5, at 46, 54.
10. R. Reese, *supra* note 2, at 36-63; Clark & Zaunbrecher, *supra* note 7, at 8-16. *See also Ecosystem Management for Parks and Wilderness* (J. Agee & D. Johnson eds. 1988).

11. Examining the Greater Yellowstone Ecosystem Symposium, Univ. of Wyoming, Laramie, Apr. 13–15, 1989 [hereinafter Greater Yellowstone Ecosystem Symposium] (presentation by Ed Lewis, executive director, Greater Yellowstone Coalition; available from author). For a description of the Greater Yellowstone Ecosystem Symposium, see the Preface to this volume. *See also* Wilderness Society, *Management Directions for the National Forests of the Greater Yellowstone Ecosystem* (1987).

12. *See generally* A. Haines, *The Yellowstone Story: A History of Our First National Park* (1977); R. Bartlett, *supra* note 2; R. Righter, *Crucible for Conservation: The Creation of Grand Teton National Park* (1982).

13. Aggregation Report, *supra* note 3, at 2-5, 3-54, 3-65, 3-94; CRS Ecosystem Report, *supra* note 3, at 67–111.

14. Aggregation Report, *supra* note 3, at 2-5, 3-27 to 3-34; CRS Ecosystem Report, *supra* note 3, at 83–109.

15. Greater Yellowstone Ecosystem Symposium, *supra* note 11 (presentation by Michael Sullivan, governor of Wyoming; available from author).

16. *Id.*

17. Greater Yellowstone Ecosystem Symposium, *supra* note 11 (presentation by Bill Schilling, executive director, Wyoming Heritage Society; available from author).

18. *Id.*; Wyo. Stat. Ann. § 9-1-207(d) (1989 Supp.).

19. *See* Budd chapter 6 in this volume.

20. Greater Yellowstone Ecosystem Symposium, *supra* note 11 (presentation by Fernando Blackgoat, exploration geologist, Exxon Company, U.S.A., and public lands chair, Rocky Mountain Oil & Gas Ass'n; available from author). *See also* Leal, Black, & Baden, Oil and Gas Development, in *The Yellowstone Primer: Land and Resource Management in the Greater Yellowstone Ecosystem* 117 (J. Baden & D. Leal eds. 1990).

21. U.S. Forest Serv., Final Bridger-Teton Land and Resource Management Plan Environmental Impact Statement 1, 201-204, 738-740 (1989); 36 C.F.R. § 228.102 (1989). *See also* Sierra Club v. Peterson, 717 F.2d 1409 (D.C. Cir. 1983); Conner v. Burford, 848 F.2d 1441 (9th Cir. 1988), *cert. denied sub nom.*; Sun Exploration & Prod. Co. v. Lujan, 109 S. Ct. 1121 (1989); Keiter, *supra* note 2, at 975-82.

22. *See, e.g.,* Mountain States Legal Found. v. Andrus, 499 F. Supp. 383 (D. Wyo. 1980); Mountain States Legal Found. v. Hodel, 668 F. Supp. 144 (D. Wyo. 1987). *See also* Brooks, Multiple Use versus Dominant Use: Can Federal Land Use Planning Fulfill the Principles of Multiple Use for Mineral Development? 33 Rocky Mtn. Min. L. Inst. 1 (1988).

23. Greater Yellowstone Ecosystem Symposium, *supra* note 11 (presentations by Frank Gladics, representing the Intermountain Forest Industry Ass'n, and Bill Schilling; available from author).

24. *Id.*

25. *See* O'Toole chapter 4 in this volume; Wilderness Society, *supra* note 11, at 21-29. *See also* Leal, Saving an Ecosystem: From Buffer Zones to Private Initiatives, in Baden & Leal, *supra* note 20, at 25.

26. CRS Ecosystem Report, *supra* note 3, at 115-32; D. Amato & D. Whetmore, *Status Report on Yellowstone Grizzly Bear* 60-64, 84 (1989).

27. *See* Thorne, Meagher, & Hillman chapter 18 in this volume; Keiter & Boyce chapter 24 in this volume.

28. Budd chapter 6 in this volume; G. Reynolds, *Promise or Threat? A Study of "Greater Yellowstone Ecosystem" Management* 115-24 (1987). *See also* Wyoming Heritage Found., White Paper: Wyoming's Federal Lands (May 1987).

29. Greater Yellowstone Ecosystem Symposium, *supra* note 11 (presentation by Bill Schilling); G. Reynolds, *supra* note 28, at 151-161.

30. Greater Yellowstone Ecosystem Symposium, *supra* note 11 (presentation by Bill Schilling).

31. *Id. But see* O'Toole chapter 4 in this volume.

32. *See* Intermountain Forest Industry Ass'n v. Lyng, 683 F. Supp. 1330 (D. Wyo. 1988).

33. Aggregation Report, *supra* note 3, at 2-5; CRS Ecosystem Report, *supra* note 3, at 95–101.

34. Greater Yellowstone Ecosystem Symposium, *supra* note 11 (presentation by Bland Hoke, Teton County commissioner, Jackson, Wyo.; available from author).

35. *Id.*

36. *See, e.g.,* Craighead chapter 3 in this volume; Minshall and Brock chapter 10 in this volume; Singer chapter 21 in this volume.

37. *See* Sax chapter 7 in this volume.

38. *See* Lockhart chapter 5 in this volume; Budd chapter 6 in this volume.

39. *See* O'Toole chapter 4 in this volume. *See also* Baden & Leal, *supra* note 20.

40. Greater Yellowstone Ecosystem Symposium, *supra* note 11 (presentations by Robert Barbee, superintendent, Yellowstone National Park, and Susan Consolo, Resource Management Office, Yellowstone National Park; available from author).

41. *Id.* (presentation by Robert Barbee).

42. *Id.*

43. *Id.*

44. *Id.*

45. Greater Yellowstone Ecosystem Symposium, *supra* note 11 (presentation by Lorraine Mintzmyer, regional director, National Park Service, and co-chair, Greater Yellowstone Coordinating Committee; available from author).

46. Greater Yellowstone Ecosystem Symposium, *supra* note 11 (presentation by Brian Stout, supervisor, Bridger-Teton National Forest; available from author).

47. *Id.*; Budd chapter 6 in this volume.

48. Greater Yellowstone Ecosystem Symposium, *supra* note 11 (presentation by Brian Stout).

49. *Id.*

50. Aggregation Report, *supra* note 3, at vii, 5-2. The Greater Yellowstone Coordinating Committee is composed of the following officials: the regional foresters of the Intermountain, Northern, and Rocky Mountain regions of the Forest Service; the regional director of the Rocky Mountain region of the Park Service; the forest supervisors of the Beaverhead, Custer, Gallatin, Shoshone, Targhee, and Bridger-Teton national forests; and the superintendents of Grand Teton and Yellowstone national parks.

51. *See* Aggregation Report, *supra* note 3, at 4-1 to 4-3; Keiter, *supra* note 2, at 984-88. *See also* Varley, Managing Yellowstone National Park into the Twenty-first Century, in *Ecosystem Management for Parks and Wilderness, supra* note 10, at 216-25; Salwasser, Schonewald-Cox & Baker, The Role of Inter-Agency Cooperation in Managing for Viable Populations, in *Viable Populations for Conservation* 160 (M. Soulé ed. 1987).

52. Greater Yellowstone Ecosystem Symposium, *supra* note 11 (presentation by Lorraine Mintzmyer).

53. *See* Aggregation Report, *supra* note 3. After the Aggregation Report was published, the GYCC recognized a need to address some problems promptly, so it initiated Phase Two, Stage One of the coordination process, which involves coordination efforts on such pressing issues as fire management policies, park winter-use plans, and mineral leasing standards. *Id.* at 4-2; Greater Yellowstone Coordinating Committee, Phase II-Applying the Aggregation (1988) (prepared by the GYCC team leader and staff).

54. Greater Yellowstone Ecosystem Symposium, *supra* note 11 (presentation by Lorraine Mintzmyer); Aggregation Report, *supra* note 3, at 4-2; Keiter, *supra* note 2, at 987.

55. Greater Yellowstone Ecosystem: Oversight Hearing before the Subcomm. on Public Lands and the Subcomm. on National Parks and Recreation of the House Comm. on Interior and Insular Affairs, 99th Cong., 1st Sess. (1985).

56. CRS Ecosystem Report, *supra* note 3.

57. *Id.* at 48-52, 65-66, 77-82, 101-106, 177.

58. *Id.* at 123-29, 177-78.

59. *Id.* at 143-46, 177-79.

60. Greater Yellowstone Coordinating Committee, Vision for the Future: A Framework for Coordination in the Greater Yellowstone Area (Draft) iii (1990) [hereinafter Draft Vision for the Future].

61. *Id.* at 3-1.

62. *See, e.g.*, U.S. Forest Serv., Final Bridger-Teton Land and Resource Management Plan (1989); U.S. Forest Serv., The Forest Service Program for Forest and Rangeland Resources: A Long-Term Strategic Plan (1990).

63. Greater Yellowstone Ecosystem Symposium, *supra* note 11 (presentation by

Ed Lewis); Wilderness Society, *supra* note 11, at 15-20; Sierra Club, *Yellowstone under Siege: Oil and Gas Leasing in the Greater Yellowstone Region* (1986).

64. Greater Yellowstone Ecosystem Symposium, *supra* note 11 (presentations by Bill Schilling, Fernando Blackgoat, and Frank Gladics). *See also* Budd chapter 6 in this volume.

65. Greater Yellowstone Ecosystem Symposium, *supra* note 11 (presentation by Gov. Michael Sullivan).

66. *Id.*

67. A. Leopold, *A Sand County Almanac* 262 (1949).

68. *See Ecosystem Management for Parks and Wilderness, supra* note 10; Report of the President's Commission on Americans Outdoors, *Americans Outdoors: The Legacy, the Challenge* 168-69 (1987); Draft Vision for the Future, *supra* note 60, at 4-1.

69. Patten chapter 2 in this volume.

70. Craighead chapter 3 in this volume.

71. O'Toole chapter 4 in this volume.

72. Lockhart chapter 5 in this volume.

73. Budd chapter 6 in this volume.

74. Sax chapter 7 in this volume.

CHAPTER 2   **Defining the**
Greater Yellowstone
Ecosystem
Duncan T. Patten

         The Greater Yellowstone Ecosystem—these words conjure up scenic beauty, wildlife, and geysers. That is one perception. Another identifies the Greater Yellowstone Ecosystem as an area that includes Yellowstone and Grand Teton national parks, national forests and wildlife refuges, and private lands. Neither of these perceptions actually defines the Greater Yellowstone Ecosystem; one is aesthetically oriented, the other geopolitically conceived. The Greater Yellowstone Ecosystem is more than an assemblage of aesthetic wonders. It has no definite boundaries, and yet it is bound by its ecological unity or cohesiveness.

ECOSYSTEM CONCEPT

The use of the term *ecosystem* to describe the Greater Yellowstone region has created controversy. To understand the controversy, the concept of an ecosystem should be examined. An ecosystem is a dynamic, functional ecological unit. Within it, biotic and abiotic factors interact through a wide variety of processes. These interactions maintain a relative balance among four basic components: living organisms, water, atmosphere, and earth.

    The complexity of ecosystems has been illustrated as a weblike diagram (Billings 1952). The web includes all environmental factors around its edge and their influence on organism distribution and growth at the center of the web, as well as their influence on each other through interlaced strands of the web. The interactions among all these factors are controlled, in part, by time. The web analogy is useful to describe an ecosystem because it demonstrates how any point (environmental factor) along the edge of the web (ecosystem) can be changed, thus altering but not necessarily breaking the system. Although this weblike diagram is theoretical, Patten (as shown in Strain and Billings 1974) created a web diagram from actual vegetation and environmental data from research in Yellowstone National Park. It demonstrated the interactions among vegetational cover and such influencing factors as soil, elk (*Cervus elaphus*), pocket gophers (*Thomomys* spp.), and topography.

ECOSYSTEM STRUCTURE

Knowing that ecosystem processes occur within Greater Yellowstone and that we can call the area an ecosystem still does not define it. The Greater Yellowstone Ecosystem is said to encompass about 5,600,000 ha (14 million acres). It includes unique assemblages of wildlife and vegetation and has a high biological diversity for a temperate region. The area also includes 60 percent of the geothermal regions of the world and is the origin of three major continental river systems. It includes an area at elevations above about 1,500 m (5,000 ft.) around Yellowstone and Grand Teton national parks that was uplifted during very old volcanic periods (Absaroka-Beartooth $40-50 \times 10^6$ BP) and more recent ($< 2 \times 10^6$ BP) geothermal plateau building (the Yellowstone Hotspot).

The Greater Yellowstone Ecosystem area is presently divided into many different jurisdictional units that have little to do with the ecological diversity or unity of the system. Examples of boundaries that divide this system are those establishing the national parks and forests. The area also has been divided into wilderness, undeveloped, and developed areas. Moreover, land ownership partitions the system into lands that are owned by the federal and state governments, as well as privately. Ownership may establish jurisdictional authority, but it does not help define the Greater Yellowstone Ecosystem. Indeed, these legal boundaries are quite unlike biotic boundaries; they do not define an area that is necessary to maintain existing ecological processes or a given assemblage of species (Newmark 1985).

The natural components of the area may help to define the system. But these components either do not cover the whole area under consideration or are compartmentalized. Groundwater basins and recharge aquifers within the Greater Yellowstone region, for example, show a mosaic pattern that transcends all jurisdictional boundaries (Williams 1987, chart 6). The pattern of aquifers, however, does reveal interrelationships between basins and that changes in one basin may influence others.

Another natural component is the grizzly bear (*Ursus arctos*). The present range of grizzly bear in the Yellowstone area also overlaps jurisdictional boundaries, extending beyond Yellowstone National Park into adjacent national forests and private lands (Williams 1987, chart 48). Indeed, the range of up to 7 percent of all mammals in eight western national parks extends beyond legal boundaries (Newmark 1985).

ECOSYSTEM DYNAMICS

The Greater Yellowstone Ecosystem is an island of suitable conditions for the biotic and abiotic components and processes that make up this system. The edge of the island is controlled by increased human activities that have altered the primary characteristics of the system. Newmark (1987), in studying mammal extinctions in national parks, found that a high percentage of mammal species that existed when a particular park was established have vanished from it. The primary reason attributed was lack of sufficient size and habitat, that is, the islands were too small (Schonewald-Cox and Bayless 1986). However, by aggregating geographical and jurisdictional components, the Greater Yellowstone Ecosystem creates a bigger "island" than is found elsewhere in the coterminous forty-eight states. This is why it is often referred to as "the largest, single, essentially intact, functional 'natural' ecosystem in the lower forty-eight."

Grizzly bear range represents a concept that is applicable to the Greater Yellowstone Ecosystem. Although grizzly bears occupy much of the habitat in the Greater Yellowstone region suitable for their maintenance, their range appears to be expanding. Limitations on available habitat are primarily those of human activity. Consequently, grizzly bear habitat in the Yellowstone area is actually an island surrounded by inhospitable habitat. The size and conditions of the island control the reproductive and foraging capabilities of the bear, thus putting limits on its population (MacArthur and Wilson 1967). Grizzly bear range thus also demonstrates the need to understand the edge effects of national parks and the dynamics of the processes of exchange across the boundaries (Schonewald-Cox and Bayless 1986).

Only a few of the components and processes of the Greater Yellowstone Ecosystem have been noted; others deserve mention. The ecosystem is, in part, driven by geothermal phenomena that account for the actual park topography, volcanics, the buried and now exposed fossil forests, and the geyser basins and hot springs. The hydrological cycle and its components make up another driving force in the ecosystem. Precipitation, runoff, streams, and wetlands influence land formation and create habitat for many of the ecosystem's biota. Lack of precipitation can create drought, which in turn promotes the potential for fires. This process has molded the vegetational mosaic presently found in the ecosystem.

The biota of the ecosystem include all trophic levels, although removal of some predators has created an incomplete assemblage of large mammals. The "charismatic megafauna" such as elk, bear, moose (*Alces alces*), bison (*Bison bison*), deer (*Odocoileus* spp.), and coyote (*Canis latrans*) are the obvious faunistic components of the ecosystem. The avifauna has its own charismatic representatives, such as the trumpeter swan (*Cygnus buccinator*) and eagles. Hundreds of species of fish, small mammals, birds, insects, and other invertebrates are also necessary components of the ecosystem. Such ecosystem processes as trophic dynamics and decomposition would not function without these biota.

The vegetation (or flora) of the Greater Yellowstone Ecosystem is most critical to its survival as a functioning ecosystem. Plants are the foundation of all food webs or trophic pyramids. To maintain the dynamic processes within ecosystems, conditions must exist that promote plant establishment, growth, and maintenance.

All of the abiotic and biotic components separately do not make an ecosystem. There must be interactions among them. Figure 2.1 represents a conceptual model of the Greater Yellowstone Ecosystem showing some of these interactions and interrelationships. This model shows only the more obvious components of the system. The left side of the model shows geological phenomena, indicating geothermal processes creating past volcanism and present geyser basin activities. The left center of the diagram demonstrates the hydrological influences on the system, including phenomena that cause erosion and create aquatic and riparian habitats. The right side of the diagram shows successional processes resulting from fire and forest dynamics. The right center of the diagram represents the dynamics among some of the fauna of the system.

The arrows in the diagram represent influences or flows of such resources as energy and nutrients. In actuality, many of the arrows should go in two directions, as positive feedback occurs between components of the system. This positive feedback (or "bootstrapping") (Perry et al. 1989) is represented by many relationships shown in the diagram. One example is the predator-prey relationship between elk and coyotes (or other predators). The predator is dependent on the elk as an energy source, but the elk are dependent on the predator for population control. Positive feedback can also be found between abiotic processes. For example, riparian vegetation is dependent on stream flow for water, but stream channel stability is a

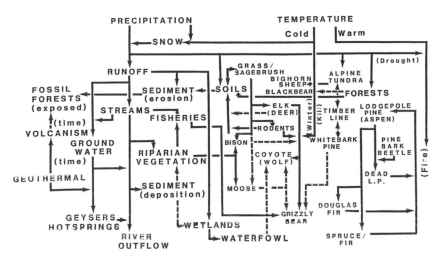

Figure 2.1 A conceptual model of the flows and interactions among many of the major components of the Greater Yellowstone Ecosystem.

result of riparian vegetation growth. Many similar dynamic relationships are represented in the conceptual model and can be easily documented from research within the Greater Yellowstone region.

URBAN ANALOGY

An understanding of a functional ecosystem such as the Greater Yellowstone Ecosystem, as well as the necessity for cooperative management arrangements, can be illustrated by using an analogy. The analogy is that of a metropolitan area, which represents, in effect, an urban ecosystem. The Phoenix, Arizona, metropolitan area is used because it is composed of many different jurisdictional units that are closely aligned. Like all urban areas, it functions as an ecosystem and reflects all the appropriate components and processes that are attributed to "natural" ecosystems.

Although many analogies can be drawn between the Phoenix metropolitan area and the Greater Yellowstone region, only a few will be suggested. The Phoenix urban ecosystem contains a network by which resources flow between and among the various units. Energy flows along these routes, and products of the ecosystem also are carried throughout the system. The streets and freeways are the network that creates a grid overlaying the city. The rates of flows within this network and the size of the pathways are managed, in part, by a cooperative program among the different jurisdictional units.

Within the Greater Yellowstone Ecosystem, a similar network allows flows between and among the different natural and jurisdictional components. The hydrological network of rivers and streams (Williams 1987, chart 7) is, in a sense, "managed" by the ecological factors that govern hydrological inputs and flow rates. It is also directly influenced by management decisions made by the different jurisdictional entities through which the system flows. These management decisions thus should be coordinated in much the same way as those in the urban system.

There are also biological analogies between "natural" and urban ecosystems. In the Phoenix metropolitan system, each day many people commute, or migrate, from one point to another to earn a livelihood. In much the same fashion, wildlife and birds migrate from night resting areas to feeding areas within the Greater Yellowstone Ecosystem. Both natural and urban ecosystems usually experience evening return migrations.

Moreover, there are seasonal migrations in both urban and natural systems. Many people throughout the world travel to the Phoenix metropolitan area for the winter, finding the environment more conducive to their general well-being. Within the Greater Yellowstone Ecosystem there are seasonal migrations of wildlife, represented by the extensive fall and spring migrations of elk. The converging of migration routes at the National Elk Refuge in Jackson Hole is a prime example (Williams 1987, chart 35). Migration patterns are not an easily managed ecosystem phenomenon. All jurisdictional units must understand the routes, causes for the routes, and timing of migration, whether the system is urban or the Greater Yellowstone Ecosystem.

The urban analogy can be carried into other ecosystem processes. For example, just as there are nutrient flows (effluent) between units within the Phoenix metropolitan area, there are also nutrient flows between units in the Greater Yellowstone Ecosystem. Runoff and streams carry wastes, or ash from fires, from one watershed down through the drainage basin.

The important concept of cumulative impacts can best be explained by the urban analogy. There is increasing concern that within relatively pristine ecosystems, effects from human activities may be compounded if they are too closely situated or too numerous for a particular system. A similar concern arises in residential neighborhoods within a city when commercial areas are developed. One commercial area within a neighborhood generates a certain level of traffic. If two or more commercial developments are located near each other, however, the impact of the attractions is much greater than the sum of the individual impacts. Although this may make economic sense, it creates major disruptions in the adjacent neighborhoods.

Resource development activity within the Greater Yellowstone Ecosystem can be considered similar to urban commercial developments in residential neighborhoods. As resource development activities increase, the cumulative impacts increase to the ultimate ecological detriment of the system. Management decisions, therefore, must take cumulative impacts into account for both urban and natural systems.

This discussion of the Greater Yellowstone Ecosystem is based on the premise that the system is still relatively undisturbed. Compared with highly manipulated agricultural and ranching systems surrounding the ecosystem, it is. The Greater Yellowstone Ecosystem is not, however, a system devoid of human presence. Indeed, the analogy with the urban ecosystem was purposely used to demonstrate the need to acknowledge human presence and to manage the entire system, recognizing that ecosystem processes do not stop at jurisdictional boundaries.

The Greater Yellowstone Ecosystem is unique, with two national parks as a central focus and a great variety of outstanding natural resources. With these resources the system should be wisely managed, which may mean "letting nature take its course" or utilizing additional environmental protections. Management is difficult because the system defies exact definition. No definite boundaries exist, and the components and processes are myriad and yet constantly changing. Its unifying character, however, requires us to consider it as a large single system rather than a mosaic of smaller ecosystems. Separate management might cause the system as a whole to fragment or collapse.

REFERENCES

Billings, W. D. 1952. The environmental complex in relation to plant growth and distribution. Q. Rev. Biol. 27:251–265.

MacArthur, R. H., and E. O. Wilson. 1967. The theory of island biogeography. Princeton Univ. Press, Princeton, N.J.

Newmark, W. D. 1985. Legal and biotic boundaries of western North American national parks: A problem of congruence. Biol. Conserv. 33:197–208.

———. 1987. Animal species vanishing from U.S. parks. Int'l Wildl. 17:1–25.

Perry, D. A., M. P. Amaranthus, J. G. Borchers, S. L. Borchers, and R. E. Brainerd. 1989. Bootstrapping in ecosystems. BioScience 39:230–237.

Schonewald-Cox, C. M., and J. W. Bayless. 1986. The boundary model: A geographical analysis of design and conservation of nature reserves. Biol. Conserv. 38:305–322.

Strain, B., and W. D. Billings. 1974. Vegetation and environment. Handbook of vegetation science, vol. 6. W. Junk, The Hague.

Williams, R. G. 1987. The Greater Yellowstone area: An aggregation of national park and national forest management plans. U.S. Dept. Interior, U.S. Dept. Agric., U.S. For. Serv.

CHAPTER 3   **Yellowstone in Transition**

John J. Craighead

For more than one hundred years, Yellowstone National Park has worn a coat of many colors, serving as a scientific research laboratory, a national recreation site, and a wilderness area contiguous to other wilderness areas. Can it continue this threefold function into the future? If so, how can this be achieved? Yellowstone is now in a state of transition biologically and administratively. What will it be like a hundred years from now? This is anybody's guess, but past trends and present events provide a basis for speculation and constructive criticism. To look ahead we must first look back.

Pre-Columbian Yellowstone was indeed a pristine wilderness. Animals were abundant, and native Americans were an important member of the biota. Blackfoot, Shoshone, and Crow Indians visited the area, but only a small band of Shoshones, or "sheep eaters," lived there year-round (Haines 1977, vol. 1). In the early 1800s Yellowstone's landscape diversity was high as a result of large fires in the 1700s, some probably due to prescribed burning and incendiarism by native Americans. This diversity of landscape was reflected in the diversity of plant communities making a vegetational mosaic of lowland coniferous forests in all stages of plant succession, sagebrush parks, aspen woodlands, subalpine meadows, and upland coniferous forests, with alpine or subalpine meadows, spruce "snow mats," and boulder fields at the higher elevations.

A full complement of animal populations occupied the Yellowstone habitat, their numbers regulated by natural processes. Elk summered on the high plateaus and migrated to distant winter ranges. Wolves and cougars preyed on the elk and other large mammals—deer, moose, bighorn, and bison. Lynx, marten, wolverines, and coyotes were common carnivores that preyed on the small mammals. Beaver were relatively abundant. Both black and grizzly bears were well distributed throughout the ecosystem, utilizing a wide range of plant and animal foods. The avifauna was probably not significantly different in species diversity than we find today, but some species no doubt occurred in greater numbers, such as the peregrine falcon, great gray owl, harlequin duck, bald eagle, trumpeter swan, whooping crane, and various species of woodpeckers.

HUMANS AND WILDERNESS

On March 1, 1872, Congress approved a bill creating Yellowstone National Park. And in 1916 Congress directed the National Park Service "to conserve the scenery and the natural and historic objects and the wildlife therein, and to provide for the enjoyment of the same in such manner and by such means as will leave them unimpaired for the enjoyment of future generations." This mission, both to use and to preserve Yellowstone National Park, spawned over the years numerous operational policies, sometimes conflicting, which have had major impacts on the park's resources.

In its early years the park was managed by a civilian administration without cost to the government. During this period, corruption, abuse, and destruction flourished. Thousands of elk, deer, and large predators were legally killed or poached. Such species as the lynx, wolf, and cougar were brought to the verge of extinction. To remedy this situation, Congress in 1886 authorized the U.S. Army to administer the park. A period of intense preservation and law enforcement ensued for the next thirty years. The establishment of the National Park Service in 1916 brought back civilian administration. The military left its imprint on the park and on the newly created National Park Service in the form of a rigid and authoritarian style of administration that has survived to the present day.

Since Yellowstone National Park was created, great changes have occurred in the plant and animal communities, some natural, others human induced. Plants and animals have been particularly hard hit by policies stemming from the conflicting mandate of preservation versus use. Changes also occurred that have left an administrative legacy of unresolved resource and management problems. The examples abound: a predator control policy, operational between 1916 and 1935, eliminated the wolf and brought the cougar nearly to extinction; a policy of overprotecting large ungulates, intermittently applied, has resulted in some drastic changes in plant succession; a road construction program designed to encourage visitation has altered or denied wildlife access to much of the park's limited riparian habitat; a wildfire policy that initially sought to suppress fires and then to encourage them has confused the goal of forest management; an operational policy that failed to integrate humans into the biota has left the human ecologic role in the park poorly defined; and finally, the most critical legacy of all, an artificial boundary that when surveyed in 1871 did not and could not recognize biotic boundaries or entities. The future ecologic health of Yellowstone will depend on whether the National Park Service can correct or compensate for these problems.

In recent years several prominent committees have offered specific advice and have suggested operational policies to cope with these legacies and guide the National Park Service into the future. The two most comprehensive were the Robbins and Leopold committee reports ("A Report by the Advisory Committee to the National Park Service on Research," W. J. Robbins, chairman, 1963; "Wildlife Management in the National Parks," A. S. Leopold, chairman, 1963). The Robbins report presented the pressing need for research in the national parks and offered twenty specific recommendations. The Leopold report addressed the problem of wildlife management in national parks by discussing specifically what should be the goals, the policies, and the methods of managing park wildlife and its habitat. Unfortunately, many of the most important recommendations from these committees for scientific research and natural resource management have received scant attention or have been ignored by Yellowstone administrations. Park administrations have remained inflexible and resistant to change. Agency control of the production and release of scientific knowledge has created a credibility gap and, frequently, an adversarial relationship with concerned scientists. Bureaucratic staffs have aggravated this further with an "in-house" paranoia that has discouraged and effectively prevented "outside" criticism and assistance, especially in the area of big-game management.

More rigid adherence to the committee recommendations and greater response to outside critiques could, in the future, bring about a more ecologically harmonious relationship between wildlife and its habitat within Yellowstone National Park. The crippling legacies can be ameliorated, but only if the National Park Service recognizes their importance and formulates policies to cope with them.

COPING WITH THE LEGACIES

By 1924, park administrators of the newly created National Park Service generally agreed that both wolves and mountain lions had been eliminated from Yellowstone. The effective loss of these two highly evolved predators altered the ecology in many important but unrecorded ways. Obvious changes, credited to intensive predator control, were the expansion of elk herds and the proliferation of rodents (Bartlett 1985). Steps are now being taken to reintroduce the wolf and to restore the cougar, but political, social, and biological hurdles must first be overcome. If successful, these large carnivores should be enacting their ecologic role early in the next century. Modern research techniques can restore these species, but fine-tuned management will be necessary to keep them in check. Ongoing research will be essential to determine how these predators integrate with such existing predators as the coyote and grizzly bear. Rapid proliferation of any one species could affect the population viability of the others within the geographically isolated Yellowstone ecosystem.

Loss of Wildlife Habitat from Roading

The legacy of roads within the park (a road system essentially completed by the army engineers in 1906) and the growth of campgrounds and visitor centers represent problems more difficult to rectify. Roads were built to provide scenic views and to take advantage of favorable terrain; wildlife habitat values were not considered. Campgrounds and developed areas were inadvertently placed in the highest quality riparian habitat (Bartlett 1985; Haines 1977, vol. 2). It has long been recognized that the road system reduced the amount of available habitat and increased wildlife conditioning to human presence. The loss of habitat resulting from these developments has had its greatest effect on the grizzly bear population. For more than eighty years grizzlies have had only limited use of habitat along the park's streams and lake shores. Those bears that did use it rapidly became habituated to people and frequently had to be destroyed as nuisance bears. Conversely, such species as elk and bison, not too shy to utilize riparian roadside habitat, have heavily overgrazed these areas. Closure or zoning of some roads could have alleviated these conditions, but this is not now a feasible option. Such options as closure of campgrounds and reduction of public service areas are being pursued.

The Role of Man in the Biota

How to integrate humans (park visitors) into the Yellowstone biota has been a problem since the park was founded. Decreed both a pleasuring ground and a preserve, it could not sustain the impact of millions of people and remain ecologically unaltered. Yet an illusion of the park as wilderness has persisted, and it became the basis for operating procedures and for the formulation of all major resource policies. The biological effect of humans as transient visitors has not been adequately addressed. For over three months each year, more than 2.5 million people become part of the park's biota and impact both park wildlife and its habitat. The problem of steadily increasing human visitation is partly the result of a budgetary policy whereby park appropriations increase in direct proportion to visitor numbers. The tendency over the years has been for park administrators to encourage visitation in order to increase appropriations. Yet, because the carrying capacity for native wildlife and transitory humans is limited, visitor quotas or some type of zoning will no doubt be necessary in the future.

How best to integrate these visitors with the native wildlife has become an increasingly acute problem. As more people visit the park, their impact on wildlife habitat and the sanitation problem become continually greater. Prior to 1970, for example, human refuse was deposited in garbage cans and land-filled garbage dumps within the park. The latter became "ecocenters" that attracted and held grizzly bears throughout the summer months. Research has shown that grizzlies were not people conditioned at the isolated garbage dumps. For nearly one hundred years, these ecocenters were ecologically beneficial to the grizzlies. Visitor impact on habitat was offset in part by biotic utilization of garbage (ecologic wastes); human refuse substituted for unrestorable grizzly habitat (Craighead 1971, 1982). Unfortunately for the bears, habituation to food at these sites was confused by park officials as habituation to the presence of humans. The two were not mutually interdependent. This long-term ecologic relationship in which grizzlies aggregated to feed (largely in isolation from 1959 through 1968) was upset suddenly and arbitrarily by a mandate that ignored scientific facts (Craighead and Craighead 1971; Craighead, Varney, and Craighead 1974). Recommendations for a gradual phaseout of the dumps over a ten-year period, accompanied by close scientific monitoring of effects on the bear population (Craighead and Craighead 1967), were not accepted. Instead, the major dumps at Rabbit Creek and Trout Creek were closed over a period of one year, and follow-up monitoring of the bear population was poor. The documented increases in bear mortalities and control actions, however, clearly suggested a population crisis.

Managing the Wildlife

How to manage the wildlife to prevent both extinction and overabundance has always been a knotty issue. Management controversies can be highly inflammatory, and thus the tendency of park administrators has been to keep them "in house" as much as possible and, recently, to let nature do the regulating. Natural processes could not be easily faulted; management actions could.

Over the years, many competent scientists and committees have offered suggestions for managing park wildlife, but few of these have moved officials to take effective action. In recent times, the problems of managing ungulates and other wildlife were addressed by the Leopold committee. Their report did not advocate a "hands-off" management policy, but rather urged active management of park resources using the most advanced techniques. Unfortunately, the committee's advice has been too frequently ignored or misinterpreted. A well-designed long-range program of wildlife management to meet specific biological objectives, recognized as such by the scientific community, has yet to be formulated and carried out. Instead, a "hands off, let nature take its course" policy has prevailed. This policy of "naturalism" rests on a misinterpretation of the committee's advice to maintain or re-create "the primitive conditions" of pre-park times. It has been based on the erroneous notion that biotic communities can regulate themselves within artificial boundaries and in areas where man is a massive intruder. The result has been a serious overpopulation of elk and bison, with corresponding decline in whitetail, mule deer, beaver, and other species. Strangely, this hands off, or natural regulation, policy has not been applied to black bears and grizzly bears. Both species have been intensively researched and the results variously interpreted. The numbers of grizzly bears are greatly reduced, and there is no firm evidence that the population has stabilized. The black bear population is the lowest since scientific records have been kept.

THE GREATER YELLOWSTONE CONCEPT AND NATURAL REGULATION

Many Park Service policies developed and implemented since the Leopold and Robbins reports assume that Yellowstone is a large enough area to regulate itself. This assumption derives from empirical studies of intact natural ecosystems that, if not disturbed, do appear to be self-regulated. The problem with natural regulation policies in Yellowstone National Park is that the area is not an intact natural ecosystem. Moreover, with its road system, developments, and annual infusion of more than 2 million visitors, the area is far from being undisturbed.

That Yellowstone National Park boundaries did not delineate a self-contained, independent ecosystem has long been recognized. As early as 1882, Gen. Philip Sheridan suggested that the Yellowstone preserve was not nearly large enough to provide adequate protection for its wildlife. He proposed doubling the size of the park to include land used by migrating ungulates. The areas he proposed eventually became, instead, part of the national forest system; his proposal of a single management entity became lost in the bureaucratic struggle for turf (Haines 1977, vol. 2). Again, in 1918, an addition of 3,275 square kilometers (1,265 square miles) east and south of the Yellowstone boundary was proposed. Instead, this later became part of Grand Teton National Park and the Teton National Forest. And again, the original intent of creating a single biological entity was lost. The concept of a Greater Yellowstone, however, has remained alive.

When the park was surveyed more than a century ago, there were no ecologists and the concept of an ecosystem was unknown; thus, in spite of the best intentions, the boundaries were arbitrarily drawn and never revised as perceived by early planners. It is time for the Park Service to acknowledge fully the implication of this and to recognize the severe flaws in their hands-off natural regulation style of management. The Yellowstone elk herds provide a dramatic case in point.

When the park was created, herds of elk used it and adjacent areas as summer ranges. In the autumn, they left this deep-snow country and migrated to winter ranges far beyond the park boundaries. The fences, roads, and communities that sprang up outside the park effectively blocked the migratory elk routes and usurped their traditional winter ranges. With adequate winter ranges no longer available, at least five distinct elk herds were forced to winter in areas within and immediately adjacent to the park that could not provide their nutritional needs. Clearly, the herds had to be managed, but how and to what end? These questions have spawned numerous controversies for many decades. Self-regulation has been supported by some individuals, whereas others have advocated the extreme of sport hunting within the park. Administration after administration has failed to resolve this complex issue, and it may take a major collapse of the elk herds for the hard choices to be made.

The biotic regulation of Yellowstone by natural processes disappeared as a viable management option when the park boundaries were drawn and when visitor numbers greatly exceeded the total of the entire megafauna. People have become an integral part of the Greater Yellowstone biota, whether park officials recognize this or not. The Yellowstone ecosystem can, and must, be managed as an entity in which human presence and impact are properly recognized.

The Vegetation Mosaic and Fire

Vegetation is the biotic foundation of any land area. It provides both stability and diversity to the pyramid of different organisms that live upon it. Since plant communities are in a constant state of change, operational policies designed to preserve, modify, or retard ecological stages, and thereby to attain predetermined goals, are essential to the management and preservation of natural areas. This means that a growing body of scientific knowledge must be continually applied both within the park and outside its borders.

The Leopold committee report recommended, as a long-range park objective, the maintenance "of large examples of relatively stable climax forest communities which under protection perpetuate themselves indefinitely." This would require fire suppression and the application of forest management practices, in other words, an active program of vegetation and landscape management.

In Yellowstone National Park the climax forest vegetation for the prevailing climate is spruce, fir, and whitebark pine. The development of plant communities composed of one or more of these species is dependent on soil factors, moisture, seeding conditions, and, especially, altitude. When Yellowstone was established, well over half the park was covered with young stands of lodgepole pine, a successional stage that is eventually replaced by Engelmann spruce, subalpine fir, Douglas fir, and whitebark pine. This successional process can occur naturally, or with the aid of active fire suppression. Well-planned, carefully controlled prescribed burns can provide scenic and biologic diversity and set the stage for the development of a mosaic of climatic climax forest communities. Large, uncontrolled intense burns are more likely to set the whole process back two to three hundred years than either to initiate or to stabilize climatic climax communities.

Yellowstone's lodgepole forests (about 77 percent of the entire forest complex) have been protected from fire for nearly one hundred years. Fire suppression has been successful, and some would say, too successful. Lodgepole forests represent a fire climax, that is, a forest destined to burn periodically that seldom, if ever, attains the climatic climax condition over extensive areas. In Yellowstone, large-area burns have occurred on a three- to four-hundred-year cycle. The subalpine forests are characterized by long-term cyclic changes in landscape composition and diversity (Romme 1982). Throughout the entire park and greater ecosystem, early, middle, and late forest successional stages provide landscape diversity. Both biotic and landscape diversity decline, however, as lodgepole forests mature. These mature or overmature forests contain heavy loads of both dead and live fuel. During the summer of 1988, they presented a serious fire threat. Had they not burned (and barring future fires), they would have been successionally replaced by the understory of climatic climax species—spruce, fir, and whitebark pine. In general, such mixed-species stands support a greater diversity of birds and mammals than do single-species stands.

The 1988 wildfires drastically altered the entire ecosystem in just a matter of weeks, creating conditions that will take years to evaluate fully. To those familiar with the park, the aesthetic impacts were immediately apparent and are likely to persist for decades. At such landmarks as Gibbon Falls, Virginia Cascades, the Firehole River gorge, Roaring Mountain, Bunsen Peak, Mount Holmes, Dunraven Pass, the Lewis River canyon, and elsewhere—now charred landscapes—pre-fire landscapes will not be missed by our grandchildren, only because they will not have a basis of comparison. The spotty nature of the burns in some areas will provide both landscape and vegetative diversity, and even the large-area intense burns will have some long-term beneficial effects. But to call the results of the fire a "regeneration" or "renewal" of Yellowstone, as some have, is euphoric and may close the bureaucratic mind to a critical review of what occurred and what must be done in the future. Interdisciplinary science researchers will focus their efforts on how the Yellowstone ecosystem responds to the devastating fires. Perhaps even more important for the future of Yellowstone is a much needed public review of operational policies.

Some general responses of animals to the fires are evident or amenable to short-term predictions. Where the burns cover large areas, small-rodent populations will not recover for years. Repercussions will be felt by all the raptors and mammalian carnivores, the most immediate being a fall feast and a spring famine. The large populations of elk and bison will decline rapidly or slowly in response to immediate climatic conditions. A severe winter will cause heavy winter and early spring mortality among all the ungulates, and herd reductions will continue until new vegetation is stabilized. The small interior herd will be severely stressed, and high winter losses are a certainty. Fire-charred and partially burned trees will attract and harbor insects, which will attract woodpeckers and other insect eaters.

The omnivorous grizzly, at the top of the food web, will be hard hit for a number of years. The availability of forbs, sedges, and palatable grasses for the grizzly may not change significantly. Rodents, berries, and pine nuts will be less common in its diet, however, and winter-killed ungulates more so. Movements to "remembered" seasonal feeding sites within home ranges will be disrupted or blocked by the extensive burns, and many food sites will no longer exist. Reproductive efficiency could drop, and with increased movement in search of food, bear-human encounters could become more frequent, with an inevitable rise in bear deaths. Such factors would prove significant to the well-being of a threatened or endangered species.

The grizzly is probably the best indicator of terrestrial ecosystem health. A continuing decrease in adult females will indicate serious trouble for a population already in decline and serious problems for the entire ecosystem. Over the long term of one hundred years or more, however, the ecosystem will adjust, especially if scientific management lends a hand. It will be an altered ecosystem, but the grizzly should still be a viable member of its megafauna.

The recent fires in Yellowstone point out only too well the potential flaws in the "let nature take its course" policy. Clearly, there is a limit to naturalism. What do we want Yellowstone to be one hundred years from now? To what extent and on what scale are we willing to guide natural processes? What is the proper balance between nature having its way and the skillful application of scientific management? Before other unmanageable events occur, Yellowstone National Park needs a "hands-on, let science guide its course" policy. Specifically, it needs a more precise vision of its future forests as well as the wildlife they will support, and a scientific program for attaining them.

RECOMMENDATIONS FOR THE FUTURE

What concepts and what policies should be challenged, and what policies altered or developed to give Yellowstone a rebirth and to guide the entire ecosystem into the future?

First, the area must be kept as natural as possible, but skillfully managed. Even within the Greater Yellowstone Ecosystem, there are too many renewable resource conflicts to allow nature to take her course. Goal-oriented management, for both wildlife and its habitat, is the key and will be into the foreseeable future. A clear statement of sustainable management objectives is needed, as well as a blueprint for achieving them. These can be realized only through the participation of the private as well as the government sector. In addition, management must be sustained on a time scale of decades and on a spatial scale of thousands of square kilometers. Synecology must supplant autecology in our ecological thinking.

Second, the Park Service must restate its purpose. Managing recreationists and preserving the resources are not enough. It must preserve the dynamic processes and components of the park environment, yet include human involvement, too. A realistic statement of purpose would indicate that human involvement is essential, the objective being application of modern scientific knowledge to guide ecological processes in attaining specified goals. As we gain scientific knowledge of the totality of wild areas (synecology), we must apply this knowledge, even if it forces us to alter our concepts of the pristine and to redefine wilderness.

Third, there must be a scientifically credible vision of future landscape diversity and methodologies for attaining it. How much climatic-climax versus fire-climax forest is desirable or possible, how should these areas be distributed, and how can this distribution be realized? What type of management is needed to retain open parks and meadows and to ensure healthy riparian and lake-shore plant communities? Can vegetation diversity be "engineered" with the aid of mechanized equipment by prescribed burns at appropriate times and places? Should artificial seeding of large-area burns with climax species be undertaken immediately to shortcut the fire-climax succession? If so, what degree of mechanical aid would be tolerable? What hypothetical vegetational mosaic can, in one hundred or two hundred years, give the maximum in landscape and biotic diversity and at the same time provide ecologic stability? Can continuity of effort and purpose be maintained to attain such a long-range goal?

Fourth, research should be undertaken to better understand wilderness ecology, especially fire ecology. This research should include the response and recovery of the biota to the recent burns, changes in stream flow and sedimentation, nutrient cycling, aquatic productivity, and changes in landscape diversity, to mention only a few. Should this research be highly structured and administered by committees, or open and flexible with emphasis on individual initiative? How much should be government sponsored and how much by the private sector? How can we ensure that knowledge arising from research will be incorporated into management programs? Are oversight committees essential, and how should their members be selected?

Fifth, a fire management policy must be integrated with wilderness preservation. Fire, along with climate and soils, determines vegetative cover. When wildfires are effectively suppressed, plant succession throughout the landscape is less diverse, but proceeds slowly to the climatic-climax forests. The policy of allowing natural-caused fires to run their course permits lightning strikes rather than scientific management plans to determine where successional changes occur and, to a large extent, the size of the burn and the type of vegetation that will follow. This is the natural process that existed in pre-Columbian times. But is it defensible in the late twentieth century, when "pristine" wilderness areas constitute only 14 percent of all public lands and less than 4 percent of total land area in the lower forty-eight states?

Vegetative recovery and plant succession vary greatly with climatic

zones. But wildfires know no boundaries. The successional process following fire is more rapid in the transition zone and becomes progressively
slower in the higher elevational subalpine zones. Do we need more precise
guidelines tailored specifically for climatic zones, for wildfire and for
prescribed burns as well? Should all wildfire be suppressed in the higher
elevational zones? Can a semblance of the primitive ecological situation be
re-created by prescribed, controlled burns only? If so, how extensive must
they be to provide the landscape composition and diversity of long-term
cyclic fire changes? Are human-induced changes of this magnitude feasible
and, if so, on what time scale?

Sixth, our concept of wilderness must be revised. Much of Yellowstone
is wilderness, as is much of the surrounding forest land. But even when
originally set aside, wilderness areas were not pristine, unaltered by human
use. Now threatened by oil and gas development, increased radiation from
ozone depletion, acid rain, the spread of exotic plants, and radioactive
fallout—all effects of human activity—is wilderness, as described in the
Wilderness Act (1963), really "a place to be visited, but left untrammeled
by man"? Can we separate people from nature or draw a line between
pristine and non-pristine? Or is wilderness in the traditional sense an
illusion at the end of the twentieth century? Have we simply been warding
off the more obvious human impacts? Should we, therefore, be actively
managing the Greater Yellowstone Ecosystem to counteract the disruptive
processes at work? Can naturalness be restored? If so, can the bureaucra-
cies cooperate to shape one vision, one policy, and one coordinated management plan for this unique area?

If Yellowstone is to remain "the jewel in the crown" of our national park
system, its natural resources must be actively managed. For this to be done
properly, the Greater Yellowstone Ecosystem will have to be biologically
defined and delineated, and management policies formulated for the entire
area. Because the area includes lands under the jurisdiction of several
public agencies and private individuals, common goals and operational
policies must be agreed upon and implemented. In turn, such policies
must be translated into local action if they are to produce the necessary
ecosystem-wide impact. However, this will happen only if the National
Park Service revamps its own organizational structure and becomes more
open, flexible, and cooperative. It needs the right organizational structure
for the job ahead—a system with flexibility to match its responsibilities;
and the other land management agencies must respond in kind.

In sum, Yellowstone National Park policies must provide a clear view of
the future. The task of managing the park throughout the next century for

those functions it has served in the past—an outdoor research laboratory, a pleasuring ground for our people, and a wilderness refuge—is enormous. Even more difficult will be the task of managing the park as a portion of a biological whole. But this is no more visionary or difficult than the task of creating the world's first national park.

REFERENCES

Bartlett, R. A. 1985. Yellowstone: A wilderness besieged. Univ. of Arizona Press, Tucson.

Craighead, J. J., and F. C. Craighead, Jr. 1967. Management of bears in Yellowstone National Park. Unpublished report.

———. 1971. Grizzly bear–man relationships in Yellowstone National Park. BioScience 21:845–857

Craighead, J. J., and J. A. Mitchell. 1982. The grizzly bear. Pages 515–556 in J. A. Chapman and G. A. Feldhamer, eds. Wild mammals of North America. Johns Hopkins Univ. Press, Baltimore.

Craighead, J. J., J. R. Varney, and F. C. Craighead, Jr. 1974. A population analysis of the Yellowstone grizzly bears. For. Conserv. Exp. Sta. Bull. 40. School of Forestry, Univ. Montana, Missoula.

Haines, A. L. 1977. The Yellowstone story. 2 vols. Colorado Associated Univ. Press, Boulder.

Leopold, A. S., et al. (Advisory Board on Wildlife Management). 1963. Wildlife management in the national parks. Am. Forests 69:32–35, 61–63.

Robbins, W. J., et al. 1963. A report by the Advisory Committee to the National Park Service on research. National Research Council, National Academy of Sciences, Washington, D.C.

Romme, W. H. 1982. Fire and landscape diversity in subalpine forests of Yellowstone National Park. Ecol. Monogr. 52:199–221.

Wilderness Act. 1964. Pub. Law 88-577. Washington, D.C.

CHAPTER 4 **Recreation Fees and the Yellowstone Forests**

Randal O'Toole

When Gifford Pinchot founded the U.S. Forest Service more than eighty years ago, he believed that scientifically trained forest managers paid out of public funds would automatically work in the public interest. Yet there is strong evidence that the national forests in the Greater Yellowstone Area are not being managed in the public interest.

The Forest Service estimates that more than 80 percent of the annual benefits of the Yellowstone forests come from recreation (figure 4.1). When net benefits are considered, recreation probably provides close to 100 percent. Yet national forest budgets and management activities do not reflect the importance of recreation.

Plans for the Yellowstone forests propose to spend only 18 cents out of every resource-management dollar on recreation, while spending about 60 percent of the resource dollar on timber (figure 4.2). Yet most timber sales on all of the Yellowstone forests lose money. These sales are not justified by the side benefits they provide to recreation, wildlife, and other resources. Instead, timber sales often conflict with those more valuable resources.[1]

The Forest Service's recent analysis of timber sales, the "Timber Sale Program Information Reporting System," ignored many timber-related costs. Even so it reported that the seven forests in the Greater Yellowstone Area lost $5.7 million on timber sales in 1988. When road and management costs that were ignored by the timber sales analysis are added, along with expenditures by regional and Washington offices apportioned to the Yellowstone forest timber programs, this loss increases to $12.2 million.[2]

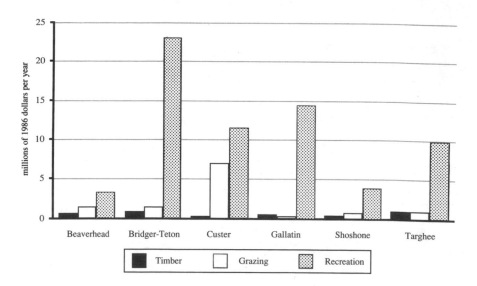

Figure 4.1 Projected benefits of timber, grazing, and recreation. Recreation produces far more benefits than timber or grazing on the Yellowstone forests. Source: Cascade Holistic Economic Consultants, *Economic Database for the Greater Yellowstone Forests* 21 (1987).

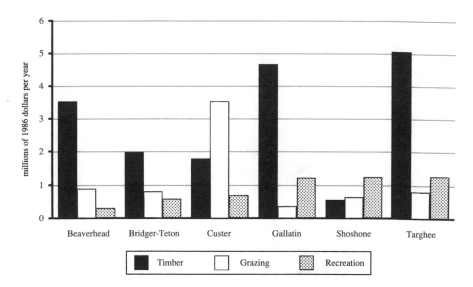

Figure 4.2 Planned expenditures on timber, grazing, and recreation. Timber has the lion's share of funds, whereas recreation is often the least well funded. Source: Cascade Holistic Economic Consultants, *Economic Database for the Greater Yellowstone Forests* 22 (1987).

Why do Yellowstone forest managers lose so much money on timber sales that conflict with recreation, wildlife, fisheries, and water quality? The answer reveals that Pinchot's ideal of the altruistic scientific forester working in the public interest has not been achieved.

INCENTIVES FOR LOSING MONEY ON TIMBER

Two major factors tend to sidetrack forest managers from the public interest. First, although Congress nominally supports multiple-use management, many members of Congress like some uses more than others. Timber sales, whether they make or lose money, produce many jobs—and therefore votes—in a state or congressional district. By comparison, recreation, even if it is worth much more than timber, does not produce many local jobs because recreationists often buy most of their supplies near their homes rather than near the recreation areas. Congress is thus more likely to fund below-cost timber sales than valuable recreation. A 1972 Forest Service study, for example, found that Congress tends to fund more than 95 percent of the Forest Service's timber budget requests but only about 70 percent of its recreation, fish and wildlife, and soil and water budget requests.[3] These figures were even more disparate during the Reagan administration.

The second factor is the result of a law known as the Knutson-Vandenberg Act and of several related laws that allow forest managers to keep an unlimited share of gross timber receipts for forest management activities in the timber sale area.[4] These activities include slash burning, reforestation, precommercial thinning, herbicide spraying, road maintenance, timber salvage sales, and improvements to wildlife habitat, recreation facilities, and watershed conditions.

Most of the costs of actually arranging timber sales, including road engineering and construction, marking of trees, and surveying property boundaries, are paid for out of funds appropriated from the U.S. Treasury. The Forest Service believes that it has no obligation to return an equal amount of timber receipts to the Treasury. In fact, the Yellowstone forests often keep more than 75 percent of the gross timber receipts. When this happens, the Treasury fails not only to recover its costs, but also to collect enough to pay the 25 percent share of gross receipts that it is obligated to pay the counties.[5] In short, the congressionally designed budgetary process actually rewards forest managers who lose money on timber sales. Managers receive no similar awards for emphasizing wildlife, watershed, or dispersed recreation.

This does not mean that Forest Service officials are intentionally defrauding the public by losing money in order to increase their budgets. Most, if not all, Forest Service employees are sincerely interested in "caring for the land and serving the people." But different people have different ideas about the best way to manage the national forests. Through a process of natural selection, those people whose ideas tend to increase the agency's budget will be promoted over people whose ideas tend to shrink that budget. Since World War II, the Forest Service has become dominated by timber managers, whereas those managers who want to emphasize wilderness or other resources that conflict with timber have fallen by the wayside.

Today, many people still believe that public forest managers ought to automatically work in the public interest. But they will do so only if the incentives are correctly designed. People who think incentives play no role in national forest management are not only ignoring reality, they are also missing an opportunity to use an extremely powerful tool for improving Yellowstone forest management.

One obvious way to improve incentives for Yellowstone forest managers is to repeal the Knutson-Vandenberg Act and the other laws that reward forest managers for losing money. Funding timber and other commodity uses out of a share of the net income from those activities will give managers an incentive to sell timber only when it makes money.

RECREATION FEES AS INCENTIVES

But we cannot simply rely on Congress to provide more funds for recreation and other amenity resources, because those resources simply do not "bring home the pork" the way timber does. Instead, we have to give forest managers new incentives to promote recreation, wildlife habitat, and clean water. The best way to do this is to charge a fee for all national forest recreation and allow managers to keep a share of those fees. To discourage below-cost activities and to keep recreation on an even par with timber and other resources, almost all forest management should be funded out of a fixed share of the net income that each national forest produces.

Past proposals for recreation fees have emphasized the need to recover costs. Few people have mentioned the most important reason to have recreation fees: the incentives that they can provide for forest managers. This has been graphically illustrated in the Forest Service, which is not allowed to collect fees for dispersed recreation and until 1988 was not allowed to keep any of the recreation fees it did collect.

But in 1987 Congress decided to allow forest managers to keep 75 percent of the campground fees that they collected. The Forest Service's response was rapid, with forest managers throughout the country making efforts to maintain and staff campgrounds that had previously been neglected. The chief established a policy encouraging recreation "partnerships," which in essence allowed private recreation companies like Kampgrounds of America to improve and operate national forest campgrounds.[6]

Recreation fees have also profoundly influenced many private forest land managers, particularly in the South, where there are fewer public lands that provide free or nearly free recreation. In 1980, International Paper began charging fees for hunting deer, turkey, and waterfowl in its 1 million hectares (2.5 million acres) of forests in Arkansas, Louisiana, and Texas. Since then, the company has reduced the average size of its clearcuts by 70 percent and leaves buffer strips around all lakes and streams.[7] Environmentalists in many states have unsuccessfully attempted to use regulatory methods to force private forest managers to reduce clear-cut size and to leave buffer strips. Recreation fees worked in this case where prescriptive legislation had failed because those fees produce 25 to 35 percent of International Paper's local profits.

Several different types of fees could be collected from national forest recreationists without tollgates or an expensive enforcement program. Most recreation would probably be covered by a basic and very modest dispersed recreation fee. After all, national forest recreation capacities are two orders of magnitude larger than current use, and there is little reason to charge a high fee for abundant forms of recreation.

Some forms of recreation are near capacity, however, and additional fees could be collected for these premium uses. Special fees could be charged for hunting, fishing, wilderness use, river running, developed sites, and such concentrated-use areas as popular cross-country ski and snowmobile sites. Setting fees at market rates would mean that trophy moose hunting or running the Gallatin River, for example, would incur a higher fee than deer hunting or backpacking into a remote wilderness area.

Monitoring of fees could be accomplished by requiring recreationists to display a visible permit indicating that they had paid their fees. Cars driving on forest roads would have a bumper sticker showing payment of the dispersed recreation fee. Backpackers and hikers would carry a ski-lift-type tag, perhaps color coded to indicate the kind of recreation permit they hold. Permits could be sold on an annual basis or, for short-term visitors, on a daily or weekly basis. Overall, the average fee collected would probably be about $3 per visitor day. Of course, some fees would be much less than this while others will be more.

The biggest obstacle to recreation fees is the belief that the public will resist paying for something that traditionally has been free. On the contrary, most recreationists I meet say they would not object to paying a fee if they knew that their money was being used to promote more recreation opportunities. Any resistance that did develop could be reduced with an educational program describing the benefits of fees.

A second common objection is that user fees might price poor people out of the market for recreation. In fact, the opportunities for national forest recreation are so numerous that some forms of recreation will always be accessible to all people, regardless of their income. Forest Service figures indicate that the national forests can supply about 10 billion visitor days of recreation per year, whereas current use is only about 3 percent of that level. The forms of recreation that are in short supply would of course require higher fees.

Such higher fees might prohibit low-income people from paying market rates to hunt a bighorn sheep or other trophy animal, but neither could they pay the market rate for a redwood or cedar home. Just as most people can find affordable housing made of less valuable materials, so most people will be able to find affordable recreation. Recreation is already so costly that fees would add only a small amount to anyone's recreation budget. Although a few Americans might not be able to afford that small amount, the Forest Service is probably not the best agency to help them.

The third most common objection to user fees is that they will encourage forest managers to overdevelop the national forests. Yet the danger of overdevelopment is remote, because developed recreation requires very little land. In fact, it is developed and motorized recreation that is available in such abundant supply, whereas primitive forms of recreation tend to be in short supply. Developed recreation does require lots of money, and forest managers who are funded out of net receipts will be unwilling to invest that money unless they can be assured of a return. Dedication of a small percentage of national forests to motorized or other developed recreation would completely saturate the demand for those types of recreation, leaving the remaining forests to dispersed recreation.

Even after hearing these arguments, some people object to recreation fees on plain moral grounds: They believe that recreation is a right, not a privilege. But the hard, cold fact is that recreation fees are the best, if not the only, way of giving national forest managers an incentive to consider recreation and other amenity values. Being morally right but ineffective accomplishes nothing.

OTHER NECESSARY REFORMS

Recreation fees alone cannot solve all the problems of national forest management. In connection with the repeal of the Knutson-Vandenberg Act and related laws and the use of recreation fees, I suggest:

- That preservation groups be allowed to purchase conservation easements on the national forests if they can outbid potential developers. This would provide protection for critical wildlife habitat and for recreation and other important areas that is now available only on private land.
- That wilderness- and river-use fees be dedicated to special trust funds that would be used to purchase conservation easements on other parts of the national forest system. Decisions about the use of these funds would be made by wilderness "boards of trustees" elected by holders of wilderness permits and others who donate money to the funds. As people use wilderness they would thus contribute to expansion of the wilderness system without the current political turmoil. Moreover, people who support wilderness but do not visit it could express their support by donating money to the funds.
- That the Endangered Species Act be maintained to ensure that old-growth forests and other habitat are available for grizzly bear, spotted owls, and other animals that do not have a high recreation value. To give land managers an incentive to protect rare species, Congress might offer a bounty to public agencies or private landowners whose land successfully breeds endangered species in the wild.
- That to minimize economic dislocations and compensate displaced workers, a fund equal to about $100,000 per lost job be created. This fund would be used to train and place workers in new jobs. I estimate that at most 40,000 workers will lose their jobs due to these proposals, so such a fund would be less than $4 billion.
- Finally, since appropriations nearly always emphasize pork-barrel developments, that national forest appropriations be virtually eliminated. Most national forest activities could be funded instead by user fees. This would save taxpayers some $2 billion per year, which would pay off the displaced workers fund in less than two years.[8]

Even without these additional proposals, recreation fees would have a profound effect on Yellowstone forest management. When combined with a program of funding resource management out of a fixed share of net forest income, forest managers would quickly find recreation to be their main source of funds. Conflicts between timber and other resources would decline as timber sales diminished and were confined to developed areas not needed for other purposes. Finally, fees would save taxpayers millions of dollars per year since users would be paying as they go rather than being subsidized by the U.S. Treasury.

NOTES

1. For a more detailed description of these conflicts, see CHEC reviews of the Beaverhead, Custer, Gallatin, Shoshone, and Bridger-Teton forest plans.
2. U.S. Forest Serv., *Statement of Timber Sale Revenues and Expenses as of 9/30/88* (1989), pages for cited forests and regions.
3. R. Alston, FOREST: *Goals and Decisionmaking in the Forest Service* 63 (1972).
4. The Knutson-Vandenberg Act allows the use of timber receipts for reforestation, 16 U.S.C. § 576. The Act of Aug. 11, 1916, allows the use of timber receipts for brush disposal, 16 U.S.C. § 490; the National Forest Roads and Trails Act of 1964 allows the use of timber receipts for road maintenance and erosion control, 16 U.S.C. § 537; and the National Forest Management Act of 1976 allows the use of timber receipts for timber salvage sales, 16 U.S.C. § 472h, and wildlife habitat and other forest improvements, 16 U.S.C. § 576b.
5. Act of May 23, 1908, 16 U.S.C. § 500.
6. U.S. Forest Serv., Fee Legislation, memorandum from the Washington office to regional offices, Dec. 22, 1987.
7. Presentation by Tom Bourland, International Paper wildlife ecologist, at the Political Economy Research Center Journalists Conference, Big Sky, Mont., September 1988.
8. These and other reforms are described in detail in R. O'Toole, *Reforming the Forest Service* 213–18 (1988).

CHAPTER 5   **"Faithful Execution" of the**
Laws Governing
Greater Yellowstone:
Whose Law? Whose Priorities?
William J. Lockhart

The public at large, the scientific community, and
resource managers increasingly are recognizing that the uniqueness, diversity, and interdependence of Greater Yellowstone's natural systems demand
sensitive, integrated, and well-coordinated management. Unfortunately,
the human-centered administrative systems that govern land management
do not duplicate the selective accommodations that temper and strengthen
Greater Yellowstone's natural systems. There is a resemblance: Like natural systems, the established land management systems pursue a myriad of
different, often conflicting courses. Unlike natural systems, however, governing principles of survival in the bureaucratic and political wilderness
tend to discourage, rather than reward, the establishment of priorities that
can produce a healthy, regenerative balance. As a result, especially because
its natural systems and resources transcend many administrative boundaries, Greater Yellowstone is threatened by the familiar failure of our
political institutions to establish or respect priorities compatible with preservation of natural values. Even for Yellowstone National Park, theoretically the protected core of Greater Yellowstone, the key question is
whether existing institutions are capable of making decisions that responsi-
bly address, rather than avoid, the need to establish and respect priorities
compatible with a regenerative natural order.

Highlighting the problem of priorities is the central institutional problem that Greater Yellowstone shares with other important natural areas whose core, both physically and institutionally, is a national park. That central problem is whether practical application of current (or strengthened) park organic legislation will recognize an authoritative priority for protection of park values and resources. The crucial test of priorities is upon us as the park faces increasing adverse impacts from development activities on adjacent lands, primarily activities proposed or encouraged by other federal agencies. Current approaches to decision making in those agencies strongly suggest that priorities adequate to protect the park—and crucial to protecting Greater Yellowstone—will be established only by creative and aggressive efforts, through administrative challenges and litigation, to compel implementation of statutory priorities.

AVOIDANCE OF RESPONSIBLE PRIORITY SETTING

The pending or approved plans for national forests surrounding Yellowstone National Park propose to authorize timber sales and oil and gas leasing and to tolerate hard-rock mining on almost all lands not designated wilderness.[1] The lands subject to these developments include large areas acknowledged to be important to the park's wildlife, including migration routes and prime grizzly bear habitat, as well as areas where development may have significant visual, noise, and other impacts on the park. These are lands, in other words, where roads and road construction, drill pads, shuttling of equipment, drilling and blasting, and the constant whine of saws—the cumulation of industrial and human activity—will inevitably have detrimental consequences for park wildlife and visitors.

When pressed on these issues, the Forest Service falls back on the traditional claim that its legal mandate requires approval for a full range of multiple-use activities. Furthermore, that mandate is so broadly asserted that the range of discretionary choice appears limitless, permitting infinite evasion of any duty to recognize or establish priorities.

Typical of the Forest Service's discretion-reserving posture, for example, is the Shoshone Forest response to Department of the Interior comments on its proposed forest plan. Interior had expressed concern that planned activities on lands adjacent to Yellowstone National Park "could adversely affect efforts to protect the grizzly bear, maintain a healthy elk population, or perpetuate naturally-occurring levels of geothermal activity in the park." Responding in a comment-response document, as required by the National Environmental Policy Act, the Shoshone Forest offered the conclusory justifications that "mineral operations are by law a viable use of public land" and that "our charter is to manage for multiple-use, not just preservation."[2]

Superficially, such responses do not manifest illegal disregard for statutory duties to protect the park and its resources. Indeed, the responses claim to be rooted in law and imply an effort by the Forest Service to "balance" a multitude of development and conservation objectives that, in its view, are all justified under its multiple-use mandate. But what the Forest Service response does not disclose is how—under what priorities—the Forest Service will apply its diverse mandates when specific proposals for mineral development or logging threaten direct conflict with the legal mandate to protect the park and its resources. Indeed, the Forest Service response does not indicate whether it *recognizes* a mandate of equal dignity requiring forest managers to protect the park. This, then, is the central problem confronting Greater Yellowstone, because the critical problem of priorities is not addressed by any of the plans for the forests surrounding Yellowstone.

Nor is the problem of priority setting addressed, or even overtly recognized, by the recently developed program of the Greater Yellowstone Coordinating Committee to establish "common goals and visions" for the future of the Greater Yellowstone Area "which can be shared by all who have an interest in the area."[3] Indeed, the problem is demonstrated by a preliminary GYCC statement on the "Mission of National Parks and National Forests." Noting that "abrupt differences are evident on some boundaries between Parks and Forests, for activities such as timber harvest, livestock grazing, motorized vehicle use, and mineral leasing," the GYCC explained that those disparities were simply "the result of different legislated purposes and management requirements."[4] There was no hint that those "abrupt differences" in management practices at park boundaries might involve impacts on the park inevitably requiring choices among conflicting priorities.

Similarly, the inevitable problems of choice among priorities are not addressed by the GYCC's formal statement of goals in its August 1990 draft "Vision for the Future" of Greater Yellowstone document. Emphasizing the need for expanded "coordination" among the Yellowstone management agencies, the GYCC's "Vision" completely ignores the priority setting that, case by case, will emerge from "coordinated" decisions to implement its inherently contradictory goals.

Furthermore, there are troubling indications that, in the absence of considered assessment of priorities, the GYCC effort to "coordinate" the missions of Greater Yellowstone management agencies could result in compromising well-established protections against impairing activities within the park. A troubling harbinger is reflected in the preliminary National Park Service position on a Forest Service proposal that would have allowed commercial logging trucks to use the park's primary road system for hauling timber salvaged from the fires of 1988. Explaining that the "USFS needs to fulfill its mandate for timber production," the Park Service's draft environmental assessment cited the GYCC as authority for the "need . . . to coordinate and cooperate" with other agencies in the Greater Yellowstone Area.[5] This approach, if adopted, would turn the GYCC program on its head, converting it into a justification for least-common-denominator management of all of Greater Yellowstone—even the park—despite severe impacts on the park's "different legislated purposes and management requirements."

This is not to suggest that the GYCC's unique and farsighted effort to improve coordination of Greater Yellowstone land management programs should begin by drawing a provocative line in the dust. But one might reasonably expect frank recognition, at least in principle, of the need to modify or tailor conflicting programs to accommodate established statutory priorities.

FAILURE TO RECOGNIZE CONGRESS'S PRIORITY
FOR PARK PROTECTION

The Council on Environmental Quality was recently so troubled by the problem of conflicts between parks and other land-use demands that it offered some advice to Congress on the subject of priority setting. That advice was provoked when the National Park Service sought CEQ intervention in a dispute with the U.S. Marine Corps under regulations providing that disagreements over environmental issues between federal agencies may be referred to the CEQ.[6] The Marines had proposed to conduct training flights in a "military operating area" over Cape Lookout National Seashore. The proposed flights, twenty-one high-speed, low-altitude training missions per day, would have taken place over a 4-mile-wide (6.4 km) swath of airspace directly over Cape Lookout. Originally designed for an elevation of 100 feet (30.5 m), at subsonic speeds exceeding 250 knots, the proposal was later modified, raising the altitude of the overflights to 500 feet (152.4 m), and to 3,000 feet (914.4 m) on weekends between Memorial Day and Labor Day.

Most of Cape Lookout is wild and managed as wilderness, with important colonies of nesting shorebirds, as many as five hundred endangered eastern brown pelicans, overwintering populations of the endangered Arctic peregrine, and significant nesting areas for the threatened Atlantic loggerhead turtle. Concerns about noise impacts on both wildlife and visitors prompted the Park Service to challenge, before the CEQ, the Marine Corps' environmental impact statement on the proposal, contesting the adequacy of analysis of adverse impacts and the failure to consider alternatives.

Because the park is located within the 75-mile (120.7 km) operating range of the Harrier aircraft stationed at Cherry Point Air Station, and the CEQ could find "no alternative locations for such flights," it concluded that the training flights were "critical to national defense needs." For that reason, the CEQ recommended approval, subject to more adequate analysis of cumulative actions and cumulative impacts.[7]

That result would appear to be just another disputed application of the National Environmental Policy Act, if it were not for some troubling comments, and a striking omission, in the CEQ decision. First, the council emphasized that it recommended approval only because of the "extraordinary" fact that no alternative operating area could be found in the vicinity of the Marine Corps training center at Cherry Point. Recognizing that the park had been created long after the 1942 authorization of the training center, the CEQ commented that when the park was established in 1966, "Congress made no reference to the earlier [training center] designation or to the possibility for conflict between two compelling national interests."[8]

Second, stressing that "federal lands are a valuable resource, the varying uses of which must be carefully weighed and balanced," the CEQ was apparently provoked to offer advice to Congress "with respect to the need to consider competing uses of federal resources." Although not likely to create a legislative stampede (it is located in a footnote in the *Federal Register*), the CEQ recommended "that the Congress take these potential impacts into account when setting aside lands such as national recreation areas, seashores, national trails, wilderness areas, and other specialized designations." The council went on to advise Congress about the setting of priorities: "Congress should also offer some guidance as to how conflicts in use should be resolved. . . . The need to foresee such clashes is an issue which deserves more extensive consideration by Congress."[9] What is mystifying and troubling about this advice is its apparent innocence of any recognition that Congress has already spoken on the subject, and the CEQ's resulting failure to grapple with the adequacy or inadequacy of established priorities.

The Council on Environmental Quality is the president's chief adviser and ultimate referee for resolving interagency conflicts over issues of environmental protection. It has authority to seek the president's direct and personal resolution of interagency environmental disputes through exercise of his constitutional authority to "execute the laws." Yet the CEQ approached this problem as if there were no "law" to apply; as if Congress had never mandated, in the 1916 National Park Service Organic Act, that units of the national park system are to remain "unimpaired for the enjoyment of future generations";[10] as if Congress had never reacted to the ineffective protection of Redwoods National Park by strengthening the Organic Act to require that no "authorization of activities" may cause any "derogation of the values and purposes" of our national parks.[11] Furthermore, regardless of when the Cherry Point Marine training center was established, the CEQ apparently did not consider the likelihood—at least a reasonable presumption in this instance—that Congress knew the Organic Act's statutory protections would be triggered by legislation setting aside Cape Lookout as a national seashore.

What is troubling is the CEQ's apparent assumption that Congress had carelessly created competing programs without any guiding priorities, leaving it to the competing agencies to accommodate their conflicting mandates through discretionary ad hoc balancing of legitimate competing uses, guided by political priorities. In spite of explicit statutory mandates that create a substantial interpretive basis for prioritizing protection of our parks, the CEQ failed to recognize or acknowledge that Congress had already weighed in; that where decisions affect national parks, the balance struck by Congress may require, at the very least, explicit demonstration of a strong and specific legal basis for overriding that statutory priority.

As in the Cape Lookout dispute, the central issue in any of the impending disputes over forest plans affecting Greater Yellowstone is not initially a question of the exact standards governing the level of protection to be established for the parks. Rather, the key question that must first be addressed is whether any authoritative priority will be recognized for application of existing statutory standards as the basis for restraining activities outside park boundaries that may impact the resources and values of the parks. Robert Keiter and the author, among others, have written on this question of the "transboundary" reach of the National Park Service Organic Act, emphasizing the substantial legal basis for bringing that act to bear on threats from adjacent lands, particularly those sponsored by other public land management agencies.[12]

Even if the Organic Act were generally accepted as having application to threats originating outside the parks, of course, a difficult and important question would remain. That is, to what extent the priority established by the Organic Act may override (or "trump") specific activities and programs undertaken to carry out the statutory missions of other agencies from which threats may originate.

REJECTION OF ADJACENT-LAND PROTECTION BY THE BUREAU OF LAND MANAGEMENT

Concern about the extent of the park protection priority, however, may be somewhat hypothetical at this point. Other land management agencies, like the Marines and the Forest Service, with missions they view as legitimately conflicting, do not easily concede that any authoritative park protection priority is applicable outside park boundaries. Too often they behave as if the Organic Act establishes no such priority; they are often explicit in saying it does not—sometimes in stark terms.

Particularly troubling has been the response of the Bureau of Land Management—another Department of the Interior agency—to direct requests that park protection be considered in designing management stipulations to control the types of development activities permitted on lands adjacent to national parks. Although its position, in part, reflects the BLM's characteristic dispersal of authority to local offices, the bureau in Utah threw down the legal gauntlet in unqualified language. To requests from the Park Service and others that the BLM's recent San Juan resource management plan provide protective management of key lands adjacent to Canyonlands National Park, the bureau directly responded that "we do not manage public lands as a 'buffer zone' to the park." Confidently—albeit, without legal support—the BLM offered only the following explanation: "The NPS Organic Act, as amended, states that NPS is to leave [parks] 'unimpaired for the enjoyment of future generations.' This law does not address the administration of [BLM] public lands, whether in proximity to an NPS unit or not; *it does not require the Secretary to leave [BLM] lands unimpaired to preserve park values.* To the contrary, Congress provided that [BLM] lands are to be managed for multiple use and sustained yield, whether in proximity to an NPS unit or not."[13]

More recently, the bureau asserted a similar position in a less confrontational statement generated by a continuing dispute over the protection of Hovenweep National Monument, which straddles the Colorado-Utah border. The Park Service (as well as certain environmental groups)[14] had contested repeated BLM approval of oil and gas operations on lands surrounding the small detached units that make up the monument. The Park

Service contended that drilling, drill pads, and road construction would violate protections established for a "resource protection zone" around the monument under a memorandum of agreement between the BLM and the Park Service. Following a heated exchange, the bureau responded to the Park Service, introducing its response as follows: "We in BLM remain committed to the idea that multiple use can be performed in a manner which is compatible to the needs of adjoining national parks and monuments. To achieve this, however, we must have a mutually clear understanding of each others legislative mandates, budget constraints, and goals and objectives, as well as an understanding of the impacts of valid existing rights and what revisions to procedures and policies are practicable."[15] Although the BLM recognized that a key determinant of the dispute involved the agencies' respective legal mandates, it conceded no weight or priority for park protection. Rather, the bureau's response clearly assumed that the relationship between the agencies is governed by statutory mandates that have equal legal priority on their respective lands.[16]

"FAITHFUL EXECUTION OF THE LAWS" AT HIGHER LEVELS

The Bureau of Land Management's insistence on the unprioritized equivalence of statutory mandates, like the similar though less provocatively phrased Forest Service position, guarantees continued disregard of any statutory priority for protection of park resources from adjacent-land impacts. Particularly under the current policies of the Department of the Interior, which provide that intradepartmental disputes are to be solved by "anticipation, avoidance and resolution,"[17] the practical effort of an operative standard of "equality of mandates" foredooms internal administrative efforts to avert adjacent-land impacts. Nevertheless, the disposition of interagency disputes over conflicting mandates and statutory priorities might be decisively affected if senior officials at an appropriate level of the executive branch would take explicit legal and political responsibility for resolving issues relating to the statutory priority for park protection. In the case of disputes between the Bureau of Land Management and the Park Service, that official presumably would be the secretary of the interior.

It is true, of course, that park protection advocates would not necessarily be pleased with the immediate result if the secretary of the interior did decide to take responsibility for determining that legal-policy question. But it is unlikely that the decision would be an unqualified disaster, because the secretary would have to buck some reasonably current and explicit statements in which the department expressed the view that it does have adequate authority to address external threats.[18] Nevertheless, disaster is certainly a possibility; short of disaster, compromise positions could severely undercut important pending efforts at park protection that rest, in part, on legal predictions about the department's authority.

In spite of the risks, however, long-term improvement is likely to come from such accountable decision making. To the extent that the decision favorably recognized authority to protect park values from transboundary impacts, it would provide a substantial legal basis on which to build more explicit protection for the parks, whereas the present legal uncertainties invite conflict and "least-common-denominator" negotiated resolution. If, however, the decision diminished transboundary protections, its consistency with statutory standards could then be determined through careful pursuit of judicial review, which might well result in a favorable ruling. And an unfavorable decision, even if affirmed by the courts, would provide a concrete political rallying point for the huge national constituency that supports protection of our national parks.

Unfortunately, the omens are not promising for that sort of responsible upper-level determination of these conflicting claims of authority. Even where senior officials accept such direct responsibility, their decisions often reinforce rather than reduce the tendency toward ad hoc discretionary determinations. And at least one important recent policy decision suggests that the Interior and Justice departments prefer to avoid clarification or strengthening of park protection priorities.

If the views expressed by former Secretary of the Interior Donald Hodel are any guide, the secretary is no more likely than subsidiary agency officials to resolve resource conflicts by analysis of relative statutory priorities. More likely, Hodel's successors will see their roles much as he did in a 1986 decision where an Alaskan native land claim conflicted with protection of wilderness and wildlife values in Tuxedni National Wildlife Refuge. Taking personal responsibility for the decision, Hodel focused on the question of "how much" land should be granted. Hodel's view of the problem was dominated by his perception of the competing interests, rather than by statutory priorities:

> The Secretary of the Interior is daily faced with many decisions wherein there are significant competing interests, not just between the Department of the Interior and other governmental agencies or private groups or individuals, but within the Department itself. The Department is composed of bureaus and agencies which share in common an interest in public and/or trust lands, but whose responsibilities and duties with respect to those lands are widely divergent. Interests vary from preservation to development. Statutory mandates

impose on the Secretary management responsibilities which range from one end of the spectrum to the other.[19] With such mandates, choosing between conflicting and competing interests is a significant inherent responsibility of the Secretary of the Interior.[20]

Hodel's decision reflected a balancing of his "trust" obligations to native claimants with a highly discretionary view of his other statutory duties. Although Hodel recognized that the claimants' rights might be limited by his statutory duties under the National Wildlife Refuge Act and the Wilderness Act, he offered no analysis or explanation of the respective statutory priorities. Rather, his decision carefully preserved a maximum of discretion, declined to address those legal conflicts, and based judgment primarily on "a balancing of all the competing interests involved in this case."[21]

It is understandable that a decision maker facing a wide range of competing claims would easily come to think primarily in terms of ad hoc weighing of those "conflicting and competing interests" rather than in terms of legal priorities. Yet legal standards can legitimately ease, rather than complicate, the problems of choice facing administrators. Indeed, it should be obvious that faithful execution of the laws begins with a careful identification of applicable legal priorities and the extent of their reach or possible conflict.

The prospects for clarification are seriously undercut by a disturbing executive branch refusal even to assert the statutory priority for park protection in the context of litigated conflicts with external interests. A striking example arises from a recent executive decision affecting the course of important litigation involving a serious external threat to Everglades National Park. In an apparently joint decision by the Interior Department and the Justice Department, the agencies calculatedly declined to pursue a nearly ideal opportunity to obtain a judicial interpretation that could have significantly clarified and strengthened recognition of the transboundary protective reach of the National Park Service Organic Act.

The case, still pending, involves a challenge to actions taken by the South Florida Water Management District, which is alleged to be transmitting large quantities of nutrient pollutants from huge corporate agricultural developments into the critical Everglades water supply. The case offered a clear opportunity to strengthen judicial precedents, along lines suggested in an earlier legal opinion by the solicitor of the Department of the Interior. Explaining his analysis of the transboundary reach of the Organic Act, the solicitor had concluded that the logic of the act and the limited case law, though not conclusive, do suggest applicability to external threats. The solicitor went on to observe—prophetically, for the Everglades case, that to a certain extent the effectiveness of existing law to deal with this problem will be determined case by case in the litigation process. Statutory mandates will have to be interpreted by the Secretary in the context of specific problems. Ultimately, those judgments will be tested and resolved in the courts, where the Justice Department is responsible for defending the interests of the United States. *How those actions are prosecuted and defended will play a role in the development of the law for the protection of NPS units from [external threats].*[22]

Fulfilling his role in the solicitor's scenario, the United States attorney had originally included a claim under the Organic Act when the Everglades suit was filed. But, without explanation, the Justice Department subsequently amended the complaint to delete any claim under the Organic Act.

In view of the nearly indisputable prospect of impacts on the park from externally generated pollutants, there seemed little basis for withdrawing the Organic Act claim except political disagreement with the substance of the claim itself, presumably because it reached out to seek relief against external sources of the pollution. That speculation, unfortunately, is strongly supported by a later filing in the case. In a footnote to an otherwise unrelated brief in the case, the Justice Department explained that the Organic Act claim "was dropped for policy reasons."[23] In light of the circumstances prompting the suit, it is difficult to imagine a credible "policy" basis for dropping this substantial and legitimate claim.[24] Apparently the governing "policy" simply involved a lack of high-level political support for applying or extending the transboundary reach of the Organic Act.

ENFORCING "FAITHFUL EXECUTION" OF STATUTORY PRIORITIES

Is lack of political support, then, a proper legal basis for the executive branch to disregard, or refuse to address, the Organic Act's statutory priorities in resolving the continuing interagency disputes that arise from adjacent-land threats to park resources? Since that lack of political support suggests that current political decision makers will not choose to give authoritative effect to park protection priorities, what legal grounds might compel a responsible determination? Obviously, traditional avenues of judicial review should be pursued to challenge disregard of statutory priorities by administrative decision makers, and to test the legal boundaries of claimed agency discretion. But the effectiveness of judicial review in correcting operative priorities is limited by the layers of delegated authority that insulate high-level decision makers from public political accountability for institutional decisions.

One respected theorist has suggested that undemocratic agency autonomy, otherwise encouraged by broad delegations of discretionary power, is
offset—democratized—by each president's election-year accountability
for the policy content infused into vague agency mandates by his executive
branch appointees.[25] But that political purification can operate only if
workable legal or political devices can convert faceless institutional decisions into focal points of policy accountability. Our legal system has not
developed ready approaches to that problem; aggressive conservationists
may find possible solutions in the answers to questions such as the following at the boundaries of existing law:

- Is it possible to raise both the legal and political stakes for the cabinet-
  level or subcabinet decision makers by formally appealing to the president when their ad hoc decisions disregard statutory priorities or fail to
  decide important questions? A series of attorney generals' opinions are
  conflicting about whether such an appeal is entitled to review, or whether
  it is precluded by the president's constitutional authority or valid delegations of power.[26] Surely, however, it is worth exploring whether there
  may at least be grounds for demanding some sort of response to requests
  for such a review.[27]
- Can judicial review ever compel the president to take direct legal responsibility for decisions made at the cabinet or subcabinet level, hence
  focusing political responsibility? When it makes administrative decisions, at least if it should purport to decide specific conflicts by interpreting statutory priorities, the office of the president would appear to meet
  the definition of an "agency" whose decisions are technically subject to
  judicial review under the federal Administrative Procedure Act.[28] Although the limited judicial precedent is conflicting and murky,[29] one
  federal court recently held that the president's Office of Management and
  Budget was subject to judicial review where its efforts to limit and control
  agency rule making were calculatedly interfering with development of
  regulations mandated by Congress.[30]
- Where procedures for higher-level resolution of interagency disputes do
  succeed in producing an executive branch determination, is it feasible to
  obtain judicial review reversing an unfavorable determination that dis-
  regarded statutory priorities? In at least one case, despite a formal opinion of the attorney general resolving an interagency jurisdictional dispute
  in favor of the Forest Service and against the Bureau of Indian Affairs, a
  federal district court overrode and reversed that determination based on
  its independent assessment of the applicable law.[31]

These and similar questions raise ancient and continuing problems about adherence to law, the extent of executive authority to interpret as well as execute the laws, the appropriate scope of executive discretion, and the proper role of judicial review. Our legal system has gradually generated some evolving answers, grist for the fields of administrative and constitutional law. But the impending conflicts over unresolved agency priorities in management of Greater Yellowstone will turn on crucial questions, like these, that remain to be answered. Like other citizens, conservationists must create the answers at the very boundaries of established law.

NOTES

1. *See* Keiter, Taking Account of the Ecosystem on the Public Domain: Law and Ecology in the Greater Yellowstone Region, 60 U. Colo. L. Rev. 923 (1989).
2. U.S. Forest Serv., Shoshone National Forest, Land and Resource Management Plan, *Final Environmental Impact Statement,* vol. 2, ch. 6, pp. 474 and 70 (undated; responses to comments dated September–October 1985).
3. Greater Yellowstone Coordinating Committee, Public Participation Plan for the Greater Yellowstone Area, Phase II—Plan Aggregation, at Introduction. A coordinating body established by regional officials of the Park Service and Forest Service to address land management problems in the Greater Yellowstone Area, the makeup of the GYCC is described in Keiter, chapter 1 in this volume.
4. Greater Yellowstone Coordinating Committee, The Greater Yellowstone Area: An Aggregation of National Park and National Forest Management Plans, at 1-2 (1987).
5. Nat'l Park Serv., Commercial Log Haul from the Northeast Entrance to the North Entrance, Yellowstone National Park, at 3 (draft environmental assessment June, 1989). Although Park Service regulations expressly forbid use of park roads by commercial vehicles except in emergencies (36 C.F.R. § 5.6(h)), the draft environmental assessment evaluated the proposal on the basis of the additional "criteria" cited in the text. Ultimately, the Park Service denied the Forest Service request.
6. 40 C.F.R. § 1504.1 (1990).
7. Findings and Recommendations by the Council on Environmental Quality Regarding the Establishment of the Cherry I and Core Military Operating Areas over Cape Lookout National Seashore, North Carolina, 53 Fed. Reg. 36,357 (Sept. 19, 1988).
8. *Id.* at 36,359 n.6.
9. *Id.* at 36,362 n.24.
10. 16 U.S.C. § 1.
11. 16 U.S.C. § 1a-1.

12. Keiter, On Protecting the National Parks from the External Threats Dilemma, 20 Land & Water L. Rev. 355 (1985); Keiter, National Park Protection: Putting the Organic Act to Work, in *Our Common Lands: Defending the National Parks* 75 (D. Simon ed. 1988); Hiscock, Protecting National Park System Buffer Zones: Existing, Proposed, and Suggested Authority, 7 J. Energy L. & Pol'y 35, 48–49 (1986); Lockhart, External Park Threats and Interior's Limits: The Need for an Independent National Park Service, in *Our Common Lands, supra,* at 27–36. The solicitor of the Department of the Interior, albeit grudgingly, has agreed (*id.* at 28–29), as has the Congressional Research Service (*id.* at 30).

13. Response by Utah BLM State Director Roland Robison, Mar. 6, 1985, to the author's comment on BLM preplanning analysis of issues for the resource management plan for the San Juan Resource Area; response by Moab District BLM, in final San Juan Resource Management Plan/EIS, September 1987, at 2-10, to detailed comments by the National Park Service and the National Parks and Conservation Association on the earlier draft plan. Both comments had insisted that the BLM was obligated, in its planning process, to address the consistency of BLM plans with national park plans and policies. *Id.* at 2-8 to 2-19 (emphasis added). These and similar examples are detailed in Lockhart, *supra* note 12, at 18–21.

14. The National Parks and Conservation Association and the Colorado Environmental Coalition.

15. Memorandum, Mar. 15, 1989, from BLM State Directors, Colorado and Utah, to Regional Director, National Park Service, concerning General Management Plan, Hovenweep National Monument.

16. It required an administrative appeal to the Interior Department's Board of Land Appeals simply to establish that the need for special protections recognized in the memorandum of agreement compelled the BLM to consider cumulative impacts on the monument from all of the drilling proposed for the area before approving a permit to drill within the agreed protection zone. Colorado Environmental Coalition et al., 108 IBLA 1 (Mar. 20, 1989).

17. This policy was the product of a "park protection working group" originally established by the undersecretary to deal with the problem of external threats to parks arising from activities on adjacent lands managed by other agencies. When that objective was abandoned in favor of the above policy, Chairman Bruce Vento of the House Subcommittee on National Parks and Recreation protested that this approach improperly assumed that "equal weight of law" was to govern resolution of these conflicts, whereas Congress had intended that parks receive "the highest possible level of protection." U.S. Department of the Interior, Report of the Subgroup of the Park Protection Working Group (1985); Congressman Bruce F. Vento to Undersecretary Ann Dore McLaughlin, Department of the Interior, Oct. 9, 1985. *See* Lockhart, *supra* note 12, at 22–24.

18. When asked at oversight hearings to provide a posthearing statement on "what additional tools are necessary to avoid critical *external* threats," the Park Service responded: "We do not believe that any new tools are needed. We believe existing authorities provide us with sufficient tools to continue to successfully fulfill the mandate of the National Park Service" (emphasis added). *Hearings on Department of the Interior and Related Agencies Appropriations for 1987 Before the Subcomm. on the Department of the Interior and Related Agencies of the House Comm. on Appropriations,* 99th Cong., 2d Sess. 801 (1986) (written questions and answers accompanying hearing transcript, question 3e). And when asked in the same inquiry, "what are your currently-available tools to mitigate or eliminate these critical *external* threats," the Park Service responded: "Utilization of injunctive and other legal tools can prevent others from conducting activities that are demonstrably harmful to park resources." *Id.* at 800, question 3d (emphasis added).

19. The secretary cited at this point his obligation to manage public lands for "multiple use," reciting the Federal Land Policy and Management Act definition of that concept at 43 U.S.C. § 1702(c), which offers an eclectic catalog of inevitably conflicting objectives. That broadly discretionary concept accentuated the discretion claimed in his preliminary determination in this matter that the Alaskan Native Claims Settlement Act permitted him to award the claimant less than the statutory maximum of 160 acres.

20. *In re* Appeals of the U.S. Fish and Wildlife Service, 94 Interior Dec. 339, at 346 (1986).

21. *Id.* at 349.

22. Opinion letter, Sept. 20, 1985, from Associate Solicitor Keith E. Eastin to Director, National Park Service, at 18 and 31 (emphasis added).

23. Memorandum, "United States Opposition to Motion to Stay Discovery and to Exempt This Action from Local Rule 14," at 5 n.1, United States v. South Florida Water Mgmt. Dist. (No. 88-1886-CIV-Hoeveler) (S.D. Fla. 1988).

24. The credibility of the Organic Act claim is supported by the court's subsequent order rejecting a motion under Fed. R. Civ. P. 11 for sanctions against the United States for having included the Organic Act claim and certain other claims in the original complaint. Contrary to defendants' contentions that these claims were "frivolous" and "contrary to existing precedent," the court recognized that there are plausible grounds for "extending" the existing law applicable to these claims. Order Denying Motion for Sanctions, at 2, in United States v. South Florida Water Mgmt. Dist., *supra* note 23.

25. Mashaw, Prodelegation: Why Administrators Should Make Political Decisions, 1 J. Law, Econ. & Org. 81, 95–96 (Spring 1985).

26. See list of conflicting attorney generals' opinions in Gellhorn, Byse, Strauss, Rakoff, and Schotland, Administrative Law, Cases and Comments 159 (8th ed. 1987).

27. The federal Administrative Procedure Act expressly requires that a federal

agency give "prompt notice . . . of the denial in whole or in part of a written application, petition, or other request of an interested person made in connection with any agency proceeding" together with "a brief statement of the grounds for denial." 5 U.S.C. § 555(e). In some appropriate circumstances, at least, the office of the president may well be held to be an "agency" bound by the obligation of reasoned response. See note 29, *infra*.

28. Unless exempted by law or unreviewable discretion, all "agency" action is subject to judicial review. 5 U.S.C. §§ 701(a), 706. "Agency" is defined in 5 U.S.C. § 551(1) as "each authority of the Government of the United States," · and the sole exclusions from the definition do not mention the president. See K. Davis, 1 Administrative Law Treatise 4 (1978).

29. *See, e.g.,* Kissinger v. Reporters Committee for Freedom of the Press, 445 U.S. 136 (1980); Chicago & Southern Air Lines, Inc. v. Waterman Steamship Corp., 333 U.S. 103 (1948); United States v. George S. Bush & Co., 310 U.S. 371 (1940); Soucie v. David, 448 F.2d 1067 (D.C. Cir. 1971); Amalgamated Meat Cutters & Butcher Workmen v. Connally, 337 F. Supp. 737 (D.D.C. 1971).

30. Environmental Defense Fund v. Thomas, 627 F. Supp. 566 (D.D.C. 1986); *see also* Public Citizen Health Research Group v. Brock, 823 F.2d 626 (D.C. Cir. 1987). It may, however, be difficult to obtain judicial review, because (1) the president has effectively delegated final authority on most issues such as these to his cabinet officers, and (2) presidential decisions may frequently be considered "committed to discretion" and thus beyond review under the Administrative Procedure Act, 5 U.S.C. § 701(a)(2), Heckler v. Chaney, 470 U.S. 821 (1985), particularly where they are central to exercise of the president's specified constitutional powers. Chicago & Southern Air Lines, Inc. v. Waterman Steamship Corp., 333 U.S. 103, 111 (1948).

31. Pueblo of Taos v. Andrus, 475 F. Supp. 359 (D.D.C. 1979).

CHAPTER 6

Ecosystem Management: Will National Forests Be "Managed" into National Parks?

Karen J. Budd

The U.S. Forest Service and the National Park Service are "re-creating" the land management policies for several million hectares of National Park Service, Forest Service, Bureau of Land Management, state of Wyoming, and privately owned land in Wyoming, Idaho, and Montana through the coordination efforts of the Greater Yellowstone Coordinating Committee. The GYCC was formed in response to what the Forest Service claimed was criticism from members of Congress and environmental groups about the disjointed land management policies by the federal agencies in the so-called Greater Yellowstone Ecosystem. Lands within the Greater Yellowstone Ecosystem include two national parks and six national forests, as well as state, federal, and privately owned lands. Membership in the GYCC consists of the Forest Service regional foresters from the Northern, Intermountain, and Rocky Mountain regions; the Forest Service supervisors from the six affected national forests; the Rocky Mountain regional director of the National Park Service; and the Park Service superintendents for the Grand Teton and Yellowstone national parks.

PROCESS FOR ECOSYSTEM MANAGEMENT

"The Greater Yellowstone Aggregation Report"

In December 1987 the GYCC published the Greater Yellowstone Aggregation Report. The purpose of this document was to describe the current land management patterns of the federal lands surrounding Yellowstone National Park and to project the future land management direction contemplated by the surrounding Forest Service land-use plans. The report included a series of maps delineating range use and condition, oil and gas potential, the location of lands with timber stands suitable for harvest, the location of lands slated for land sale or exchange purposes, and so on.[1]

Commodity interests dependent on federal lands for livestock grazing, oil and gas development, and timber production were assured that the Aggregation Report was a one-time publication and would not be used to supersede current land management policy established through the Forest Service land-use planning processes. In fact, the Forest Service agreed that the report was inaccurate because the information gathered from each forest came in so many different forms that it was difficult to synthesize.[2]

Upon completion and publication of the Aggregation Report and accompanying maps, the GYCC determined that its land management efforts should continue. Although the original report listed only four areas requiring additional coordination among the federal land management agencies in the Greater Yellowstone Ecosystem, the GYCC has since included four more areas.[3] The areas of specific concern to the GYCC now include uniform oil and gas leasing standards and stipulations, park winter-use plans, scenic byway designations, information management systems, noxious weed management programs, management of off-road vehicle use, management of native and exotic fish, and fire suppression and fire prescriptions.[4] The GYCC is also focusing on the coordination of silvicultural systems for timber production, buffalo and elk herd migration patterns, winter wildlife range acquisitions, and migration of wildlife away from Yellowstone National Park.[5]

The GYCC also hired two full-time staff coordinators to "facilitate communication" between the Forest Service and the National Park Service, and to represent the public before the committee.[6] Both staff coordinators are current employees of the federal bureaucracy (one from the Park Service and the other from the Forest Service), who will return to their respective agencies at the end of this assignment.

"Vision for the Future: A Framework for Coordination in the GYA"

The determination of the need for additional coordination has become a two-stage process, which will eventually lead to the revision of the individual land and resource management plans promulgated by the Forest Service and the National Park Service. Based on an ad hoc and informal public opinion process, the Forest Service and Park Service have published an umbrella document called "Vision for the Future: A Framework for Coordination in the GYA." Although informal comments from some members of the public were solicited for use in drafting this document,[7] there are no plans to issue formal agency responses to any of the public comments received.[8] Instead, the public participation plan adopted by the GYCC will "provide an opportunity for consensus building and mediation between polarized interests."[9]

The stated purpose of the "Vision" document is to describe the desired future condition of the GYA through a coordinated management process. The "Vision" document specifically emphasizes preservation of the area's natural resources over other commodity or local community needs and above multiple-use management. The document states, for example, that livestock grazing, timber production, and oil and gas development "will continue only where it is compatible with other GYA goals and values, such as wildlife habitat improvement and vegetation management."[10]

This "Vision" process also addresses the areas identified by the GYCC as needing additional intergovernmental coordination and includes "a set of goals representing a reasonable consensus on the major points that will influence [the management] direction [in the Greater Yellowstone Ecosystem] for the foreseeable future."[11] In addition, the GYCC states that "difficulties will revolve around philosophy and values instead of interpretation of rigorous data."[12]

Finally, the GYCC claims that the "Vision" document is not a regional land-use plan or guide and that evaluation of its alternatives or contents under the National Environmental Policy Act will not be required.[13] However, the "Vision" document contains "standards and guidelines" that implement the goals or "points of reasonable consensus" adopted by the GYCC.[14]

At this time, the "Vision" document has been presented to the public as a draft. Because of the strong criticism directed against this document, the GYCC has not decided if it will issue a final "Vision" report or a second draft document.

The next step in the GYCC ecosystem management process is a comparison of the land management goals, standards, and guidelines of the six legally adopted Forest Service land-use plans,[15] the three Forest Service regional guides, and the two National Park Service land management plans within the Greater Yellowstone Ecosystem. The inconsistencies among and within these previously adopted plans will be contrasted with the goals, standards, and guidelines in the GYCC "Vision" document in order to identify the conflicts among and between the individual land-use plans and the "areas of agreement for management of the GYA" in the "Vision" document.[16] Resource task forces would then be appointed to "staff out" the conflicts between the documents and recommend a solution. The GYCC concludes that "completion of the above step should result in a series of recommended amendments/revisions to Regional guides, Forest plans, and Park GMP's."[17]

PROBLEMS WITH ECOSYSTEM MANAGEMENT

Congress does not intend that national forests should be managed like national parks. National forests are to be managed for multiple-use values. Multiple use means that commodity uses, such as oil and gas development, timber production, and livestock grazing, must be considered important and legitimate uses of the federally managed lands.[18] In fact, the national forest system was created for two primary multiple-use purposes: to furnish a continuous supply of timber for the citizens of the United States and to protect and improve favorable conditions of water flows.[19] The Organic Administration Act, the act creating the national forest system, has never been repealed or amended and the primary purposes stated in that act have not been diminished.[20]

Multiple use also means that federal agencies must consider the economic stability of those surrounding communities dependent on the use of the lands within the national forest system. The notion of "community stability" grew out of congressional concern for the impact on local communities as thousands of acres were unexpectedly withdrawn and reserved for national forests by President Grover Cleveland. The president, ignoring Congress's right of consultation, used his authority under the Creative Act of 1891[21] to establish many of the national forests. At that time Congress repeatedly expressed its concern that the communities adjacent to these newly created forests have access to the forests for timber, minerals, and agricultural purposes.[22]

Additional evidence of congressional concern for the local economies dependent upon use of the national forest lands was demonstrated during the debates surrounding the passage of the Twenty-five Percent Fund Act in 1908.[23] Under that act, 25 percent of the gross revenues generated from commodity development on national forest lands is to be returned to the states for distribution to local counties. These monies are to be used for local schools and county roads. The basis for this legislation was the acknowledgment that the revenues generated for the U.S. Treasury from the uses of the national forests are paid by westerners, and that these revenues should be returned to the states in which they were generated. Republican Congressman Frank Mondell of Wyoming suggested that the rate of return to the states should be set at a level near what the states would receive if the lands were in private ownership and taxed.[24] The Twenty-five Percent Fund Act also has not been diminished or repealed.[25]

National parks, on the other hand, are to be managed for preservation purposes, wildlife habitat, and recreation values.[26] Multiple use and commodity development are not a part of the congressional mandate for management of the national park system. Additionally, legislation directing national park planning does not contain any requirements to address community stability. The different missions envisioned for the Park Service and Forest Service dictate that the goals implemented through their independent land-use planning efforts differ and that the standards and guidelines implementing those goals also differ. In other words, these two agencies cannot manage their lands in the same manner and for the same purposes.

Besides recognizing the difference between the missions of these two agencies, the GYCC must also acknowledge the difference between the definitions of *coordination* and *consistency.* Coordination, which is required by the National Forest Management Act,[27] means to "put in the same order or rank; to bring to common action or movement or condition," whereas consistency is marked by harmonious regularity or steady continuity; free from irregularity, variation, or contradiction. Not only did Congress intend that national forests and national parks be managed differently, but Congress also used the word *coordination,* not *consistency,* to describe that difference.

Although the GYCC is continuing to implement its "ecosystem management program" as outlined above, several outstanding issues must be considered.

1. *Purpose of the "Vision" document.* The purpose of the GYCC "Vision" document is to establish broad goals that will guide the future management direction of the Greater Yellowstone Ecosystem.[28] But what kind of management goals will be established, given the different functions and different missions of the Forest Service and the National Park Service? The goal of better cooperation in carrying out each agency's independent function is important, but not enough to warrant combining the missions and goals of these two separate federal agencies into a single management plan. Again, Congress did not intend that the lands administered by the two agencies be managed as a single unit.

2. *Consistency versus coordination.* Congress created the mechanism to "coordinate" the land-use planning processes of the National Park Service and the Forest Service in the National Forest Management Act. The act requires that Forest Service land-use plans be "*coordinated* with the land and resource management planning processes of State and local governments and *other federal agencies.*"[29] Each of the Forest Service land and resource management plans, which have been legally promulgated for every forest in the Greater Yellowstone Ecosystem, contains a section discussing the coordination efforts between that land-use plan and neighboring land-use plans, including Park Service resource management plans. Not one Forest Service or Park Service land or resource management plan has ever been overturned for failure to coordinate with other land-use plans. If the Forest Service and the Park Service are failing to coordinate, they need only to follow already existing law. There is no need to create a new process for "ecosystem management," which is outside the authority granted by Congress and goes beyond the legal mandates of the NFMA.

3. *Compliance with the National Environmental Policy Act.* Even more disturbing is how the GYCC will effect the goals stated in the "Vision" document. To this end, the GYCC proposes to develop "standards and guidelines, criteria and coordinating requirements which will support and implement the overall goals in the Vision document."[30] Under the Forest Service planning regulations, goals, standards, and guidelines drive and control all uses and activities on national forest lands.[31] Because these goals, standards, and guidelines determine how the lands of the national forest system are to be managed, Forest Service planning regulations mandate that the public participate in their establishment.[32] In addition, these same regulations, established pursuant to the NFMA, state that before effecting final standards and guidelines, a "broad range of reasonable alternatives" be formulated and considered pursuant to the National Environmental Policy Act.[33]

4. *Compliance with public participation mandates in the National Forest Management Act.* The process that the GYCC will use to assess public comments on the "Vision" document is also disturbing. The GYCC's public relations plan states that there will be "continuing public contact." Does "continuing public contact" mean that the GYCC will formally respond to the comments received on the draft and revised goals in the "Vision" document?[34] If a formal response to the public's comments is not issued, will the "Vision" document be legally deficient?[35] If a formal response is not issued, what kind of continuing public contact is envisioned? As stated above, the NFMA requires that the public be given the opportunity to

participate early and often in the Forest Service land-use planning process.[36] Will the NFMA's mandate for early public participation be ignored under the "ecosystem planning" process?

5. *Philosophy versus technical data.* The GYCC also states that the goals, standards, and guidelines in the "Vision" document will "revolve around philosophy and values instead of interpretation of rigorous data."[37] Forest Service regulations state, however, that land-use planning documents must be based on the best available technical data.[38] That the Forest Service and the Park Service would issue goals, standards, and guidelines without considering technical data violates the spirit and intent of those regulations. Also, the practicality and usefulness of the goals, standards, and guidelines in the "Vision" document are questionable if they are not based on realistic technical data.

6. *Role of a facilitator.* The GYCC, in a memorandum of understanding, has agreed that its members cannot force, convince, threaten, or impose their opinions, management directives, goals, or mission statements on other members of the GYCC.[39] In addition to the "staff coordinators" already employed by the GYCC, however, the committee is considering hiring a "facilitator" to bring consensus to the goals of the differing organizations.[40] Congress has mandated specific goals in the enabling legislation for each agency. Will the GYCC facilitator rewrite those goals while creating consensus among the parties?

Even if the role of the facilitator is only to assist the Forest Service and the National Park Service in negotiation of those goals, the same blurring of agency missions will occur. The negotiation of agreements means a give and take between differing parties. How is that give and take going to occur, without confusing the congressional mandates of the two agencies?

7. *Membership of the GYCC Committee.* The so-called Greater Yellowstone Ecosystem is owned or administered by many different federal and state land management agencies and private individuals. Yet of the twelve members of the GYCC, nine are Forest Service employees and the remaining three are employed by the National Park Service. The GYCC states that it does not want to add additional committee members because it would make decision making too cumbersome. However, the limited membership of the GYCC can, in effect, influence the land management policies for the Bureau of Land Management, the state of Wyoming, and numerous private citizens who also own or manage property within the Greater Yellowstone Ecosystem. The GYCC might determine, for example, that one of the goals in the "Vision" document should be to limit access to certain land areas within the ecosystem. That limitation on access through the implementa-

tion of standards and guidelines in the "Vision" document could severely impair the use and development of other Bureau of Land Management, state of Wyoming, or privately owned lands located in the same area.

One of the stated purposes for the creation of the GYCC is to correct the "disjointed land management" problems in the region. This goal cannot be achieved unless all land uses within the ecosystem are considered. If the GYCC is truly interested in land management within the entire ecosystem, the membership of that committee should be more broadly distributed among all affected parties.

8. *Consistency review.* The GYCC must also reconsider the legality of completing the comparative analysis of the standards and guidelines in existing Forest Service and Park Service plans. The Forest Service land and resource management plans within the Greater Yellowstone Ecosystem have been legally adopted through a lengthy process, including a congressionally mandated public comment period, NEPA compliance, and coordination review.[41] Under this process, should an outside party or appellant wish to challenge a forest plan, the burden of proof is on the appellant to show why that land-use plan is faulty. In other words, the plan is judged innocent and must be proven illegal or inadequate.

Now the GYCC is planning to again review these planning documents in a manner directly opposite to the one described above. Through this extra-procedural review, the GYCC is assuming that all planning inconsistencies are in error and that each forest supervisor must produce evidence to defend his or her decision. In other words, the plan inconsistencies are judged as illegal and must be proven innocent. This shifting of the burden of proof is cause for concern. Since the Forest Service plans now in place have already survived numerous administrative challenges, this additional review is unnecessary.

9. *Park Service review of Forest Service plans.* Additionally alarming is that the Forest Service plans are being reviewed for inconsistent standards and guidelines with the involvement of the National Park Service. The Park Service does not have the legal authority to validate Forest Service land and resource management plans. The Forest Service merely is required to coordinate its land-use plans with the National Park Service resource planning process. That process was completed when the Forest Service plans were adopted as final, and should not be disturbed now.

10. *Grizzly bear recovery plan justification.* Finally, the GYCC is seeking to justify its authority for general land management planning by touting its success in the coordination of the grizzly bear recovery plan. This comparison is inappropriate, however, because the legal mandates involved

with general land-use planning are completely different from those governing the grizzly bear listing under the Endangered Species Act.[42] The ESA, which protects all federally listed species, applies to all federal and state agencies and private individuals and supersedes all existing legal mandates, including the congressionally designated missions of individual agencies.[43] In other words, legal designation of the grizzly bear as a threatened species, and the subsequent adoption of the grizzly bear recovery plan, mandated that all federal agencies coordinate their efforts to assist in the recovery of that species.

There are no statutes, however, that allow multiple use, wildlife preservation, or roadless recreation to be elevated above the mission or goals of a congressionally created agency. These matters are not governed by an overriding statute, such as the ESA, and cannot be elevated to that level by consistency or ecosystem planning. Again, the Forest Service and the Park Service should coordinate, but only to the extent of the law.

The idea for ecosystem planning is spreading. Areas in California and Utah have requested the GYCC consistency planning model and are establishing ecosystem planning systems of their own. The Forest Service says that even if it does not have the authority for ecosystem planning, it is just trying to head off federal legislation that would mandate this type of land-use management. Frankly, I would rather take my chances with Congress.

NOTES

1. The list of resource issues and maps contained in the Aggregation Report includes landforms and characteristics; landownership and adjustment; general geology; unstable soil and rock patterns; groundwater aquifer recharge areas; major riparian areas; areas with seismic activity; existing and planned roads and trails; administrative and transportation facilities; developed recreation facilities; recreation uses authorized by permit; existing and proposed wilderness, wilderness study, recommended wilderness, and undeveloped areas; a description of existing and proposed livestock grazing areas; locations and types of noxious and exotic plants and weeds; vegetation classifications; existing and planned tree age classifications; locations of trees killed by mountain pine beetles; location of lands suitable for timber production; fire management; geologic potential for minerals; location of mining claims, mines, and mineral rights; location of mineral leases, lease applications, and applications for permits to drill; seasonal range condition and trend for elk, mule deer, white-tailed deer, bighorn, antelope, moose, and bison; grizzly bear, trumpeter swan, and osprey habitat locations; fishery resource classifica-

tions; air resource management; and planned visual resource management. Greater Yellowstone Coordinating Committee, *The Greater Yellowstone Area: An Aggregation of National Park and National Forest Management Plans* 3-1 to 3-172 (1987).

2. *Id.* at 1-3.
3. Memorandum from U.S. Forest Serv., Phase 2—Applying the Aggregation, 1 (1988) [hereinafter Applying the Aggregation].
4. *Id.*
5. Agenda of Greater Yellowstone Coordinating Committee semiannual meeting, Cheyenne, Wyo., Apr. 4–6, 1989.
6. Minutes of Greater Yellowstone Coordinating Committee semiannual meeting, Cheyenne, Wyo., Apr. 4–6, 1989.
7. It is not clear whether and which parts of the "Vision" document will be published in the *Federal Register* and therefore available for general public comment.
8. Memorandum to Greater Yellowstone Coordinating Committee, Public Participation Plan for the Greater Yellowstone Area—Phase II—Plan Aggregation (March 1989).
9. Applying the Aggregation, *supra* note 3, at 2.
10. Greater Yellowstone Coordinating Committee, Vision for the Future: A Framework for Coordination in the Greater Yellowstone Area (draft) (1990).
11. Applying the Aggregation, *supra* note 3, at 2.
12. *Id.*
13. 42 U.S.C. §§ 4321 *et seq.* (1989).
14. Applying the Aggregation, *supra* note 3, at 2.
15. *E.g.*, U.S. Forest Service, Bridger-Teton National Forest Land and Resource Management Plan and Record of Decision (1990).
16. Applying the Aggregation, *supra* note 3, at 3.
17. *Id.*
18. *See* Multiple Use, Sustained Yield Act, 16 U.S.C. §§ 528–531; National Forest Management Act, 16 U.S.C. §§ 1600 *et seq.*; Forest Service regulations, 36 C.F.R. §§ 219.1 *et seq.*
19. Organic Administration Act of 1897, 16 U.S.C. § 475.
20. The U.S. Supreme Court has also recognized that the primary purposes for creating national forests have not been repealed or diminished by subsequent actions of Congress. In United States v. New Mexico, 438 U.S. 696 (1978), the Supreme Court refused to grant reserved water rights to the U.S. Forest Service for any purposes other than those specifically named in the Organic Administration Act of 1897. The Court stated: "The legislative debates surrounding the Organic Administration Act of 1897 and its predecessor bills demonstrate that Congress intended national forests to be reserved for only two purposes—[t]o conserve the water flows and to furnish a continuous supply of timber for the people. . . . National forests were not to be reserved for aesthetic, environmental, recreational, or wildlife-preservation purposes."

21. 16 U.S.C. § 471 (repealed in 1976).
22. 30 Cong. Rec. 984 (1897).
23. 16 U.S.C. § 501.
24. J. Ise, *The United States Forest Policy* (1920); G. Robinson, *The Forest Service* (1975).
25. Under the Twenty-five Percent Fund Act, Wyoming receives approximately $1.4 million from the Forest Service each year. Revenues generated during fiscal year 1988 for counties within the Greater Yellowstone Ecosystem include:

County	National Forest	Hectares	Payment per Forest ($)	Total County Payment ($)
Fremont	Bridger	13,933	4,981.95	
	Shoshone	342,407	105,140.45	
	Teton	40,792	8,175.40	118,297.80
Hot Springs	Shoshone	22,019	6,761.11	6,761.11
Lincoln	Bridger	316,202	113,061.26	
	Targhee	24,336	21,717.00	
	Teton	21,092	4,227.19	139,005.45
Park	Shoshone	615,583	189,022.58	
	Teton	71,034	14,236.39	203,258.97
Sublette	Bridger	369,083	131,969.22	
	Shoshone	3,926	1,205.50	
	Teton	100,422	20,126.32	153,301.04
Teton	Bridger	2,655	949.49	
	Shoshone	1,086	333.42	
	Targhee	109,773	97,959.14	
	Teton	441,210	88,426.13	187,668.36
Total		2,054,343	719,866.42	808,292.83

Source: M. Brokaw, *The Economic Impact of Commodity Development on National Forest Lands in Wyoming Counties, Schools and Roads*, at appendix 2 (1989).

26. *See, e.g.*, 16 U.S.C. §§ 1, 41d, 47.1, 90a, 90a-1, and 90c-1.
27. National Forest Management Act, 16 U.S.C. § 1604.
28. Applying the Aggregation, *supra* note 3, at 2.
29. 16 U.S.C. § 1604(a) (emphasis added).
30. Examining the Greater Yellowstone Ecosystem Symposium, Univ. of Wyoming, Laramie, Apr. 13–15, 1989 (presentation by Lorraine Mintzmyer, regional director, National Park Service).
31. Goals are defined as concise statements that describe a desired condition to be achieved some time in the future. They are normally expressed in broad, general terms and are timeless in that they have no specific date by which they are to be fulfilled. Forest Service regulations require that planning goals be

promulgated through NFMA public participation requirements and NEPA compliance. 36 C.F.R. § 219.3.

Standards and guidelines are the methods that will be used to accomplish a particular goal. They determine the resource management practices, levels of resource production and management, and availability and suitability of lands for resource management. Standards and guidelines usually apply to each individual management area of the forest. Again, Forest Service planning regulations require that standards and guidelines be promulgated through public participation and after considering alternative measures under the National Environmental Policy Act. 36 C.F.R. §§ 219.1, 219.11.

32. 36 C.F.R. § 219.6.
33. National Environmental Policy Act, 42 U.S.C. § 4321; 40 C.F.R. §§ 1502.14, 1502.16.
34. Memorandum to Greater Yellowstone Coordinating Committee, Public Participation Plan for the Greater Yellowstone Area—Phase II—Plan Aggregation (March 1989).
35. *See* Natural Resources Defense Council v. Clark, No. 86-0548G (E.D. Ca. Aug. 13, 1987) (setting aside regulations for failing to adequately respond to public comments).
36. 16 U.S.C § 1604; 36 C.F.R. §§ 219 *et seq.*
37. Applying the Aggregation, *supra* note 3, at 2.
38. 36 C.F.R. § 219.12(d).
39. Memorandum of Understanding between the Rocky Mountain Region of the National Park Service and the Northern, Rocky Mountain, and Intermountain Regions of the Forest Service, Sept. 24, 1986.
40. Discussion at Greater Yellowstone Coordinating Committee semiannual meeting, Cheyenne, Wyo., Apr. 4–6, 1989.
41. 16 U.S.C §§ 1600 *et seq.*
42. 16 U.S.C §§ 1531 *et seq.*
43. Hill v. Tennessee Valley Authority, 437 U.S. 153 (1978).

CHAPTER 7   **Ecosystems and Property Rights
In Greater Yellowstone:
The Legal System in Transition**
Joseph L. Sax

It is hardly surprising that such issues as wolf reintroduction and natural fire management should generate profound controversy. In each instance we appear to be permitting, even welcoming, the
risk of danger to life and property. Such policies run contrary to conventional intuitions, which are to save and to protect. They are antithetic also to
centuries of learning and legend: fires are to be put out; wolves are vicious.
I leave it to others to correct folkloric errors. I should like to respond to
these issues from the perspective of the law, for modern resource management issues contravene fundamental presuppositions of the legal system as
well.

THE LEGAL SYSTEM AND NATURAL SYSTEMS IN CONFLICT

Perhaps I can best introduce the subject with a slightly shocking statement:
A fundamental purpose of the traditional system of property law has been to
destroy the functioning of natural resource systems. What I mean is this.
Under our legal system we cut up the land into arbitrary pieces (such as
square 160-acre tracts) and then endow the owner with the right, indeed
with every encouragement, to enclose the land and make it exclusive. Why
have we done this? Because our dominant purpose was to transform the
American landscape from what it was—in effect a wilderness and a wildlife economy—into an agricultural (and later industrial) economy.[1]
    If that is the goal, as certainly it was, enclosure and exclusion is a

perfectly sensible strategy; indeed it may be essential. What fencing accomplishes is the severance of wildlife lifelines and the destruction of wildlife habitat. That is what the law, as the handmaiden of the new settlers' incipient economy, sought to accomplish, and it succeeded.

Elements of this same goal reappeared in one context after another. In 1850, for example, Congress enacted a law called the Swamplands Grant Act.[2] The purpose of that law was to give the states the opportunity to put to economic use what were thought to be useless lands—lands that were then called swamplands or wastelands, or even "noisome mosquito-infested lands." Today we call these same places our precious wetlands. The idea was that such lands could be made productive by filling and building on them. In other words, the federal purpose was to promote the destruction of those places as functioning biological systems. That act of destruction was called reclamation. In this respect the statute was a roaring success (though the law is also famous for the frauds committed under its auspices).[3] Millions of acres of wetlands were duly disposed of as a prelude to obliteration-reclamation.[4]

Perhaps the most visible example of the legal system's goals is the appropriation system of western water law. Its purpose was to destroy river systems; not for the pleasure of destruction, of course, but to permit miners and ranchers to take water out of rivers so it could be applied on the land. Two of the standard terms of western water law are *waste* and *beneficial use*. What was beneficial use? It was the abstraction of the water from the river, often to the point of totally drying up river systems downstream. And what was waste? It was leaving water in the river to be "wasted" by running into the sea without having been "productively" used.[5]

To be sure, most of us don't think this way anymore, and that is precisely the point. Public attitudes and values about the use of natural resources have been undergoing a dramatic change. The direction of that change is toward maintenance and restoration of the functioning of natural systems: free-flowing rivers and land allowed to support wildlife, unfilled coastal wetlands, and even forests left to the effects of lightning-caused fires. Not everyone, by any means, has fully embraced the value of restoring functioning natural systems, and there are people whose thinking is still locked into traditional patterns. A recent article in the *High Country News* quoted a lawyer who had for many years represented the water interests of Denver: "[F]orgetting . . . the civilization on which the good life exists in Colorado, many people often referred to as environmentalists have now come to the attitude that water should be wasted by leaving it in streams for the fish and the stream fishermen."[6] Today most of us laugh at such a statement, but not long ago it represented mainstream opinion. Indeed, the job of lawyers like this gentleman was, in effect, to help dewater riverine eco-systems so that the water would not be wasted "by leaving it in streams for the fish."

The difficulty is that generations of this sort of thinking, and of a legal system that implemented it, have created ownership patterns, expectations, and claims of rights that build on the destruction and severance of function-ing natural systems, which included fire and predators. Yet now we have in Yellowstone the leading edge of a new sort of thinking that relies to a great extent on the reconnection and restoration of these same systems.[7] There are significant costs associated with these changes. Even fires that are permitted to burn within prescription can, and sometimes will, get out of control, damaging persons or property and causing ensuing losses to the local tourist economy.[8] Bear and wolf populations also will cause some damage. Our legal system is not yet prepared to cope with these changes. It has no established way to respond to the risks and changes generated by new laws and policies aimed toward restoring natural systems. The reason is, as I have explained, that our legal system was built essentially on the assumption that these sorts of risks should be averted.

YELLOWSTONE AS A TESTING GROUND

A parenthetical observation is called for at this point. In describing the current changes in public values and resource management, I do not mean to suggest we are moving toward a point where the restoration of natural systems will or should dominate all other considerations. Nor do I mean to suggest that all of the destruction of natural systems in the past was a bad thing. Who would deny that some interference with natural systems was justified in order to create Rome and Paris (if not Los Angeles and Miami)? Instead, I have sought to describe a change in values and goals of consider-able significance that will require significant adjustments. That change is a desire to maintain and restore more functioning natural systems, not to abolish all human intervention in such systems. Because the Yellowstone ecosystem is in the forefront of such change, it may be a primary testing ground for the adjustments that will have to be made.

What sort of adjustments will be required? Let me start with what will not do the job. Merely acquiring more public land or compensating prop-erty owners will not be sufficient. Certainly some land acquisition would be helpful in the Yellowstone region, such as the ranchland just north of Yellowstone National Park.[9] And some provision authorizing compensation of ranchers for stock losses from wildlife predation may also be desirable.[10] But even if the public bought up all the land in the United States and started all over again, we would not have solved the problem. The reason is that the central question is how our land is going to be used, and not simply who owns it. How much of the productiveness of the conventional economy are we willing to give up in order to have wolves and bears and natural fire and free-flowing rivers? The proof that ownership alone is not the issue can be seen in the controversy over the national forests, which we, the public, already own. The issues there are not proprietorship or compensation, but how to allocate the land between such competing demands as timber production, hydrocarbon or geothermal development, and wilderness and wildlife.

No one can say with certainty exactly how the new allocations will be made, but at least the direction, and the area of institutional or legal adaptation, is clear. The direction favors more maintenance of natural systems and the processes sustaining them. And the adaptation will require us to define and manage resources as parts of systems and not as inter-changeable commodities seen only in terms of development value. In other words, the law will be used less to encourage cutting natural links and more to require the protection of public trust values in functioning natural systems.[11]

One striking illustration can be seen in the area of western water law. In California the courts have said that the maintenance of downstream water quality sets a limit on the amount of water that can be abstracted from a river upstream, and that this constraint applies to existing water users who may have to release water in order to protect the function of the natural aquatic system below.[12] As I indicated earlier, such rulings are a sharp departure from the past.

These water cases stand for the proposition that the legal rights one can obtain are limited by the nature of the resource system in which they are found. One cannot obtain a right to abstract so much water that it destroys the capacity of downstream areas to withstand saltwater incursion, for example. We are increasingly seeing this approach in the courts and legislatures and will see more of it in the future. The resource, rather than the perception that one acre is like another, will be the focus of attention. Recent cases involving regulation of floodplain land,[13] of coastal wetlands,[14] and of fragile lands[15] are all illustrative of a system of use rights that grow out of an analysis of the resource. Inevitably, therefore, people who live and work in a place like the Yellowstone ecosystem will be seen as having different rights of use than those of people who live in places without such crucial wildlife habitat and wilderness. The future in the Yellowstone region will be one of uses compatible with the functioning of natural systems in a relatively pristine state. The traditional notion that every landowner of every acre, wherever located, has identical rights of use will not, I am confident, prevail much longer. Such claims will bend to a changing conception of property that affirmatively values the sustenance of natural systems.

LOOKING (BACKWARD) TO THE FUTURE

Oddly enough, such a change would not be nearly as radical as it may at first seem. Because of extensive land use regulation in urban areas, owners in such places as New York City already have different rights than owners in rural Wyoming. Those regulations have not been treated as changes in the nature of property rights attuned to the ecosystems in which the resource is found, but they may well be conceived that way.[16] (Indeed, the wolfishness of New York probably imposes more limitations on the opportunities of property owners than would the putative wolves of Yellowstone.)

One desirable approach to smooth the transition that is under way is to discourage incompatible developments in regions like Greater Yellowstone. There are many appropriate ways to do this. In the North Fork region on the west side of Glacier National Park, for example, a decision not to go forward with public infrastructure of the sort that would incite a developmental rush (improved roads, increased telephone and electric service) keeps this island of private land—which is sandwiched between primitive park and forest land—as a compatible, but still productive, private use.[17] In the Yellowstone region, the Forest Service's reluctance to grant permission for a high-density ski resort in important grizzly bear habitat may avoid incompatibility problems before they arise.[18] In the same region, some timely and modest local land use controls might have deterred the acquisition and development of a church property that raises a variety of incompatibility problems and may well end up requiring an expensive public acquisition.[19] Notably, the much publicized and very expensive condemnation of land at Manassas National Battlefield in 1989, occasioned because of proposed incompatible use, was identified as an emerging problem in congressional hearings in 1973.[20]

Even with the most astute efforts, however, a transition as fundamental as the one I have been describing—from a legal system and economy set on destruction of natural systems to a determined public effort to restore and recover those systems still extant—cannot help but be disruptive of existing arrangements. No doubt some of the rough ride will be felt most keenly at places like Yellowstone. Perhaps it will be some consolation, and provide perspective, to observe that we are not experiencing the first such transformation in human history.

We need only go back to the beginning of the nineteenth century and look at the owner of a tract of riparian land in England. Natural flow was the law governing water rights at the time, which meant that if a river flowed past your property you had a right to demand its continued flow undiminished in quantity or quality. And that had been the law for a long time, as one might expect in a preindustrial world. Then something happened, namely the industrial revolution. Coal began to be mined, mills were built. Demand grew to put rivers in service as waste sinks and as sources of energy. So rivers were dammed up and mine owners released contaminated drainage into them. But the landowners said, "You can't do this to us, you are violating our rights. We have a right to the continued flow of the river as it was in a state of nature. And we can invoke the old legal maxim that each person must use his own property so as not to harm the property of others."

The courts, however, quite uniformly rejected such claims and remade the rules so as to favor industrialization.[21] They usually gave some technical justification for what they were doing, and often they refused to admit just how dramatically they were changing things. But one doesn't have to read very deeply between the lines to appreciate the implicit message of those cases to landowners: You are a little worse off in the immediate sense, but you shouldn't worry because as a result of what is going on here we are all going to be better off, you included. We are all beneficiaries of coal mining. The industrial revolution is going to make a better world in which everyone will share. You must think of yourself as a member of a community, part of a new and modern world.[22]

Maybe something like that will happen as contemporary courts come face to face with the implications of such issues as natural fire management, wolf reintroduction, and the protection of wild lands. Perhaps they, too, will say: Yes, there are some rights you landowners used to have that we are no longer going to recognize because we are engaged in maintaining and restoring the function of some natural systems that we did not previously value sufficiently. But don't despair; when it's all over we will all be better off, happier and healthier and wiser than we used to be. As that increasingly happens the legal system will be remaking itself in congruence with modern efforts to restore the functioning of natural systems.

NOTES

1. For an eloquent explanation of how this transformation was effected, see W. Cronon, *Changes in the Land: Indians, Colonists and the Ecology of New England* (1983).
2. Act of Sept. 28, 1850, ch. 84, 9 Stat. 519, 43 U.S.C. § 982 (1988).
3. P. Gates, *History of Public Land Law Development* 326–30 (1983).
4. *Id.* at 325.
5. *See generally* J. Sax & R. Abrams, *Legal Control of Water Resources* 329–43 (1986).
6. High Country News, Mar. 13, 1989, at 3.
7. *See, e.g.,* T. Clark & A. Harvey, *Management of the Greater Yellowstone Ecosystem: An Annotated Bibliography* (1988).
8. See the unpublished internal report on one of the Yellowstone fires of the summer of 1988, Greater Yellowstone Coordinating Committee Managers, Clover-Mist Fire Review, Dec. 1, 1988.
9. U.S. Urged to Take Guru's Land near Yellowstone, New York Times, May 27, 1989, at 7, col. 2 (Western ed.).
10. See Montana Legislative Council, Wildlife Damage to Agriculture, Joint Interim Subcommittee on Agricultural Problems (December 1986).
11. The public trust describes a long-standing obligation of government to maintain and manage navigable and tidal waters and the lands beneath them for public purposes only, including navigation, fishing, recreation, and ecosystem protection. For the background of the doctrine, see Sax, The Public Trust Doctrine in Natural Resources: Effective Judicial Intervention, 68 Mich. L. Rev. 471 (1970).
12. National Audubon Soc'y v. Superior Court of Alpine County, 33 Cal. 3d 419, 189 Cal. Rptr. 346, 658 P.2d 709, *cert. denied,* 464 U.S. 977 (1983); United States v. State Water Resources Control Board, 227 Cal. Rptr. 161, 182 Cal. App. 3d 82 (1st Dist. 1986).
13. J. Kusler, 3 *Regulation of Flood Hazard Areas to Reduce Flood Losses* (1982); Baram & Miyares, Managing Flood Risk, 7 Colum. J. Envtl. L. 129 (1982). *Cf.* First English Evangelical Lutheran Church v. Los Angeles, 482 U.S. 304 (1987). On remand the California court held that the floodplain ordinance did not constitute a taking of property. 258 Cal. Rptr. 893 (1989).
14. *See, e.g.,* Moskow v. Commissioner, 427 N.E.2d 750 (Mass. 1981); Graham v. Estuary Properties, Inc., 399 So. 2d 1374 (Fla. 1981), *cert. denied sub nom.* Taylor v. Graham, 454 U.S. 1083 (1981).
15. *See, e.g.,* Mears, Municipal Avalanche Zoning, Ekistics 309, November–December 1984. For an excellent discussion of avalanche law, see Marty, Les Avalanches, 20 Droit et Ville 89 (Toulouse, 1985).
16. *See* Patten chapter 2 in this volume.

17. Sax & Keiter, Glacier National Park and Its Neighbors: A Study of Federal Interagency Relations, 14 Ecology L.Q. 207, 233 (1987).

18. *See, e.g.*, Lovett, The Role of the Forest Service in Ski Resort Development: An Economic Approach to Public Lands Management, 10 Ecology L.Q. 507, 548–49 (1982).

19. *See* New York Times, *supra* note 9. For a general discussion of this issue, *see* Sax, Buying Scenery: Land Acquisitions for the National Park Service, 1980 Duke L.J. 709. *See also* H.R. 2535 (101st Cong., 1st Sess.), 135 Cong. Rec. H2783, H2265 (daily ed. June 1, 1989) (appropriating federal funds to purchase the church property).

20. The acquisition law is PL 100-647 (Nov. 10, 1988). *See* Sax, Helpless Giants: The National Parks and the Regulation of Private Land, 75 Mich. L. Rev. 239, 240 n.9 (1976).

21. J. Sax & R. Abrams, *supra* note 5, at 160–75.

22. *See, e.g.*, Pennsylvania Coal Co. v. Sanderson, 113 Pa. 126, 6 A. 453, 459 (1886).

PART II   **FIRE POLICY AND MANAGEMENT**

Research has shown that natural fires have been a part of Yellowstone's environment for thousands of years prior to the arrival of modern man. Large fires burned at average intervals of 20 to 25 years in the low grasslands, at intervals of perhaps 250–400 years in the forests, and less frequently in the alpine areas. . . . Natural fires are allowed to burn in zones not endangering life or property, or not threatening [to] spread from the park where agreements with neighboring agencies do not allow for such. All man-caused fires are extinguished as soon as practicable.
Yellowstone National Park Natural Resources Management Plan and Environmental Assessment, 1982.

Overleaf: *Natural fire burning in Yellowstone National Park, August 1988. Photo courtesy of Yellowstone National Park, Mammoth, Wyoming.*

CHAPTER 8   **The Yellowstone Fire Controversy**

Dennis H. Knight

There have been many controversies over resource management in the Greater Yellowstone Area, but few have evoked so much emotional debate as the question of what role fire should play. Most of the debate on this subject occurred in 1988, when raging fires swept across the GYA landscape. Although research suggests that large areas burned in the 1700s (Romme and Despain 1989a), few envisioned the awesome power and high costs that would be faced if this occurred again. Indeed, fire management in Yellowstone National Park had been a comparatively simple matter since 1972, when the National Park Service decided that lightning-caused fires in the back country should be allowed to burn if they did not threaten human life and property. Most fires went out without human intervention after burning a few hectares or less (Romme and Despain 1989a; Varley and Schullery chapter 9 in this volume).

Flammability, however, is dependent on climatic conditions as well as fuel accumulation (Chandler et al. 1983; Pyne 1984, Heinselman 1985), and by any standard 1988 was unusually dry and windy (Trenberth, Branstator, and Arkin 1988). Ignitions by lightning were common, and humans caused fires as well. Fuel accumulations proved sufficient under drought conditions to sustain the largest fires experienced in the GYA during the past two centuries or more (Romme and Despain 1989a). The fires could not be stopped with the resources available until light rain and snow fell in

I am especially grateful to the following individuals for excellent suggestions on an earlier version of this chapter: Stephen F. Arno, James K. Brown, John F. Chapman, Robert B. Keiter, William H. Romme, and Paul Schullery.

September (Davis and Mutch 1989; Varley and Schullery chapter 9 in this volume).

Large fires have been common in western North America during the 1900s, primarily because often-flammable coniferous forests are a predominant feature of the landscape. Residents of the Rocky Mountains are accustomed to haze caused by fires to the west that burn out of control every few years, despite immediate attempts to suppress them. More forests burned in the Pacific Northwest during 1910 than in Yellowstone during 1988 (Pyne 1982), but memories of raging widespread fires had waned. Furthermore, there were fears that Yellowstone National Park, the "crown jewel" of the national park system, was being destroyed along with a tourism industry critical to the regional economy. Such fears were fostered inadvertently by managers and scientists with insufficient information, editors approving overly dramatic headlines, public leaders making premature pronouncements, and smoke in the air for miles around that made life unpleasant if not intolerable.

Everyone was happy when the 1988 fires finally were extinguished. A truly significant event had been experienced with minimal loss of personal property and no more human casualties than occur in the GYA during a normal summer. Newspaper headlines and public pronouncements moderated after the 1988 fires were extinguished. Although approximately 36 percent of YNP (less than 10 percent of the GYA) had been subjected to some burning, only about 15–20 percent of the park was subjected to the crown fires that give the impression of devastation (Despain et al. 1989). From the standpoint of highway observers, who compose more than 95 percent of park visitors, less than 30 percent of the park's roads pass through forest burned in 1988. The geologic features that attract so many tourists are apparently unscathed and the large mammal populations appear to be thriving (Singer et al. 1989; Van Dyke et al. chapter 13 in this volume). Sales tax revenues were up in surrounding counties during 1988 because of business created by fire fighters (McVeigh 1989), and the number of park visitors in 1989 and 1990 was higher than ever before (YNP, personal communication).

Yet the fire controversy continues. Following the advice of an interagency panel (Fire Management Policy Review Team 1988), the secretaries of interior and agriculture mandated the immediate suppression of all fires in the GYA (and federal lands elsewhere) until fire management plans have been reviewed and, if necessary, revised. Before being approved, the plans probably will be subjected to public hearings, thus assuring debate over whether the potential impacts of future fires have been properly assessed.

Some disagreements may be resolved in court. Scientists will debate research priorities, a necessity because of limited funding and uncertainty over the kind of research that can and should be accommodated in the GYA; and natural-area managers will continue to debate the best management strategies for parks and other preserves that have become so important to the world.

CONTROVERSIAL ISSUES

Before considering controversial issues, it is important to review four points on which there seems to be agreement. First, no one doubts that fire over the years has played a significant role in creating the mosaic of different vegetation types in the GYA (Taylor 1973, 1974; Houston 1973, 1982, Arno 1980; Romme 1982; Romme and Knight 1982; Pyne 1989; Romme and Despain 1989a; Despain n.d.). Sharp transitions from young to old forest are readily apparent from the air, marking the boundaries of old fires. Fire-scarred trees are common. Furthermore, the plants are well adapted to fire through such features as serotinous cones, as found in some populations of lodgepole pine, and the capacity for sprouting exhibited by aspen and many shrubs and herbaceous plants (Knight and Wallace 1989). Such adaptations suggest that fire has been an important factor in natural selection for thousands of years.

Second, no one would dispute that fires can occur in the absence of humans. Lightning ignitions are common. On June 27, 1986, for example, lightning struck the ground in YNP 786 times in two and a half hours (determined using triangulation on the radio waves emitted by each individual strike; Don G. Despain, pers. comm.). Five fires were started, but as observed so often, none continued to burn, because of the prevailing climatic conditions.

Third, there is little disagreement that animal population sizes and the GYA landscape have changed in the past and will continue to change in the future. Even without human influences, which have been many (Haines 1977; Bartlett 1985; Chase 1986), Yellowstone landscapes will continue changing in response to climatic change and the continual fluctuations of plant and animal populations. Ecosystems of all kinds are characterized by change, sometimes gradual and sometimes the result of episodic disturbances (Pickett and White 1985; Agee and Johnson 1988).

Finally, all agree that the suppression of every fire only leads to fuel accumulations of such magnitude that suppression becomes impossible. As concluded by an interagency team (Fire Management Policy Review Team

1988), fires will and must continue to play a major role in the management of most wildlands.

Significant disagreement continues, however, on 1) the importance of fire suppression in creating unnaturally high flammability, 2) the desirability and potential of prescribed burning, and 3) the need for changing the fire management policy. Each of these issues provides a classic opportunity for considering the relevance of basic ecological research to wildland management and public policy.

FIRE SUPPRESSION, INDIAN-CAUSED FIRES, AND FLAMMABILITY

Until the early 1970s, fire management in the GYA was simply a matter of suppression (Taylor 1974; Pyne 1982; Davis and Mutch 1989). Fire was viewed by the National Park Service and the Forest Service as an undesirable event with few, if any, positive effects. Even in YNP, where wood production was not a management objective, fires were suppressed whenever possible.

In the 1970s Park Service and Forest Service managers became concerned that the elimination of fires was leading to increased fuel accumulation, as had been experienced in the sequoia redwoods of California (Pyne 1982). The difficulties of suppressing all fires also led to the adoption of fire management rather than control as a guiding principle (Kilgore 1976; Butts 1985). Some benefits of fire were being recognized, including the preservation of biological diversity (Taylor 1973; Wright 1974; Heinselman 1981). Encouraged partly by observations that most fires had burned rather small areas with little threat to visitor centers and gateway communities, GYA agencies adopted the policy of letting some lightning-caused fires burn in parks and wilderness areas if there was no apparent threat to human settlements or unique natural features (Pyne 1982; Davis and Mutch 1989; Varley and Schullery chapter 9 in this volume). By allowing such fires to burn, fuel accumulations would be reduced and a natural process—fire—would be restored to the ecosystem.

The new policy appeared to be well conceived; most fires burned only a small area and created no obviously adverse impacts. For sixteen years there was little evidence of excessive fuel accumulation caused by fire suppression (Varley and Schullery chapter 9 in this volume; Schullery 1989) because only a small portion of the GYA burned each year. Most fires went out by themselves. The program proceeded in such an orderly and predictable manner that there was little incentive to investigate what might happen during a truly dry year, one that exceeded in flammability the other dry years recorded during the comparatively long history of YNP. Some criticized the YNP fire management program (Pyne 1989), but the Park Service and others saw no compelling reason to change.

Several fire-history studies were conducted in the GYA during the 1970s. Houston (1973, 1982) and Arno and Gruell (1983) studied the low-elevation Douglas fir forests, finding that fire suppression had led to an increase in tree density and sagebrush cover in some areas. Suppression undoubtedly had created more flammable conditions. Romme (1982), on the other hand, studied a 73-square-kilometer tract of high-elevation forests (above 2,200 m) in YNP dominated by lodgepole pine, Engelmann spruce, and subalpine fir. He found evidence of large-scale fires in the 1700s and concluded that the slow rate of tree growth and succession at the higher elevations was an important factor in causing long fire-return intervals. He calculated that highly flammable conditions required 250–300 years to develop in his study area. Fire suppression, he reasoned, probably had little influence on the high-elevation forests because fuels there accumulate so slowly. His data led him to predict, however, that large-scale fires would occur again in the next century.

Recognizing that extrapolating to all of YNP based on Romme's initial research was risky, Romme and Despain (1989a) obtained similar data on fire history for a much larger area—15 percent of the park. Their conclusions, published with the experience of the 1988 fires behind them, were modified only slightly. Fire suppression, they concluded, had some influence on the spread and severity of fires in 1988, but it was less important in creating the large scale of the fires than the coincidence of an extremely dry and windy summer with fuel accumulation developed through natural succession during the past 250–300 years. They did observe that never in the past 300 years had so much of their study area burned in one year as burned in 1988. In contrast, the large areas burned in the late 1600s and early 1700s resulted from several large fires during a period of two decades or more (figure 8.1). Only time will tell if the same occurs during the late 1900s; there could be additional large fires in the near future.

Two other dimensions to the fire suppression issue must be considered. First, although fire suppression in the back country of Yellowstone and Grand Teton national parks may have been difficult prior to the 1940s, due to inaccessibility and limited resources (Romme and Despain 1989a), fire suppression on adjacent better-roaded land probably was effective. Fires on adjacent land can burn into the parks. Therefore, suppression outside park boundaries is essentially fire suppression within.

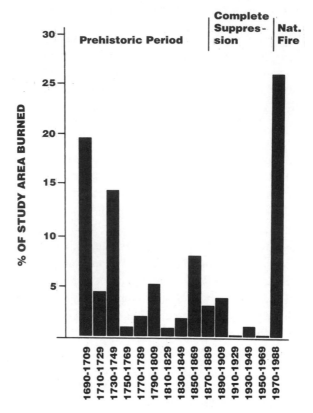

Figure 8.1 Land area burned during 20-yr intervals for a 1,295 km² portion of the Yellowstone plateau, as determined from tree-ring data and an analysis of the landscape mosaic by Romme and Despain (1989b). For the last period (1970–1988), most of the forest burned in a single year (1988), in contrast to previous periods when the burning occurred during several years. When the data are grouped in 50-yr intervals, approximately the same amount of land burned in 1690–1739 as burned during 1940–1988 (fig. 3, Romme and Despain 1989b). The comparatively large amount of land burned during the period 1850–1869, and the smaller amount burned thereafter until the most recent period, suggests that attempts at complete suppression (from 1872 to 1972) may have prevented extensive burns until the record drought year 1988. Another plausible interpretation, however, is that climatic conditions were especially favorable for fires just prior to the establishment of YNP in 1872. Romme and Despain (1989b) suggest that, without fire suppression, some of the area burned in 1988 might have burned during a series of smaller fires after about 1940, but a large area would nevertheless have burned in 1988 (Figure from Romme and Despain 1989b; reprinted with permission of the authors and *Western Wildlands*).

Second, Indian-started fires have been eliminated in the GYA. Some evidence suggests that fire frequency was higher in areas of Indian occupation than elsewhere (Barrett and Arno 1982; Arno 1985; Gruell 1985), and a few have argued that the elimination of Indian fires created very unnatural fuel accumulations in YNP because fires caused solely by lightning would be less frequent (Chase 1986; Bonnicksen 1989). Although plausible, two factors must be considered in resolving this issue: First, little evidence is available on the effect of Indian fires in the GYA. The study by Barrett and Arno was done in western Montana at lower elevations. Arno (1985) and Gruell (1985) concluded that Indian-caused fires probably were less important at higher elevations, though fires could have spread into the higher mountains from the foothills. Second, fires occur when fuel and climatic conditions are right, the source of ignition being relatively unimportant.

Given the abundance of fish and game, Indians must have used the GYA and they surely started some fires, accidentally if not intentionally. However, contrary to what is predicted by persons who maintain that Indian fires preserved a more open, less flammable condition, the forests in the interior of Yellowstone at higher elevations could be quite dense. Gen. W. E. Strong wrote after his trip there in 1875 (Strong 1968):

> The trees have been falling here for centuries, and such a network of limbs, trunks, and stumps has been formed, that to face it with a horse . . . is enough to appall the stoutest heart . . . and add to this a perfect labyrinth of fallen timber, with limbs and branches entwined in every imaginable shape. . . . The pine leaves were lying so thickly upon the surface of the ground, that the tracks of nearly forty horses . . . trailing one another, were hardly discernible two hours after they were made.

Although General Strong may have been writing about one small area, other explorers also commented on the dense forests (Haines 1977).

Thus the large-scale 1988 fires could have been a "natural" event, in spite of the large area burned in one year, or a "near natural" event, as concluded by Romme and Despain (1989a) after considering the possibility of effective fire suppression in the GYA. Such distinctions are fraught with ambiguity (Kilgore 1985). Furthermore, to categorically label the fires as natural or unnatural is not possible because studies on the rate of fuel accumulation with and without fire suppression, and with and without insect epidemics (for example, the mountain pine beetle), have not been done. The contrasting results of Houston (1973) and Romme and Despain (1989a) in YNP, combined with other predictions, suggest that the effects of suppression will vary considerably in relation to topography and elevation, and that attempts to generalize for the entire GYA are futile. Fire management policies must consider this variability. Further research is necessary before anyone can state confidently that the large-scale fires of 1988 were either an artifact of poor management or an essentially natural event triggered by climatic phenomena.

USING PRESCRIBED FIRES TO AVOID WILDFIRE

Prescribed fires traditionally are those that are ignited intentionally by managers under climatic conditions that are of moderate or low fire hazard. Usually the goal is to reduce fuel loads, improve wildlife habitat, or enhance conditions for the growth of certain trees. The Forest Service and the Park Service also recognize another kind of prescribed fire, namely, lightning-caused fires that are evaluated by managers and allowed to burn if certain conditions are met (Davis and Mutch 1989). Both kinds of prescribed fires are used in the GYA, though only lightning-caused prescribed fires have been allowed to burn in YNP (with the exception of a few small experimental fires). Regardless of origin, fires that cannot be controlled at will, such as those that occurred in 1988, are classified as "wildfire" and are avoided whenever possible. Some prescribed lightning fires undoubtedly have been uncontrollable at times, but the risks to human life and property were sufficiently low that they were allowed to burn. Such fires frequently start late in the summer or early fall and, despite burning briefly at intensities comparable to 1988 (Romme and Despain 1989a), are soon extinguished by autumn rains and snow.

Prescribed burning is comparatively simple in Douglas fir and ponderosa pine savannas at lower elevations, where many of the trees are not killed by surface fires because of thick bark, but the logistical problems are substantial in the denser forests dominated by spruce, fir, and lodgepole pine. Crown fires often develop in such forests and are difficult to contain within designated boundaries, especially if unexpected winds develop. Burned forests with heavy fuel accumulations also may smolder until weather changes allow the crown fires to continue spreading (J. K. Brown, pers. comm.). Thereby, some prescribed fires may end up burning under weather conditions more hazardous than at the time of ignition.

Human-ignited prescribed fires typically are used only in circumstances where managers are confident of containing the fire within designated boundaries. Restricting the fires to the burning of surface fuels is often preferred, though canopy fires are sometimes prescribed in western coniferous forests (J. K. Brown, pers. comm.). In Rocky Mountain subalpine forests, restricting prescribed burning to surface fires, even if it were possible, would change dramatically the nature of the fire disturbances that probably prevailed in presettlement times. Herein lies the dilemma that makes prescribed fire difficult to implement in the GYA and elsewhere (Lopoukhine chapter 12 in this volume): To preserve fire as a natural process in GYA wildlands, some unpopular and possibly expensive wild-fires must occur.

Though permitted by park policy, human-caused prescribed fires have not been used in Grand Teton and Yellowstone national parks, partly because of a desire to minimize human influences (Schullery and Despain 1989). It seemed better to let meteorologic and fuel conditions determine where fires occur rather than depending on human decisions. The Park Service was committed to this policy, even though it frequently led to difficult questions about the difference between fires caused by humans and those caused by lightning. Although not different physically, there can be differences in fire location and whether the fire burns at all. Humans with drip torches can elevate temperatures to ignition points in several locations through prolonged exposure to flames, greatly increasing the chances that a fire will occur in an area that a lightning strike would fail to ignite. On the other hand, some lightning ignitions will occur at a time when human-caused prescribed fires would not be approved because of extreme fire hazard conditions. As more is learned, it may be possible to more faithfully mimic lightning fires through prescribed burns.

Right or wrong, the Park Service goal was to maintain a landscape mosaic, away from visitor centers, that was subject primarily to modifications brought about by lightning-caused fires. Although the Park Service had difficulty addressing questions about whether the mosaic was indeed "natural," there seemed little need to modify the policy until substantial evidence was presented that the existing mosaic was artificial, perhaps because of fire suppression, or that human-caused prescribed fires were necessary to protect human life and property.

For some observers, the need for human-caused prescribed fires was made eminently clear in 1988. Noting that gateway communities and visitor centers were threatened because the adjacent forests were too close and too flammable, they argued that human-caused prescribed fires during moderate fire hazard conditions, in the vicinity of human habitations, could have minimized the anxiety created by the 1988 fires. Brown (chapter 11 in this volume) substantiates these claims, suggesting that the cost of fuel reduction in the vicinity of developments would have been reasonable compared to the cost of fighting the 1988 wildfires. Some fuel reduction could have helped protect developed areas, even though fires can be started by embers blown in from more than a mile away (Davis and Mutch 1989).

Brown did not conclude, however, that the scale of the 1988 fires would have been reduced significantly with a program of human-caused pre-scribed burns, given the traditional resources and attitudes of both the Park Service and the Forest Service. Large areas of young forests, with com-paratively little fuel, were burned in 1988 as well as older forests with abundant fuel (Romme and Despain 1989a). Human-caused prescribed fires would have been set only during moderate fire conditions, with the result that only small areas would have been burned. Yet the resources required to contain such fires, if weather conditions and fire intensity changed quickly, would be large enough that only a few such fires could be afforded each year. And not every year would be acceptable climatically. Even assuming that human-caused prescribed fires had been used since 1972, when fire was officially accepted as a necessary process in the GYA, Brown concluded that too little forest away from human habitations would have been burned to prevent the large scale of the 1988 fires.

The current fire management policy does not preclude human-caused prescribed fire for the purpose of reducing hazardous fuels, and fuel has been removed manually with saws in some areas. Policy changes thus are unnecessary for the purpose of creating broader fuel breaks around visitor centers and gateway communities. Some may not like the more parklike surroundings this creates, but there is no other choice, short of removing visitor centers altogether, if easier protection from fire is desired. The experience gained in 1988 provides a basis for calculating with greater confidence just how much fuel reduction is needed. The results should be helpful throughout the Rocky Mountain region.

THE CURRENT FIRE MANAGEMENT POLICY
IN GYA WILDLANDS

The current fire management policy for parks and wilderness in the GYA can be summarized as follows: (1) Permit lightning-caused fires to burn in designated areas unless there is a high potential for wildfire and the destruc-tion of human life, human property, or special features of the area; (2) suppress all nonprescribed human-caused fires (and any natural fires whose suppression is deemed necessary) in as safe, cost-effective, and environmentally sensitive a way as possible; and (3) resort to prescribed burning when and where necessary and practical to reduce hazardous fuels or restore certain types of vegetation. Full suppression remains the policy near human habitations or on national forest lands where wood production is an important goal. Human-ignited prescribed fires have been used by the Forest Service to control sagebrush, to experiment with aspen management, and to reduce logging slash. These fires have not been used in coniferous forests, apparently because it did not seem necessary or because the chances of a crown fire were high and the resources for controlling the prescribed fires were judged inadequate.

Many have questioned why more extensive fuel reduction was not done in YNP around human habitations, considering that it was allowed by policy. Conversations with YNP officials suggest a two-part answer. First, past experience indicated that lightning-caused fires could be controlled, as they had been prior to the unusual climatic conditions of 1988. Second, YNP differed from most national parks because of its large size, which was a compelling reason for managing the park with a minimum of human intervention —the unwritten "natural regulation policy." Human-caused prescribed fires seemed unnecessary, and preventing them was one way of maintaining a higher order of naturalness. There was also the potential for considerable embarrassment if a human-ignited fire escaped control. The resources required for controlling prescribed fires often were inadequate, or simply not known. Furthermore, appealing for additional funds for the purpose of burning in national parks has not been popular because of the stigma attached to fire and because diverting funds from other activities would have been necessary. Such difficulties might have been resolved if the Park Service had been more aggressive in making requests for an augmented fire research and management program.

The natural regulation policy has been criticized sharply by Bonnicksen and Stone (1982), Chase (1986), and Bonnicksen (1989). They argue that Yellowstone has been subjected to so many adverse human impacts that allowing natural disturbances to occur without proactive management can lead only to further declines in park resources. Commonly mentioned among the adverse impacts are the loss of the gray wolf, the declines in beaver and aspen, the elimination of Indian fires, an unnatural forest structure, an allegedly excessive fuel accumulation due to fire suppression, and the presence of too many large ungulates. Aldo Leopold recognized the dilemma of managing parks in 1927, when he wrote to the superintendent of Glacier National Park, "The balance of nature in any strict sense has been upset long ago. . . . The only option we have is to create a new balance objectively determined for each area in accordance with the intended use of that area." His son Starker later chaired a committee that recommended the restoration of parks to something close to the conditions they were in prior to European settlement (Leopold et al. 1963). In general, critics of the Park Service want proactive management plans with specific goals and a scientifically sound program for assuring that progress is being achieved.

Such recommendations seem highly appropriate for many national parks and natural areas, especially those of small size and low ecological diversity. In fact, a recent workshop that involved Park Service employees also recommended improved management goals and more careful monitoring (Agee and Johnson 1988). However, wildlands like those in the GYA may be large enough and "natural" enough for semipassive management. Perhaps large size and complexity, as well as an inadequate research effort, have hampered the establishment of goals that could withstand the criticism of being too human-centered. Moreover, human values and goals change over time. For example, there is now considerable support for reintroducing the wolf, but at one time predators were controlled because the parks were viewed as being a place for elk, deer, and bison. The wolf is still suffering from a bad image.

Taking a passive or semipassive approach to wildland management often has merit because exercising active management with precise goals preempts the opportunity to learn about ecological phenomena that have occurred for millennia. This in itself is one of the major scientific values of wildlands that could be lost by so-called scientific management, especially when the knowledge base is small. Preserving such scientific values does not preclude large parks from serving "for the enjoyment of the people" during most years.

Critics of the passive, or natural regulation, policy maintain that the 1988 fires proved their point, contending that the fires "destroyed" too much of the world's first and most famous national park. But what has been destroyed? Western coniferous forests have evolved in the presence of fire, and some plant and animal species are favored by it. Those that are not favored by fire persist elsewhere in unburned forests. The landscape mosaic has changed, as it undoubtedly has in the past, but insufficient information is available to state that the changes will be detrimental or that the new mosaic is an artifact of human intervention. Large mammal populations were down in 1989, due partially to drought and a severe winter (not simply because of the fires), but the prognosis for these animals and others is favorable (Christensen et al. 1989; Singer et al. 1989). Nutrient losses, erosion, and even occasional mud slides are taking place in some burned areas, but such events apparently occurred in presettlement times as well, as indicated by layers of charcoal and other sediments in lake-bottom sediments (Mehringer 1985). Mud slides also occur in unburned forest (P. E. Farnes, pers. comm.). Such erosion events seem inappropriate outside of parks because of already elevated rates of soil loss, sedimentation, and eutrophication caused by human activity; but background levels of erosion in large GYA wildlands usually are quite low. Furthermore, erosion must be viewed as a natural process in such wildlands.

To be sure, some effects of the 1988 fires remain unknown. A team of scientists concluded that known rare species were not affected adversely (Christensen et al. 1989), but such statements can only be tentative. Also, although the landscape mosaic has changed, predicting the long-term consequences of these changes for terrestrial and aquatic biota is difficult and constitutes one of the challenges of landscape ecology (Knight 1987; Knight and Wallace 1989). Predicting the long-term effects on aquatic ecosystems also is uncertain (Minshall, Brock, and Varley 1989; Minshall and Brock chapter 10 in this volume), and the potential exists for higher than normal flooding of rivers draining the park (Knight and Wallace 1989). Such uncertainties are unfortunate, but they are a reality in managing the GYA and other wildlands (Parsons et al. 1986; Agee and Johnson 1988). Because definitive statements about adverse ecological effects are not yet possible, significant changes in fire management policies at this time seem unnecessary. Moreover, adoption of a policy that attempts to eliminate uncertainties, even if that were possible, creates an inherently unnatural situation.

If change in the policy does occur, the reason will probably be adverse public opinion rather than adverse ecological effects. Regardless of ecological impacts, the costs and anxiety of fighting the fires were high. In addition, part of the GYA landscape is now less attractive for those who perceive forest as more significant than the communities of plants and animals that become abundant following fire. Similarly, many people think a stand of lodgepole pine is worthier than a population of the native mountain pine beetle, which can kill trees. Such distinctions may be appropriate for forests where wood production is the goal, but they are not valid in large parks where the maintenance of biological diversity and a primeval landscape is the goal. Forests are more than trees and large mammals. Indeed, the survival of trees and large mammals depends on many other organisms and ecological processes. Fortunately, wildlands in the GYA appear to be large enough that visitors can enjoy a landscape mosaic consisting of stands of green trees as well as stands of other plants and animals—all of which are important. The forest ecosystem survives because of this diversity, and maintaining that diversity depends on periodic disturbance (Wright 1974; Pickett and White 1985).

But must the disturbances be as large and costly as in 1988? Some argue no, maintaining that the required disturbances can be "scaled down" with prescribed burning and manual fuel manipulation, and without losing important ecological features. Others argue that humans should not expect to control all natural phenomena, that doing so in large wildlands with currently available information precludes further learning about wildland ecology, and that being too eager to establish specific goals and proactive management conflicts with the purposes for which some wildlands were established. This controversy has emerged because of the high costs of visitor center and gateway community protection in a landscape that seems to be characterized by large-scale fires. Perhaps users of such centers should be taxed to help cover the periodic costs of fire protection. The rate of taxation could be quite low, because the fires are so infrequent.

The debate about changing the fire management policies of GYA agencies will continue. Policies will continue to evolve, too slowly for some and too rapidly for others. Regardless of one's perspective, the cost and anxiety of protecting gateway communities must be balanced with the economic benefits of being a gateway community. The regional economy has benefited for many years from Yellowstone and Grand Teton national parks. It appears that the 1988 fires were caused as much by uncontrollable climatic conditions as by fuel accumulation. If that proves to be true, then some businesses must be prepared for occasional lean years when large fires will occur again—just as ski resorts must be prepared for low snowfall years and farmers must be prepared for drought years. Fortunately, such adverse climatic events are infrequent, and large fires are the most infrequent of all.

In conclusion, human influences in the last century have changed the character of most wildlands. Whether or not these changes have been subtle or dramatic in the GYA is a matter of debate and depends on the specific area being considered. To a large degree, disagreement persists on some issues because there is still insufficient information to be confident about some conclusions, and because participants in the debate are attempting too many generalizations or are confounding the management of parks and wilderness with the management of forests for wood production. There is now a clear mandate to learn from the surprising 1988 fires through careful analysis and new research initiatives. The results will be relevant to wildland management throughout western North America.

REFERENCES

Agee, J. K., and D. R. Johnson, eds. 1988. Ecosystem management for parks and wilderness. Univ. of Washington Press, Seattle.

Arno, S. F. 1980. Forest fire history in the northern Rockies. J. For. 78:460–465.

———. 1985. Ecological effects and management implications of Indian fires. Pages 81–86 in J. E. Lotan, B. M. Kilgore, W. C. Fischer, and R. W. Mutch, tech. coords. Proceedings: Symposium and workshop on wilderness fire. U.S. For. Serv. Gen. Tech. Rep. INT-182.

Arno, S. F., and G. E. Gruell. 1983. Fire history at the forest-grassland ecotone in southwestern Montana. J. Range Mgmt. 36:332–336.

Barrett, S. W., and S. F. Arno. 1982. Indian fires as an ecological influence in the northern Rockies. J. For. 80:647–651.

Bartlett, R. 1985. Yellowstone: A wilderness besieged. Univ. of Arizona Press, Tucson.

Bonnicksen, T. 1989. Fire gods and federal policy. Am. Forests 95:14–16, 66–68.

Bonnicksen, T., and E. C. Stone. 1982. Managing vegetation within U.S. national parks: A policy analysis. Envtl. Mgmt. 6:101–102, 109–122.

Butts, D. B. 1985. Fire policies and programs of the National Park Service. Pages 43–48 in J. E. Lotan, B. M. Kilgore, W. C. Fischer, and R. W. Mutch, tech. coords. Proceedings: Symposium and workshop on wilderness fire. U.S. For. Serv. Gen. Tech. Rep. INT-182.

Chandler, C., P. Cheney, P. Thomas, L. Trabaud, and D. Williams. 1983. Fire in forestry, vol. 1. Forest fire behavior and effects. John Wiley and Sons, New York.

Chase, A. 1986. Playing God in Yellowstone: The destruction of America's first national park. Atlantic Monthly Press, New York.

Christensen, N. L., J. K. Agee, P. F. Brussard, J. Hughes, D. H. Knight, G. W. Minshall, J. M. Peek, S. J. Pyne, F. J. Swanson, J. W. Thomas, S. Wells, S. E. Williams, and H. A. Wright. 1989. Interpreting the Yellowstone fires of 1988. BioScience 39:678–685.

Davis, K. M., and R. W. Mutch. 1989. The fires of the Greater Yellowstone Area: The saga of a long hot summer. W. Wildlands 15:2–9.

Despain, D. Yellowstone vegetation: Consequences of environment and history in a natural setting. Roberts Rinehart, Boulder, Colo. In press.

Despain, D., A. Rodman, P. Schullery, and H. Schovic. 1989. Burned area survey of Yellowstone National Park: The fires of 1988. Internal report. Yellowstone National Park.

Fire Management Policy Review Team. 1988. Report on fire management policy. U.S. Department of Agriculture and U.S. Department of the Interior, Washington, D.C.

Gruell, G. E. 1985. Indian fires in the interior west: A widespread influence. Pages 68–73 in J. E. Lotan, B. M. Kilgore, W. C. Fischer, and R. W. Mutch, tech. coords. Proceedings: Symposium and workshop on wilderness fires. U.S. For. Serv. Gen. Tech. Rep. INT-182.

Haines, A. 1977. The Yellowstone story. 2 vols. Colorado Associated Univ. Press, Boulder.

Heinselman, M. L. 1981. Fire intensity and frequency as factors in the distribution and structure of northern ecosystems. Pages 7–57 in H. A. Mooney, T. M. Bonnicksen, N. L. Christensen, J. E. Lotan, and W. A. Reiners, eds. Fire regimes and ecosystem properties. U.S. For. Serv. Gen. Tech. Rep. WO-26.

———. 1985. Fire regimes and management options in ecosystems with large high-intensity fires. Pages 101–109 in J. E. Lotan, B. M. Kilgore, W. C. Fischer, and R. W. Mutch, tech. coords. Proceedings: Symposium and workshop on wilderness fire. U.S. For. Serv. Gen. Tech. Rep. INT-182.

Houston, D. B. 1973. Wildfires in northern Yellowstone National Park. Ecology 54:1111–1117.

———. 1982. The northern Yellowstone elk: Ecology and management. Macmillan, New York.

Kilgore, B. M. 1976. From fire control to fire management: An ecological basis for policies. Trans. N. Am. Wildl. Nat. Resources Conf. 41:477–493.

———. 1985. What is "natural" in wilderness fire management? Pages 57–66 in J. E. Lotan, B. M. Kilgore, W. C. Fischer, and R. W. Mutch, tech. coords. Proceedings: Symposium and workshop on wilderness fire. U.S. For. Serv. Gen. Tech. Rep. INT-182.

Knight, D. H. 1987. Parasites, lightning, and the vegetation mosaic in wilderness landscapes. Pages 59–83 in M. G. Turner, ed. Landscape heterogeneity and disturbance. Springer-Verlag, New York.

Knight, D. H., and L. Wallace. 1989. The Yellowstone fires: Issues in landscape ecology. BioScience 39:700–706.

Leopold, A. S., S. A. Cain, C. M. Cottam, I. N. Gabrielson, and T. L. Kimball. 1963. Wildlife management in the national parks. Trans. N. Am. Wildl. Nat. Resources Conf. 28:28–45.

McVeigh, B. 1989. The Yellowstone fires of 1988: An analysis based on sales tax collections and various park related data. Wyo. Q. Update 8:26–32.

Mehringer, P. J., Jr. 1985. Late-Quaternary pollen records from the interior Pacific Northwest and northern Great Basin of the United States. Pages 167–189 in F. M. Bryant, Jr., and R. G. Holloway, eds. Pollen records of late-Quaternary North American sediments. Am. Ass'n Stratigraphic Palynologists, Dallas.

Minshall, G. W., J. T. Brock, and J. D. Varley. 1989. Wildfires and Yellowstone's stream ecosystems. BioScience 39:707–715.

Parsons, D. J., D. M. Graber, J. K. Agee, and J. W. van Wagtendonk. 1986. Natural fire management in national parks. Envtl. Mgmt. 10:21–24.

Pickett, S. T. A., and P. S. White, eds. 1985. The ecology of natural disturbance and patch dynamics. Academic Press, New York.

Pyne, S. J. 1982. Fire in America: A cultural history of wildland and rural fire. Princeton Univ. Press, Princeton, N.J.

———. 1984. Introduction to wildland fire. John Wiley and Sons, New York.

———. 1989. The summer we let wild fire loose. Natural History (August):45–49.

Romme, W. H. 1982. Fire and landscape diversity in subalpine forests of Yellow-stone National Park. Ecol. Monogr. 52:199–221.

Romme, W. H., and D. H. Knight. 1982. Landscape diversity: The concept applied to Yellowstone Park. BioScience 32:664–670.

Romme, W. H., and D. G. Despain. 1989a. Historical perspective on the Yellow-stone fires of 1988. BioScience 39:695–699.

———. 1989b. The long history of fire in the Greater Yellowstone Ecosystem. W. Wildlands 15:10–17.

Schullery, P. 1989. The fires and fire policy. BioScience 39:686–694.

Schullery, P., and D. G. Despain. 1989. Prescribed burning in Yellowstone Na-tional Park: A doubtful proposition. W. Wildlands 15:30–34.

Singer, F. J., W. Schreier, J. Oppenheim, and E. O. Garten. 1989. Drought, fires, and large mammals. BioScience 39:716–722.

Strong, W. E. 1968. A trip to the Yellowstone National Park in July, August, and September, 1875. Univ. of Oklahoma Press, Norman.

Taylor, D. L. 1973. Some ecological implications of forest fire control in Yellow-stone National Park, Wyoming. Ecology 54:1394–1396.

———. 1974. Forest fires in Yellowstone National Park. For. Hist. 18:69–77.

Trenberth, K. E., G. W. Branstator, and P. A. Arkin. 1988. Origins of the 1988 North American drought. Science 242:1640–1645.

Wright, H. E., Jr. 1974. Landscape development, forest fires, and wilderness management. Science 186:487–495.

CHAPTER 9   **Reality and Opportunity**
in the Yellowstone Fires
of 1988
John D. Varley and
Paul Schullery

We must be grateful to the founders of Yellowstone
for their vision in creating the world's first national park, but we must also
be realistic about the clarity of that vision. The Organic Act of Yellowstone, it has been said, raised more questions than it answered about the
goals and future of this remarkable preserve (Schullery 1984).

The park founders' foremost intent was to protect the area's unique
geothermal and geological features, features made more valuable by their
sublime setting of mountains, forests, and lakes (Haines 1977). The preservation of plants and animals in the park was soon considered equally
important by Yellowstone managers; by the late 1800s, many of these
species were becoming rare, or even extinct, throughout other parts of the
Rocky Mountains (Trefethen 1975).

Through a century-long process of legislative definition, scientific inquiry, and public dialogue, it has become widely recognized that the
primary purpose of Yellowstone and other national parks as natural areas is
to maintain these representative and unique ecosystems in as near pristine
condition as possible (Leopold et al. 1963; Houston 1971; Schullery 1984;
McNamee 1987). This grand and often controversial purpose has been
superimposed on the original goal of preserving the park's geothermal and
geological features, and in many ways complements that original goal. In

Portions of this paper previously appeared, in substantially different form, in
Northwest Science 63 (1989):44–54.

addition to preserving ecosystems for their cultural and scientific values, the park, as an international biosphere reserve, is now seen as a reservoir of biological diversity and as an environmental base line to which more exploited systems may be compared (Barbee and Varley 1985).

For park managers, the challenge of presiding over such natural areas as Yellowstone is to maintain natural processes, indeed large parts of whole ecosystems, in a near-pristine condition while providing for, as the park's founding legislation states, the enjoyment of the people. This challenge has long been recognized (Schullery 1984). The extent and type of management required to meet these objectives is of considerable public and scientific interest and not without controversy. Few parks have as colorful a history of debate as Yellowstone does (Despain et al. 1987).

Ecological processes, including plant succession, fluctuations in relative abundance of animals, and a wide variety of natural disturbances, are now widely acknowledged as an essential part of a proper national park setting; modern human influences are generally considered inappropriate, and modern human uses are for the most part restricted when possible to nonconsumptive activities (Houston 1971; Varley 1988). As Yellowstone Plant Ecologist Don Despain has put it, Yellowstone's resource is wildness (Schullery 1984). These unique land-use objectives require park managers to manipulate park settings only when such intervention is necessary to compensate for the influence of modern man on ecosystem processes, or when such overriding concerns as the protection of a threatened or endangered species takes priority over other goals.

Criteria used to manage vegetation and wildlife as sustainable, harvestable crops thus are clearly inappropriate within national parks (Houston 1971). This inappropriateness, though it may seem obvious at first glance, is in fact an extremely complex matter, and managers and park interest groups frequently find themselves at odds, or at loose ends, over just what criteria should be used to judge and direct park management (Houston 1988). Until relatively recently, for example, the management of fires in many U.S. national parks was nearly indistinguishable from the corresponding programs of other land management agencies, such as the U.S. Forest Service and the Bureau of Land Management (Kilgore 1976; Pyne 1982).

Appropriate management criteria for natural areas are typically quite difficult to develop because such criteria are trustworthy only when based on extensive ecological and historical information. Ecosystems are dynamic, and individual plant and animal populations routinely coexist in continuously varying states in which the fate of any individual element of the setting depends on a suite of factors that are themselves the result of many environmental variables (Forman and Godron 1986). Managers thus must resist the temptation to manage natural ecosystems with a view toward maintaining some arbitrary status quo; the risk inherent in trying to manage for stability rather than for dynamic change is, quite simply, the risk of turning the parks into static displays of life forms divorced from the rich assortment of evolutionary processes that shaped them. A further risk lies in assuming that a set of management criteria that work well for one area in the national park system will work well in all others. The same uniqueness that caused us to set these areas aside, each for its own distinctive qualities, compels us to be prepared to manage each area by equally unique guidelines that will accommodate its peculiar character within the greater goals of the system (Schullery 1989a).

NATURAL-FIRE POLICY AND THE WILDERNESS MOVEMENT

The absolute necessity for a management policy that accommodates the role of fire seems to be recognized by most participants in the scientific and political dialogues generated by the Yellowstone fires of 1988. The extent to which fires should be allowed to exercise their power the way they may have prehistorically is, however, hotly debated. There are great differences of opinion over how "free" fire should be in modern parks. The sorting out of this issue—determining how true we can afford to be to natural processes on the scale of major fires—promises to be instructive, stimulating, and entertaining. A century of evolution in national park thinking is being put to a stern test, and much is at stake, culturally, politically, and scientifically.

As interesting in the long run will be the effect of the fires and fire-related dialogue on public opinion and understanding about wilderness processes and natural resource management. As controversial and important as federal fire policy is, the fires have stimulated discussion and debate about much larger topics. The fires, perceived by all too many misinformed people as a failure of vision among wilderness protectionists, may well be used as political leverage in other fields of natural resource protection. A great many special-interest groups, with a diverse assortment of goals and motivations, are attempting to use the fires to advance their agendas regarding federal natural resource management policies and direction. For example, we have already heard from people who believe that if we had had the foresight to clearcut the park and crisscross it with roads and human-set burns, we could have prevented the fires of 1988. But if we treated the park like that, who would care if it burned?

A reasonable perspective on the Yellowstone fires and their possible consequences requires an accurate portrayal of the actual fire event. A summary of the fire season and the events that led up to it sheds light on the issues surrounding the future of wildland management.

Since early in this century, plant ecologists have recognized the significant role of fire in many plant communities. Prior to the arrival of Europeans, fire—whether set by lightning or by native Americans—was nearly as important as sun, rain, and soils in determining the vigor and the composition of many habitats (Wright and Bailey 1982). Fires often burned in a patchwork, or mosaic pattern, sometimes small, sometimes large, creating and maintaining a diversity of habitats for both plants and animals. Most landscapes in North America were in fundamental ways the result of fire.

Fire suppression was the order of the day on public and private lands until relatively recent times, when several federal agencies and private landowners began to experiment with prescribed burns; that is, fires allowed to burn, whether human or lightning caused (Pyne 1982). Farmers, of course, have been setting their fields on fire for agricultural reasons for hundreds of years. The Forest Service began using human-set prescribed burns to improve forests in the 1940s and 1950s, eventually allowing lightning-caused fires to burn in some forests to preserve wilderness values (Kilgore 1976).

The National Park Service, with its legislative mandates oriented toward natural processes, was perhaps even more aggressive in attempting to reestablish the role of lightning and fire in its wilderness settings. By 1978, twelve areas in the national park system had programs that allowed at least some lightning-caused fires to burn. The goal of these programs was substantially different from that of other private or public fire programs: A state of primitive wildness—and its resulting biological diversity and dynamic processes—was usually the most important aspect rather than specific "improvements" directed toward an individual species or specialized habitats (Kilgore 1985).

The terminology of fire management has confused many observers and some commentators, but it is both precise and efficient once understood. In the language of professional fire management, a natural fire is one not caused by humans; the usual source is lightning. A prescribed fire is a fire that, whatever its source (human or lightning), is burning within established prescriptions that define what humans have decided fire will be allowed to do in the setting in question, and is therefore acceptable to management. A wildfire is a fire that is burning out of prescription; it has, in effect, "gone wild." A wildfire may have been started initially by humans or by lightning, and it may have been burning initially within or outside of prescription. "Wild" only defines its current status in relation to the fire management plan of the area in question.

Yellowstone National Park initiated its first experiment with natural prescribed fire (that is, with lightning-caused fire allowed to burn if within defined prescriptions acceptable to managers) in 1972. By 1976 about 688,500 of the park's 891,000 hectares were included in natural fire zones. The park's fire management plan required suppression of all fires that showed any threat to human life, property, historic and cultural sites, special natural features, or threatened and endangered species.

In the first sixteen years of the plan's existence in Yellowstone, 235 fires were permitted to burn. Literally thousands of lightning strikes were observed to go out on their own without burning any measurable acreage. The 235 fires burned a total of 13,851 hectares (an average of 60.75 hectares per fire). The largest burned 2,997 hectares. Only 15 fires burned more than 41 hectares, and the vast majority burned an acre or less before they extinguished naturally, without human involvement (Renkin 1988).

By almost anyone's standards, the natural fire program during that sixteen-year period was considered successful public policy. It restored fire as an ecological force in Yellowstone; it took no human lives, nor did it cause any significant injuries; it destroyed no private property or significant historical and cultural resources: it did no harm to threatened and endangered species; and it was certainly cost effective. At the conclusion of each fire season, experts evaluated new data and applied them to future fire planning. In short, going into 1988 we had every reason to believe that we were working with a solid, professionally researched and maintained program, and that we were therefore entitled to considerable confidence about the future. As it turned out, the fire management plan was without question solid and professionally researched and maintained. But Yellowstone's fire regime operates on a scale of centuries, and sixteen years' experience clearly did not prepare us for every eventuality. Among other things, it did not prepare us for the truly grand scale of primitive fire, a scale that could readily exceed agency boundaries and any scenario imagined to that time by managers and fire behavior specialists.

FIRE MANAGEMENT IN THE GREATER YELLOWSTONE AREA

Fire, whether natural or human caused, is not compelled to conform to political boundaries of the sort that crisscross the Greater Yellowstone

Area. Greater Yellowstone, with Yellowstone Park at its core, includes roughly 4.9 million hectares of wildlands, 95 percent of which are publicly owned and managed. Within the ecosystem are portions of six national forests, two national parks, and two national wildlife refuges. In the past fifteen years, progress has been made coordinating management across agency boundaries so that management might make some ecological sense. Management of such free-ranging animals as grizzly bears, elk, and migratory waterfowl reflects an increased appreciation for ecological, rather than political boundaries. Progress was also made through the development of agreements between the Park Service and some national forests regarding the cross-boundary acceptance of natural fires. In principle, this meant that a natural fire starting on one agency's land could be monitored jointly and could conceivably be welcome to cross a boundary. In fact, the agencies differed considerably over what was an acceptable fire size, and what was acceptable fire behavior.

It can be fairly stated that the National Park Service was the less conservative party in these deliberations. Whereas Forest Service fire plans typically established maximum size limits on fires, Park Service prescriptions were aimed at allowing fire to replicate its prehistoric behavior. In prehistoric times, no arbitrary limitations or ceilings were placed on how large a fire might grow. Considering the Park Service's accumulated legislative and cultural mandates, it seemed appropriate to allow nature to act now as it had then, as long as fires did not threaten human life, developments, or other unusual values in the area.

It is ironic, considering the enormous controversy generated by the Yellowstone fires of 1988, that for the most part the terms of the fire management plan were met. Not only did the fires exercise their primitive prerogatives on the landscape, but also human life, developments, and other values were almost always (with a few tragic exceptions) protected successfully.

CLIMATE AND FIRE CONDITIONS IN 1988

The northern Rocky Mountains were in a drought throughout most of the 1980s. The driest previous year in the sixteen-year history of the natural fire policy was 1981, when lightning-ignited fires burned 8,181 hectares, without any adverse political, public, or scientific response.

Although the Greater Yellowstone Ecosystem did not escape the overall effects of the drought, it experienced a peculiar weather pattern that our lowland neighbors missed altogether. In the past decade the Greater Yellowstone Area had winter droughts—that is, below-normal snowfall—but the summers were unusually wet. Precipitation in July, for example, averaged 200 percent of normal between 1982 and 1987, and most of the other months were frequently above average (National Park Service 1988). This pattern was not confined to the park, but included nearby communities as well. Between 1982 and 1987, Driggs, Idaho, experienced July rainfalls averaging 289 percent of those for 1940–1970, and in Jackson, Wyoming, July rainfalls averaged 195 percent of those in 1951–1980 (climate data presented in this paper are taken from monthly climatological reports of the National Climatic Data Center). While the northern Rocky Mountain region was suffering through the great and economically stressful drought of the 1980s, the rainfall in Yellowstone was more than enough to subdue lightning-caused fires; from 1982 to 1987, natural fires in Yellowstone Park burned only about 450 hectares (Renkin 1988).

Part of the lesson learned in the first sixteen years of the fire policy was that in most years, including those with normal or average weather patterns, very little will burn. Every once in a while a year comes along that is dry enough to burn at least some of the landscape. And then, as we saw in 1988, comes a rare year that allows the burning of a lot more landscape than any manager or observer expected or even wanted burned. Predicting fire season conditions is very difficult for fire experts, although the knowledge base grows each year, especially in "learning years" like 1988.

During the 1988 fire season, the monitoring of fire conditions began in early April, when Forest Service and Park Service fire specialists activated their regular measuring system. By June 15, eighteen such measures were being computed daily at twelve locations in the park. By July 1, they were being computed at twenty-six locations. Why then were fire specialists caught by surprise? The answer is simple: There was no technology or data set that could predict an unprecedented event (that is, one that had not happened since scientists began measuring such phenomena).

The fire season began normally. Long-range drought indexes suggested that the Greater Yellowstone Area was in at least a moderate drought by the end of April, but local conditions in the park reveal the difficulties of interpreting such information. April and May were very wet in the park; about 155 percent of normal rainfall fell in April, and May rainfall was 181 percent of normal. The spring flood peak of the Yellowstone River at Corwin Springs, usually a good reflection of the whole watershed's condition, was also quite high. As late as July 11, the National Weather Service long-term forecast, as published in the *Billings Gazette*, predicted normal precipitation for July.

These indicators ultimately were cancelled out by others, but observers who, with the luxury of hindsight, accuse fire experts of ignoring obvious warning signs are themselves guilty of choosing only the indicators that support their accusations. As later events in the summer of 1988 would prove, fire conditions are extraordinarily difficult to anticipate even a few days in advance. The world's foremost experts in fire behavior were regularly unable to predict the behavior of the fires even forty-eight hours in advance. Predicting them weeks or months ahead is beyond science.

During late May and June some twenty fires started; eleven died out of their own accord. The others behaved more or less as in previous years. But June rainfall was only 20 percent of normal, and there was little rain in early July. By mid-July it was becoming obvious that unprecedented conditions had developed. We also knew, however, that even a modest summer rain could extinguish the few relatively small fires then burning.

The critical period of decision making, as identified by postfire review boards, occurred roughly from July 1 until July 21. By July 15, when a total of about 3,483 hectares had burned in the park, Park Service and Forest Service fire specialists were aware that fire conditions were extremely dangerous, whatever sort of precipitation forecasts were being made by the National Weather Service. It was unclear, however, just what that danger meant. By July 21, managers decided to suppress all existing and new fires as resources would allow. On that day, the total perimeter of all fires enclosed a little less than 6,885 hectares.

The extreme dryness, as unprecedented as it was, would not have been enough to create the situation that then developed. In July, August, and September, a series of six dry cold fronts passed through the Yellowstone area, with winds of 60 to 100 kilometers per hour that fanned the fires and moved them great distances very quickly. During these episodes of high wind the fires performed most spectacularly, consuming dry forest fuels by the hundreds of thousands of acres.

Extreme fire behavior became the order of the day. Fires ran as many as 16 kilometers in an afternoon. High winds sent burning embers as much as a mile and a half ahead of the main fire to create dozens of independent spot fires. The presence of so many spot fires, along with the rapid and wide advance of the main fires, made fighting the fires head-on impossible without risking lives. Uncharacteristically, the fires did not "lie down" at night because humidity stayed low; fires continued to move even in darkness. Hundreds of kilometers of fire line were constructed, but standard hand lines and bulldozer-built lines were no obstacle to fire movement.

Fires routinely jumped such major barriers as rivers and roads, and even the Grand Canyon of the Yellowstone. During the fire season a commonly repeated witticism was that the only line that held was Yellowstone Lake.

By September 26 the burned area in Greater Yellowstone was estimated to be about 567,000 hectares. Coarse-resolution aerial mapping in October suggested that more than 400,000 hectares in the park were affected by fire; some in canopy burn, some in surface burn under canopy, and some in meadow burn (Shovic et al. 1988). Finer-resolution mapping completed in December 1989 employed a combination of aerial photography of satellite-image interpretation, which indicated that about 322,000 hectares in the park were in some way affected and that about half of this was in the canopy burns that produce the stereotypical blackened forest (Despain et al. 1989). Media typically —and perhaps predictably—used the largest numbers they could find at any given time. In spite of daily published statements by agency staff that all figures were preliminary estimates of the perimeter of the fires, the media routinely used maximum estimates as if they were final numbers, worsening an already poor public understanding of the fires and their effects.

Substantial portions of the burned area, especially in the surface burns and meadow burns, regrew in native vegetation so quickly that by midsummer of 1989 most visitors were probably unable to identify it as recently burned. The pace of regrowth varied greatly from site to site, depending upon intensity of burn, soil characteristics, aspect, slope, moisture, and other factors; Yellowstone will move into its new vegetative era with at least equal the variety and diversity it had prior to the fires of 1988.

At the peak of the fire-fighting efforts, 9,500 civilian and military fire fighters, dozens of water-dropping helicopters and retardant bombers, and more than one hundred fire engines were involved in a massive interagency struggle. The cost is now estimated at about $120 million. The logistical efforts of fighting the fires, including decision-making processes, fire modeling procedures, and many other aspects of the fire season, were professionally evaluated, which resulted in recommendations not only for improving interagency coordination, but also for refining fire policies.

Many controversial decisions were made during the fire season, and these will no doubt be the subject of debate for years. At least one fire behavior specialist has hypothesized formally what a number of us have suggested informally, that the fire suppression effort, for all its heroic achievements in protecting cultural resources and villages, did not significantly reduce the total area the fires would have burned had we not fought them at all (Brown 1989). Perhaps the most humbling single piece of information to come out of the fire suppression effort has received scant attention: A *quarter inch* of precipitation, in rain and snow, on September 11, 1988, essentially accomplished what the largest, most expensive, and most technologically sophisticated fire-fighting effort in American history could not.

The ecological effects of the fires were also assessed, both by agency personnel and by an independent panel of ecological authorities (Mills 1989; Christensen et al. 1989). It is not overstating the findings of these studies to say that they indicate what park ecologists have long assumed: Nature cannot destroy itself in Yellowstone. The processes that gave us the Yellowstone landscape we enjoy today have simply continued to function, so that tomorrow's Yellowstone will be as dynamic, fascinating, and even inspiring as today's.

Central to any discussion of the fires is the matter of fire source. The fires were almost invariably called the "Yellowstone fires" by the media. Though all fires were directly and explicitly associated, especially by television reporters, with the National Park Service fire management plan, the reality of the fires was far more complex and revealing. Nothing more powerfully demonstrates the ecological unity of Greater Yellowstone than a review of how and where the largest fires started.

Most of the area affected by fire was encompassed within the perimeters of seven fires, five of which started outside the park and were initially managed under the fire plans of various national forests. Of those five, three, including the largest fire of all, were human caused and were fought from the day of their ignition. The other two were initially managed as natural prescribed fires in the national forest of their origin (U.S. Department of Agriculture and U.S. Department of the Interior 1988).

Within Yellowstone Park, roughly half of the burned area was the result of lightning-caused fires, and half was the result of human-caused fires. All human-caused fires started outside the park and burned in. Once ignited, for better or worse, human-set fires behaved and affected the landscape exactly as did lightning-caused fires. It has been suggested, based on known lightning strikes that occurred within the perimeters of human-caused fires, that large portions of those burns would possibly have been duplicated by natural fires even had the human fires not been set (Romme and Despain 1989; Christensen et al. 1989). This conjectural exercise opens fertile fields for philosophical rumination, fields that will probably be plowed repeatedly and to a variety of depths by researchers and commentators of many persuasions.

THE FIRES IN PERSPECTIVE

From the political and social perspectives, the fires were enormously disruptive in the Yellowstone area. Some elements of the regional economy suffered (others benefited from increased income due to fire-fighting needs), many residents were inconvenienced and suffered threats to their homes and property, and visitors were frequently displaced from sections of the park. A total of sixty-seven structures were destroyed, and another twelve damaged, in the Greater Yellowstone Area. Most of these structures were small, including eighteen guest and employee cabins in Yellowstone Park, but a number of private residences, including seventeen mobile homes, were destroyed by the Clover-Mist fire in the Crandall, Wyoming, area. About 12,150 hectares of timber suitable for harvest was burned in national forests of Greater Yellowstone. Other damages included the loss of power lines and the destruction or damage of such minor facilities as picnic areas (Mills 1989). A political fire storm followed the real ones, and aftershocks are still being felt in many political circles.

Viewed from the distance that objective ecological study demands, however, a calmer and more dispassionate perspective emerges. At most, 10 percent of Greater Yellowstone was affected by fire. As already mentioned, leading fire researchers believe that, for all the variety of source of ignition, the fires came close to replicating a natural event. Greater Yellowstone survived the fires just fine ecologically, however much political and social upheaval may have resulted. This is not to suggest that the fires were without ecological effect; the effects were profound, and we are busy analyzing them. We will, with a little luck, continue to find the 1988 fires scientifically instructive for decades, perhaps forever, or at least until the current fire interval is to some extent concluded and Yellowstone once again experiences fires on such a grand scale. As of late 1989, at least 103 research projects relating to the fires were under way.

Perhaps the most intriguing element of the fire story from the social perspective is the creation of public perceptions. The events of the fire season passed through a series of "filters," including agency public information offices and the media, before being received by the public. Extensive research and the observations of a variety of people indicate that at best the media did a mediocre job of reporting the fires (Smith 1989a; Smith 1989b; Smith 1989c; Reid 1989; Schullery 1989b). It now appears that the public may not avoid Yellowstone Park because of the fires (Snepenger 1989), but it is equally clear that their understanding of the fires, of fire policy, and of natural resource management in national parks in general is less sophisticated than we would hope.

For example, following the fire season there was widespread interest in helping Yellowstone to "recover" from the fires. For a sizable element of the public, "recovery" meant restoring nature to its prefire state. Park scientists and advisers, including the independent panel of scientists convened to consider the ecological implications, have generally agreed that only for purposes of landscaping around villages should any reseeding take place in the park (Christensen et al. 1989). This may seem puzzling, but the reasons are sound ecologically. Extensive soil testing in the autumn showed that less than one-tenth of 1 percent of the soils in burned areas received heat extreme enough to kill seeds, roots, rhizomes, and other regenerative plant parts more than an inch under the surface. This means that the vegetative organisms are alive and well.

The energy that drives Yellowstone's vegetative systems was not depleted or erased by the fires. It simply resides in a different place, below the surface of the soil in roots, seeds, and other forms. By the fall of 1988, newly cast lodgepole pine seeds from the burned parent trees were covering the forest floor at densities ranging from 20,000 to 400,000 seeds per hectare, and many new seedlings were seen in the spring and summer of 1989 (D. Despain and P. Schullery, personal observation). More immediately visible and popular with visitors was a spectacular wild-flower show that many agreed was the most dramatic in living memory—the result of ash fertilization and the generally wet conditions that prevailed throughout the summer. Yellowstone's long history of regrowing vegetation following fires seemed sufficient proof for most observers that the park's vegetation would regrow naturally and at its own pace.

Concern was widespread, both in public and scientific circles, about other fire effects, such as increased erosion or sedimentation in streams. Again, Yellowstone's landscape had experienced such processes countless times before. In the summer of 1989, in fact, major debris flows blocked some park roads and added to sediment flow in some streams. These were initiated by unusually heavy rains, but were certainly heightened by reduction of vegetative cover due to fire. Future levels of erosion and sedimentation will depend on the rate and amount of spring snow melt and precipitation for one to three years. Mud slides are almost as difficult as fires for the uninformed to keep in perspective. To our agriculturally directed minds, moving earth is always bad. To nature, the mud slide is an opportunity, a new seed bed that may promote diversity in that locality.

Ecologists generally agree that the long-term contributions of nutrients released into streams and lakes by the fires will at least temporarily enrich many aquatic systems. Whether that occurs or not, it will be important for future observers to keep in mind that in Yellowstone, such processes as nutrient releases and erosion are natural consequences of fire, and should not be viewed as something to be prevented, repaired, or encouraged.

Another concern, one with more complicated consequences in our quest for a healthy Yellowstone, involves the risk of non-native vegetation or weeds invading burned areas, especially pristine wilderness areas. This is of particular concern in the hundreds of kilometers of fire line built during the fires, where native vegetation has been removed or destroyed and soil is easily recolonized by unwanted species. Here, unlike the revegetation of natural burns or the erosion of burned slopes, we are dealing with a threat to the primitive ecological integrity of the area, and almost all observers agree that aggressive prevention measures are in order.

Probably no topic generated more urgent public concern than the welfare of park wildlife. We now know, based on paleontological research, that the Yellowstone area has hosted a similar assortment of fauna for much of the past two thousand years (Hadly 1990). Park wildlife, like park vegetation, evolved and adapted with Yellowstone's fire regime, so the likelihood that even extensive fires could entirely drive a species from the area is extremely low. But few observers were prepared for what we witnessed when Yellowstone wildlife encountered the fires. Wildlife losses were remarkably light. The large herds of grazing animals that are a major attraction in Yellowstone displayed behavior not at all like that in such traditional portrayals of forest fires as the movie *Bambi*. Animals were caught in the fires only in the ten or so days when wind storms caused the fires to make fast, wide runs. A number of animals were caught in human-started backfires. Most of the time, animals more or less just stepped aside. Photographs and films show bison and elk grazing calmly in a meadow while the forest behind them burns.

Extensive autumn surveys of carcasses in the park revealed about 250 dead elk—less than 1 percent of the park's summering population of about 32,000—9 bison from a population of about 2,700, 2 moose, and 4 mule deer (Mills 1989; Singer and Schullery 1989; Singer et al. 1989). Most died of smoke inhalation, not flames (French and French 1989). Similarly light losses were reported on surrounding national forest lands. Except for the possible loss of four grizzly bears, no threatened or endangered animals were known lost in the fires (R. Knight and B. Blanchard, pers. comm.).

An even more challenging issue in public perception of the fires is the aesthetic one. To the wilderness "purist" who is fully tuned in to the processes of wildlands, the results of a fire are viewed neither as good nor bad, but as process. Semantic and rhetorical problems have arisen since the beginning of the dialogues over the fires, some of which have been analyzed (Barbee and Schullery 1989). Some people term a burned forest "destroyed," whereas others point out that it has only moved along to a new stage in its ongoing life process. Some find blackened trees ugly or tragic, whereas others see them as an opportunity to stretch our perceptions of natural settings. Educating the public to the aesthetics and language of natural process will not be easy.

In these instances—revegetation, erosion, wildlife, aesthetics—and in others, we have discovered a wide gap between ecological reality and public understanding. Inasmuch as public understanding is often a direct impetus for political action, those of us intimately familiar with Greater Yellowstone, and deeply concerned that its future management course be based on the best possible knowledge, have our work cut out for us. Greater Yellowstone is always at many crossroads, but the fires brought it to an unusually perilous one, one where public education will play a critical role in determining future direction.

Current deliberations over fire policy are only a manifestation of broader dialogues about the general direction of wildland management. The fires, as mentioned earlier, were perceived by some as proof that the wilderness movement has faltered and has lost a realistic vision of its own future. Others perceive the fires as proof that our vision needs fine tuning in some ways. Yet others see the fires as a vindication of nature as the real manager of Yellowstone. On one end of the opinion spectrum are people who would turn Yellowstone into a stagnant garden or a large-scale zoo. On the other end are people who, during the fire season, joked that we had built the fire line on the wrong side of Grant Village.

Of all these perspectives, the most worrisome may be the ones that favor intensive husbandry of the Yellowstone setting. We have struggled, debated, and often fought for several decades to reach the point where the natural processes that gave us Yellowstone are respected; the point where we will admit that Yellowstone can generally take care of itself, if only we will let it. Could it be that the fires of 1988 will be used as a lever, to halt or even reverse the singularly creative movement that has brought us so far? That is a far more ominous prospect than any possible consequences of the current fire policy debates.

But those debates do require our attention. Although almost all parties seem to agree that we must allow fire some role in our wildlands, opinions differ greatly over what that role should be. It has been pointed out that a fire policy could be developed for Yellowstone that was in every way a model of accommodating language and affirmative philosophy, but that would establish such tight controls and "ceilings" on allowable fire size as to effectively eliminate fire from the park (Schullery 1989c). This is no time for mincing bureaucratese that bows politely toward the principle while backing away from the reality.

This is, therefore, a time of great risk for Yellowstone. But it is also a time of great opportunities. Although we must be aware of the opportunities for political hay making, we can take comfort in knowing that the wild assortment of polemic and commentary the fires have caused will be largely self-cancelling, as supporters of all viewpoints will inadvertently neutralize one another. The very volume and diversity of opinion are probably the best tempering influences on it, and the best guarantees that no one viewpoint will prevail.

Promoters of travel and recreation in the Yellowstone region are emphasizing the distinctive opportunity the fires present. Only once in several generations can visitors view such huge ecological "beginnings." And, as already suggested, opportunities for education, learning, and scientific research are almost limitless. But for those who enjoy ecological implications more than political and social consequences, the finest opportunity belongs to the resource. The biotic communities of the Greater Yellowstone Area have just received a dynamic jolt of prehistoric dimensions, and the members of those communities will be doing all that evolution will allow to take advantage of the new order. For nature, and for those of us who love nature and find enrichment and inspiration in her workings, opportunity rarely knocks this loudly in Yellowstone.

REFERENCES

Barbee, R., and P. Schullery. 1989. Yellowstone: The smoke clears. Nat'l Parks 62:18–19.

Barbee, R. D., and J. D. Varley. 1985. The paradox of repeating error: Yellowstone National Park from 1872 to biosphere reserve and beyond. Pages 125–130 in J. D. Peine, ed. Proceedings of the conference on the management of biosphere reserves, 1984. National Park Service, Uplands Field Research Laboratory, Great Smoky Mountains National Park, Gatlinburg, Tenn.

Brown, J. K. 1989. Could the 1988 fires in Yellowstone have been avoided with a program of prescribed burning? Paper presented at the 155th annual meeting of the Am. Ass'n for the Advancement of Science, San Francisco, Jan. 19, 1989.

Christensen, N. L., J. K. Agee, P. F. Brussard, J. Hughes, D. H. Knight, G. W. Minshall, J. M. Peek, S. J. Pyne, F. J. Swanson, S. Wells, J. W. Thomas, S. E.

Williams, and H. A. Wright. 1989. Ecological consequences of the 1988 fires in the Greater Yellowstone Area. Final report. Greater Yellowstone Postfire Ecological Assessment Workshop. Yellowstone National Park.

Despain, D., M. Meagher, D. B. Houston, and P. Schullery. 1987. Wildlife in transition: Man and nature on Yellowstone's northern range. Roberts Rinehart, Boulder, Colo.

Despain, D., A. Rodman, P. Schullery, and H. Shovic. 1989. Burned area survey of Yellowstone National Park: The fires of 1988. Yellowstone National Park, Division of Research and Geographic Information Systems Laboratory.

Forman, R. T. T., and M. Godron. 1986. Landscape ecology. John Wiley and Sons, New York.

French, S., and M. French. 1989. Yellowstone bear behavior during and after the fires. Yellowstone Grizzly J. 1:1–3.

Hadly, E. 1990. Late Holocene mammalian fauna of Lamar Cave and its implications for ecosystem dynamics in Yellowstone National Park, Wyoming. M.S. thesis, Northern Arizona Univ.

Haines, A. 1977. The Yellowstone story. Colorado Associated Univ. Press, Boulder.

Houston, D. B. 1971. Ecosystems in national parks. Science 172:648–651.

———. 1988. Managing national parks in the twenty-first century: Can we find our way? Twenty-fourth Paul L. Errington Memorial Lecture, Iowa State University, Ames, Apr. 14, 1988.

Kilgore, B. 1976. From fire control to fire management: An ecological basis for policies. Trans. N. Am. Wildl. Nat. Resources Conf. 41:477–493.

———. 1985. The role of fire in wilderness: A state-of-knowledge review. Intermountain Res. Station Gen. Tech. Rep. INT-182, Ogden, Utah.

Leopold, A. S., S. A. Cain, C. M. Cottam, I. N. Gabrielson, and T. L. Kimball. 1963. Wildlife management in the national parks. Trans. N. Am. Wildl. Nat. Resources Conf. 28:28–45.

McNamee, T. 1987. Nature first. Roberts Rinehart, Boulder, Colo.

Mills, S., ed. 1989. The Greater Yellowstone postfire assessment. Greater Yellowstone Coordinating Committee, Yellowstone National Park.

National Park Service. 1988. The Yellowstone fires: A primer on the 1988 fires season. Yellowstone National Park.

Pyne, S. 1982. Fire in America: A cultural history of wildland and rural fire. Princeton Univ. Press, Princeton, N.J.

Reid, T. R. 1989. When the press yelled "fire!" Washington Post, July 23, 1989, D5.

Renkin, R. 1988. Fire seasons summary, Yellowstone National Park, 1972–1987. In National Park Service, The Yellowstone fires: A primer on the 1988 fire season.

Romme, W. H., and D. G. Despain. 1989. Historical perspective on the Yellowstone fires of 1988, BioScience 39:695–699.

Schullery, P. 1984. Mountain time. Nick Lyons Books/Schocken, New York.

———. 1989a. Feral fish and kayak tracks. George Wright Forum 6:41–47.

———. 1989b. The story itself: Lessons and hopes from the Yellowstone fire media event. George Wright Forum 6:17–25.

———. 1989c. The Yellowstone fires: A preliminary report. NW Sci. 63:44–54.

Shovic, H., et al. 1988. Preliminary burned area survey of Yellowstone National Park and adjoining national forests, project summary and tabular areas, December 1988. National Park Service and U.S. Forest Service, Yellowstone, Wyo.

Singer, F., et al. 1989. Drought, fires, and large mammals. BioScience 39:716–722.

Singer, F., and P. Schullery. 1989. Yellowstone wildlife: Populations in process. W. Wildlands 15:18–22.

Smith, C. 1989a. Reporters, news sources, accuracy, and the Yellowstone forest fires. Paper presented at the annual meeting of the International Communications Ass'n, San Francisco, May 1989.

———. 1989b. Flames, firefighters and moonscapes: Network television pictures of the Yellowstone forest fires. Paper presented at Third Annual Visual Communications Conference, Park City, Utah, June 26, 1989.

———. 1989c. Brave firefighters, endangered national icons and bumbling land managers: Network TVC myths about the 1988 Yellowstone wildfires. Paper presented to the Ass'n for Education in Journalism and Mass Communication, Washington, D.C., Aug. 13, 1989.

Snepenger, D. 1989. Projecting visitation to Yellowstone National Park after the fires of 1988. J. Travel Res. 28:39–40.

Trefethen, J. 1975. An American crusade for wildlife. New York, Winchester Press and the Boone and Crockett Club.

U.S. Department of Agriculture and U.S. Department of the Interior. 1988. Greater Yellowstone area fires of 1988: Phase II report. Interagency Task Force, U.S. For. Serv. Region 2, Denver, Colo., and Nat'l Park Serv. Rocky Mountain Region, Lakewood, Colo.

Varley, J. 1988. Managing Yellowstone National Park into the twenty-first century: The park as an aquarium. Pages 216–225 in J. K. Agee and D. R. Johnson, eds. Ecosystem management for parks and wilderness. Univ. of Washington Press, Seattle.

Wright, H. A., and A. W. Bailey. 1982. Fire ecology, United States and southern Canada. John Wiley and Sons, New York.

CHAPTER 10   **Observed and Anticipated**
Effects of Forest Fire
on Yellowstone Stream
Ecosystems

G. Wayne Minshall and

James T. Brock

In 1988, fires burned extensively in numerous watersheds of the Greater Yellowstone Area ecosystem, a 4.86-million-
hectare area of federally owned lands in northwestern Wyoming, south
central Montana, and east central Idaho. Yellowstone National Park is the
heart of the GYA and, although it constitutes only 19 percent of the area, 68
percent of the land burned in 1988 is there. Most of the vegetative cover
burned (95 percent) was forest, and the remainder was a mix of meadow,
grass land, and sagebrush (Shovic et al. 1988). Roughly 5 percent (45,000
ha) of YNP is covered by water in the form of more than 150 lakes and 4,300
km of streams. Of the park's water area 95 percent is found in only four
lakes, and the watersheds of these were burned to varying degrees: Heart
(50 percent), Lewis (33 percent), Yellowstone (28 percent), and Shoshone
(8 percent) (J. D. Varley, pers. comm. 1989). In addition, approximately 32
percent of the park's stream system was influenced by the fires. Twenty
separate river basins or major subbasins were affected by the fires to various
degrees (figure 10.1). Because of differences in landscape morphology and
in the nature of the fires, streams in the Madison, upper Yellowstone (above
Yellowstone Lake), and Snake River drainages are less likely to be affected
by the 1988 fires than the other main river systems in the GYA.

Our thanks to Robert E. Gresswell, Ronald D. Jones, and John D. Varley for
helping us to obtain the firsthand knowledge of the 1988 fires reported here.

WATERSHEDS AFFECTED BY 1988 GYA FIRES

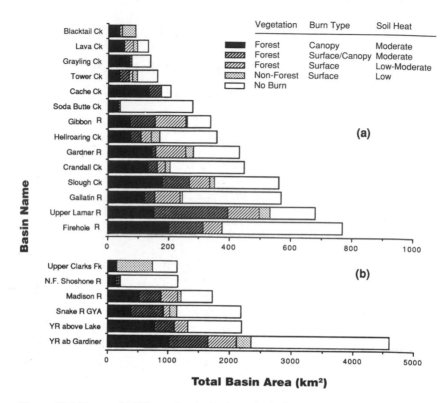

Figure 10.1 Extent of 1988 GYA fires by drainage basin for catchment areas (a), less than 1,000 km², and (b), greater than 1,000 km². Portion of bar that is shaded indicates amount of basin burned by vegetation type and burn intensity. Data from Hydrology Assessment Team 1988.

The 1988 fires present several challenges to those interested in ascertaining the effects of fires on aquatic environments and their inhabitants in the Greater Yellowstone Area. The main problems involve (1) the lack of published information on the effects of fires on aquatic environments and their inhabitants, especially for the Rocky Mountain region, (2) the large scale and spatial heterogeneity of the fires, and (3) the delayed impacts and long-term recovery that are likely to be involved. In addition, the impacts of the fires are expected to vary with the type and size of the aquatic habitat and as a result of differences among sites in watershed conditions (including aspect, slope, soil development, and bedrock geology), heat intensity of the fires, and climate. In spite of these difficulties, it seems worthwhile to derive a set of generalizations that can be used to guide aquatic scientists, resource specialists, and policy makers as they address the problems and opportunities afforded by this unique event.

The treatment that follows is predicated on several simplifying assumptions. We expect that smaller bodies of water will be impacted more strongly than larger bodies because of their lesser ability to temper the heat from the fire or to dilute the physical and chemical effects of the ash and eroded sediments. Likewise, we anticipate that flowing waters (creeks and rivers) will be affected more severely than standing waters (ponds and lakes) because of their generally greater direct exposure to the fire and its aftermath. For example, streams receive the full brunt of the runoff from burned hill slopes, including high concentrations of chemicals and sediments and erosion of the stream channel, whereas lakes dissipate the effects of runoff through reduction of current velocities and dilution and deposition of chemicals, organic matter, and inorganic sediments. Furthermore, in many lakes the enrichment by nutrients released by fires should be masked by the recirculation, during spring overturn, of nutrients stored in the hypolimnion. Because we expect streams to show a more dramatic response to the 1988 fires and because we are more familiar with their likely responses (Minshall, Brock, and Andrews 1981; Minshall, Brock, and Varley 1989; Minshall et al. 1990), our focus is on flowing-water ecosystems.

SPATIAL VARIATION AND THE RESPONSE OF STREAMS TO FIRE

Most of the area burned (90 percent) was spread among six fires: North Fork (>202,000 ha), Clover-Mist (>129,000 ha), Snake River Complex (>70,000 ha), Huck (>43,000 ha), Storm Creek (>38,000 ha), and Hell-roaring (>27,000 ha). Adding to the complexity was that even within the burned areas the intensity of the fire varied from "hot" canopy fires (61 percent of burned area), to cooler ground fires, to unburned patches of 50 ha or less. Although the percentage of each burn type was remarkably similar among fires, the extent of patchiness varied considerably. Fires that burned earlier in the summer, when fuel-moisture levels were higher, generally were patchier than those that burned later. Those that burned between July 21 and September 26 frequently were driven by 65–95 km/h winds and tended to include wide swaths of continuous canopy burn and spot fires along the sides and in front.

As noted earlier, the response of streams to fire will vary with respect to their size and the spatial heterogeneity of the landscape. Stream size can be differentiated in terms of "orders," where the headwater-most unbranched tributary is designated a first-order stream, the joining of two or more first orders forms a second-order stream, and so on. After the recent fires in Yellowstone it is relatively easy to find numerous first-order streams where the entire watershed has burned. However, it is almost impossible to find watersheds above fourth order where this is so. This suggests the generalization that in natural wildfires covering large areas (for example, those with 300-year recurrence frequencies in Yellowstone), low stream-order watersheds tend to burn extensively or not at all, whereas higher stream-order watersheds tend to burn partially. Consequently, fires will tend to increase the among-stream patchiness (beta diversity) of low-order streams relative to higher-order streams; however, the within-stream patchiness (alpha diversity) of high-order streams should be greater than that of low-order streams. High-order watersheds that contain a large number of burned tributaries also will be more severely affected by wildfire than those of similar order in which a smaller proportion of the watershed burned. As the size of the watershed increases, greater percentages of the area remain unburned and greater volumes of water feeding the streams and lakes serve to dissipate the effects of the fire. Changes in stream geomorphology and reduction of the influences from the riparian vegetation (that is, shading, overhanging cover, and litter inputs) superimpose additional differences in stream ecosystem response with increasing stream size (Vannote et al. 1980; Minshall et al. 1983, 1985). Aquatic habitats in or adjacent to forested areas generally are more severely affected than those buffered by meadows or other wetlands. Many of the latter should experience no lasting adverse effects; in fact, a stimulation of stream and riparian vegetative growth occurred following the fire probably due to the release of nutrients formerly bound up as plant biomass.

In Yellowstone, although a significant number of the smaller (headwater) watersheds burned, it was by no means the majority. Almost none of the larger drainages in the Greater Yellowstone Area burned completely, and because of the reduced direct impact and dilution effect from a mix of upstream sources, discernible immediate or long-term adverse effects probably will not be seen. We are aware of only two (Cache Creek and Hellroaring Creek) watersheds greater than third order in size that suffered substantial impact over their whole areas, and only a few others (for example, Upper Lamar River and Slough Creek) might possibly fall into this category. Most of the streams in Yellowstone that support a major sport fishery (Firehole, Gardner, Gibbon, Lamar, Madison, and Yellowstone) are all fifth order or greater.

In general, the fires in the southern portion of the park were patchier and fewer entire watersheds burned there than in the western and northern parts. This is because the fires in this area occurred earlier in the season, when fuel-moisture levels were higher and winds more moderate. Thus watersheds in the Madison and Lamar River drainages, for example, tended to be more severely impacted than those in the Upper Yellowstone (above Yellowstone Lake) and Snake River drainage basins. The greater the severity, the greater the potential for alteration of an aquatic ecosystem from its prefire condition.

CLIMATE, RUNOFF, AND EROSION

Climatic conditions, especially temperature and precipitation, affect the type and density of plant cover on the watershed, the intensity and areal extent of the fire, and the amount and timing of runoff. Once a fire has occurred, it is the runoff that is of major immediate concern from the standpoint of aquatic ecosystems. Watershed aspect, slope, and bedrock geology are some of the major variables that control the rate of runoff. Soil and snow moisture content and depth of winter snowpack also strongly influence snow-melt soil erosion. Fire results in increased overland flow and greater peak and total discharge (Helvey 1973; Anderson, Hoover, and Reinhart 1976; Helvey, Tiedemann, and Fowler 1976; Wright 1976; Schindler et al. 1980; Campbell and Morris 1988). The lack of vegetation to hold the soil combined with an enhanced runoff from reduced transpiration and impedance of flow commonly leads to increased erosion and transport of sediments from burned watersheds. These probably are the most dramatic and important deleterious water-quality responses associated with fire (Tiedemann et al. 1979).

Snow melt generally constitutes the majority of runoff in Rocky Mountain streams, resulting in peak erosion and channel alteration at that time. In Yellowstone in 1989, however, snow melt was more gradual than usual due to a cool, extended spring, and spring runoff peaks were much reduced (J. D. Varley, pers. comm. 1989). Instead, summer rainstorms produced a substantial portion of the annual runoff and appear to have been responsible for a large portion of the erosion and change in channel conditions during the first postfire year. Runoff volumes in the park may increase 10–40 percent as a result of the fire (P. E. Farnes, pers. comm. 1989; Stottlemyer 1987). Peak discharge may increase by tenfold or more (Tiedemann et al. 1979). Snow-melt runoff tends to occur earlier (Helvey 1973; Jaynes 1978), and all runoff will be more "flashy" in burned watersheds than in unburned ones. Factors contributing to early runoff include increased solar energy input to the snowpack due to reduced shading and lower snow albedo caused by dust from the blackened timber. Runoff from burned watersheds that is earlier than that from unburned ones appears to be partly responsible for the attenuation of spring runoff peaks in the downstream reaches (sixth order or greater) of large watersheds, such as the Yellowstone River at Corwin Springs, Montana (J. D. Varley, pers. comm. 1989).

Large changes in the timing and magnitude of runoff may adversely affect populations that lack the genetic or reproductive capacity to adjust. Increases in flow magnitude could destabilize stream systems and, at least over the short term, decrease biotic diversity and production (Resh et al. 1988). In the long run, however, such changes probably are well within the range of conditions periodically experienced by aquatic organisms, and no lasting damage should result. Such disturbances are all part of a grand erosional-depositional "cycle" (Chorley, Schumm, and Sugden 1984) associated with periodically recurring fires (Houston 1973; Arno 1980; Romme 1982), to which the organisms must be able to adapt or they would not have survived to the present. In fact, in the broader perspective, the fire should actually enhance aquatic production over prefire conditions due to the increased input and availability of light and nutrients and improved fish habitat conditions (Minshall et al. 1990). Chance storm events (for example, heavy snowpack, rapid snow melt on frozen ground, spate, and summer drought) can magnify damage, impede recovery, and set new (lower) equilibrium levels in fire-ravaged watersheds, just as they do in those not affected by fire.

Sheet erosion, rill and gully formation, and mass movement of material were observed on various burned watersheds in Yellowstone during the first postfire summer (Minshall, personal observations). Probably the most spectacular were periods of widespread "black water" conditions and debris torrents following heavy rains. Three major mud slides and a dozen smaller ones caused by a rainstorm in August 1989 carried large volumes of silt, sand, and stones into the Gibbon River a short distance above Gibbon Falls. Suspended sediment levels increased measurably in streams in burned watersheds throughout Yellowstone following runoff from both snow melt and rain; such events extended from spring through summer in 1989 and 1990. Burned watersheds are most vulnerable to erosion during the first two years following fire (Helvey 1973; Packer and Williams 1976; Lyon 1984). Thereafter, regrowth of native vegetation progressively reduces runoff and erosion. High discharge and erosion could result in substantial impact on stream ecosystems (Minshall et al. 1990). This is particularly true in the heavily burned areas on steep slopes having low moisture-absorption capacity, such as found in watersheds in the Absaroka mountain range along the northeastern edge of the park (Clover-Mist, Hellroaring, and Storm Creek fires). Erosion, sediment loads, and channel movement are likely to increase significantly in these areas, resulting in substantial decreases in algal, insect, and fish populations. Considerable recovery is likely to be seen as the redevelopment of terrestrial vegetation begins to slow the rate of runoff. Even in more moderately impacted areas, however, three to ten years may be required (depending on local weather conditions and the rate of forest regeneration) for significant recovery of stream and riparian ecosystems. In more severely impacted watersheds with shallow soils, little terrestrial plant regrowth, or heavy precipitation, return to prefire aquatic conditions may require fifty years or more. In Yellowstone some of the watersheds most susceptible to severe postfire impact were already subject to substantial physical disturbance prior to the fire (Mohrman, Ewing, and Carty 1988). The added impacts due to fire consequently may be much less dramatic in these areas than normally expected.

IMPLICATIONS FOR RESOURCE MANAGEMENT

As noted above, the disturbance of streams resulting from wildfire should decrease over time (see also Minshall, Brock, and Varley 1989), and low-order streams should be affected more severely than higher-order ones because the removal of vegetation will be greatest there. The response of aquatic invertebrates provides an index of expected changes in stream conditions over time (figure 10.2). Total invertebrate numbers and biomass should initially decrease and then gradually increase following average fire conditions in Yellowstone. Both features should eventually persist above prefire levels for up to twenty years or so (figure 10.2, circles) because of enhanced primary production and high quality allochthonous input during that period (Newbold, Erman, and Roby 1980; Duncan and Brusven 1985; Murphy et al. 1986; Noel, Martin, and Federer 1986). Species richness is expected to follow a similar pattern. The extent of postfire depression of total abundance or species richness and the rate of return to prefire condi tions depend largely on the degree of disruption of the watershed and stream channel in the first few years (figure 10.2). The difference (for a given environmental region) appears to be due primarily to the size of the watershed burned and the intensity of the fire. The chance occurrence of intense summer storms, which are common in this area, also will be a factor. In streams that are not subjected to high-intensity scouring dis-

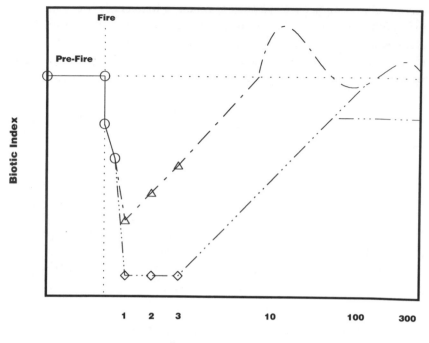

Figure 10.2 Expected changes in total abundance (numbers or biomass) or species richness of stream organisms following wildfire. Three possible recovery trajectories are shown Dashed line depicts expected response for moderately disturbed streams. Broken line indicates expected response for more severely impacted streams. The latter may eventually recover to prefire conditions or be displaced to a new, lower quasi-equilibrium. The actual pattern of recovery will be determined largely by the extent of disturbance of the watershed and stream channel from runoff in the first few years following fire.

charges, species richness and abundance are not depressed so severely and the recovery process begins soon after a fire. In such cases, the stream ecosystems are expected to return relatively quickly to prefire conditions (figure 10.2, dashed line). In those streams in which the watershed becomes heavily eroded and the bed severely scoured, recovery will be delayed and may ultimately follow a different trajectory altogether (figure 10.2, broken line). In severe cases, such as when disturbances of the stream channel occur repeatedly over a long period, levels for abundance and richness lower than those of prefire may be established.

A number of dead trout were found in the Blacktail Deer Creek, Cache

Creek, and Hellroaring Creek drainages soon after the 1988 fires (Minshall, personal observations). The reason for this mortality is not known. Given the size of some of the streams (third order), it is unlikely that temperatures reached lethal levels (Cushing and Olson 1963; Ice 1980) although water temperatures near 30°C have been observed during wildfire in Glacier National Park (F. R. Hauer, pers. comm. 1990). Toxic chemical conditions from smoke or ash seem more likely to have been responsible (Cushing and Olson 1963; F. R. Hauer, pers. comm. 1990). However, laboratory tests of Yellowstone ash leachate and early life-stage cutthroat trout over a three-week exposure showed no acute toxicity effects (Woodward 1989). In addition to mortality related to fire, almost total mortality of trout occurred on a section of the Little Firehole River due to an accidental drop of fire retardant (ammonium phosphate) directly on the stream (E. D. Koch, pers. comm. 1988). Only one other direct release of retardant on a stream in the park was reported (R. E. Gresswell, pers. comm. 1989). Although wildfire and attempts at its suppression can directly eliminate substantial numbers of fish, especially in streams up to about third order, many survived the immediate influence of the fire. Their fate and subsequent reproduction will be determined by the extent to which abnormally high flows and sediment conditions develop. These impacts are likely to be most pronounced during the first few postfire years. Over the next several years the abundances of trout and sculpin are expected to increase in association with the opening of the riparian canopy and increases in algal and invertebrate production (Hawkins et al. 1983; Minshall et al. 1989). Following this, trout and sculpin production should gradually decline to prefire conditions as the riparian canopy closes and the forest reaches maturity (Minshall, Brock, and Varley 1989; Minshall et al. 1990). These responses will be most pronounced in smaller streams (generally less than fifth order). As stream size increases, an influx of nutrients and other ions from the fire should be diminished by dilution and biotic uptake, and the effects on the solar regime will be minor, so the immediate (deleterious) and midterm (enhancement) effects of the fire on fish populations could be minor or nonexistent. Because most of the fishing pressure in the park is on larger streams (U.S. Fish and Wildlife Service annual reports), the impacts of fire on sport fishing and water quality of streams in the park and adjacent wilderness should be imperceptible to the majority of visitors. Postfire management actions, if instituted at all, should be restricted to controlling runoff and erosion during the first few years following a fire. Woody debris entering streams due to fire should be maintained and even actively increased or stabilized during these early stages. This material will stabilize the stream channel, retain organic matter and inorganic sediments, reduce stream temperatures, enhance environmental heterogeneity, and provide habitat for fish (Brown 1971; Heede 1972; Megahan and Nowlin 1976; Keller and Tally 1979; Bilby 1981; Likens and Bilby 1982; Marston 1982; Megahan 1982; Hawkins et al. 1983, Murphy et al. 1986; Minshall et al. 1990; Smock, Metzler, and Gladden 1989).

Viewed from broad spatial and temporal perspectives, the recent fires appear to provide a mechanism for rejuvenating productivity, maintaining or enhancing high systemwide diversity, and (because of their patchy nature) tempering the impact of physical disturbance in lotic ecosystems. The effects of prescribed burning, in place of wildfire, depend on a number of factors, but the restriction of prescribed fires to small individual watersheds and wide separation in time and space could simulate the beneficial midterm effects of wildfire while reducing the detrimental short-term effects. Because of the effort and expense required to operate such a program on even a drainage-basin scale (Brown chapter 11 in this volume), however, this may not be a feasible alternative.

REFERENCES

Anderson, H. W., M. D. Hoover, and K. G. Reinhart. 1976. Forest and water: Effects of forest management on floods, sedimentation, and water supply. U.S. For. Serv. Gen. Tech. Rep. PSW-18.

Arno, S. F. 1980. Forest fire history in the northern Rockies. J. For. (August):460–465.

Bilby, R. E. 1981. Role of organic debris dams in regulating the export of dissolved and particulate matter from a forested watershed. Ecology 62:1234–1243.

Brown, G. W. 1971. Water temperature in small streams as influenced by environmental factors. Pages 175–181 in J. T. Krygier and J. D. Hall, eds. Forest land uses and stream environment. Oregon State Univ. Press, Corvallis.

Campbell, W. G., and S. E. Morris. 1988. Hydrologic response of the Pack River, Idaho, to the Sundance fire. NW Sci. 62:165–170.

Chorley, R. J., S. A. Schumm, and D. E. Sugden. 1984. Geomorphology. Methuen, New York.

Cushing, C. E., and P. A. Olson. 1963. Effects of weed burning on stream conditions. Trans. Am. Fish. Soc. 92:303–305.

Duncan, W. F. A., and M. A. Brusven. 1985. Benthic macroinvertebrates in logged and unlogged low-order southeast Alaskan streams. Freshwater Invert. Biol. 4:125–132.

Hawkins, C. P., M. L. Murphy, N. H. Anderson, and M. A. Wilzbach. 1983. Density of fish and salamanders in relation to riparian canopy and physical habitat in streams of the northwestern United States. Can. J. Fish. Aquatic Sci. 40:1173–1185.

Heede, B. H. 1972. Influences of a forest on the hydraulic geometry of two mountain streams. Water Resources Bull. 8:523–530.

Helvey, J. D. 1973. Watershed behavior after forest fire in Washington. Pages 403–422 in Proceedings of the Irrigation & Drainage Division Specialty Conference. American Society Civil Engineers. Available from author.

Helvey, J. D., A. R. Tiedemann, and W. B. Fowler. 1976. Some climatic and hydrologic effects of wildfire in Washington State. Proc. Tall Timbers Fire Ecol. Conf. 15:201–222.

Houston, D. B. 1973. Wildfires in northern Yellowstone National Park. Ecology 54:1111–1117.

Hydrology Assessment Team. 1988. Water resource assessment. Greater Yellowstone Post-fire Resource Assessment and Recovery Program. National Park Service and U.S. Forest Service, Yellowstone, Wyo.

Ice, G. G. 1980. Immediate stream temperature response to a prescribed burn. Special report. National Council of the Paper Industry for Air and Stream Improvement, New York.

Jaynes, R. A. 1978. A hydrologic model of aspen-conifer succession in the western United States. U.S. For. Serv. Res. Pap. INT-213.

Keller, E. A., and T. Tally. 1979. Effects of large organic debris on channel form and fluvial processes in the coastal redwood environment. Pages 169–197 in D. D. Rhodes and G. P. Williams, eds. Adjustments of the fluvial system. Kendall/Hunt, Dubuque, Iowa.

Likens, G. E., and R. E. Bilby. 1982. Development, maintenance, and role of organic-debris dams in New England streams. Pages 122–128 in F. J. Swanson, R. J. Janda, T. Dunne, and D. N. Swanston, eds. Sediment budgets and routing in forested drainage basins. U.S. For. Serv. Gen. Tech. Rep. PNW-141.

Lyon, L. J. 1984. The Sleeping Child burn: Twenty-one years of postfire change. U.S. For. Serv. Res. Pap. INT-330.

Marston, R. A. 1982. The geomorphic significance of log steps in forest streams. Annals Ass'n Am. Geog. 72:99–108.

Megahan, W. F. 1982. Channel sediment storage behind obstructions in forested drainage basins draining the granitic bedrock of the Idaho Batholith. Pages 114–121 in F. J. Swanson, R. J. Janda, T. Dunne, and D. N. Swanston, eds. Sediment budgets and routing in forested drainage basins. U.S. For. Serv. Gen. Tech. Rep. PNW-141.

Megahan, W. F., and R. A. Nowlin. 1976. Sediment storage in channels draining small forested watersheds in the mountains of central Idaho. Pages 115–126 in Proceedings of Third Federal Inter-agency Sedimentation Conference, Denver, Colo., March 1976.

Minshall, G. W., J. T. Brock, and D. A. Andrews. 1981. Biological, water quality, and aquatic habitat responses to wildfire in the Middle Fork of the Salmon River and its tributaries. Final report. U.S. Forest Service, Ogden, Utah.

Minshall, G. W., D. A. Andrews, J. T. Brock, C. T. Robinson, and D. E. Lawrence. 1990. Changes in wild trout habitat following forest fire. Pages 111–

119 in F. Richardson and R. H. Hamre, eds. Wild trout IV: Proceedings of the symposium. 774–173/25037. GPO, Washington, D.C.

Minshall, G. W., J. T. Brock, and J. D. Varley. 1989. Wildfires and Yellowstone's stream ecosystems: A temporal perspective shows that aquatic recovery parallels forest succession. BioScience 39:707–715.

Minshall, G. W., K. W. Cummins, R. C. Petersen, C. E. Cushing, D. A. Bruns, J. R. Sedell, and R. L. Vannote. 1985. Developments in stream ecosystem theory. Can. J. Fish. Aquatic Sci. 42:1045–1055.

Minshall, G. W., R. C. Petersen, K. W. Cummins, T. L. Bott, J. R. Sedell, C. E. Cushing, and R. L. Vannote. 1983. Interbiome comparison of stream ecosystem dynamics. Ecol. Monogr. 53:1–25.

Mohrman, J., R. Ewing, and D. Carty. 1988. Sources and quantities of suspended sediment in the Yellowstone River and selected tributary watersheds between Yellowstone Lake outlet, Yellowstone National Park, Wyoming, and Livingston, Montana: 1986 annual progress report. U.S. Fish and Wildl. Serv., Yellowstone Fish. Off. Tech. Rep. no. 4.

Murphy, M. L., J. Heifetz, S. W. Johnson, K. V. Koski, and J. F. Thedinga. 1986. Effects of clear-cut logging with and without buffer strips on juvenile salmonids in Alaskan streams. Can. J. Fish. Aquatic Sci. 43:1521–1533.

Newbold, J. D., D. C. Erman, and K. B. Roby. 1980. Effects of logging on macroinvertebrates in streams with and without buffer strips. Can. J. Fish. Aquatic Sci. 37:1076–1085.

Noel, D. S., C. W. Martin, and C. A. Federer. 1986. Effects of forest clearcutting in New England on stream macroinvertebrates and periphyton. Envtl. Mgmt. 10:661–670.

Packer, P. E., and B. D. Williams. 1976. Logging and prescribed burning effects on the hydrologic and soil stability behavior of larch/Douglas fir forests in the northern Rocky Mountains. Proc. Tall Timbers Fire Ecol. Conf. Land Mgmt. Symp. 14:465–479.

Resh, V. H., A. V. Brown, A. P. Covich, M. E. Gurtz, H. W. Li, G. W. Minshall, S. R. Reice, A. L. Sheldon, J. B. Wallace, and R. Wissmar. 1988. The role of disturbance theory in stream ecology. J. N. Am. Benth. Soc. 7:433–455.

Romme, W. H. 1982. Fire and landscape diversity in subalpine forests of Yellowstone National Park. Ecol. Monogr. 52:199–221.

Schindler, D. W., R. W. Newbury, K. G. Beaty, J. Prokopowich, T. Ruscznski, and J. A. Dalton. 1980. Effects of a windstorm and forest fire on chemical losses from forested watersheds and on the quality of receiving streams. Can. J. Fish. Aquatic Sci. 37:328–334.

Shovic, H., et al. 1988. Preliminary burned area survey of Yellowstone National Park and adjoining national forests. Greater Yellowstone Post-fire Resource Assessment and Recovery Program. National Park Service and U.S. Forest Service, Yellowstone, Wyo.

Smock, L. A., G. M. Metzler, and J. E. Gladden. 1989. The role of debris dams in the structure and functioning of low-gradient headwater streams. Ecology 70:764–775.

Stottlemyer, R. 1987. Ecosystem nutrient release from a large fire, Yellowstone National Park. Pages 111–118 in Proceedings of Am. Meteorological Soc. Ninth Conference on Fire and Forest Meteorology, San Diego, Calif., April 1987.

Tiedemann, A. R., C. E. Conrad, J. H. Dicterich, J. W. Hornbeck, W. F. Megahan, L. A. Viereck, and D. D. Wade. 1979. Effects of fire on water: A state-of-knowledge review. U.S. For. Serv. Gen. Tech. Rcp. WO-10.

Vannote, R. L., G. W. Minshall, K. W. Cummins, J. R. Sedell, and C. E. Cushing. 1980. The river continuum concept. Can. J. Fish. Aquatic Sci. 37:130–137.

Woodward, D. F. 1989. The Yellowstone fires: Assessing the potential for ash in runoff water to reduce survival and growth of cutthroat trout. U.S. Fish and Wildlife Service, National Fisheries Contaminant Research Center, Jackson Field Research Station, Jackson, Wyo.

Wright, R. F. 1976. The impact of forest fire on the nutrient influxes to small lakes in northeastern Minnesota. Ecology 57:649–663.

CHAPTER 11   **Should Management Ignitions Be Used in Yellowstone National Park?**

James K. Brown

In the aftermath of the 1988 fire season, one question repeatedly arises: Would a program of management-ignited prescribed fires have eliminated the undesirable consequences of wildfire in Yellowstone National Park? (Management-ignited prescribed fires are ignited by managers rather than by such uncontrolled sources as lightning.) More specifically, would the fires have been prevented from threatening major visitor facilities and from crossing park boundaries? Would the fires have been less intense, and would they have burned less acreage? Are management-ignited prescribed fires compatible with the park policy of maintaining natural ecosystems?

FIRE POLICY

The management goal for Yellowstone National Park is to maintain as near as possible a natural ecological system. From 1972 to 1988, Yellowstone's fire management policy called for allowing lightning fires to burn so long as they did not threaten human lives, property, cultural and special natural features, or endangered species (Despain and Sellers 1977). All human-caused fires were to be suppressed. Management-ignited prescribed fire was permitted for reducing hazardous fuels, but not when intended primarily to mimic natural fire. To date, management-ignited prescribed

The help of the following individuals in developing this chapter is greatly appreciated: John Chapman, Steve Frye, John Krebs, Rod Norum, Ron Pierce, Dennis Quintilio, and Dave Thomas.

burning has not been utilized. The natural-fire program has instead relied strictly on lightning-caused fires. A policy of allowing natural fires to burn can be expected to prevail again in the future, but with tighter controls on when fires will be permitted to burn.

In carrying out this policy in the future on the national park and national forest lands of the Greater Yellowstone Area, the proper mix of lightning ignitions and management-ignited prescribed fire must be determined. Should management-ignited prescribed fire be used to reduce fire hazard? Do management-ignited prescribed fires mimic natural fire and should they be used specifically for that purpose?

In natural-fire management programs, goals tend to be either process oriented or structure oriented. The aim of process-oriented goals is to re-create the range of fire frequencies, intensities, and patterns that existed before European settlement. Whether Indian ignitions should be considered natural is a debated issue (Kilgore 1985), but in Yellowstone National Park and Forest Service wildernesses, only lightning-caused fires are considered natural and allowed to burn. Structure-oriented goals call for maintaining the composition and structure of vegetation that existed prior to the influence of Europeans. Although management-ignited prescribed fires can meet both process and structure goals, they have been used primarily to attain structure goals.

Achieving a completely natural fire process is not possible in Yellowstone National Park, or anywhere in the United States, except perhaps portions of Alaska. Constraints are needed to avoid threats to human life and property. In many situations, fires originating outside the parks and wildernesses are suppressed, even though historically they burned into such areas, thus eliminating one source of ignition. In Yellowstone National Park this may not be critical because the park's large size allows many fires to originate within its boundaries. In addition, many fires originating in adjacent Forest Service wilderness will be allowed to burn into the park. Nevertheless, in smaller wildernesses and parks, elimination of such ignitions seriously limits a natural-fire regime.

The structure-oriented approach is appropriate for short-interval fire regimes (up to twenty-five years between fires) such as the mixed conifer forest of the Sierra Nevada (Kilgore 1973), where excessive fuel buildup presents an unnatural situation. Carefully executed prescribed fires may be necessary to restore vegetation and fuels to a primeval condition, after which naturally occurring fires may be allowed. The structural approach is also appropriate for obtaining vegetation compatible with a natural-fire regime. Here, one must clearly define conditions of naturalness so that clear objectives can be set for management-ignited prescribed fires (Bon-nicksen and Stone 1985). Knowledge of natural-fire regimes, however, is often inadequate to set such standards.

The lodgepole pine forests of Yellowstone National Park have long-interval fire regimes (Romme 1982) and probably are best managed under a process goal. The process-oriented approach is more appropriate for long-interval fire regimes where fires typically are of high intensity and result in stand replacement (Agee and Huff 1986). Fuels have not had time to accumulate to significantly unnatural amounts during more than a half-century of fire suppression (Romme and Despain 1989).

An important issue is whether management-ignited prescribed fires should be used to meet a process goal for the long-interval fire regime. Management-ignited prescribed fires can be used for two purposes. (1) to mimic natural fire, and (2) to reduce hazardous fuels. The decision to use management-ignited prescribed fire to mimic natural fire rests on the ac-cepted definition of *natural*. A review of the fire ecology literature offers little help in characterizing what is natural wilderness fire management (Kilgore 1985). The critical consideration appears to be whether a human-caused ignition is acceptable as natural. If a manager ignites a fire and lets it burn unconstrained until it extinguishes on its own, it produces natural-fire effects, including postfire pattern on the landscape. The only arguably unnatural element is that the fire was started by a manager at a chosen location according to a plan. The primary objection to management-ignited prescribed fires thus is man's control over the origin. By accepting light-ning as the only natural source of ignition, managers are freed of the responsibility of determining when and where natural fires start. Disagree-ments over whether a fire was natural or whether it may have been ignited to serve such resource goals as improvement of wildlife habitat are elimi-nated. The debate about what constitutes a naturally occurring fire will no doubt continue.

A process-oriented approach, relying solely on lightning ignitions, en-counters trouble when fires threaten human lives or property, as witnessed during the 1988 fires in the Yellowstone area. To avoid unwanted fire behavior, which jeopardizes public acceptance of a natural-fire program, fuels must be managed in critical locations. Management-ignited pre-scribed fires should be considered for reducing hazardous fuels, even though only lightning-caused fires are defined as natural in an organiza-tion's fire management plan. Management-ignited prescribed fires should be conducted near areas requiring protection against wildfires. They should be scheduled only if effective fuel reduction can be achieved. In addition to reducing fuels, management-ignited prescribed fires closely mimic natural-fire effects.

Fuels can also be effectively managed by mechanical removal. Thinning to break crown continuity and removing dead woody surface fuel greatly mitigate the threat of wildfire. Physical treatment of fuels near facilities and developments should be given high priority regardless of whether prescribed fires are conducted.

FUEL TYPES AND FIRE BEHAVIOR

Moving from low to high elevation, major cover types include sagebrush-grass, Douglas fir (*Pseudotsuga menziesii*), lodgepole pine (*Pinus contorta*), Engelmann spruce (*Picea engelmannii*), subalpine fir (*Abies lasiocarpa*), and whitebark pine (*Pinus albicaulis*). These cover types can be grouped into three fuel classes that display different fire behavior potential: (1) sagebrush-grass, (2) continuous forest, and (3) open forest at high elevations. The potential for using prescribed fire in these fuel groups varies substantially.

The sagebrush-grass type occurs in the northern portion of the park. This type consists of fine fuels and supports rapid rates of fire spread when the grasses are cured. Fire intensities are intermediate among wildland fuels and depend partly on the amount of sagebrush present. The practice of prescribed burning is well established in this type (Bunting, Kilgore, and Bushey 1987). Opportunities to use management-ignited prescribed fire occur annually, except where intensive grazing has markedly depleted the herbaceous fuels. Grass fuels recover after one growing season. The benefit of hazard reduction is primarily reduced intensity, because fire can still spread rapidly in areas burned the previous year.

Continuous forest, primarily of lodgepole pine, occupies nearly 80 percent of the park. Potentials for development of high-intensity fire and spread of fire vary greatly, depending on the amount of dead vegetation present and vertical continuity of live fuels, particularly understory conifers. Fires typically spread very slowly in lodgepole pine and spruce-fir types unless long-term drying and sustained winds produce severe burning conditions. Then fire behavior changes abruptly, and fires spread by high-intensity crowning and spotting. We have limited experience in using management-ignited prescribed fire in this type. Dry-site Douglas fir stands occupy a small portion of the park. Fires in this type burn readily beneath tree canopies in grass and small-twig fuels.

High-elevation forests of whitebark pine and spruce-fir hummocks are typically of low flammability due to sparse fuels and high fuel moisture. Management-ignited prescribed fire would be impractical in most of this type because burning conditions occur infrequently and hazardous fuels are seldom a problem. The major wildfire threat to villages, improvements, and wilderness boundaries lies with the lodgepole pine forest.

Fuels and potential fire behavior change dramatically over the life span of lodgepole pine, depending upon establishment, growth, mortality, and site characteristics (Brown 1975; Brown and See 1981). Some stages during the life cycle of lodgepole pine are more flammable than others. A program of management-ignited prescribed fire to reduce fuel hazard should be applied to the more flammable stages that typically occur in overmature stands and sometimes in immature stands.

The following, based partly on Don Despain's successional classification (Despain 1987), illustrates fire behavior at different stages in the development of lodgepole pine forests:

Young stands (0–40 yr): Herbaceous plants are the major plant cover. Litter and duff are absent. Fire spread through this type is rare, although partially rotten downed logs will burn.

Immature stands (30–150 yr): Dense stands of small-diameter lodgepole pine occupy the site. Understory vegetation is sparse. Needle litter is nearly continuous, but the duff layer is shallow during most of this period. During the early portion of the period, downed woody material from the previous stand ignites readily. Under dry conditions it supports fire spread on the surface and initiates crowning in the young stand. A wildfire that occurs now (double burn) eliminates the woody fuels, and the next stand develops through the immature stage free of large woody fuels. In the latter part of the period, the downed logs from the previous stand have largely decayed, the trees are taller with crowns well above the ground, and flammability is reduced. The chance of crowning supported by surface fuels is nil.

Mature stands (150–300 yr): Closed canopy stands dominated by lodgepole pine occupy the site. Engelmann spruce and subalpine fir seedlings and saplings are frequently present. The forest floor is well covered with herbaceous and low shrubby vegetation. Litter and duff are continuous. Downed woody fuels are normally sparse. Fire spread is slow and the potential for crowning is slight. Occasional pockets of understory fuels will support torching and crowning. In the older mature stands, the mountain pine beetle (*Dendroctonus ponderosae*) may kill many trees and increase flammability.

Overmature stands (300+ yr): The overstory is predominantly occupied by lodgepole pine but some Engelmann spruce, subalpine fir, and white-bark pine are present. The canopies are ragged, and understory fuel components are usually well developed. Large-diameter downed woody fuels, perhaps the most significant fuel component in lodgepole pine forests, have accumulated. Duff is 2–5 cm deep. Ladder fuels are present, namely understory spruce and fir, and lichens in older trees. Fuels ignite readily and support torching, crowning, and spotting. Extreme fire behavior occurs typically in this successional stage.

PRESCRIBED FIRE PROGRAM

Mechanical Fuel Treatment

All of the prescribed-fire experts consulted agree that some fuel treatment around villages would be necessary before conducting any management-ignited prescribed fires near them. The management-ignited prescribed fires might cause high-intensity fire behavior that could threaten the villages unless fuels are mechanically treated. Mechanical fuel treatment is free of the risks associated with uncontrolled fire behavior and can be carried out at any time, such as during low-use visitor periods. It can be used effectively to reduce crown-fire potentials.

One way of reducing fuel is to create shaded fuel breaks completely around villages and vulnerable campgrounds. A fuel-break strip at least 150 m wide and preferably 300 m wide is needed. Within the strip, all standing and downed dead woody fuels larger than about 3 cm should be removed, and the live trees should be thinned to break up continuity of the crown canopy. Thinning can be feathered into the stands, with the widest tree spacing occurring toward the protected areas. Approximately one-third to one-half of the trees should be removed.

Costs of fuel reduction could vary greatly depending on the method used and constraints imposed to protect the environment. Costs would probably range from $1,000/ha for a mechanized operation to $3,700/ha for hand labor. To construct fuel breaks around the three major visitor centers with minimal disturbance to the site, costs of $300,000 to $500,000 should be expected. To treat fuels in the vicinity of all facilities and power lines would cost substantially more. These costs could be offset somewhat by selling trees from the thinnings.

Fire Prescription

A fire prescription states the objectives for the fire, describes the required fire, and outlines the environmental conditions under which the objectives can be met. The following sections describe the fire prescription for Yellowstone Park. It was assembled by integrating conditions suggested by seven fire behavior experts and conditions derived from several fuel consumption equations (Brown et al. 1985; Ottmar 1984; Sandberg 1980).

Objectives. Although planned ignitions should mimic a natural biological process, the purpose of management-ignited prescribed fires is to reduce fuels in critical areas so that lightning fires may be allowed to burn without posing threats to visitor centers and park boundaries. To meet these management goals, management-ignited prescribed fires should substantially reduce the potential for high-intensity fire behavior, including crowning and spotting. To accomplish this, ignitions should (1) consume 80 percent or more of 2- to 8-cm downed woody fuel and 50 percent or more of greater than 8-cm downed woody fuel; (2) consume at least 70 percent of the litter and duff; and (3) kill at least 60 percent of understory spruce, fir, and lodgepole pine. Achievement of these objectives will greatly reduce fire behavior potentials, but under extremely dry and high-velocity wind conditions, crown fires will spread even without well-developed surface fuels. To lessen the threat of crown fire, crown canopies must be opened up near visitor centers by mechanical thinning and fuel removal.

Fire treatment. Areas must be identified where high-intensity wildfire could threaten visitor centers or escape across park boundaries. Good candidates are areas of overmature lodgepole pine, particularly those supporting an understory of fir or lodgepole pine, and areas having fuel loadings that exceed 34 t/ha for material averaging 15 cm in diameter (Aldrich and Mutch 1973). Treatment areas of 800 to 2,000 ha should be identified and ignited using helicopter application of alumagel. The areas should be approximately 1.6 km wide and several km long. The 1.6-km width is recommended to eliminate risk of spotting, which commonly occurs over 0.8–1.2 km and occasionally farther with high wind speeds.

A massive ignition effort will be required to achieve ignition and good burnout of woody fuels. Within the general fire perimeter, ignition probably can be bypassed in old immature stands and young mature stands because woody fuels there will be sparse.

Fires will spread slowly in the surface fuels. Considerable torching and occasional crowning of clumps of trees and entire areas of several hectares in size will occur. Spotting can be expected up to 0.4–0.8 km.

Environmental conditions. Certain environmental parameters must be met in conducting the prescribed fires (table 11.1). Moisture content of large fuel, and related National Fire Danger Rating System 1,000 hour time-lag moisture content, are considered to be the most critical parameters

Table 11.1 Range of preferred and acceptable fire prescription
parameters

Parameter	Preferred	Acceptable
Moisture content of fine fuel (1 & 10 h time-lag fuels)	5–8%	5–12%
Moisture content of large fuel (7.6 cm and larger diameter)	10–15%	8–20%
NFDR-1,000 h time-lag moisture	< 16%	< 19%
Lower duff moisture content	< 60%	< 80%
Wind speed (6 m height), km/h	3–16	2–24
Relative humidity	18–30%	15–35%
Time of year	After 8/15	After 8/1

for meeting objectives because they control consumption of large woody fuel. Calculation of the NFDR-1,000 hour moisture content is based on the accumulated effects of temperature, relative humidity, and duration of precipitation (Cohen and Deeming 1985). In all likelihood, if moisture content of large fuels meets the prescription, moisture contents of duff will be acceptable also. Early summer fires are not considered because of the risk of prolonged wildfire conditions as experienced in 1988, and because cured herbaceous vegetation is normally needed to assist in fire spread.

Probability of meeting prescription conditions. Weather records from Old Faithful covering the period 1965 to 1987 were analyzed to determine the probability of occurrence for the prescription (table 11.2). Records for one year, 1971, were missing; thus twenty-two years of data were available. This is a short period of time, but enough to provide an idea of weather probabilities. Although precipitation and related fuel moisture vary substantially from the relatively wet southwestern corner to the dry northern portion, Old Faithful should represent fire weather reasonably well for the lodgepole pine forest.

The frequency with which date and NFDR-1,000 hour moisture content met the prescription was one in four years for preferred conditions and three in four years for acceptable conditions. When the prescription was restricted to September, preferred conditions were met three out of twenty years and acceptable conditions two out of three years.

The number of days from August 1 to September 30 that relative humidity, NFDR-10 hour time-lag moisture content, and wind speed were simultaneously in prescription averaged four days (9 percent) for preferred conditions and twelve days (24 percent) for acceptable conditions. The

Table 11.2 Number of years in which three or more consecutive days satisfy the prescription for NFDR-1,000 h moisture content and date

	NFDR-1,000 h Moisture Content			
	Preferred (< 16%)		Acceptable (< 19%)	
Prescription Occurrence	*Aug. 1– Sept. 30*	*Aug. 15– Sept. 30*	*Aug. 1– Sept. 30*	*Aug. 15– Sept. 30*
Years meeting prescription	8	5	20	16
Percentage of total years	36	23	91	73
Ratio of years in prescription	1:3	1:4	9:10	3:4

probability of all prescription parameters being met simultaneously could not be calculated with the available computer programs. But the probabilities obviously would be less than calculated just for date and NFDR-1,000 hour moisture content. Although the exact probabilities of meeting all prescription conditions remain uncertain, it is apparent that successful prescribed burning could be carried out only on an average of once every several years.

Burning Plan

What are the logistics for carrying out a program of prescribed fires, and how much would such a program cost? To answer these questions, the number of prescribed fires approximately 1,200 ha (1.5 × 8 km) in size needed to protect visitor centers and national park boundaries was first estimated. To protect Old Faithful, Grant Village, Lewis Campground, and Canyon Village from spread of fire by crowning and spotting, approximately ten prescribed fires located to intercept prevailing winds would be needed. To reduce heavy fuel accumulations within 1.5–3 km of all boundaries, approximately forty fires would be required. Not all boundaries are equally vulnerable to escapes, so this number could be reduced by concentrating prescribed fires on the boundaries most likely to be threatened. Nevertheless, twenty-five to thirty prescribed fires would be necessary.

Two or three prescribed fires are probably all that could be conducted in a single season without risking too much fire. Assuming fires could be conducted every third year, which is probably optimistic, it would take thirty to fifty years to safeguard visitor centers and boundaries. The program to safeguard the centers alone could be carried out in about ten years. Speeding up the program by conducting many burns in a single season would be possible, but logistically difficult as well as risky.

Two helicopters, each igniting 200 ha per day, would be assigned to an individual burn. A massive ignition effort would be required because surface fire could not be relied upon to adequately ignite critical fuels. Surveillance with a small airplane would be necessary during and after the ignition period until the fire was no longer active. A twenty-person holding crew should be available for a ten-day period. Under these assumptions, the cost for a 1,200 ha burn is estimated to be $67,350 (about $56/ha).

An acceptable contingency plan for each prescribed fire would be necessary to cover the likely possibility of fire moving beyond its expected perimeter. The passage of one or two dry cold fronts with high-speed winds, crowning, and spotting for 1 km or more should be assumed. The prescribed fire could easily grow to several times its planned size and even considerably larger. To guard against this event, prescribed fires would not be ignited before September in drought years such as 1988. This would shorten the period of burning during severe fire weather. A severalfold increase in fire size would presumably be acceptable in most areas of the park, but some fires might require suppression action involving a large fire organization. This could add several million dollars to the cost.

The estimated direct operational costs for a program of prescribed burning and presuppression fuel treatment are as follows: fuel breaks around centers, $500,000; prescribed fires near centers, $675,000; prescribed fires near boundaries (forty fires) $2,695,000.

Nearly $4 million would be required for this program. The costs of conducting individual prescribed fires could be reduced by one-half or more, once experience is gained, particularly for low-risk fires near boundaries. In this case, the program could be carried out for a minimum of $2.5 million. The risk of undesirable consequences should be assessed on each potential prescribed fire. Costs per burn can be held to reasonable levels by conducting burns only when risk of escape and damage is considered low. Where fires might become inordinately expensive to control or cause unacceptable damage, burning would not be conducted. Even with cautious planning, the costs could be considerably greater than budgeted if fire suppression were required to quell unexpected threats from the prescribed fires. Nonetheless, compared with the fire suppression costs of 1988, approximately $100 million within Yellowstone National Park, the cost of this program would be relatively small.

The answers to the original questions are as follows. Yes, threats to visitor centers could have been prevented or greatly reduced, assuming a program of management-ignited prescribed fires had been initiated in 1972, with considerable additional funding in the Yellowstone Park fire management budget. Some escapes across park boundaries might have been avoided, but not to a significant degree, because time was not available to complete the program along all boundaries, even with adequate funding. The amount of area burned also would not have changed significantly. Had the boundary program been completed, however, escapes on the eastern and western sides of the park probably would have been significantly reduced, though not eliminated. Less area outside of the park would have burned. Yes, management-ignited prescribed fires are compatible with a policy of maintaining natural ecosystems, particularly when used to reduce threats to human lives and property. But the appropriateness of management-ignited prescribed fires mimicking natural fire remains a debated issue.

The above questions are relevant to managing fire in wildernesses and parks throughout the West. Management-ignited prescribed fires could help assure the safety of allowing lightning-caused fires to burn over most of the wilderness area. Although the location and timing may be unnatural, management-ignited prescribed fires produce natural-fire effects. A strong argument can be made for employing management-ignited prescribed fires to mimic natural fire in the many wildernesses, parks, and natural areas that are too small to allow natural fire otherwise.

A program of management-ignited prescribed fires appears feasible, but it would require substantially more funding than is currently available for prescribed fire programs. A specially trained and experienced interagency team would probably be required to assist in planning and conducting the burns. Meeting the objectives of these prescribed fires could be difficult and tricky because rather severe burning conditions are required for success. The threshold between surface fire and crowning fire behavior is narrow. Skillful and experienced prescribed burners are necessary to successfully manage this type of fire potential. The irregular burning opportunities in any one location make it difficult for local managers to maintain needed skills. An interagency team able to provide assistance throughout the West could overcome this problem. An informed and supportive public would also be needed.

The effectiveness of this program depends on selecting the right areas for burning, achieving the desired reduction of fuels, and controlling the fires. Because current fire managers lack substantial experience with this type of prescribed burning, operational scale research and development efforts should be undertaken soon to provide guidance for managing fire in parks and wilderness.

REFERENCES

Agee, J. K., and M. H. Huff. 1986. Structure and process goals for vegetation in wilderness areas. Pages 17–25 in R. C. Lucas, comp. Proceedings national wilderness research conference: Current research. U.S. For. Serv. Gen. Tech. Rep. INT-212.

Aldrich, D. F., and R. W. Mutch. 1973. Wilderness fire management planning guidelines and inventory procedures. U.S. For. Serv. N. Region 36.

Bonnicksen, T. M., and E. C. Stone. 1985. Restoring naturalness to national parks. Envtl. Mgmt. 9:479–486.

Brown, J. K. 1975. Fire cycles and community dynamics in lodgepole pine forests. Pages 429–456 in D. M. Baumgartner, ed. Management of lodgepole pine ecosystems: Symposium proceedings. Washington State Univ. Cooperative Extension Service, Pullman.

Brown, J. K., M. A. Marsden, K. C. Ryan, and E. D. Reinhardt. 1985. Predicting duff and woody fuel consumed by prescribed fire in northern Rocky Mountains. U.S. For. Serv. Res. Pap. INT-337.

Brown, J. K., and T. E. See. 1981. Downed dead woody fuel and biomass in the northern Rocky Mountains. U.S. For. Serv. Gen. Tech. Rep. INT-117.

Bunting, S. C., B. M. Kilgore, and C. L. Bushey. 1987. Guidelines for prescribed burning sagebrush-grass rangelands in the northern Great Basin. U.S. For. Serv. Gen. Tech. Rep. INT-231.

Cohen, J. D., and J. E. Deeming. 1985. The National Fire-Danger Rating System: Basic equations. U.S. For. Serv. Gen. Tech. Rep. PSW-82.

Despain, D. G. 1987. Lodgepole pine types. Report on file at Yellowstone National Park.

Despain, D. G., and R. E. Sellers. 1977. Natural fire in Yellowstone National Park. W. Wildlands 4:20–24.

Kilgore, B. M. 1973. The ecological role of fire in Sierran conifer forests: Its application to national park management. Quarternary Res. 3:496–513.

———. 1985. What is "natural" in wilderness fire management? Pages 57–67 in J. E. Lotan, B. M. Kilgore, W. C. Fischer, and R. W. Mutch, tech. coords. Proceedings: Symposium and workshop on Wilderness Fire. U.S. For. Serv. Gen. Tech. Rep. INT-182.

Ottmar, R. D. 1984. Predicting fuel consumption by fire stages to reduce smoke from slash fires. Pages 87–106 in Proceedings of Northwest Forest Fire Council annual meeting, Olympia, Wash., Nov. 21–23, 1983.

Romme, W. H. 1982. Fire and landscape diversity in subalpine forests in Yellowstone National Park. Ecol. Monogr. 52:199–221.

Romme, W. H., and D. G. Despain. 1989. The long history of fire in the Greater Yellowstone Ecosystem. W. Wildlands 15:10–17.

Sandberg, D. V. 1980. Duff reduction by prescribed underburning in Douglas-fir. U.S. For. Serv. Res. Pap. PNW-272.

CHAPTER 12 **A Canadian View of Fire Management in the Greater Yellowstone Area**

Nikita Lopoukhine

The Canadian Parks Service was affected by the Yellowstone fires of 1988 when President Ronald Reagan permitted Canadian fire fighters to join the legion of forces fighting fires in and around Yellowstone. From that moment on, previously infrequent media reports became a daily part of the news, leading to an exploration of U.S. fire policies and comparisons with Canadian policies. The uncontrollable behavior of fires experienced in Yellowstone was not the "news," as such fires are common in Canada; instead, it was the "let burn" policy and the attention the fires were getting from politicians. As a result of the fires in Yellowstone, CPS personnel underwent numerous interviews.

This Canadian media attention regarding Yellowstone underlines that whatever happens in Yellowstone is an international news item. Of further significance is that such news has repercussions for international park management policies. The focus on fire policies governing Yellowstone gave impetus to an ongoing examination of CPS policies (Day, White, and Lopoukhine 1990).

Yellowstone's notoriety was established when it was created as the world's first national park. This event established an American leadership not only in the creation of parks but also in the formation of policies. Such leadership comes with responsibilities that extend to parks and reserves throughout the world. Canadians have benefited from American leadership, experiences, debates, research, and conferences, all of which have been invaluable for forming policies. This leadership has doubtless provided the Canadian Parks Service with justification for many management actions. At times, it has also given us reason to try a different route.

CPS FIRE MANAGEMENT HISTORY AND POLICIES

The Canadian Parks Service traces its origins to the creation of Banff National Park in 1885, thirteen years after the creation of Yellowstone. From the start the CPS also suppressed fires, killed predators, and developed parks with "improvement" in mind. It was during this period that access routes and town sites were established. Policies to the contrary were introduced slowly as demand necessitated and, unfortunately, not because of an internal desire to lead in "preservation," the term of endearment at the time. The purpose and role of national parks in both countries have a common pattern (figure 12.1).

In the formative years, the Canadian Parks Service did lead other Canadian agencies in the development of fire suppression techniques and equipment. The development of the first portable fire pump in Canada, for example, is attributed to the CPS. The Warden Service (equivalent to the U.S. National Park Service Ranger Service) was established in part to deal with fires that marred the scenic greenery of the parks and upset visitors' expectations (White 1985). Perhaps it was the fortuitous circumstances of climate and fuel arrangement rather than the effectiveness of

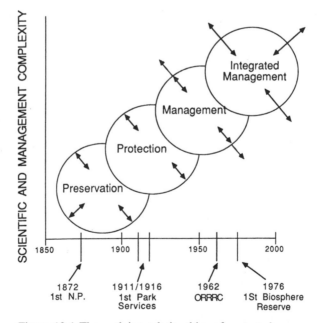

Figure 12.1 The evolving relationships of protected areas, from isolation to integration (Eidsvik 1985).

suppression techniques, but prevention and suppression efforts have been linked to the drop in fire occurrences such as that in Banff National Park (table 12.1) and elsewhere. Whether it was fire prevention, climate, or a combination that resulted in the paucity of fires greater than 40 hectares is unclear.

Reduced fire occurrence made it easier to justify diverting the resources dedicated to fire. Limited resources and the growing diversification in park management responsibilities led to changes in the orientation of park wardens. When it became clear that fire was to be managed and not just suppressed, our resource managers were found specializing in more "important" and, unfortunately, more fragmented issues. Major fires in 1968 and 1980 began to alter some perceptions, but the CPS continued to ignore the changing landscapes, and their root cause, park management.

At present, there is agreement that most of the vegetation in Canadian national parks owes its origin to fire and that exclusion has caused change (Resource/Environment Management Systems Research Ltd. 1988). Nevertheless, efforts are still primarily directed at keeping fire out of most of our parks. A few parks have initiated experimental prescribed burning programs. Integrated management (figure 12.1), however, which was to be launched with cabinet approval of the Parks Canada Policy (1979), has not yet been fully implemented.

Table 12.1 Random ignition fires (> 40 ha) in Banff National Park

Decade	Area Burned (ha)	Fires No.	Average Fire Size (ha)
1880–1889	37,050	> 6	—
1890–1899	18,600	10	1,860
1900–1909	16,850	12	1,404
1910–1919	3,300	6	550
1920–1929	10,500	9	1,167
1930–1939	8,050	6	1,342
1940–1949	4,200	2	2,100
1950–1959	0	0	0
1960–1969	500	1	500
1970–1979	45	1	45
1980–1989	0	0	0
Totals	99,095	53	

Source: White 1985.

SIMILARITIES AND DIFFERENCES IN CPS AND NPS FIRE MANAGEMENT

Perhaps it was the absence of internal scientific input that delayed the implementation of modern integrated fire management. Unlike the U.S. National Park Service, there were and are no scientists within the CPS. Also, the CPS has only a few professional resource managers to lead the initiative. In contrast to the NPS, within the CPS the Warden Service is expected to manage natural resources while also attending to public safety, law enforcement, and public relations functions; all this at a technician's classification and wage. Besides such obvious differences in our division of labor there are other equally fundamental differences in regard to our respective fire management approaches.

Policies

The institutional framework by which the CPS manages parks consists of a recently amended National Parks Act, a cabinet-approved policy (under review), and where more detail is necessary, directives (figure 12.2). The latter not only provide specific direction but also assign responsibilities.

The fire management directive specifies the following major points, which differ from the policies governing NPS fire management policies. First, the directive states that the effects of a fire are a more important consideration than the source of ignition. Second, fires cannot be pre-scribed outside of objectives for vegetation as defined by an approved vegetation plan (Van Wagner and Methven 1980; Lopoukhine 1985; Lopoukhine and White 1985). The plan justifies managing vegetation. It is the governing medium for the approval of suppressing fires or of prescribing fire or any other techniques for managing vegetation.

A prescribed fire is one that fits into predetermined objectives for the park's natural resources. Both planned fires and unplanned fires (random lightning and accidental fires) are possible prescribed fires. The objectives correspond to the purpose of the national park as a representative of the element of the Canadian landscape or natural region within which the park is situated.

For objectives to be realized and their realization monitored, they must be quantifiable. Furthermore, the objectives must be accompanied with costs and an implementation schedule. Such a schedule would also incorporate the required studies (for example, fire history, human and other disturbances, and of course a basic inventory) and research where basic information is lacking.

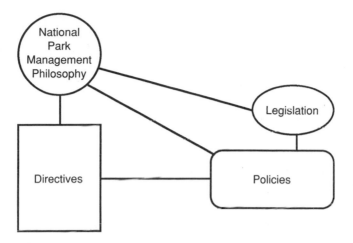

Figure 12.2 The institutional framework for park management.

The preparation of a vegetation management plan is required not only by the fire management directive, but more important, it can be argued that it is now required also by our amended legislation. Section 5(1.2) of the National Parks Act, amended in 1988, now states: "Maintenance of ecological integrity through the protection of natural resources shall be the first priority when considering park zoning and visitor use in a management plan."

"Ecological integrity" is as yet undefined and as such suffers from the same problems associated with using the term *natural*. Yet it is a step forward, since the stifling debate over naturalness based on presence or absence of man has now been replaced by a debate over ecological principles and their application to park management.

The concept of vegetation planning for purposes of ecological integrity is easy to invoke, but writing a plan is more difficult, and implementing one even more so. At present only three vegetation plans are in existence in the CPS (Blyth and Hudson 1987; Mosquin 1986; Lopoukhine 1989). These plans are first editions, which will require revision over time as the appropriateness of each vegetation objective is evaluated and as each plan is implemented.

Although "ecological integrity" offers a clearer framework for resource management, it does not alleviate the realities of the ever-present problems affecting the management of natural resources within national parks. The holy grail, ecological integrity, is compromised by fixed "straight" park boundaries, existing facilities, concerns for different land uses exterior to national parks, and "traditional use" interests. These compromisers of ecological integrity justify planning and active management, and they also serve as good examples of why park managers cannot avoid making moral and ethical judgments. This reality further enforces the need to have all management actions governed by quantifiable objectives accompanied by a rigorous and constant monitoring program.

Ecosystem Factors

Most of Canada's national parks have a vegetation that has been determined by high-intensity fires. Certainly all Canadian parks in the boreal forest and the subalpine of the Rocky Mountains have vegetation with such characteristics (Heinselman 1981). Although this differentiates most of our respective parks from U.S. parks, the events of 1988 indicate that there are similarities with Yellowstone National Park's fire regime.

High-intensity fires are a large-scale decomposer, a short-term nutrient cycler, and the dominant determinant of vegetation structure and species distribution. Such fires have burned most parts of the boreal forest, on average, one hundred times in the past ten thousand years (Bailey 1985). The pattern of the burns can either be in the form of a very large individual fire, exceeding 500,000 ha (Bailey 1985), or as in northwestern Ontario where in 1983 twenty-five fires in two days burned 400,000 ha (Kincaid 1985), the equivalent of the Greater Yellowstone Ecosystem 1988 burn area.

To manage such fires within the scope of a national park compounds the difficulty, as previously explored by among others Heinselman (1985) and Alexander and Dubé (1983). The issues of public safety and values at risk are primary concerns, given that under extreme weather conditions fire behavior is not dependent on the age of the forest, site, or indeed aspect. Severe drought as experienced in the GYE in 1988 was also a precursor to major fires in other national parks in previous years. In what is now Pukaskwa National Park, fires in 1931, 1936, and 1942 were all preceded by drought (Alexander 1985).

To re-create such intense fires or to permit such fires to burn under a sanctioned fire management plan would not currently be approved in most Canadian parks. The current art and science of fire-control cannot justify such a plan, and the values at risk in some parks are considered too high on the societal scale to even consider risking their loss by prescribed burning. The dilemma this poses, of course, is that the natural-fire regime, the essence of ecological integrity, which the Canadian Parks Service is mandated to perpetuate, is being altered.

The matter is complicated further by the scale of such intense fires. Few if any of our parks are large enough or were designed to capture the grain of such fires (Baker 1989). The landscape fragmentation exterior to parks has altered the natural-fire return interval and upset the temporal distribution of the natural patchwork pattern that characterized, for example, the boreal zone. This is unfortunate, since in relation to other biogeographic regions of the world, the boreal zone is still only slightly affected by human impact (Hamet-Ahti 1983).

Van Wagner (1978) recognized that in the boreal forest regeneration occurs at the community level and as such can be tracked by plotting age-class distributions on a landscape scale. Where fires burn randomly, regardless of age, the age classes or fire intervals or both (nonlethal fire regimes) will represent a negative exponential distribution where the frequency of age classes or intervals decreases with age. A random pattern is associated with a natural-fire-dependent forest and is therefore an appropriate model for parks intent on perpetuating a vegetation renewed by fire at the community level. Some critical decisions are involved, however.

To achieve and then maintain an age-class distribution reflecting a random fire pattern when the park clearly encompasses only a part of the landscape is a de facto decision to try to fit a microcosm of the original landscape into the park. Rejecting this decision leads to accepting the other alternative, which is to have the age-class distribution oscillate between a bell and a negative exponential shape. Oscillation is an inescapable reality given that the bell-shaped curve is impossible to retain as a long-term goal. In time, such a distribution will eventually dramatically convert to a negative exponential distribution. The oscillation alternative is exemplified by the Greater Yellowstone Ecosystem.

Unfortunately, the oscillation alternative is the only short-term option available to most Canadian park managers. Fiscal resources and human resources with the requisite ability to maintain a negative exponential distribution of age classes within all parks are currently insufficient. The right amount of fire or an approximation of a negative exponential curve by the age classes must of course be in congruence with predetermined objectives stated in the vegetation plan. Pursuing the oscillation option in a fire-dependent ecosystem has the effect of continuing to modify fire-dependent vegetation, eroding ecological integrity, and losing representativeness. Furthermore, the haunting specter of a conflagration is not appeased.

Nahanni National Park in Canada's North West Territories has few capital investments requiring protection either within or outside the park. The oscillation alternative as a long-term objective is appropriate for this park. In contrast, the oscillation option is risky for the parks with investments within or exterior to the park. Fire suppression thus becomes a preoccupation, which has the effect of extending the range of the oscillation, increasing biomass accumulation, and certainly not eliminating the possibility of a major conflagration. Asbestos forests are a myth.

Putting aside the utilitarian question of capital investments in favor of issues of ecological integrity, this option must also be evaluated in the light of the effect it may have on the components of an ecosystem that have become wholly dependent on the park area for survival. Will society permit oscillations that exceed the bounds of tolerance for a particular species or a community relegated to existence solely on a reserve?

These are the issues facing Canada's national parks, and apparently we now share them with Yellowstone managers. Indeed, the managers of the GYE have a basic question before them. What will the objectives be for the GYE? This is a particularly appropriate question since the area burned in 1988 has in effect pushed Yellowstone National Park's age-class distribution into a negative exponential trace.

Even if the decisions are not taken in the context of age-class distribution, that distribution provides a record of the decisions. Will the decision in effect be to create a mosaic of small burn areas (a negative exponential distribution), or will the large burn area not be broken up by smaller burns until another "nearly natural event" pushes the bell-shaped distribution back into a negative exponential distribution?

Philosophy

The lag in the establishment of our first national park perhaps reflects the Canadian philosophy of being cautious and dependent on others to take the lead. There are many advantages to being cautious as we enter the stage of integrated management (figure 12.1) in national parks. With such caution we may avoid some of the pitfalls that number at least as many as the different values placed on national parks (Bratton 1985).

There are also drawbacks, however. Being cautious has held the CPS back in delivering on our mandate of assuring ecological integrity. Public safety and capital assets continue their hold over our operational decisions. True, many past decisions presently compromise our options and in fact are dominating the reasoning behind resource management decisions. For instance, Banff Townsite represents some $3 billion worth of real estate. In deference to these assets and the visitors in wooded campgrounds, prescribed fires within the Bow Valley where these facilities are situated are now prohibited. Instead, mechanical fuel modifications are becoming a priority. The vegetation of Banff's Bow Valley, which was to be regulated

Table 12.2 Random ignited fires and area burned within Canadian parks in the past twelve years

Year	Total No. of Fires	Area Burned (ha)
1978	69	52
1979	150	70,762
1980	108	175,002
1981	145	680,173
1982	104	9,113
1983	93	5,209
1984	161	14,207
1985	128	5,646
1986	90	2,662
1987	93	140
1988	73	331
1989	131	834

by prescribed burns (Lopoukhine and White 1985), thus for the moment at least is being relegated to an anthropocentrism governed by the well-being of a town site and other capital developments. This decision, incidentally, came on the heels of 1988 events in Yellowstone.

Ironically, the diversion of prescribed burning away from the Bow Valley comes at a point where statistically the CPS prescribed burning program was gaining stature. The total yearly area burned by random ignitions (table 12.2) in the past three years was surpassed by planned-ignition burns. In 1988, a total of 2,600 ha were burned in three parks at a total cost of $25,000. The largest (1,500 ha) of these fires, in the Bow Valley, burned primarily as a crown fire and formed a convection column of several thousand meters (Day, White, and Lopoukhine 1990). In 1989, CPS staff burned 1,937 ha in seven fires.

Financial Considerations

Resource management within the CPS, as I believe is the case with the NPS, represents but a minor component (5 percent) of the overall budget. This, of course, excludes the emergency funding system for paying the costs of suppression and most presuppression activities directed at wildfires.

The similarity ends, however, if the comparison is made in actual dollars. We have not had a $120 million year. In 1981, when 15 percent of Wood Buffalo burned (670,000 ha) only $2.6 million was expended and only one hundred fire fighters were mobilized. These exceptional expenditures aside, the CPS budget dedicated to fire consists of only twenty-six person years and $220,000 operating dollars (White 1988).

Park Values

North American society has developed a spectrum of park values, which at both ends are quasi-religious. As such their adherents are categorizable as either fundamentalists, those who fervently defend natural areas against man, or as restoration ecologists, those who wish to shield and perpetuate specific natural-area features from the impacts of a globally omnipresent man through active management (Bonnicksen 1988). The debates among and within these two groups over the issue of fire in Yellowstone is, unfortunately, not always constructive, as both sides seem to have taken unbending positions. Each accuses the other of "gardening" and thus of being destroyers of wilderness. It would be unfortunate if further acrimony develops since only through a healthy open debate based on free-flowing information can the issue be resolved. Such a debate would keep the purpose of national parks near the top of North American society's consciousness. Only then will our society, which demanded that parks be created and has guided policy development to date, continue guiding the evolution of our respective policies. An exclusion of information or of elements of our respective societies from this critical debate could jeopardize future park values.

Yet one must question whether the debate is relevant in light of some of the predicted near-future impacts from human-accelerated climate (Peters 1988). If ecosystems will be unable to keep up with the rate of climate change, can either camp profess a relevant standard of naturalness? Any rapid climatic change will likely affect the role of parks and, perhaps, render the debate on fire management irrelevant. Instead, we will soon be, and some already are, debating how to use our North American park systems as arks or nodes for the predicted movement of species in response to changes in climate (Peters 1988). The function of parks may shift from perpetuators of landscapes and ecosystems to perpetuators of species and new human-induced associations for the benefit of future generations. I only hope that society retains park values while undergoing the stress of climate change.

Management Philosophy

To be optimistic, I am confident that the second centennial of our respective park systems will be realized. There is a caveat, however. To continue,

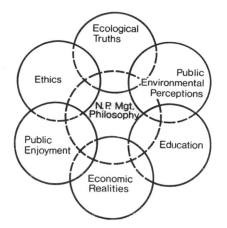

Figure 12.3 Spheres of influence on park management philosophy.

there must be a management philosophy that complements the integrated stage of park management mentioned earlier (figure 12.1). Essentially it must be a philosophy divorced from the controls of anthropocentric economics, that is, the perception of parks only in terms of their utility. Society's growing perception of our environment's jeopardy is helping this transformation in our respective countries.

Parks are increasingly brought forward in the media and elsewhere as examples of where ecocentric economic principles must dominate. Such principles are of course based on ecological truths and ethics (figure 12.3). The former is the recognition of park management's impact on critical interrelationships within and without parks. Ethics consists of choosing whether parks are intended for man's sole enjoyment or truly for the protection of ecosystems and their elements, including their controlling forces, with whom we share this planet.

Economic realities, enjoyment, and education are not going to be eliminated as determinants of the philosophy of North American park management. They must, however, become subservient in the age of integrated management.

Philosophical musings and crystal gazing aside, the events of 1988 in Yellowstone and the ongoing reviews of policies have had repercussions for the Canadian Parks Service. A prescribed burning program has been delayed and the CPS fire management program has received limited media attention. Since our organization is only in the stage of developing the expertise to use fire (Day, White, and Lopoukhine 1990), we are vulnerable to such events. If, for instance, a decision were reached that the GYE had experienced enough fire, warranting a suppression policy, the CPS efforts to reintroduce fire would soon be affected.

The view from Canada is that if Yellowstone is required to change policies, not only other NPS parks are affected but Canadian parks as well. Any changes in NPS overall policies will cause a reexamination of the CPS policy. For that reason, Yellowstone is important to the Canadian Parks Service in regard to policies in general and to our fire policy in particular.

Canadians have chosen a path for using fire that differs from that of its U.S. counterpart. Where fire operates as a renewal agent in a Canadian park, the use of fire to achieve a predetermined vegetation is the guiding principle. Nevertheless, this principle is still far from being widely accepted throughout the CPS. More fundamental is that the debates have yet to be completed over the appropriateness of specific objectives for vegetation in a park.

In the struggle to meet the national park mandate an important point must be retained. To be cavalier with the resources we are managing for future generations is unacceptable. Whatever management regime is applied has immediate repercussions on a park's resources as well as on the options available for future managers. This should spur us to carefully document our resource management objectives and this methods used to achieve them.

Nevertheless, I do not believe that our goals are different. Both agencies recognize that fire belongs in national parks and both are striving to assure that our vegetation does not lose its pyric characteristics. We must now determine how best to do this. Each agency has different circumstances that must be taken into account, but our resolve to deliver on the objective of ecological integrity cannot waver. It is a matter of ethics; ethics that are concerned not only for humanity, one part of the functional organism of our globe, but for all such parts. Such ethics send out a strong signal that our society is not wholly subjugated to human economic values and the artificial.

REFERENCES

Alexander, M. E. 1985. The forest fire environment of Pukaskwa National Park: Analysis, evaluation, and assessment guidelines. Report prepared for Parks Canada, Ontario Region, Cornwall

Alexander, M. E., and D. E. Dubé. 1983. Fire management in wilderness areas,

parks, and other nature reserves. Pages 273–298 in R. W. Wein and D. A. Mac-
Lean, eds. Role of fire in northern circumpolar ecosystems. Scientific Committee on Problems of the Environment 18, John Wiley and Sons, New York.

Bailey, R. 1985. Managing large fires in the Northwest Territories. Pages 41–44 in
D. E. Dubé, comp. Proc. Intermountain Fire Council Fire Mgmt. Workshop
1983. Can. For. Serv., N. For. Res. Centre Info. Rep. NOR-X-271. Edmonton,
Alta.

Baker, W. L. 1989. Landscape ecology and nature reserve design in the boundary
waters canoe area, Minnesota. Ecology 70:23–35.

Blyth, C.. B., and R. J. Hudson. 1987. A plan for the management of vegetation
and ungulates, Elk Island National Park. Report prepared for Canadian Parks
Service.

Bonnicksen, T. M. 1988. Restoration ecology: Philosophy, goals, and ethics.
Envtl. Professional 10:25–35.

Bratton, S. P. 1985. National park management and values. Envtl. Ethics 7:117–
134.

Day, D., C. A. White, and N. Lopoukhine. 1990. Keeping the flame: fire manage-
ment in the Canadian Parks Service. Pages 35–47 in M. E. Alexander and G. F.
Bisgrove, tech. coords. Proc. Interior West Fire Council Annual Meeting,
Oct. 24–27, 1988, Kananaskis Village, Alta. Can. For. Serv., N. For. Res.
Centre Info. Rep. NOR-X-309. Edmonton, Alta.

Eidsvik, H. K. 1985. Biosphere reserves in concept and in practice. Pages 8–19 in
J. Peine, ed. Proceedings of the conference on the management of biosphere
reserves, 1984. National Parks Service, Uplands Field Research Laboratory,
Great Smoky Mountains National Park, Gatlinburg, Tenn.

Hamet-Ahti, L. 1983. Human impact on closed boreal forest (taiga). Pages 201–
211 in W. Holzner, M. J. A. Weyer, and I. Ikusima, eds. Man's impact on
vegetation. W. Junk, The Hague.

Heinselman, M. L. 1981. Fire intensity and frequency as factors in the distribution
and structure of northern ecosystems. Pages 7–57 in T. M. Bonnicksen, N. L.
Christensen, J. E. Lotan, and W. A. Reiners, eds. Fire regimes and ecosystem
properties. U.S. For. Serv. Gen. Tech. Rep. WO-26.

———. 1985. Fire regimes and management options in ecosystems with large
high-intensity fires. Pages 101–109 in J. E. Lotan, B. M. Kilgore, W. C.
Fischer, and R. W. Mutch, tech. coords. Proceedings: Symposium and workshop on wilderness fire. U.S. For. Serv. Gen. Tech. Rep. INT-182.

Kincaid, R. 1985. Managing large fires in Ontario. Pages 55–58 in D. E. Dubé,
comp. Proc. Intermountain Fire Council Fire Mgmt. Workshop 1983. Can. For.
Serv., N. For. Res. Centre Info. Rep. NOR-X-271. Edmonton, Alta.

Lopoukhine, N. 1985. Guiding philosophy in fire and vegetation management in
Canadian parks. Pages 16–20 in J. E. Lotan, B. M. Kilgore, W. C. Fischer, and
R. W. Mutch, tech. coords. Proceedings: Symposium and workshop on wilder-
ness fire. U.S. For. Serv. Gen. Tech. Rep. INT-182.

————. 1989. A vegetation plan for Pukaskwa National Park. Report prepared for Canadian Parks Service, Ontario Region, Cornwall.

Lopoukhine, N., and C. A. White. 1985. Fire management options in Canada's national parks. Pages 59–68 in D. E. Dubé, comp. Proc. Intermountain Fire Council Fire Mgmt. Workshop 1983. Can. For. Serv., N. For. Res. Centre Info. Rep. NOR-X-271. Edmonton, Alta.

Mosquin, T. 1986. A vegetation management plan for St. Lawrence Islands National Park. Mosquin Bio-Information Ltd. Report to Canadian Parks Service, Ontario Region, Cornwall.

Parks Canada. 1979. Parks Canada Policy, Can. Dep't Indian N. Affairs Publ. QS-7079-000-EE-A1. Ottawa.

Peters, R. L., II. 1988. The effect of global climatic change on natural communities. Pages 450–461 in E. O. Wilson, ed. Biodiversity. Nat. Acad. Press, Washington, D.C.

Resource/Environment Management Systems Research Ltd. 1988. Fire management in the Canadian Parks Service: Evaluation and recommendations. Report to the Canadian Parks Service.

Van Wagner, C. E. 1978. Age class distribution and the forest fire cycle. Can. J. For. Res. 8:220–227.

Van Wagner, C. E., and I. R. Methven. 1980. Fire in the management of Canada's national parks: Philosophy and strategy. National Parks Occ. Pap. no. 1. Parks Canada, Ottawa.

White, C. A. 1985. Wildland fires in Banff National Park. Environment Canada-Parks Occ. Pap. no. 3. Ottawa.

————. 1988. Keepers of the flame: Implementing fire management in the Canadian Parks Service. Report prepared for Canadian Parks Service.

CHAPTER 13   **Vegetation and Elk Response to Prescribed Burning in South-Central Montana**

Fred G. Van Dyke,

Jeffrey P. Dibenedetto, and

Steven C. Thomas

The benefits of fire may be difficult to assess when fires are extensive, unplanned, and uncontrolled, like the Yellowstone National Park fires of 1988, and when they are obscured by negative public reaction to loss of wildlife (Singer and Schullery 1989) and property. When limited, planned, and controlled as a management tool in the form of prescribed burning, the benefits may be more directly measurable and public reaction more favorable. Burning changes the amount, composition, and nutritional quality of vegetation. The most common short-term response to burning on western range lands is an increase in grass and forb production at the expense of shrubs. This response would be expected to be especially favorable to elk, which make greater use than other ungulates of

Our thanks to G. A. Weldon, for design and supervision of prescribed burning in 1988–1989, and to B. Anderson, for contributing pre- and postburn data from prescribed burning conducted under his supervision in 1984. C. H. Goodall assisted with collection of information in 1989 This study was administered by the Montana Department of Fish, Wildlife, and Parks. Major funding was provided by the U.S. Forest Service, the Montana chapter of Safari Club International, the Amoco Oil Corporation, and the Phillips Petroleum Company. R. Brownson assisted with interpretation of nutritional results. P. Jacquith, L. J. Lyon, C. Eustace, L. D. Hayden-Wing, and H. G. Shaw reviewed this chapter.

grasses and forbs and are better able to digest them (Boyd 1978; Hobbs et al. 1979; Hobbs et al. 1981; Hobbs, Baker, and McGill 1983; Baker and Hansen 1985).

Vegetation on burned areas has been shown in some cases to be greater in amount and higher in nutritional value than similar vegetation from unburned areas (Asherin 1976; Hobbs and Swift 1985). These findings are of particular significance on winter ranges, which are typically inadequate in both amount and quality of forage for animal maintenance (Torbit et al. 1985). Animals endure winter conditions partly by catabolism of stored energy reserves. Therefore winter range, which can minimize losses of energy reserves acquired on summer range, could contribute disproportionately to big game carrying capacity and associated survival and reproductive patterns (Van Horne 1983). Any technique, such as prescribed burning, that could improve the amount and quality of forage on winter range could enhance the condition, productivity, and survivorship of local big game populations.

Elk can make functional or numerical responses to changes that burning causes in plant populations. Elk use of burned areas has been observed to increase after reestablishment of herbaceous forage (Rowland et al. 1983). Rounds (1981) was able to demonstrate a positive preference of elk for burns, as well as higher elk densities on ranges with a greater grassland component. Rowland et al. (1983) documented that elk in New Mexico ate more grass on burned areas compared with unburned areas. Few field studies, however, have been able to quantify both the functional and the numerical responses of individual populations to burns within a specific time frame, or to relate such responses to changes in vegetation.

Our objectives were (1) to quantify changes in amount and nutritional quality of vegetation following burning; (2) to determine diets of elk that use the winter range in terms of the amounts and proportions of plant species found on burned versus unburned areas; and (3) to quantify elk use of burned areas. We sought to provide a quantitative measurement of these responses to better assess the possible impacts and uses of prescribed burning on vegetation and on ungulate populations.

STUDY AREA

Burns were conducted on U.S. Forest Service lands in the North Line Creek Basin (45°1'00"N to 45°1'30"N, 109°16'30"W to 109°16'00"W) and in Mill Draw (45°2'00"N to 45°2'30"N, 109°15'00"W to 109°14'00"W), Carbon County, Montana (figure 13.1). Major ridges and drainages in and

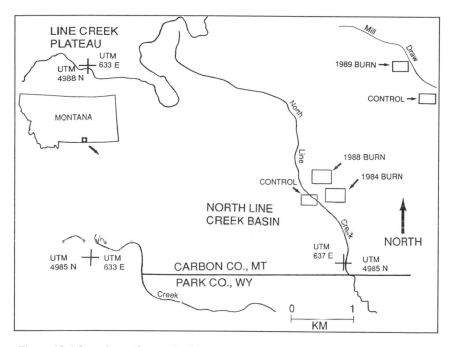

Figure 13.1 Locations of prescribed burns and unburned (control) plots on elk winter range in North Line Creek Basin and Mill Draw, 1984–1989.

around the basin run northwest to southeast, with slopes generally having southwestern and northeastern aspects. Average January temperature in Red Lodge, Montana, near the study area, is −6°C, and average annual precipitation is 56 cm. Precipitation is typically in the form of snow from November through May (Montana Department of Commerce 1986, unpubl. data).

Vegetation on winter range is typical for *Artemisia tridentata–Festuca idahoensis* habitat (Mueggler and Stewart 1980). Black sagebrush (*A. nova*) is common on colder, drier sites. A scattered overstory of limber pine (*Pinus flexilis*) is present near crests and upper ends of ridges. Idaho fescue (*Festuca idahoensis*) and bluebunch wheatgrass (*Agropyron spicatum*) are the most common grasses, with scattered associations of Sandberg bluegrass (*Poa sandbergii*), needle-and-thread grass (*Stipa comata*), and king fescue (*Hesperochloa kingii*). Common forbs include milk vetch (*Astragalus* spp.), prickly pear (*Opuntia* sp.), and phlox (*Phlox* spp.).

Winter game surveys from 1975–1988 and relocations of telemetered elk from March 1988 to October 1989 confirmed that both the North Line Creek Basin and Mill Draw received use as winter range by the Line Creek elk herd (approximately 140 animals), which summers on the Line Creek plateau in south-central Montana. The Bennett Creek elk herd (approximately 200 animals), which summers in Wyoming, also spends part of each winter in North Line Creek Basin. Heaviest use by both herds occurs from late December to mid-April. Land in the study area is administered by the Beartooth District of the Custer National Forest. No livestock grazing is permitted on Forest Service land in either area.

METHODS

Controlled burns of similar size and intensity were conducted in the North Line Creek Basin in October 1984 (40 ha) and March 1988 (30 ha) by Forest Service personnel. Burns were on the same side of the same ridge, had similar aspects (southwestern) and slopes, and similar vegetation and disturbance histories. In April 1989 a 50-ha area was burned in the upper end of Mill Draw.

Five 20.1 m × 20.1 m permanent plots were established in each burn, all with slopes ≥15%≤26%, except for one plot in Mill Draw, which had a slope of 31%. Sites with less slope were not available. Sites with greater slopes were not used because previous observations of elk in this and other local areas indicated that animals did the majority of feeding on slopes ≤ 30%. A control plot with characteristics similar to plots in the North Line Creek Basin burns was established on an unburned ridge in the basin. Five control plots were established in Mill Draw that had slopes, aspects, preburn vegetation, and disturbance histories similar to permanent plots in burned areas.

One macroplot in each burn was used to measure vegetation response. Following Forest Service ECODATA procedures (U.S. Forest Service 1988), each macroplot consisted of six 20.1 m × 66 cm belts established at random intervals along the plot base line. Plant-species composition and percent cover were then determined in five 25.4 cm × 50.8 cm microplots placed randomly along each belt (thirty microplots per plot). Shrub cover was measured using line-intercept canopy-cover method. Grasses, forbs, and shrubs were clipped separately in each microplot and weighed after drying. Protein, fat, crude fiber, phosphorous, and calcium content of plants in each category were determined by chemical analysis at the Analytical Laboratory of the Agricultural Experiment Station of Montana State University, Bozeman. Samples from both study areas were used in calculations of plant nutrient levels and of proportional production (percentage) of grasses, forbs, and shrubs. Mill Draw data were not sufficient to be included in calculation of total production estimates.

Elk-pellet groups were counted along previously established belts in each plot in the North Line Creek Basin. After counting, pellets were removed from the belt and spray painted to eliminate the possibility of double counting in subsequent surveys. Differences in pellet-group densities were compared between plots of different treatments using t tests (Lapin 1975:426). Differences in plant production and nutritional values were compared using multifactor and one-way analysis of variance (ANOVA) (Lapin 1975:479–493, 462–470). In all cases $p < .05$ was considered significant.

Food habits and dietary protein levels of Line Creek elk were determined by fecal analysis. Ten independent samples of fresh pellets from individuals in this herd were collected on seven different dates between November 15, 1988, and April 18, 1989. Two pellets were selected from each sample for food-habits analysis and two from each sample for determination of fecal nitrogen. Plant parts were identified by histological examination. Plant identification and chemical determination of dietary percentages of nitrogen and protein (fecal nitrogen, $X = 6.25$) were conducted at the Wildlife Habitat Laboratory, Washington State University, Pullman.

We recognize that relating elk food habits to the burn is limited by two factors: individual samples may have come from individuals that did not forage in the burns; and individuals that did use the burns also used other foraging areas. Our objectives in examining the food habits and dietary protein levels of these elk were (1) to determine the relation of seasonal food habits to plants available in the burned and control areas, and (2) to compare plant protein levels from the burned sites with actual dietary protein levels in the elk.

RESULTS

Plant Response

Total plant production since the 1984 North Line Creek Basin burn has followed a pattern of steady increase, after an initial decline in the first year after burning (figure 13.2). Production levels in 1989 were slightly more than twice those of preburn production levels in 1984. In 1988, the 1984 North Line Creek Basin burn had higher production of graminoids and forbs, and lower production of shrubs, than the control (table 13.1, $p < 0.5$, t tests). Compared to the drought year of 1988, above-average rainfall in 1989 contributed to substantial increases in plant production on both burned and unburned areas. Plant production in 1989 was still highest in the 1984 burn, but differences between it and control production were less, and production in the 1988 burn and the control plot was nearly identical (figure 13.2).

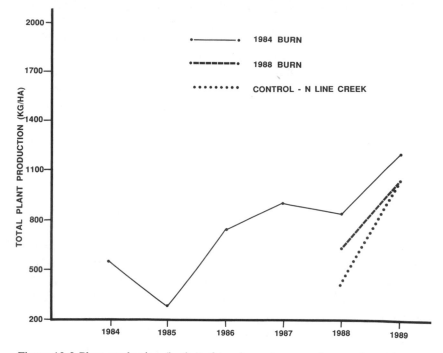

Figure 13.2 Plant production (kg/ha) of two burned areas and one unburned area on bunchgrass-sagebrush sites on elk winter range in North Line Creek Basin, 1984–1989. Initial values on burned sites reflect preburn production.

Table 13.1 Average annual production of graminoids, forbs, and shrubs on a 1984 burned plot and an unburned (control) plot on elk winter range, 1988

Plot	Plant Category	Average Production (kg/ha)	SE	95% CI
1984 burn	Graminoids	594.3[a]	30.4	562.3 to 626.2
	Forbs	178.5[a]	30.4	146.6 to 210.5
	Shrubs	77.5[a]	45.7	29.6 to 125.5
	Total production	850.3		
Control	Graminoids	155.0		
	Forbs	49.3		
	Shrubs	218.4		
	Total production	422.8		

[a]Different from control, 95% confidence interval.

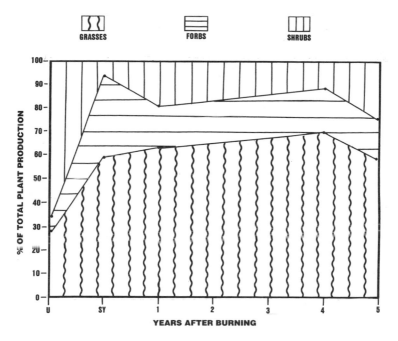

Figure 13.3 Proportional production of grasses, forbs, and shrubs following burning of bunchgrass-sagebrush sites on elk winter range in North Line Creek Basin and Mill Draw, 1984–1989. U = unburned sites, SY = same year production (late-summer estimate) following early spring burn.

Though total production varied by site and appeared strongly influenced by annual variations in temperature and moisture, proportional contribution to total production by different plant categories followed predictable patterns after burning (figure 13.3). In the same year after burning, grasses and forbs experienced increases in production with correspondent declines in shrubs. In the first year after burning, grasses and shrubs made slight increases in contribution to total production at the expense of forbs. Grasses continued to increase their proportional contribution to nearly 70 percent of total production through the fourth year after burning, but began declining in the fifth year as shrubs again began to increase. The proportional contribution of forbs to total plant production remained relatively constant from the second through the fifth year after burning.

Overall plant nutrient levels were also related to time since burning. Protein levels were most strongly affected, showing significant increases over preburn levels up to two years after burning, but declining to preburn levels in five years or less (figure 13.4, multifactor ANOVA, $p < .05$).

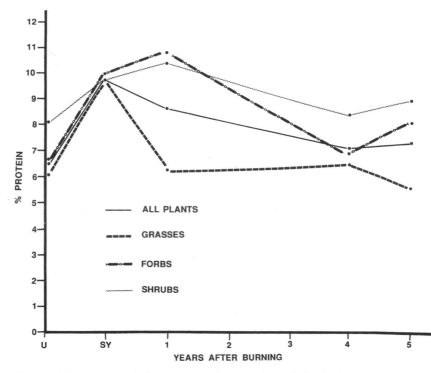

Figure 13.4 Protein levels in grasses, forbs, and shrubs following burning of bunch-grass-sagebrush sites on elk winter range in North Line Creek Basin and Mill Draw, 1984–1989. U = unburned sites, SY = same year protein levels (late-summer estimate) following early spring burn.

Grasses declined in protein levels most rapidly, dropping to preburn levels less than two years after burning (multifactor ANOVA, $p < .05$). Forbs and shrubs reached peak protein levels one year after burning. Both declined from peak levels in the second through fifth years after burning, with the decline being more pronounced in forbs. In plants generally, calcium (Ca), phosphorous (P), total digestible nutrient (TDN), and Ca/P ratio levels did not change following burning, although some significant changes did occur within plant types (table 13.2). Grasses showed increases in Ca and P in the same year after burning, and a significant decline in both from the first to the fourth year after the burn. Forbs showed increases in TDN following burning. After burning, forbs and grasses had consistently higher TDN than shrubs. Grasses were consistently lower than forbs in Ca after burning, and lower than shrubs as well by the fourth year after burning. Both grasses and shrubs had lower Ca/P ratios than forbs by the fourth year after burning.

Table 13.2 Mean percentages of calcium (Ca), phosphorus (P), and total digestible nutrients (TDN) and mean Ca/P ratios of plants on unburned sites, sites sampled < 1 year after burning, and sites sampled 4 years after burning, elk winter range, 1984–1989

Treatment	Plant Category	No.	Ca X̄	Ca SE	P X̄	P SE	TDN X̄	TDN SE	Ca/P X̄	Ca/P SE
Unburned	All plants	2	1.27	0.94	0.06	0.0	37.6	18.5	24.4	19.7
	Grasses	1	0.33	—	0.07	—	56.0	—	4.7	—
	Forbs	1	2.20	—	0.05	—	19.1	—	44.0	—
	Shrubs	—	—	—	—	—	—	—	—	—
< 1 year after burning	All plants	5	1.18	0.31	0.12	0.01	49.7	3.2	10.8	3.6
	Grasses	2	0.63[ab]	0.04	0.10[a]	0.01	55.2[c]	0.4	6.4	0.3
	Forbs	2	1.90	0.30	0.12	0.04	49.9[a]	2.7	17.9	6.5
	Shrubs	1	0.84	—	0.16	—	38.3	—	5.3	—
4 years after burning	All plants	8	0.88	0.23	0.07	0.01	49.9	3.1	14.6	5.1
	Grasses	4	0.43[bcd]	0.02	0.07[d]	0.01	53.1[c]	3.6	6.6[b]	0.5
	Forbs	2	1.90[c]	0.10	0.05	0.00	55.4[ac]	0.6	38.0[d]	2.0
	Shrubs	2	0.76	0.09	0.12	0.05	38.1	2.4	7.1[b]	2.2

[a] Different from unburned sites, same plant category. $p < .05$, multifactor ANOVA, confidence interval tests.

[b] Different from forbs, same treatment. $p < .05$, t tests.

[c] Different from shrubs, same treatment. $p < .05$, t tests.

[d] Different from sites sampled < 1 year after burning, same plant category. $p < .05$, multifactor ANOVA, confidence interval tests.

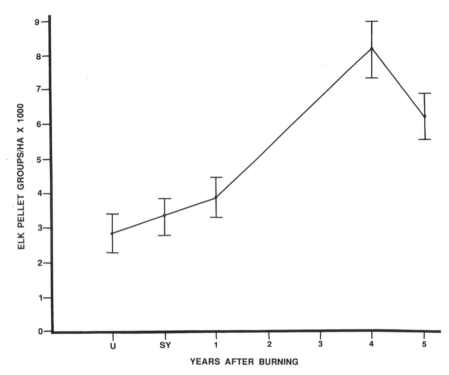

Figure 13.5 Elk-pellet densities/ha following burning of bunchgrass-sagebrush sites on elk winter range in North Line Creek Basin, 1984–1989. U = unburned sites, SY = same year estimates of elk-pellet densities following burning. Bars indicate 90% confidence interval.

Animal Response

Elk-pellet densities on burned areas did not show significant increases from those on unburned sites until the fourth year after burning (figure 13.5, $p <$ .05, t tests), although densities increased steadily after burning and approached significance in the second postburn year ($p < .10$, t test). By the fifth year, elk use on burns had begun to decline ($p < .05$, t test). Peak elk use in the fourth year after burning was equivalent to 629.2 elk-use days compared with a two-year average of 217.1 elk-use days on control areas in 1988 and 1989 (pellet group density/13, Hayden-Wing 1979).

Elk diets (figure 13.6) showed patterns typical of seasonal dietary shifts in Rocky Mountain elk (Kufeld 1973). Grasses increased from fall through winter to more than 70 percent of total diet at the expense of forbs. Shrub consumption increased from January through April at the expense of grasses. The most commonly consumed grasses were those that tended to

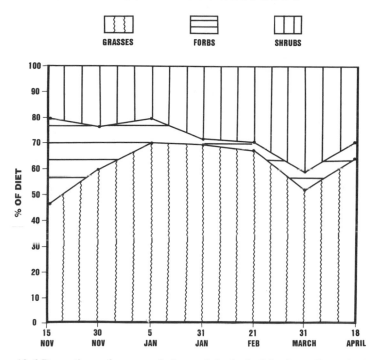

Figure 13.6 Proportions of grasses, forbs, and shrubs in fall-winter diets of elk using North Line Creek Basin, 1988–1989.

be most common on burned sites, *Poa* spp., *A. spicatum,* and *F. idahoensis* (figure 13.7). *Koeleria pyramidata* (prairie Junegrass), which was uncommon on both burned and unburned plots, began to increase in importance in diet by early winter. The most commonly consumed shrubs were those that increased after burning (*A. frigida*), those that were exploited at lower elevations in late March during early spring green-up (*Chrysothamnus visidiflorus*), and those that were not associated with either burned or control plots (*Sheperdia canadensis, Berberis repens, Vaccinium scoparius,* and *Salix* spp.) but were found in forested areas of the herd's fall and winter range or on wetter sites. *A. tridentata,* the dominant plant on unburned areas, was usually absent from elk diet, but contributed up to 6 percent of the total elk diet from late January to late February.

Dietary protein in Line Creek elk (figure 13.8) followed a typical winter pattern of decline, but remained well above the 3.6 percent level documented as the probable maintenance requirement for elk (Mould and Robbins 1981). Overall decline in dietary protein levels continued through late winter, but began increasing after February 21, 1989.

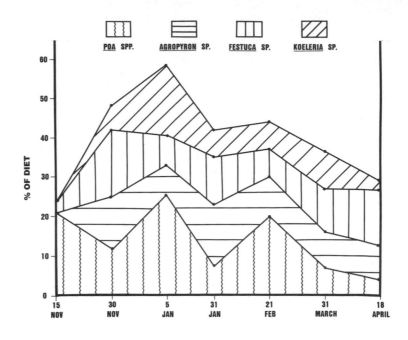

Figure 13.7 Proportions of four most commonly consumed grasses in fall-winter diets of elk using North Line Creek Basin, 1988–1989.

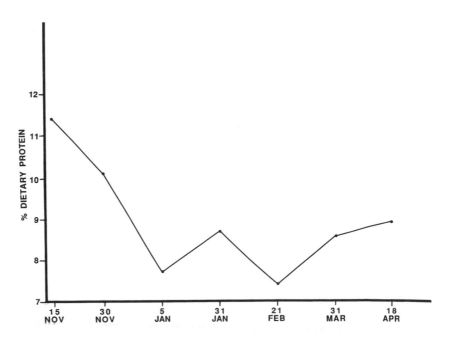

Figure 13.8 Percentage of fall-winter dietary protein in elk using North Line Creek Basin, 1988–1989.

CAUSES OF ANIMAL RESPONSE

The increase in elk use on burned plots is probably a response to increased production and increased nutritional quality of graminoids. Following methodology adapted from Stockwell, Bateman, and Berger (1991), we have documented also that elk have higher winter foraging efficiencies (percentage of time eating per five-minute feeding bout) and lower stepping rates (steps per minute) on bunchgrass-forb sites than on bunchgrass-sagebrush sites. Burning changes the latter into the former and may offer elk the opportunity to increase food intake while concurrently reducing energy expenditure.

Although forbs showed greater ability than grasses to retain improved protein levels after burning, there was no corresponding increase in forb consumption in winter diets of elk using burned areas. The most likely reasons for the continued dominance of grasses in elk winter diets, in spite of declining protein levels, were (1) the higher total production of grasses on burned plots, making it a more efficient food resource; (2) the respective growth forms of forbs and grasses, making grass easier to find during winter on snow-covered sites; and (3) the higher Ca/P ratios in forbs, making them less digestible than the lower-protein grasses (Wise, Ordoveza, and Barrick 1963).

MANAGEMENT IMPLICATIONS

As Torbit et al. (1985:84) noted, "it is probable that winter ranges will always be incapable of meeting nutritional requirements." Forage quality and digestibility typically decline throughout winter, and declines tend to be greatest in grasses most frequently consumed by elk (Hobbs et al. 1979). We did not evaluate forage quality throughout the winter in this study, but dietary protein decline in elk was evident. Prescribed burning can increase both amount and quality of forage, and its application on big game winter ranges could be of positive benefit to elk. Hobbs and Spowart (1984) documented elevated protein concentrations in the winter diets of bighorn (*Ovis canadensis*) and mule deer (*Odocoileus hemionus*) feeding in grassland and mountain shrub communities subjected to burning. Elk in this population, which had access to the burned areas, had significantly higher dietary protein levels than those examined by Hobbs et al. (1979) for the same period of year, and protein levels in grasses on sites one year or less after burning were as high as or higher than protein levels on the same herd's summer range (Van Dyke 1990). No winter mortality was observed or suspected, even though February and March weather was unseasonably cold and snowy. The high-quality forage available to this population in the burned areas may have contributed to high protein levels and survivorship. At no time did dietary protein levels in the Line Creek herd fall below 3.6 percent, which has been shown to be near or at the critical maintenance level for elk (Mould and Robbins 1981).

Short-term results suggest that prescribed burning can be an effective tool for increasing the quantity and quality of elk winter feed for at least five years after burning, and can contribute to holding large concentrations of elk on traditional winter range. Because elk cope with changing forage conditions by exploiting different forage classes at different times (Hobbs et al. 1981), prescribed burns are likely to be most effective if they are relatively small ($\geq 30 \leq 200$ ha) and widely spaced throughout a mosaic of habitat types.

The ideal schedule for burning selected areas will depend on management objectives. If the objective is to maximize plant (especially grass) nutritional quality, burns should be conducted every year. Our results indicate, however, that total plant production, grass production, and elk use continue to increase on burned areas up to five years after burning. This suggests that (1) elk use of burns may be a response learned over several years, (2) elk may be as attracted to quantity of vegetation as to quality, and (3) peak elk use may not coincide with peak plant nutrition. Hobbs and Spowart (1984:554) noted that elevations in dietary protein levels in bighorn and mule deer on burned areas occurred mainly from changes in diet selection rather than improvements in forage quality. This may also be the case with elk, and may help to explain why elk continued higher use in burns even after overall forage quality had declined to preburn levels. Therefore, if the manager's objective is simply to maintain some positive benefit for elk at minimal cost, burning intervals up to six years may be acceptable. Moreover, although elk use had begun declining by the fifth year after burning, both elk use and grass production were significantly higher than on unburned plots.

PRESCRIBED BURNING AND THE YELLOWSTONE ELK HERD

Singer et al. (1989) noted that although fire-induced successional changes in lodgepole forests on higher plateaus may create additional elk summer range for up to thirty years, improved nutritional levels in burned grass lands in YNP will probably last only three years or less. Most of the 1988 YNP fires were in forested areas, and only 9 percent of grass lands normally used by elk on the northern winter range were burned (Boyce and Merrill 1989).

Enhanced summer forage quality following the 1988 fires led Boyce and Merrill (1989) to project, from stochastic population modeling, growth in the Yellowstone elk herd peaking in the mid-1990s. Such projected growth leads us to recommend that the Park Service consider a program of carefully monitored controlled burning in dry grass-land areas used by elk. Such an approach would appear to be the only practical way to improve range quality for a growing elk population that cannot be regulated by hunting within the park and that probably will not receive supplementary artificial feeding (Singer and Schullery 1989). The short-term nutritional response of vegetation to grass-land fires noted in this study and others (Hobbs and Spowart 1984; Wood 1988) does not argue against controlled burning, but only for repeated burning on key sites at one to six year intervals. Because ungulates are able to significantly elevate dietary protein levels on burns by selective feeding, even when actual plant protein levels are not improved, we agree with Hobbs and Spowart (1984:558) that attempts to determine ungulate benefits from fire by considering forage condition alone may severely underestimate those benefits. A combination of burned and unburned areas, which could be maintained by prescribed burning, could provide two distinct flushes of new growth in spring, prolonging the period when young forage would be available to ungulates and effectively shortening the nutritional deprivation of winter (Hobbs and Spowart 1984:558).

REFERENCES

Asherin, D. A. 1976. Changes in elk use and available browse production on Idaho winter ranges following prescribed burning. Pages 122–134 in S. R. Hieb, ed. Proceedings of elk-logging-roads symposium. Univ. of Idaho, Moscow.

Baker, D. L., and D. R. Hansen. 1985. Comparative digestion of grass in mule deer and elk. J. Wildl. Mgmt. 49:77–79.

Boyce, M. S., and E. H. Merrill. 1989. Effects of the 1988 fires on ungulates in Yellowstone National Park. Paper presented at Tall Timbers Fire Ecology Conf., Tallahassee, Fla., May 18, 1989.

Boyd, R. J. 1978. American elk. Pages 11–29 in J. L. Schmidt and D. L. Gilbert, eds. Big game of North America: Ecology and management. Stackpole Books, Harrisburg, Pa.

Hayden-Wing, L. D. 1979. Distribution of deer, elk, and moose on a winter range in southeastern Idaho. Pages 122–131 in M. S. Boyce and L. D. Hayden-Wing, eds. North American elk: Ecology, behavior, and management. Univ. of Wyoming Press, Laramie.

Hobbs, N. T., D. L. Baker, J. E. Ellis, and D. M. Swift 1979. Composition and quality of elk diets during winter and summer: A preliminary analysis. Pages 47–53 in M. S. Boyce and L. D. Hayden-Wing, eds. North American elk: Ecology, behavior, and management. Univ. of Wyoming Press, Laramie.

———. 1981. Composition and quality of elk winter diets in Colorado. J. Wildl. Mgmt. 45:156–171.

Hobbs, N. T., D. L. Baker, and R. B. McGill. 1983. Comparative nutritional ecology of montane ungulates during winter. J. Wild. Mgmt. 47:1–16.

Hobbs, N. T., and R. A. Spowart. 1984. Effects of prescribed fire on nutrition of mountain sheep and mule deer during winter and spring. J. Wildl. Mgmt. 48: 551–560.

Hobbs, N. T., and D. M. Swift. 1985. Estimates of habitat carrying capacity incorporating explicit nutritional constraints. J. Wildl. Mgmt. 49:814–822.

Kufeld, R. C. 1973. Foods eaten by Rocky Mountain elk. J. Range Mgmt. 26:106–113.

Lapin, L. L. 1975. Statistics: Meaning and method. Harcourt Brace Jovanovich, New York.

Mould, E. D., and C. T. Robbins. 1981. Nitrogen metabolism in elk. J. Wildl. Mgmt. 45:323–334.

Mueggler, W. F., and W. L. Stewart. 1980. Grassland and shrubland habitat types of western Montana. U.S. For. Serv. Gen. Tech. Rep. INT-66. Ogden, Utah.

Rounds, R. C. 1981. First approximation of habitat selectivity of ungulates on extensive winter ranges. J. Wildl. Mgmt. 45:187–196.

Rowland, M. M., A. W. Alldredge, J. E. Ellis, B. J. Weber, and G. C. White. 1983. Comparative winter diets of elk in New Mexico. J. Wildl. Mgmt. 47:924–932.

Singer, F. J., W. Schreier, J. Oppenheim, and E. O. Garten. 1989. Drought, fires, and large mammals. BioScience 39:716–722.

Singer, F. J., and P. Schullery. 1989. Yellowstone wildlife: Populations in process. W. Wildlands 15:18–22.

Stockwell, C. A., G. C. Bateman, and J. Berger. 1991. Helicopter effects on bighorn sheep foraging behavior at Grand Canyon National Park. Biol. Conserv. In press.

Torbit, S. C., L. H. Carpenter, D. M. Swift, and A. W. Alldredge. 1985. Differential loss of fat and protein by mule deer during winter. J. Wildl. Mgmt. 49:80–85.

U.S. Forest Service. 1988. Ecosystem classification handbook. FSH 2090.11, Interim Directive no. 1. U.S. Dep't Agric. 490-921/40119. GPO, Washington, D.C.

Van Dyke, F. G. 1990. Vegetation characteristics of elk summer range in south central Montana. Progress report, Mar. 9, 1990, Montana Dep't of Fish, Wildlife, and Parks, Billings.

Van Horne, B. 1983. Density as a misleading indicator of habitat quality. J. Wildl. Mgmt. 47:893–901.

Wise, M. B., A. L. Ordoveza, and E. R. Barrick. 1963. Influence of variations in dietary calcium: Phosphorous ratio on performance and blood constituents of calves. J. Nutr. 79:79–84.

Wood, G. W. 1988. Effects of prescribed fire on deer forage and nutrients. Wildl. Soc. Bull. 16:180–186.

PART III   **CONSERVATION BIOLOGY
                AND WILDLIFE ECOLOGY**

National parks and similar ecological reserves are special areas set aside for conservation. As such they require a different land-use philosophy from those areas used for sport hunting or other forms of exploitation.

A. R. E. Sinclair, Foreword to D. B. Houston, The Northern Yellowstone Elk: Ecology and Management. *New York: Macmillan, 1982. Reproduced by permission.*

I have heard of parks described as overpopulated when the animals and plants were demonstrably at equilibrium. It is a novel idea that a population can be at the same time both overpopulated and stable. It is not necessarily a useful idea.

Graeme Caughley, "What Is This Thing Called Carrying Capacity?" in North American Elk: Ecology, Behavior and Management, *ed. M. S. Boyce and L. D. Hayden-Wing. Laramie: University of Wyoming Press, 1979. Reproduced by permission.*

Overleaf: *A common roadside scene, Yellowstone National Park, circa 1930. Photo courtesy of Charles L. Baker Collection, American Heritage Center, University of Wyoming, Laramie, Wyoming.*

CHAPTER 14   **Natural Regulation or**
the Control of Nature?
Mark S. Boyce

Strive on—the control of nature is won not given.
—Engineering Building, University of Wyoming

Since Yellowstone National Park was established,
wildlife has been a management priority throughout the Yellowstone area.
It also has been a source of disunity and controversy. During the park's first
eleven years, hunting was allowed and even encouraged (Haines 1977;
McNaughton 1989). For thirty-three years (1934–1967), the official policy
was that removals of elk (*Cervus elaphus*) from the northern range were
necessary to keep the population within the carrying capacity of the vegetation. Bison (*Bison bison*) numbers also were regulated on the northern
range. National Park Service officials believed that the control of nature
was necessary. Beginning in the late 1960s, however, the Park Service
adopted trial guidelines for "hands-off" or natural regulation of wildlife in
Yellowstone National Park, which means that populations are permitted to
fluctuate without human intervention within the park (Cole 1969, 1971;
Houston 1982; Despain et al. 1986).

Beyond the boundaries of Yellowstone National Park, wildlife is managed quite differently. It is often viewed as a commodity, since it supports a
multi-million-dollar hunting and outfitting industry (Taylor, Bradley, and
Martin 1982). Principal game species are elk, mule deer (*Odocoileus
hemionus*), moose (*Alces alces*), and bighorn (*Ovis canadensis*). This

Thanks to Doug Houston, Dan Huff, Bob Keiter, Dennis Knight, Mary Meagher,
Jim Peek, Paul Schullery, Frank Singer, John Varley, and Fred Wagner for critical
reviews of this chapter.

commodity-oriented perspective toward wildlife is epitomized in north-western Wyoming, where the migratory Jackson elk herd is provided supplemental food during winter at the National Elk Refuge and three state-owned feed lots, and population is controlled through regulated hunting (Boyce 1989). Feeding is justified there because human developments have displaced the Jackson elk herd from portions of its traditional winter range, to a greater extent than elsewhere in the Greater Yellowstone Ecosystem.

Though disparate, these two approaches to managing wildlife in the GYE can be compatible. Management priorities for wildlife should be determined by setting goals in a particular area, and by sensitively appraising an individual agency's history of resource management. Where humans have created imbalance (for example, by usurping winter range and winter provisioning for elk in Wyoming), continued intervention may be necessary.

My purpose in this chapter is to evaluate alternative priorities for wildlife management in the GYE. A review of relevant ecological principles is necessary to clarify some of the confusing literature that addresses wildlife ecology in Yellowstone. I discuss how these ecological principles interface with management, emphasizing the controversy regarding overgrazing on Yellowstone's northern range. Other management priorities are then evaluated, including the recent emphasis on the need to protect biotic diversity.

By reconciling ecological principles and management approaches, I conclude that ecological-process management is the most logical direction for the GYE. Whenever possible, the GYE should be managed as an ecological base-line preserve, as articulated by A. R. E. Sinclair (1983). This means allowing ecological processes to govern the ecosystem, with minimal human intervention. I am confident that such a rationale will eventually diminish our urge to control nature within the Greater Yellowstone Ecosystem.

ECOLOGICAL PRINCIPLES

A long-standing controversy surrounds the role that humans should play in the management of wildlife in the GYE, particularly elk, bison, and grizzly bears (*Ursus arctos*). Some of the disagreement among ecologists and wildlife biologists stems from semantic differences, but more important is the lack of agreement about the basic ecological mechanisms functioning in large mammal populations.

One of the fundamental ideas underlying discussions in this book is the notion of the Greater Yellowstone Area as an ecosystem (see Patten chapter 2 in this volume). There are no universally accepted criteria for establishing boundaries to an ecosystem. An ecosystem can be defined as "any part of the universe chosen as an area of interest, with the line around that area being the ecosystem boundary" (Johnson and Agee 1988). Ecosystem boundaries are usually identified in the context of ecological processes or the spatial distribution of a species, although there will always be some movement of organisms, nutrients, and energy across these boundaries (McNaughton 1989). For example, we may identify the GYE in the context of (1) the distribution of selected species, such as the grizzly bear (Craighead, Sumner, and Scaggs 1982), (2) the ranges occupied by all of the elk herds that summer in Yellowstone National Park (Clark and Zaunbrecher 1987), or (3) its vegetation characteristics (Reese 1984). For my purposes, any of these criteria for establishing ecosystem boundaries will do nicely.

Dynamic Systems

Considerable confusion has developed because of semantic and conceptual issues related to natural regulation, stability, and dynamic equilibrium. Chase (1990) assumed that ecosystems tend toward an equilibrium. Indeed, such thinking pervaded early ideas on the structuring of natural communities (Clements 1936). It has long been established, however, that ecological systems in the Rocky Mountains are comparatively dynamic. They do not remain constant for long, because of trophic-level interactions, such as those between plants and herbivores (Caughley and Lawton 1981); periodic natural events, such as fire (Romme 1982; Romme and Despain 1989); and random fluctuations imposed by vagaries of the environment, such as severe winters (Houston 1982). Fluctuations in animal populations or vegetation thus can be driven by biological interactions, which may be considered "deterministic" influences, as well as by random environmental fluctuations or chance events, known as "stochastic" perturbations.

That ecosystems are inherently dynamic has important ramifications for resource management. To manage in terms of a "vignette of primitive America," as suggested by the Leopold et al. (1963) report, may not be feasible, or even desirable. Actually, Leopold et al. were fully aware of the dynamic nature of natural systems and would concur that capturing the state of the ecosystem as it was when first visited by Europeans may require unreasonable levels of manipulation. Instead, we might wish to sustain or restore the ecological processes that have shaped dynamic landscape mosaics across the GYE (Botkin and Sobel 1975). This is perhaps best illustrated by the ecological role of fire; to retain a particular site as it was in 1850 may be impossible, because occasional fires keep the landscape in perpetual flux (Knight chapter 8 in this volume).

Natural regulation. Ultimately, population growth is the outcome of births and deaths. Without environmental constraints, populations typically have the potential for exponential increase until ecological limitations become effective. As population size increases, declines in birthrates or survivorship are normally observed. Factors that change with population size are referred to as "density dependent." Density dependence contributes to a population's equilibrium density, or ecological carrying capacity (Caughley 1979).

This simple idea is commonly known as *natural regulation,* a term that is burdened with semantic and conceptual complications. The word *natural* evokes considerable controversy, most of which is more philosophical than ecological. It has been argued, for example, that native Americans may have had a significant role in population regulation prior to the arrival of Europeans in the nineteenth century (Wagner 1969; Chase 1986). Whether it is appropriate to consider hunting by native Americans as natural and thereby part of natural regulation is a subjective issue that I will not attempt to resolve.

The word *regulation* is similarly burdened with semantic baggage. One might argue that the term implies density dependence. Hundreds of scholarly papers debate the role of density-dependent versus density-independent processes in population regulation (McLaren 1971). Happily, this controversy is largely behind us, partly resolved by Horn's (1968) elegant model, which shows how population size is a consequence of both density-dependent and density-independent mechanisms. Nevertheless, there is still no consensus definition for *regulation.*

Caughley (1976) further complicated the issue of natural regulation by noting that a single-species approach was an oversimplification of reality for most animal populations. At the very least, one must consider population dynamics for ungulates to be the consequence of plant-herbivore interactions. Seemingly a trivial point, this observation has important ramifications, because models of trophic-level interactions yield complex dynamics. Suddenly, it is no longer true that we necessarily expect populations to converge on some equilibrium (Caughley and Lawton 1981). Particularly in seasonal environments, such as those of the GYE, the simplest conceivable models can yield extremely complex dynamics (Schaffer 1988).

These recent advances in theory reinforce the conclusion that any reasonable model for an ungulate population in the GYE must be nonlinear. Furthermore, given the large effect that severe winters can have (Houston 1982; Picton 1984; Merrill and Boyce chapter 17 in this volume), it is apparent that the simplest models for ungulate populations in Yellowstone must be not only nonlinear, but also stochastic. Ungulate populations, therefore, have the potential for complex fluctuations, and it is impossible to precisely predict future populations (Schaffer 1988).

Stability. Stability is another concept that has stimulated extensive academic debate in ecology, and for which there are several explicit definitions (Botkin and Sobel 1975). Perhaps most fundamental is the mathematical concept of "local stability," which defines a system as stable if it returns to an equilibrium after a small perturbation. If the system is able to return to equilibrium after arbitrarily large perturbations, it is said to be "globally stable."

Another common usage of stability involves constancy, or low variance. In other words, if a population is relatively stable it exhibits only small fluctuations in abundance. Other notions of stability include persistence, resilience, and boundedness. Because there are so many concepts of stability, it seems essential that usage be defined.

Elk populations in Yellowstone are sensitive to variations in winter severity, thereby yielding substantial population fluctuations; by a constancy definition, this would suggest instability. Yet the analysis of Merrill and Boyce (chapter 17 in this volume) suggests that elk numbers on the northern range of Yellowstone National Park are globally stable, that is, large deviations from equilibrium result in population trajectories returning to equilibrium. Although the population undergoes substantial fluctuations, it is nevertheless resilient.

Dynamic equilibriums. An equilibrium is a stable point. If a population is reduced below equilibrium density, we anticipate increased birthrates or survivorship until equilibrium is again reached. Likewise, if the population size is greater than its equilibrium density, because of reduced habitat, for example, birthrates and survivorship will drop until the population again converges on equilibrium.

Doug Houston (1982) invoked the concept of a "dynamic equilibrium" to describe elk populations on the northern range of Yellowstone National Park. He concluded that elk populations are not driven toward the same equilibrium density each year, but rather that the equilibrium point changes over time, depending on climate or influences of the environment. If elk suffer a severe winter, we thus expect the equilibrium point to be considerably lower than after a mild winter. Evaluating an explicit model of this conceptualization, Merrill and Boyce (chapter 17 in this volume) found that the equilibrium population size in the winter of 1987–1988 was 19,000, after five mostly mild winters, whereas it would have been 15,000 had the winters been average.

Likewise, the dynamics between elk and vegetation may yield a changing equilibrium population size for elk depending on the history of the elk population and the availability of vegetation at any point in time. In other words, a plant-herbivore interaction is a dynamic one, where the carrying capacity for elk does not necessarily remain constant. And it will also certainly change subsequent to wolf (*Canis lupus*) recovery (Boyce 1990). The concept of dynamic equilibrium does not distinguish between deterministic and stochastic influences on carrying capacity, but rather, it simply recognizes that carrying capacity changes over time.

These concepts of natural regulation, stability, carrying capacity, and dynamic equilibrium burden many of the discussions of wildlife ecology in the Greater Yellowstone Ecosystem. Instead of struggling with such definitions, which are not universally accepted, we can clarify our understanding of ecological processes by developing a model of the system in question. In fact, one might argue that the system cannot be clearly understood until we develop an explicit model. And as our understanding of the ecosystem improves, so, too, our models will need to be constantly refined.

Trying to Understand Nature

The conclusion of the National Parks and Conservation Association, that the National Park Service cannot manage what it does not understand (Gordon et al. 1989), provides insight into the shortcomings of current management. Mathematical models are tools that allow us to understand ecological principles, and ultimately they may help us to formulate workable ecosystem management (Walters 1986). But we are still far from any detailed understanding of ecosystem dynamics in the GYE. For example, we do not yet understand the fundamental details of plant-herbivore relations governing the population dynamics of elk on the northern range of Yellowstone National Park. A considerable research program on the ecology of the northern range is developing, partly in response to Congress's 1985 mandate to determine if overgrazing is occurring. Once a model has been developed, it can help to frame our understanding of the system as well as guide future research and, with due caution, management.

Ecosystems, being multifarious amalgamations of biological and physical elements, are possibly the most complex structures in the universe. To begin to understand an ecosystem requires a model refined by extensive research over long time periods. Any mathematical model of an ecological system is a heuristic tool, and is necessarily a simplification. But simplification does not invalidate ecological models. Indeed, simplification is needed to make the system comprehensible. One hopes to incorporate the major limiting factors or driving forces in the system so that the model mimics reality.

Chase (1986) derides mathematical developments in ecology, clearly unaware of the important conceptual advances that have been made in ecology during the past three decades. In fact, many of the confused discussions about ecological concepts presented in Chases's (1986) book could have been clarified had he used rigorous mathematical definitions. Instead, simple issues became semantic lacunae, and principles in ecology were subverted.

Although some ecologists and resource managers view mathematical and computer models as pariahs, these models can be extremely important management tools. Rigorous ecological models are essential for understanding how the GYE functions so that we can anticipate the consequences of management actions. Increasing the scientific rigor of our understanding of the GYE will enhance our ability to manage it.

MANAGEMENT AND ECOLOGY

Ecosystem management implies quite different things to different people. Some consider it jargon used by the National Park Service to justify expansion of its jurisdiction (Johnson and Agee 1988; Budd chapter 6 in this volume). Others infer that almost any natural resource management policy constitutes ecosystem management. There appears to be some consensus, however, that "ecosystem management is concerned not merely with protecting individual elements of the system but with maintaining the relationships or linkages among them" (Clark and Harvey 1988).

Etymologically, the notion of ecosystem management is at least as vague as the notion of an ecosystem (see Patten chapter 2 in this volume). Because an ecosystem can be defined within whatever geographic boundaries one chooses, the concept can be difficult to define precisely. Yet the concept of ecosystem management implies that management will embrace all of the biotic and abiotic components of an ecosystem, on a large enough scale to ensure a buffer against disturbances outside the ecosystem. This is in contrast to traditional wildlife management for one species or group of species (Wagner 1969).

Ecosystem management does not necessarily imply anything about the presence of human interference. It certainly is not an approach appropriate only for managing natural areas (contra Chase 1987). Taking account of the entire system in management decisions is not inconsistent with commodity resource management or the U.S. Forest Service's multiple-use manage ment. Ecosystem management may be a useful construct for coordinating wildland uses (Johnson and Agee 1988), but it need not be confined to wildlands.

A key step in effective ecosystem management is the identification of goals (Johnson and Agee 1988; Huff 1989). A set of clearly defined management goals will enable the manager to decide when intervention is necessary. Yet the goals must be flexible enough to change as new information becomes available and as social attitudes evolve. Management of ecosystems ultimately must achieve socially desirable conditions (Johnson and Agee 1988) and reflect widely shared values.

Ecological-Process Management

Natural-process management has important ramifications for the Yellowstone area (Keiter and Boyce chapter 24 in this volume) and is a dimension of ecosystem management. Yet so much semantic baggage is associated with the word *natural* (Chase 1986) that it may be more useful to use the terminology *ecological-process management,* where the objective is to allow ecological processes of nutrient cycling, plant succession, fire, decomposition, competition, predation, symbiosis, birth, and death to operate unimpeded by human intervention.

Is there any difference between ecological-process management and the current guidelines followed by the National Park Service in Yellowstone National Park? Within the park, often not. But human intervention may occasionally be necessary to restore or protect the functioning of ecological processes, particularly where the system has been significantly disturbed. Wolf recovery is an obvious example (Mech chapter 20 in this volume).

Curiously, the northern Yellowstone elk herd does not offer a good example of either approach because animals are still hunted outside the park. Ideally, ecological-process management ought to transcend jurisdictional boundaries, because ecological processes do not respect such boundaries. The justification for hunting migratory elk and bison immediately outside the park in the Gardiner Valley is not to protect the functioning of ecological processes, but to avoid potential conflicts with agriculture (Houston 1982; Lemke and Singer 1989).

One of the reasons for conflict between park wildlife and agriculture is the perceived threat to the cattle industry from brucellosis, which is carried by both elk and bison in the GYE (Thorne, Meagher, and Hillman chapter 18 in this volume). It is a common misconception that Yellowstone and Grand Teton national parks serve as reservoirs for animals infected with brucellosis, thereby thwarting efforts to eradicate the disease. In fact, however, eradication of brucellosis is acknowledged to be infeasible with existing technology irrespective of how the parks decide to confront the issue (Tessaro 1987; Boyce 1989). In particular, occurrence of the disease is often used as grounds for the need to cull bison when they leave park boundaries; elk are viewed as less of a threat.

Carrying through with idealistic ecological-process management in a dynamic system may present frustrations for the manager (Sweeney 1990). It is all too easy to abandon carefully planned management objectives and to intervene when ecological change is unpopular with the public, as was so clearly illustrated by the reaction to the 1988 fires (Varley and Schullery chapter 9 in this volume). Nevertheless, anticipating ecological change must be a part of management planning, especially because some ecological processes may be dependent on environmental variability per se (Hart 1990). For example, it has been argued that aspen (*Populus tremuloides*) recruitment in some areas may rely on occasional crashes in ungulate populations (DeByle 1979; Boyce 1988).

Fishing in Yellowstone National Park has long been an attraction to park visitors. Yet exploitation management for fisheries seems counter to the ecological-process management philosophy that prevails in terrestrial environments of the park (Schullery 1979; Huff 1989). Exotic species have been introduced to enhance recreational fishing, and in some areas these species have largely displaced native taxa (Varley and Schullery 1983).

One reason for the difference in management policies is the visibility of terrestrial versus aquatic wildlife. Fish are not readily seen by park visitors and thus evoke less concern than terrestrial wildlife, which afford nonconsumptive viewing opportunities. Aquatic ecosystems are literally "out of sight" and thereby "out of mind." If ecosystem preservation is an objective for the GYE, however, aquatic systems cannot logically be overlooked.

Indeed, certain populations of cutthroat trout are currently protected from exploitation, with only catch-and-release fishing allowed. In Yellowstone National Park, tighter restrictions are progressively being imposed on fishing where native populations of fishes still exist. Curiously, the park limits the take of exotic fishes as well as native taxa. In some places, restoration of streams may be possible by eliminating exotic fishes and restocking with native species. The park could certainly be more aggressive in its efforts to implement ecological-process management in aquatic systems of Yellowstone.

Overgrazing on the Northern Range

The greatest controversy regarding the application of ecological-process management in the GYE surrounds the management of ungulates, particularly elk, on Yellowstone's northern range. For many years, a number of wildlife and range managers have claimed that there are too many elk in Yellowstone National Park; a review of the concept of overgrazing is presented by Coughenour and Singer (chapter 15 in this volume). The first proclamations of elk overgrazing for Yellowstone's northern range appeared in 1914 (Houston 1982), whereas not until the 1950s did range managers claim that southern Yellowstone summer ranges, such as Big Game Ridge, were overgrazed (Beetle 1952). These claims of excessive elk populations have been challenged for both the northern (Houston 1982; Despain et al. 1986) and southern summer ranges (Gruell 1973; Boyce 1989).

Large numbers of elk have been trapped in Yellowstone in order to restock areas throughout the western United States where they have been depopulated by overhunting. And for many years, elk were culled in the park. Removals by park rangers peaked in the mid-1960s, when as many as 4,283 elk were killed in one year for the sake of saving the range from perceived abuse.

By 1967, public reaction to the culling became intense. Dramatized by CBS News documentaries, the manner in which the Park Service implemented the slaughter of elk evoked the wrath of antihunters as well as hunters who would have preferred to be involved in the removals themselves (U.S. Congress 1967; Peek 1986). Shooting within the park clearly was socially unacceptable.

The natural regulation experiment. A radical solution to the perpetual "need" to kill elk was proposed in 1967 (Cole 1969, 1971; Despain et al. 1986). The park simply considered what might happen if the culling were stopped. After all, there had been almost no harvest of elk from the Madison-Firehole herd, yet elk numbers had not gone through the roof (Cole 1983), nor had the vegetation been destroyed. Presumably when densities became high, dispersal increased, recruitment rates declined, and more elk died due to winter kill. As Glen Cole argued, natural regulation is what national parks are all about.

Thus began the natural regulation experiment. All shooting of elk within the park was terminated while studies were implemented to document the consequences of this grand-scale, albeit unreplicated, experiment. Results of the first ten years of monitoring were summarized by Houston (1982), who championed the program as a great success (see also Despain et al. 1986). Others viewed this proclamation as premature. Yet as of 1990 there was no evidence that culling of elk is "necessary," although high numbers of elk may have consequences for plant and animal communities on the northern range (Chadde and Kay chapter 16 in this volume).

Supposed tests of the natural regulation hypothesis. As originally postulated, the natural regulation hypothesis was formalized by a list of specific research hypotheses designed to evaluate the Park Service's predicted consequences of the new laissez-faire approach to management (Houston 1976). According to Lemke and Singer (1989), the hypothesis was to be rejected if any of the following premises were violated:

1. High elk numbers should have no detrimental effects on other wildlife species, particularly other ungulates, within the park.
2. Elk should not cause major changes in vegetation to exotic or less palatable plants.
3. Soil erosion should not increase in the absence of elk culling.
4. Elk populations should stabilize at some equilibrium density.

These premises were based on some notion of how a self-regulated population of elk should behave.

Existing evidence suggests that each of these premises has been violated, and therefore, one might think that the natural regulation hypothesis should be rejected. Beaver (*Castor canadensis*) and white-tailed deer (*Odocoileus virginianus*) appear to have declined on the park's northern range (Jonas 1955; Wagner 1969; Craighead chapter 3 in this volume), thereby violating the first premise. Aspen and willow (*Salix* spp.) have allegedly declined in abundance and biomass on certain portions of the northern range, suggesting that premise two has been violated (Kay 1985; Chadde and Kay chapter 16 in this volume). There are undocumented claims that soil erosion has been increased by heavy elk use of the northern range, resulting in low water clarity on the Yellowstone River (Chase 1986; Copeland 1990). And elk numbers exceeded 20,000 on the northern range in 1988, which was substantially above the carrying capacity projected by Houston (1982), leading some to conclude, once again, that the natural regulation experiment had been an abysmal failure.

I would argue, however, that each of these four premises is inappropriate or misleading. First, why should we expect that elk would not affect other wildlife species? Interspecific competition is an ecological process that ought to be expected as elk become more numerous. Beaver, indeed, do appear to have declined in much of Yellowstone. They are certainly not extinct in the park, however, and their numbers are probably tied to the availability of forage, for example, aspen and willows, which may have declined with reduced incidence of fire as well as with heavy ungulate browsing.

White-tailed deer have apparently always been rare in Yellowstone, but infrequent observations are logged annually even now. If anything, white-tailed deer are expanding their range in the western United States, and occurrences of dispersing animals might be expected to increase. Houston (1982:180–181) documented apparent competition between bison and elk. Again, this is no surprise and certainly has no bearing on whether it is acceptable to allow ungulate populations to self-regulate without culling.

The presumption that elk should not have major effects on vegetation is inconsistent with basic principles of plant-herbivore interactions as modeled by Caughley (1976). It is to be expected that vegetation should change as elk become more numerous. If indeed forage limitation is the principal mechanism underlying density dependence in elk populations, as presumed by Houston (1982), we must anticipate a dynamic interaction with the vegetation. Perhaps Houston's (1976) criterion that vegetation should not undergo "retrogressive" change is more appropriate. Despain et al. (1986) argue that alternative hypotheses may be posed to explain vegetation changes observed on the northern range, for example, fire suppression and climatic changes, but the evidence is not adequate to resolve the debate.

Although there are reasons to expect that plant communities would be altered by ungulate foraging, elk appear to have only minor effects on herbaceous vegetation on the northern range. This is attributable to seasonality in Yellowstone: during winter, when ungulates are concentrated on the northern range, herbaceous plants are dormant. Ungulates therefore remove only cured forage from the previous growing season, and the plants sprout again in spring. The ungulates move off the winter range in the spring before their grazing seriously affects herbaceous vegetation (D. Despain, personal communication).

A major source of controversy regarding elk management has been the presumed consequences of high elk numbers to aspen regeneration in Yellowstone National Park. Kay (1985), for example, found that few aspen stands in Yellowstone have been able to sustain recruitment, and he postulates that aspen may disappear on the northern range. Heavy browsing by elk indeed can reduce aspen recruitment and lead to stand decadence, as can prolonged periods without burning (DeByle and Winokur 1985). Because aspen is an attractive component of landscapes in the Rocky Mountains, some consider increases in elk at the expense of aspen to be unacceptable (Beetle 1979).

There is no evidence, however, that aspen was ever a major component of the landscape on the northern range of Yellowstone National Park. Palynological investigations by Whitlock, Fritz, and Engstrom (chapter 19 in this volume) have established that aspen has been a minor component of the flora for at least the past eleven thousand years. If the northern range has always been ungulate winter range (Houston 1982), we might expect exactly this result. Even if it could be shown that aspen has declined in recent years, I find it difficult to justify the intensive management that would be necessary to promote aspen regeneration and growth in the park, such as fencing or elk culling.

Why should an increase in soil erosion constitute a rejection of the natural regulation hypothesis? I am not aware of any ecological principle that prohibits organisms from interaction with geological processes (see Botkin, Millilo, and Wu 1981). Is there anything necessarily unnatural or undesirable about soil erosion? Anthropogenic, excessive soil erosion may be. In any case, recent research indicates that turbidity in the Gardner River and the Yellowstone River is not related to elk grazing. Instead, steep erodible slopes free from significant elk or human influence, for example, Mount Everts, are the principal source of turbidity (Mohrman, Ewing, and Carty 1988).

Finally, all available evidence indicates that elk populations on the northern range are stable, that is, converging on some equilibrium density. Much of the considerable fluctuation in elk numbers can be accounted for by variation in winter severity and summer-range forage production (Merrill and Boyce chapter 17 in this volume). That the carrying capacity (equilibrium) for the population varies with climatically governed changes in survival and recruitment does not imply that the elk population is unstable.

I must conclude, therefore, that no basis exists for rejecting the natural regulation hypothesis, although evidence may force us to revise the criteria for evaluating the consequences of natural regulation (Coughenour and Singer chapter 15 in this volume). I reach this conclusion even though wolf predation will alter the long-term average population size for ungulates in the park (Boyce 1990). We do not yet know all of the long-term consequences of allowing elk populations in the park to self-regulate, but after more than twenty years of natural regulation, none of the consequences of high elk numbers appear to be socially unacceptable. Indeed, it would be arrogant to presume that we know how many elk should be in Yellowstone National Park.

Humanity as a Part of Nature

We do not completely understand ecosystem structure and function, and we do not know if or how we should intervene. At the same time, we do not agree on our own role in the ecosystem (Smith 1990). To what extent should humans be considered a part of the ecosystem? Chase (1986) argues that we cannot accomplish true ecosystem management for the GYE until we fully understand the ecological role of aboriginal people. Of course, we do not know and can never completely learn the role of humans during prehistory. Even if we could find "proof" of substantial Indian predation on elk and other ungulates, we have no way of estimating the number of animals that should be culled to duplicate this source of mortality. Learning how ecological processes operate in Yellowstone with minimal human influence, and observing the changes that occur, seems more appropriate than arbitrary interference.

CONSERVATION BIOLOGY FOR A DEPAUPERATE BIOTA

During the past decade, a new movement in conservation biology has emphasized the preservation of genetic diversity as a top priority for conservation efforts. The protection of genetic diversity has been identified as the most important function for such parks as Yellowstone (Newmark 1985). Preservation of genetic diversity is justified because of the future benefits to humankind from uses in medicine and industrial materials, and for resistant strains of domestic organisms (Myers 1979). Recent advances in genetic engineering have actually enhanced the importance of preserving genetic diversity, because methods of genetic engineering offer even greater potential for applications of the genetic information existing in the diversity of living organisms.

Ultimately, managing to perpetuate genetic diversity is one dimension of ecological-process management, that is, to maintain and protect natural systems. Threatened and endangered species management under the Endangered Species Act is also a variant of ecological-process management since it is designed to ensure that all the natural components of the ecosystem are there. Management for threatened and endangered species transcends boundary lines and tells us when the ecosystem is being too heavily impacted by adverse activities or policies. Preservation of threatened and endangered species thus is a vital part of ecological-process management and may provide a surrogate for the preservation of ecosystems as well.

With the passage of the Endangered Species Act in 1973, threatened and endangered species of animals and plants were given legal priority over other competing interests, along with a financial commitment for research and monitoring. The ESA is perhaps the strongest piece of environmental legislation ever enacted, and it has played a powerful role in the management of the GYE. It is appropriate, therefore, to review how the ESA is influencing ecosystem-based management in Greater Yellowstone, and whether the ESA can be reconciled with the goal of ecological-process management.

Grizzly bears. One of the greatest attractions of the GYE is its charismatic megafauna, including the awesome grizzly bear. Indeed, the grizzly is a symbol of Yellowstone and of the need to manage the GYE on an ecosystem scale. But management of the species is one of the most debated issues in the GYE.

Throughout much of this century, grizzly bears were commonly associated with refuse dumps. In fact, watching bears at the dumps was a popular tourist attraction. In the late 1960s, however, the National Park Service decided that feeding bears at dumps was inconsistent with its basic philosophy, and the park's dumps were closed to bears.

This created considerable controversy, largely due to concerns expressed by Frank and John Craighead, who had been studying the bears for several years. The Craigheads insisted that dump closures should be gradual to allow the bears to adjust to reduced opportunities for foraging. They predicted that the bear population would decline precipitously if the dumps were closed (Craighead 1979; Schullery 1986).

In spite of these objections, the National Park Service proceeded with the dump closures, and for many years there was serious concern that the bears might not be able to sustain a viable population in the area (Shaffer 1978; Craighead chapter 3 in this volume). Subsequently, the bear was given threatened status under the ESA, and an aggressive interagency grizzly bear recovery effort recognized the need for ecosystem-based management (Schullery 1989). Bear population parameters now appear promising enough that federal officials are entertaining the possibility of delisting the species and reverting management to the respective state and federal agencies.

Grizzly bear recovery in the GYE will depend on continued interagency cooperation, especially efforts on U.S. Forest Service and private lands. Protection of bears on national forest lands occupied by the bears is necessary because the park may not be large enough to ensure a viable population (Shaffer 1978). Principal threats to grizzly bears in national forests entail conflicts with humans associated with livestock grazing, logging, and mining. According to the interagency recovery plan, on lands classified as Management Situation 1 the bears are to receive top priority. Yet this does not preclude development or commodity extraction as long as such activities do not result in conflicts with bears. This is currently established by using a cumulative effects model developed under the aegis of the Interagency Grizzly Bear Committee.

Unfortunately, the cumulative effects model does not fully incorporate the bears' needs. For example, the cumulative effects model probably does not give adequate attention to cover requirements (McLellan and Shackleton 1989). The Targhee National Forest used the cumulative effects model to predict minimal consequences for grizzly bears of planned logging in management unit 12 in the Squirrel Meadows area. No negative consequences were predicted, in spite of the lack of evidence of any benefit to the grizzly bear from clearcutting.

There appears to be progress in grizzly bear management by the U.S. Forest Service. The recent management plan for the Bridger-Teton National Forest proposes a new form of land classification specifically designed to facilitate the delisting process for the grizzly bear. Although the species is listed as threatened, certain types of development are allowed in situation 1 grizzly bear habitats outside of wilderness areas. In particular, oil and gas leasing can proceed, but only in accordance with the ESA; that is, such development must pose no significant threat to the bears. Once the grizzly bear is delisted, however, Bridger-Teton's leasing stipulation for oil and gas exploration and extraction requires that there be no surface occupancy (NSO). The bear thus is protected by the ESA while listed, and by an NSO stipulation if it is delisted.

It is premature to conclude that grizzly bear recovery has been successful. Because the grizzly bear is long-lived, the ramifications of an apparently high recruitment rate for the population in recent years will require several years to evaluate. But current population data based on an inadequate sample size would suggest that interagency management has been successful and that the grizzly bear is doing well in the GYE. When we can be confident that habitat for bears is secure, such population data will appear more promising.

Grizzly bear management under the ESA, therefore, is an experiment in ecosystem or ecological-process management. If we have the bear rely upon natural food sources and wish to minimize human intervention, then we need to provide bears with sufficient secure habitat, and we need clear ecosystem-wide management guidelines. Otherwise ecological-process management will not work because the bear will not respect our artificial boundaries or our presence.

Bald eagles and peregrine falcons. Quite different strategies are appropriate for other species protected by the ESA. Bald eagles (*Haliaeetus leucocephalus*), for example, are protected not only by the ESA, but also by special legislation. One of the most serious banes in the GYE of the bald eagle, as well as of the peregrine falcon (*Falco peregrinus*), was the federal spruce-budworm control program. This relied upon DDT, which accumulates through the food chain, causing eggshell thinning and consequent reproductive failure in raptors. Since DDT was banned in 1972 raptors have increased in abundance.

The current population in the GYE totals approximately seventy nesting pairs, and more than a hundred birds winter in the area. Perhaps the greatest threats to the bald eagle in the GYE occur on private lands, where a substantial proportion of the population nests. Although the species is protected everywhere in North America, human intrusions on privately owned habitat may not be adequately controlled by the ESA (Swenson, Alt, and Eng 1986).

Whereas bald eagle recovery was accomplished by protecting the birds and nesting areas, peregrine falcon recovery has required a more active process. Beginning in 1980, birds reared in captivity have been released from "hacking" sites throughout the GYE. Recovery efforts have been highly successful. As of 1990, more than twenty pairs have been defending breeding territories in the GYE.

Trumpeter swans. It is not always clear that the ESA is necessary to protect rare species. The trumpeter swan (*Cygnus buccinator*) population in the contiguous United States was seriously threatened with extinction during the 1930s, when fewer than seventy birds were thought to exist. Since then, the species has been protected from hunting and numbers have increased to the point that more than four hundred birds occupy the GYE during summer, and approximately fifteen hundred in winter. The trumpeter swan is not currently listed as a threatened or an endangered species.

Nevertheless, in recent years the breeding population of trumpeter swans has been declining throughout the GYE, despite interagency efforts to maintain the species. R. S. Gale (1987) argued that federal and state agencies have been insensitive to this decline and have failed to respond to early warning signals that the swan is in trouble.

In an effort to halt the decline, the Trumpeter Swan Subcommittee of the Pacific Flyway Council organized a program in 1987 to expand winter range for the trumpeter swan in the tristate (Idaho, Montana, and Wyoming) area. In 1988, the Wyoming Game and Fish Department initiated cooperative ventures with private landowners to set aside wintering habitat on the Salt River drainage near the Bridger-Teton National Forest in western Wyoming. A similar initiative was undertaken on the Fort Hall Indian Reservation near Pocatello, Idaho. These efforts appear to be successful in expanding the wintering range of the species.

The cold winter of 1988–1989 resulted in a freeze-up on Henry's Fork of the Snake River, where many of the swans overwinter. To alleviate stress on the birds, the Idaho Department of Fish and Game requested the U.S. Bureau of Reclamation to release additional water into Henry's Fork from Island Park Reservoir. The bureau initially refused, but eventually agreed to release water after a purchase arrangement was negotiated. Contributions to the purchase were made by the ditch companies that normally use the water for irrigation, by a private campaign organized by the Henry's Fork Foundation, and by the Idaho Department of Fish and Game (D. Lockman, pers. comm.). In spite of these creative efforts, approximately one hundred swans died that winter (Gale 1989).

Partly in reaction to this incident, in 1989 the Idaho chapter of the Wildlife Society proposed that the species be granted threatened status. Listing the swan would give federal protection to the species and would enable conservation agencies to leverage participation by federal agencies, for example, the U.S. Bureau of Reclamation, in recovery efforts. Listing also would require ESA section 6 interagency cooperation, thus ensuring an ecosystem perspective for swan management (Gale 1987).

The Wyoming Game and Fish Department, however, has officially opposed listing the trumpeter swan as threatened. The department views threatened-status listing as a possible hindrance to its efforts to secure support from private landowners in Wyoming and from other state agencies. Further, the Game and Fish Department argues that efforts to conserve the species are already in place, and that listing therefore does not afford any advantages. Whether the swan is listed or not, its future hinges upon interagency management initiatives that address its habitat needs on an ecosystem-wide basis. And for this species, cooperation by private landowners is essential to the development of a viable recovery plan because most of the swan's winter range is on private property.

Jackson Lake sucker. Aquatic environments in many areas outside the park have been altered substantially to enhance regional agriculture. The Snake River sucker (*Chasmistes muriei*), for example, apparently became extinct subsequent to the construction of the Jackson Lake dam (Baxter and Simon 1970; Miller and Smith 1981). The extinction may have been a consequence of habitat alteration (from flooding the reservoir) or interbreeding with the Utah sucker (*Catostomus ardens*) or both. Miller and Smith (1981) note that the only existing specimen of the Snake River sucker shows introgressed characters from the Utah sucker. Unconfirmed reports suggest that the species may have been rediscovered in Heart Lake (J. Varley, pers. comm)

Ross bentgrass. Although not formally listed as an endangered species, the Ross bentgrass (*Agrostis rossiae*) is probably the most vulnerable species in the GYE (Dorn 1989). Restricted to the Upper Geyser basin in Yellowstone National Park, this species is subject to large population fluctuations due to changing thermal activity. Dorn's concern about the consequences of grazing and trampling by large ungulates is highly relevant to the context of this chapter. To develop management policy, research is urgently needed on factors influencing the population size and viability of this species.

One of the alternatives for management of natural resources in Yellowstone National Park is to give top priority to management that ensures the preservation of genetic diversity to the greatest extent possible. The global loss of genetic diversity is one of the most critical issues facing humankind today (Lovejoy 1986). It is projected that by the year 2000 the world stands to lose between 500,000 and 2 million species of organisms. Most of these losses will occur in tropical forest regions, where species diversity is exceptionally high and human exploitation of natural environments is progressing at unprecedented rates.

Species diversity in the Greater Yellowstone Ecosystem is comparatively low, and very few species extinctions are projected to occur there, regardless of future management. In contrast, tropical wet forests host an incredible diversity of species, including many yet to be described. Logically, one might argue that preservation of genetic diversity in the Greater Yellowstone Area would be of comparatively low priority for management. If preservation of global genetic diversity were an important goal, conservation groups would be much better served to expend their limited resources and energies toward preservation of tropical forests and coral reefs rather than the high-elevation, low-diversity areas of the GYE!

The preservation of genetic diversity, however, is not the only concern of conservation. And it is even possible that other conservation values may be sacrificed if ultimate priority is given to the preservation of genetic diversity. The Yellowstone area has been touted as one of the largest remaining intact ecosystems in the temperate latitudes of the Northern Hemisphere. Perhaps as an indication of the health of the ecosystem, only a few rare or threatened species reside in the GYE. Surely there must be some value in the preservation of unique assemblages of species. Clearly there are social, economic, recreational, scientific, and ethical values that justify preservation of such *biotic* diversity in the Yellowstone area. And in an area as large as the GYE, preservation of genetic diversity may largely be accomplished as a subset of ecological-process management.

Yellowstone is indeed a global paradigm. Conservation in the Greater Yellowstone Area is necessary if we are to foster sound stewardship of biotic diversity in other parts of the world. The point of threatened and endangered species management is that we need all components of the ecosystem if we are to engage in ecological-process management. And we may find that there is value to humankind in ecosystem preservation as well.

IS IT TOO LATE?

Chase (1986) argues that mismanagement by the National Park Service has destroyed Yellowstone National Park. Most people who have visited the park since the publication of Chase's book would probably agree that his death knell for Yellowstone was premature. In fact, lush regrowth of vegetation subsequent to the 1988 fires is educating park visitors about the truly dynamic nature of the ecosystem (Romme and Despain 1989; Singer et al. 1989).

It has also been argued that human influence in Yellowstone National Park is so great that trying to manage it as a "natural" system is unreasonable. Some think we should admit that Yellowstone is a perturbed environment and manage it accordingly (Huff 1989; Blood 1990). But I am not convinced that, with a few exceptions, the ecological processes of Yellowstone National Park are significantly disturbed by park visitors or other human influences. Most disturbances in Yellowstone are closely tied to the road system, and the evidence of human disturbance vanishes upon getting further than 100 m from a road. A backpacking trip into any remote area of the park would be enough to convince most people that human disturbance is not as extensive as it appears from the roads. I tend to agree with Houston (1971): In spite of human intrusions into its ecology, pristine ecosystem relations in Yellowstone are comparatively intact or potentially restorable.

Rolston (1990) proposes an interesting analogy: "A broken arm, reset and healed, is relatively more natural than an artificial limb, though both have been medically manipulated." Similarly, although humans have altered the ecology of the GYE, the ecosystem is nevertheless functioning and worthy of perpetuation.

At some level, all environments in the world have been affected by human development and agriculture. But it is not always clear that these influences are great enough to require management intervention. Although ecologists tend to emphasize the interconnectedness of nature, perturbations at one link in the ecosystem do not necessarily cascade into all its dimensions. The issue is one of embeddedness, that is, how complexly a species is embedded within the ecosystem. In Greater Yellowstone there has been little research on this issue. Thus in many cases we unfortunately have no concrete basis for establishing ecosystem management policy.

Indeed, the conviction of the National Parks and Conservation Association (Gordon et al. 1989) is that the National Park Service does not understand well enough the resources it seeks to manage. Future management must depend on our developing research programs to ensure that we understand, as well as possible, the complex GYE ecosystem. Until we do, however, we should not interfere with its function while doing whatever we can to ensure that ecosystem components remain intact.

Some may view this argument as an excuse for failing to manage natural resources in national parks. Jack Ward Thomas (1979), for example, wrote in another context, "To say we don't know enough is to take refuge behind a half-truth and ignore the fact that decisions will be made regardless of the amount of information available." But it is incorrect to suggest that the National Park Service does not, or should not, manage its parks. Ecological-process management does not imply hands-off management, but rather carefully reasoned intervention with a directed goal. Restoring wolves, perpetuating grizzly bears, replacing exotic fisheries with native aquatic communities, and minimizing human impacts (for example, from recreational use) will require active management.

It is apparent that we are capable of controlling nature for the purpose of preserving and managing particular species, but there is less evidence that we are competent to accomplish ecosystem preservation. And this task will be even more difficult beyond national park boundaries, where hands-off management will certainly not suffice. Adapting a quote by F. V. Hayden from 1871, we can say that the Greater Yellowstone Ecosystem is "the greatest scientific laboratory that nature furnishes on the face of the globe."

REFERENCES

Baxter, G. T., and J. R. Simon. 1970. Wyoming fishes. Wyoming Game and Fish Dep't Bull. 4.

Beetle, A. A. 1952. A 1951 survey of summer range in the Teton wilderness area. Bridger-Teton National Forest, Jackson, Wyo.

———. 1979. Jackson Hole elk herd: A summary after twenty-five years of study. Pages 259–262 in M. S. Boyce and L. D. Hayden-Wing, eds. North American elk: Ecology, behavior and management. Univ. of Wyoming, Laramie.

Blood, T. 1990. Men, elk, and wolves. Pages 95–115 in J. A. Baden and D. Leal, eds. The Yellowstone primer: Land and resource management in the Greater

Yellowstone Ecosystem. Pacific Research Institute for Public Policy, San Francisco.

Botkin, D. B., J. M. Millilo, and L. S.-Y. Wu. 1981. How ecosystem processes are linked to large mammal population dynamics. Pages 373–387 in C. W. Fowler and T. D. Smith, eds. Dynamics of large mammal populations. John Wiley and Sons, New York.

Botkin, D. B., and M. J. Sobel. 1975. Stability in time-varying ecosystems. Am. Nat. 109:625–646.

Boyce, M. S. 1988. Elk winter feeding dampens population fluctuations at the National Elk Refuge. Proc. W. States and Prov. Elk Workshop 1988:18–25.

———. 1989. The Jackson elk herd: Intensive wildlife management in North America. Cambridge Univ. Press, Cambridge.

———. 1990. Wolf recovery for Yellowstone National Park: A simulation model. Pages 3.5–3.58 in National Park Service, ed. Wolves for Yellowstone: A report to the U.S. Congress, vol. 2. Yellowstone National Park, Mammoth, Wyo.

Caughley, G. 1976. Wildlife management and the dynamics of ungulate populations. Pages 183–246 in T. H. Coaker, ed. Applied biology, vol. 1. Academic Press, New York.

———. 1979. What is this thing called carrying capacity? Pages 2–8 in M. S. Boyce and L. D. Hayden-Wing, eds. North American elk: Ecology, behavior and management. Univ. of Wyoming, Laramie.

Caughley, G., and J. H. Lawton. 1981. Plant-herbivore systems. Pages 132–166 in R. M. May, ed. Theoretical ecology: Principles and applications. Blackwell Scientific, Oxford.

Chase, A. 1986. Playing God in Yellowstone: The destruction of America's first national park. Atlantic Monthly Press, Boston.

———. 1987. How to save our national parks. Atlantic Monthly (July):35–37, 40–43.

———. 1990. What Washington doesn't know about the national park system. Pages 139–149 in J. A. Baden and D. Leal, eds. The Yellowstone primer: Land and resource management in the Greater Yellowstone Ecosystem. Pacific Research Institute for Public Policy, San Francisco.

Clark, T. W., and A. H. Harvey. 1988. Management of the Greater Yellowstone Ecosystem: An annotated bibliography. Northern Rockies Conservation Cooperative, Jackson, Wyo.

Clark, T. W., and D. Zaunbrecher. 1987. The Greater Yellowstone Ecosystem: The ecosystem concept in natural resource policy and management. Renewable Resources J. (Summer):8–19.

Clements, F. E. 1936. Nature and structure of the climax. J. Ecol. 24:252–284.

Cole, G. F. 1969. Elk and the Yellowstone ecosystem. Research note. Yellowstone National Park, Mammoth, Wyo.

———. 1971. An ecological rationale for the natural or artificial regulation of native ungulates in parks. Trans. N. Am. Wildl. Conf. 36:417–425.

————. 1983. A naturally required elk population. Pages 62–81 in F. L. Bunnell, D. S. Eastman, and J. M. Peek, eds. Symposium on natural regulation of wildlife populations. Univ. of Idaho, Moscow.

Copeland, M. D. 1990. The new resource economics. Pages 13–23 in J. A. Baden and D. Leal, eds. The Yellowstone primer: Land and resource management in the Greater Yellowstone Ecosystem. Pacific Research Institute for Public Policy, San Francisco.

Craighead, F. C., Jr. 1979. Track of the grizzly. Sierra Club Books, San Francisco.

Craighead, J., J. S. Sumner, and G. B. Scaggs. 1982. A definitive system for analysis of grizzly bear habitat and other wilderness resources. Wildlife-Wildlands Institute Monogr. Ser. no. 2. Univ. of Montana, Missoula.

DeByle, N. V. 1979. Potential effects of stable versus fluctuating elk populations in the aspen ecosystem. Pages 13–19 in M. S. Boyce and L. D. Hayden-Wing, eds. North American elk: Ecology, behavior and management. Univ. of Wyoming, Laramie.

DeByle, N. V., and R. P. Winokur. 1985. Aspen: Ecology and management in the western United States. U.S. For. Serv. Gen. Tech. Rep. RM-119.

Despain, D., D. Houston, M. Meagher, and P. Schullery. 1986. Wildlife in transition: Man and nature on Yellowstone's northern range. Roberts Rinehart, Boulder, Colo.

Dorn, R. D. 1989. Ross bentgrass. Page 8 in T. W. Clark and A. H. Harvey, eds. Rare, sensitive, and threatened species of the Greater Yellowstone Ecosystem. Northern Rockies Conservation Cooperative, Jackson, Wyo.

Gale, R. S. 1987. Learning from the past, preparing for the future. Greater Yellowstone Rep. 4:12–14.

————. 1989. Trumpeter swan, *Cygnus buccinator*. Pages 59–60 in T. W. Clark and A. H. Harvey, eds. Rare, sensitive, and threatened species of the Greater Yellowstone Ecosystem. Northern Rockies Conservation Cooperative, Jackson, Wyo.

Gordon, J. C., et al. 1989. National parks: From vignettes to a global view. National Parks and Conservation Association, Washington, D.C.

Gruell, G. E. 1973. An ecological evaluation of Big Game Ridge. U.S. Forest Service, Jackson. Wyo.

Haines, A. 1977. The Yellowstone story. Colorado Associated Univ. Press, Boulder.

Hart, J. H. 1990. Nothing is permanent except change. Pages 1–17 in J. M. Sweeney, ed. Management of dynamic ecosystems. North Centr. Sect., Wildlife Society, West Lafayette, Ind.

Horn, H. S. 1968. Regulation of animal numbers: A model counter-example. Ecology 49:776–778.

Houston, D. B. 1971. Ecosystems of national parks. Science 172:648–651.

————. 1976. Research on ungulates in northern Yellowstone National Park. Pages 11–27 in Research in the parks. Nat'l Park Serv. Symp. Ser. no. 1.

————. 1982. The northern Yellowstone elk: Ecology and management. Macmillan, New York.

Huff, D. E. 1989. Introduction to the role and effect of fire in Greater Yellowstone. George Wright Forum 6(3):12–16.

Johnson, D. R., and J. K. Agee. 1988. Introduction to ecosystem management. Pages 3–14 in J. K. Agee and D. R. Johnson, eds. Ecosystem management for parks and wilderness. Univ. of Washington Press, Seattle.

Jonas, R. J. 1955. A population and ecological study of the beaver (*Castor canadensis*) of Yellowstone National Park. M.S. thesis, Univ. of Idaho, Moscow.

Kay, C. 1985. Aspen reproduction in the Yellowstone Park–Jackson Hole area and its relationship to the natural regulation of ungulates. Pages 131–160 in G. W. Workman, ed. Western elk management: A symposium. Utah State Univ., Logan.

Lemke, T., and F. J. Singer. 1989. Northern Yellowstone elk: The big herd. Bugle 6(4):113–121.

Leopold, A. S., S. A. Cain, C. M. Cottam, I. N. Gabrielson, and T. L. Kimball. 1963. Wildlife management in the national parks. Trans. N. Am. Wildl. Nat. Resources Conf. 28:28–45.

Lovejoy, T. 1986. Species leave the ark one by one. Pages 13–27 in B. G. Norton, ed. The preservation of species: The value of biological diversity. Princeton Univ. Press, Princeton, N.J.

McLaren, I. A. 1971. Natural regulation of animal populations. Atheron, New York.

McLellan, B. N., and D. M. Shackleton. 1989. Immediate reactions of grizzly bears to human activities. Wildl. Soc. Bull. 17:269–274.

McNaughton, S. J. 1989. Ecosystems and conservation in the twenty-first century. Pages 109–120 in D. Western and M. C. Pearl, eds. Conservation for the twenty-first century. Oxford Univ. Press, Oxford.

Miller, R. R., and G. R. Smith. 1981. Distribution and evolution of *Chasmistes* (Pisces: Catostomidae) in western North America. Univ. Mich. Occas. Pap. Mus. Zool. 696:1–46.

Mohrman, J., R. Ewing, and D. Carty. 1988. Sources and quantities of suspended sediments in the Yellowstone River and selected tributary watersheds between Yellowstone Lake outlet, Yellowstone National Park, Wyoming, and Livingston, Montana. U.S. Fish and Wildl. Serv., Yellowstone Fish. Off. Tech. Rep. no. 4.

Myers, N. 1979. The sinking ark. Pergamon, Oxford.

Newmark, W. D. 1985. Legal and biotic boundaries of western North American national parks: A problem of congruence. Biol. Conserv. 33:197–208.

Peek, J. M. 1986. A review of wildlife management. Prentice Hall, Englewood Cliffs, N.J.

Picton, H. D. 1984. Climate and the prediction of reproduction of three ungulate species. J. Appl. Ecol. 21:869–879.

Reese, R. 1984. Greater Yellowstone: The national park and adjacent wildlands. Montana Geogr. Ser., no. 6. Montana Magazine, Helena.

Rolston, H., III. 1990. Biology and philosophy in Yellowstone. Biol. and Phil. 5:241–258.

Romme, W. H. 1982. Fire and landscape diversity in subalpine forests of Yellowstone National Park. Ecol. Monogr. 52:199–221.

Romme, W. H., and D. G. Despain. 1989. Historical perspectives on the Yellowstone fires, 1988. BioScience 39:695–699.

Schaffer, W. M. 1988. Perceiving order in the chaos of nature. Pages 313–350 in M. S. Boyce, ed. Evolution of life histories of mammals. Yale Univ. Press, New Haven.

Schullery, P. 1979. A reasonable illusion. Rod and Reel, J. Am. Angling 5:1–11.

———. 1986. The bears of Yellowstone. Roberts Rinehart, Boulder, Colo.

———. 1989. Yellowstone grizzlies: The new breed. Nat'l Parks 63(11–12):25–29.

Shaffer, M. L. 1978. Determining minimum viable population sizes: A case study of the grizzly bear (*Ursus arctos* L.). Ph.D. diss., Duke University.

Sinclair, A. R. E. 1983. Management of conservation areas as ecological baseline controls. Pages 13–22 in R. N. Owen-Smith, ed. Management of large mammals in African conservation areas. Haum, Pretoria, S. Afr.

Singer, F. J., W. Schreier, J. Oppenheim, and E. O. Garten. 1989. Drought, fires, and large mammals. BioScience 39:716–722.

Smith, V. L. 1990. Man as an ecological factor within nature. Pages 187–195 in J. A. Baden and D. Leal, eds. The Yellowstone primer: Land and resource management in the Greater Yellowstone Ecosystem. Pacific Research Institute for Public Policy, San Francisco.

Sweeney, J. M., ed. 1990. Management of dynamic ecosystems. North Centr. Sect., Wildlife Society, West Lafayette, Ind.

Swenson, J. E., K. L. Alt, and R. L. Eng. 1986. Ecology of bald eagles in the Greater Yellowstone Ecosystem. Wildl. Monogr. 95:1–46.

Taylor, D. T., F. B. Bradley, and M. M. Martin. 1982. The outfitting industry in Teton County: Its clientele and economic importance. Wyo. Agric. Ext. Serv. Bull. 793. Univ. of Wyoming, Laramie.

Tessaro, S. V. 1987. Studies on brucellosis and tuberculosis in Wood Buffalo National Park. Park News (Canada) 1987:10–13.

Thomas, J. W. 1979. Wildlife habitats in managed forests: The Blue Mountains of Oregon and Washington. U.S. For. Serv. Agr. Handbk. 553. Department of Agriculture, Washington, D.C.

U.S. Congress. Senate. 1967. Hearings before a subcommittee of the Committee on Appropriations on control of elk populations, Yellowstone National Park. 90th Cong., 1st Sess.

Varley, J. D., and P. Schullery. 1983. Freshwater wilderness: Yellowstone fishes and their world. Yellowstone Library and Museum Association, Mammoth, Wyo.

Wagner, F. H. 1969. Ecosystem concepts in fish and game management. Pages 259–307 in G. M. Van Dyne, ed. The ecosystem concept in natural resource management. Academic Press, New York.

Walters, C. J. 1986. Adaptive management of renewable resources. John Wiley and Sons, New York.

CHAPTER 15   **The Concept of Overgrazing
and Its Application to
Yellowstone's Northern Range**
Michael B. Coughenour and
Francis J. Singer

Overgrazing can be defined simply as an excess of herbivory that leads to degradation of plant and soil resources. The excess of herbivory must be induced and defined by humans, however. The concept of overgrazing has no meaning in ecosystems where there are no humans to alter or evaluate natural processes.

Concern is widespread that man has altered natural processes in Yellowstone National Park and that overgrazing is, consequently, a valid possibility. In line with the goal of preservation of natural processes, Yellowstone National Park embarked in 1968 on an experimental program of natural-regulation management of the large ungulates of the park's northern range (Cole 1971; Houston 1971). Some believe that natural regulation is impossible and that uncontrolled herbivore numbers can result only in overgrazing and ecosystem degradation. In 1986 Congress directed the National Park Service to "start a study on Yellowstone to see whether there is evidence of overgrazing [and] what should be done to avoid that" (Congressional Record, Senate, S 12613, September 16, 1986). National Park Service policy states that "natural processes will be relied upon to control populations of native species to the greatest extent possible. Unnatural concentrations of native species caused by human activities will be controlled if the activities causing the concentrations cannot be controlled" (U.S. Department of the Interior 1988).

Thanks to Norman Bishop, Mark Boyce, and Paul Schullery.

Unfortunately, the demarcation between proper grazing and overgrazing is not sharp, as grazing severity varies along a continuum. Moreover, recognition and definition of overgrazing depend on understanding plant and soil responses to climate and herbivory, as well as natural interactions between plants, herbivores, and predators over both short and long time scales. Application of the concept in Yellowstone or any national park depends especially upon our ability to correctly identify natural processes and mechanisms of natural population regulation. The ability to assess overgrazing therefore depends greatly on the state of ecological science.

Our objectives in this chapter are to examine the concept of overgrazing historically in general and as applied in Yellowstone—to reveal how the concept has evolved in relation to changes in natural conditions, changes in human influence on the system over time, and scientific advances. We compare concepts of overgrazing as used by a range manager, a wildlife manager, a model of natural regulation (Caughley 1976), the Yellowstone natural-regulation hypothesis, and a model of natural regulation that is less dependent on equilibrial assumptions.

HISTORY OF THE CONCEPT OF OVERGRAZING IN YELLOWSTONE

The concept of overgrazing may have first been introduced to Yellowstone in 1887 when Lt. Elmer Lindsley estimated there was enough summer range for forty thousand elk, but only enough winter range for one-fourth that number. In 1895 Acting Superintendent George S. Anderson remarked that a series of mild winters could make elk more numerous than the food supply could support (Houston 1982). The perception was that too many elk were confined to too small an area (Graves and Nelson 1919). Later, however, Ranger James Depuis observed in the 1910s and early 1920s that range grass was plentiful and that the northern range was not overgrazed (Edwards 1931).

High wintering densities were viewed as unnatural (Skinner 1928; Cahalane 1943). This view may have arisen for three reasons. First, elk within the park had been protected from hunting since 1883. The last park wolf was eliminated in 1926 (Weaver 1978). Thus it seemed clear that elk would seek refuge from hunters and wolves by remaining within the park. Second, few elk were believed to have wintered in the park prior to 1878. Instead, the elk herd presumably had migrated out of the park area and far down the Paradise Valley every winter. Winter elk censuses were not conducted in those early days, however (Houston 1982). It is unclear what part of the herd may have moved down the valley, what the total herd distribution was, or how this would have varied in response to winter severity. Third, ranching development outside the park was assumed to have excluded elk from using these traditional winter ranges while unrestricted hunting eliminated the migration.

The summer of 1919 was very dry, and that winter "there was no forage on the winter range at all" (Rush 1932). Park staff estimated that six thousand animals starved that season (Grimm 1945). Houston (1976, 1982) later questioned the accuracy of this number. However, a significant winter kill clearly did occur. Assertions that the mortality was an indirect result of an elk population eruption was never substantiated (Houston 1979, 1982).

Dry conditions greatly influenced perceptions of overgrazing. George Whittaker, an army scout, stated that "during those years of plentiful moisture, no depletion of the range was noticed, but generally dry conditions since 1926 caused the ranges to have a look of apparent overgrazing" (Edwards 1931). Like the summer of 1919, those of 1921 and 1926 were very dry (Edwards 1931). The drought continued and intensified through 1936. Rush (1933) subjectively assessed changes since 1914. To him it appeared that one to two inches of topsoil had eroded and that the grass was badly disturbed. Browse species were being heavily used. In 1933 there was a serious grasshopper infestation (Wright 1934). LaNoue (1936) noted soil erosion, disappearance of herbaceous cover, damage to tree growth, elk in poor physical condition at winter's end, and periodic large elk winter kill. Grimm (1935) reported erosion and denudation of plant cover aggravated by elk. Willows were dying at Slough Creek. The first scientific studies using grazing exclosures indicated that the decrease in plant density from 1930 to 1937 was 43 percent inside exclosures and 59 percent outside exclosures (Grimm 1937).

Growing conditions improved in 1937 (Grimm 1937), and grass production nearly doubled by 1941 (Gammill 1941). Gammill (1940) reported a significant increase in plant density, but only 50 percent recovery from the drought. In spite of the wetter conditions aspen and willow continued to decrease, and in 1943 Grimm noted that the amount of browse from willow and aspen was too small to even factor into elk forage requirements.

Later observations suggested a dramatic decline in big sagebrush on the part of the northern range (near Gardiner) preferred by antelope (Grimm 1945). Aspen sprouts were reportedly heavily browsed and suffered a net decline in shoot height (Kittams 1949; Barmore 1968), and willows greatly declined in abundance (Kittams 1948; Wright 1934). Sparse vegetative cover and the degree of bare soil was attributed to soil erosion from overgrazing (Wright 1934; Cahalane 1943). Competition between elk and other ungulates was noted (Mills 1935; Gammill 1941), and some grasslands retrogressed from bluebunch wheatgrass to bluegrass (Kittams 1948). Jonas (1955) found that trees failed to regenerate on sites that had been harvested by beaver. Jonas also observed that elk browsed on the regrowth and that this seemed to inhibit tree recovery.

Superintendent Lemuel (Lon) Garrison decided in 1956 that a balance had to be restored between ungulates and the range. In 1962 the elk cull was increased dramatically, and elk numbers had been reduced to less than 3,200 by 1968.

NATURAL REGULATION

Artificial reductions of elk, bison, and pronghorns in Yellowstone were terminated in 1968. The object was to test the hypothesis that park elk populations would be naturally regulated (Cole 1971; Houston 1976). This Yellowstone natural-regulation hypothesis demands acceptance of the following assertions (1) that the Yellowstone area elk existed in an ecologically complete habitat; (2) that hunting by Indians could not have been sufficient to control these large elk populations (Houston 1982, based on Lahren 1976); and (3) that predation by wolves and other predators was not essential for regulation of populations (Houston 1971; Cole 1971). Potential bases for rejection of the hypothesis included: (1) eruption of the elk population; (2) retrogressive plant succession; (3) competitive exclusion of previously sympatric ungulates; (4) population eruptions among sympatric ungulates and; (5) a significant effect of natural predation on elk population fluctuations (Houston 1976).

Ecological theory provided additional reasons for testing the natural-regulation hypothesis. Caughley (1981) pointed out that culling to prevent overgrazing, especially during a population eruption, would weaken the system's feedback mechanisms and could delay the ultimate equilibrium between ungulates and plants. He argued further that culling could destabilize the system.

Some studies in the 1960s and 1970s supported the natural-regulation hypothesis. Cayot, Prukop, and Smith (1979) concluded from historical photographs and literature that most of the traditional winter range seemed intact and that vegetative conditions on zootic climax sites were natural. Barmore (1980) observed after his northern range field studies (1964–1967) that "vegetation on the winter range has either changed little since primeval times or measured changes primarily reflect factors other than natural impacts of native ungulates." Houston (1982) attributed the decline of sagebrush on the antelope winter range to removal of heavy livestock grazing, and that of willow to drier climate. He found no real evidence for widespread soil erosion and surmised that fluctuations in abundance of perennial grasses were mostly the result of precipitation variability.

Peek (1980) concluded that a test of natural regulation in Yellowstone and the existence of a natural zootic climax vegetation could not be realized as long as fire and wolves were excluded from the system. Kay (1984), however, judged that elk in Yellowstone were not being naturally regulated because he felt that willow and aspen declines were evidence of retrogressive succession and because the elk population had not stabilized even in the 1980s. Kay (1987) also argued that since no experimental control for the natural-regulation experiment had been identified, the hypothesis was not falsifiable.

RANGE MANAGEMENT VIEWS

When Theodore Roosevelt first recommended scientific management of Yellowstone elk in 1915, the science of range ecology was just emerging (Barnes 1913). Range science arose out of necessity after decades of open-range livestock exploitation. Natural revegetation of degraded range lands was studied on the bases of plant growth requirements and life histories (Sampson 1914). Concepts of a natural succession of plants toward a climax equilibrium were developed (Clements 1916), and these concepts were implemented to determine the degree to which grazing had caused retrogression from a presumed equilibrium state (Weaver and Clements 1938; Dyksterhius 1949).

Although succession-based classification may measure departure from theorized climax equilibrium, it does not necessarily establish a relationship between current stocking rate and the direction or rate of departure (trend). Determination of overgrazing is based on observing the effects of stocking rate on range trend, as determined through trial and error (grazing trials). Stocking rates are designed to achieve a balance between retrogressive effects of grazing and natural tendencies of succession toward climax (Stoddart and Smith 1955).

These concepts of overgrazing can be difficult to implement in the context of the natural-process mandate for national parks. First, such concepts presume that an ideal balance between vegetation and herbivores will be maintained by human control. If climate change shifts the appropriate balance, the manager must try to adjust stocking rate. Human mis manipulation of stocking rate may result in retrogression or range deterioration, which has no parallel in natural systems. Therefore, as stocking rate is not truly within human control in a natural system, this concept of overgrazing is ambiguous. Second, these concepts assume that the plant-herbivore equilibrium will shift continuously and reversibly. As Westoby, Walker, and Noy-Meir (1989) have argued, this may not be a valid assumption. A third problem is that there is no allowance for temporary, but natural, imbalances that arise from imperfect adjustments of herbivores to changes in climate and vegetation.

INFLUENCE OF POPULATION AND COMMUNITY ECOLOGY

Although the term *carrying capacity* was used by early range managers in reference to an appropriate stocking rate, ecological usage is more accurately traced back to Thomas Malthus's work in 1798, and Pierre-François Verhulst, who in 1838 formulated the logistic population model with a parameter (K) representing the maximum sustainable population. This theory led to the concept of intrinsic balance between the size of a consumer population and its food resources (Nicholson 1933). Nicholson argued that the controlling factor on population must ultimately be some process that acts proportionally to population density, particularly by increasing competition for limited food. Mathematical analysis (Lotka [1924]; Volterra 1926) predicted that damped cyclic population fluctuations or stable limit cycles would occur about a theoretical equilibrium between predators and prey. The mathematical conditions leading to stable oscillations, dampened oscillations, or divergent oscillations in predator-prey systems were graphically developed by Rosensweig and MacArthur (1963). Equilibrial predator-prey theory significantly influenced the formulation of the Yellowstone natural-regulation hypothesis. Caughley's (1970, 1976) equilibrial analyses of ungulate population eruptions following their introduction into new habitat predicted damped oscillations resulting in a new equilibrium, with subsequent minor eruptions due to disturbance. Sinclair (1977) found this body of theory useful in his studies of population control in African buffalo following their release from Rinderpest disease. Caughley's eruption model seemed relevant for Yellowstone because of the potential effect of release of elk from decades of artificial regulation.

An earlier, different school of thought (Uvarov 1931) theorized that climate ultimately controls population size, but acceptance of this theory waned as Nicholson's (1933) hypothesis was more widely embraced (Krebs 1972). An accumulation of empirical data later led to Andrewartha and Birch (1954) to support a climate-control theory once again. The new theory proposed that population sizes could be determined primarily by extrinsic abiotic controls affecting the time that growth rate remains positive, and by density-independent mortality.

POST-NATURAL-REGULATION HYPOTHESIS ECOLOGY

Using equilibrial predator-prey theory, Noy-Meir (1975) found that range vegetation could be forced to extinction, achieve a low-production equilibrium with livestock, or achieve a high-production equilibrium with livestock, depending on the responses of plant growth and herbivore intake to plant abundance. Sudden transitions from the high to the low equilibrium were predicted, and these have since been interpreted in the light of catastrophe theory (May 1977). Holling (1973) and Peterson, Clark, and Holling (1979) developed a theory of multiple stability domains. As long as a system remains in a given stability domain, it will tend to move toward the equilibrium in that domain. Shifts among the domains (catastrophes) result in new equilibria. The theory also allowed for continual shifting of domain boundaries due to processes of natural selection. Caughley's models also recognized multiple stability domains (Caughley 1976, 1979). Walker et al. (1981) found multiple stability domains in analyses of savanna grazing systems. Multiple equilibrial (catastrophe) theory has recently been suggested as one explanation for sudden transitions among vegetation states (Westoby, Walker, and Noy-Meir 1989). These authors maintain that it is best to acknowledge the likelihood of such changes, and to identify the sets of conditions or rules that govern the transitions.

An evaluation of the evidence needed to judge ecological stability (Connell and Sousa 1983) indicated a continuum of dynamic variability, with no clear boundary between equilibrial and nonequilibrial systems. The authors concluded that there were few examples of stable periodic oscillations, and no evidence of multiple stability domains. They suggested that long-term persistence with bounded stochastic variation was a more meaningful concept than stability about an equilibrium point.

A more recent theory is that many nonlinear feedback systems exhibit chaotic behavior (Gleick 1987). Quite different system trajectories may result from small differences in the initial state of the system. Chaotic behavior may also be induced by strong periodic forcing (for example, climatic oscillation). Predators and prey may exhibit seemingly unpredictable dynamics about an underlying "strange attractor" (Schaffer and Kot 1985). Although populations fluctuate chaotically, the dynamics are still confined to the attractor domain.

Equilibrial assumptions have come under scrutiny because abiotic density-independent population controls are often more significant than biotic interactions (Weins 1977, 1984). Weins suggested that a gradient from nonequilibrium to equilibrium systems spans the range from climatically variable habitats, which are unsaturated with competing organisms, to predictable habitats, which are nearly saturated with competing organisms. Ellis and Swift (1988) argued that assumptions of strong density-dependent feedback between livestock and plants, and resulting equilibria, have often resulted in ineffective or adverse range-management policies. They found that periodic drought inevitably reduces plant and herbivore populations irrespective of density, but that compensatory response mechanisms promote endurance, recovery, and long-term persistence.

A thorough review (DeAngelis and Waterhouse 1987) has shown that simple deterministic equilibrial models do not sufficiently explain the instabilities caused by nonlinear feedbacks and time lags in biological interactions, stochasticity and density-independent effects, and forcing by fluctuating environments. Persistence under nonequilibrium may be facilitated by herbivore movement from grazed to ungrazed areas, or by an ability of plant populations to survive at low densities (DeAngelis and Waterhouse 1987) or as an ungrazeable reserve (Noy-Meir 1975).

Nonequilibrial concepts are relevant to overgrazing in Yellowstone for several reasons. First, elk populations may be affected by density-independent variables, and by climate in particular. Winter severity affects elk (Houston 1982) and bison (Meagher 1973, 1976). Exceptionally severe winters (for example, in the mid to late 1800s, 1919–1920, 1989–1990) or mild winters (for example, 1986–1988) may cause large shifts in the number of animals per unit of plant production. Climate may act directly, or it may modify effects of density dependence (Sauer and Boyce 1983). Elk populations were affected by climate only when near carrying capacity (Picton 1984). Second, short-term climatic changes determine forage availability. Long-term climate and fire histories may have caused long-term changes in vegetation species that are not limiting to elk (or involved in density-dependent feedback) but are nevertheless heavily utilized by elk (that is, browse). Third, time lags in herbivore responses to sudden decreases in plant growth are possible; for example, drought may have reduced the ability of plants to withstand grazing in 1919–1936, before elk numbers declined. Finally, migration patterns are labile rather than immutable (Meagher 1989); increases in use of certain areas therefore may cause localized, but significant vegetation changes.

When the Yellowstone natural-regulation hypothesis was formulated, local seasonal movements were known to be important as a means of regulating animal density in relation to local spatial and temporal variability of plant resources. An ecologically complete habitat thus "provided contingencies for ungulates to obtain food and maintain relatively stable populations in variable and periodically harsh environments" (Cole 1971). Further, "interspersion of different habitats" provided a carrying capacity that was "greater than the sum of the parts" (Cole 1969, 1971).

Stable equilibrium states should not be viewed as a fundamental property of ecological systems except by extrapolation to large spatial scales (DeAngelis and Waterhouse 1987). As spatial scale increases, local instabilities are averaged, dampened, or compensated for—the idealized level of stability may be achieved only at large spatial scales. Brown and Allen (1989) similarly pointed out that although negative effects may accrue to individual plants, effects at community or ecosystem levels may be neutral or positive.

Now ecologists hypothesize that the persistence of small-scale ecosystems may depend on the states of and interactions with surrounding small-scale systems to achieve stability at the larger scale. Although intermixing of regional herds in the Yellowstone-Teton region may normally be minimal (Cole 1969; Houston 1982), infrequent local population increases can result in dispersion. It may become advantageous for individuals to avoid competition through emigration. Thus we might posit that the northern range plant-herbivore system is nonequilibrial, but that the larger-scale system of regional herds as a whole is stable.

The question of whether herbivore populations are food limited or predator controlled has not been resolved. This question is critical to the natural-regulation hypothesis, which assumes that food limitation is critical, and predation an unnecessary adjunct (Cole 1971). Food seems to limit herbivore populations in many grazing ecosystems (Bobek 1977; Sinclair 1977; Sinclair and Norton-Griffiths 1982; Sinclair, Dublin, and Borner 1985; Fryxell 1987), but predators seem to be more limiting in other systems (Caughley 1976; Smuts 1978; Bergerud, Wyett, and Snider 1983; Messier and Crete 1985; Borner et al. 1987; Fryxell, Greever, and Sinclair 1988). Multiple equilibrium theory predicts that herbivores can be held near a lower steady state by predation, but that if herbivores escape predator control, they become limited instead by food at a higher equilibrium. Predators can hold prey into the lower "predator pit" (Walker and Noy-Meir 1982; Messier and Crete 1985), but periodic eruptions may occur if herbivore intrinsic rates of increase are high and if herbivore reproduction responds rapidly to favorable climatic variation.

Whether predators do, in fact, control large mammals is a topic of debate at present (Sinclair n.d.; Bergerud, Wyett, and Snider 1983; Messier and Crete 1985). Evidence of true regulation seems to be lacking (Sinclair n.d.). Yet there is some supporting evidence. Bear predation on newborn caribou (*Rangifer tarandus*) (Singer 1986), moose (*Alces alces*) (Franzman, Schwartz, and Peterson 1980), and elk (Schlegal 1976; Singer and Harting unpubl. data) can be significant. Unregulated wolf increases coupled with severe winters and in some cases harvesting by man have resulted in decreased ungulate populations (Gasaway et al. 1983; Bergerud, Wyett, and Snider 1983; Messier and Crete 1985). Finally, significant inverse relations have been observed between wolf density and caribou recruitment rates (Bergerud 1988).

COMPARISON OF DIFFERENT HYPOTHESES RELEVANT TO OVERGRAZING

A comparison of the concepts of overgrazing employed by an idealized range manager, a wildlife manager, the Caughley model (Caughley 1970, 1976, 1979), and the Yellowstone natural-regulation hypothesis (YNRH) (Houston 1971; Cole 1971) illustrates the effects of varying underlying assumptions and management objectives on assessments of overgrazing (table 15.1). We also consider what might be termed the persistence model, which emphasizes population persistence in the face of natural instability. This model considers the effects of climatic variation, intrinsic population instability, and spatial scale (Connell and Sousa 1983; DeAngelis and Waterhouse 1987; Ellis and Swift 1988; Westoby, Walker, and Noy-Meir 1989). We will consider only the effects induced by herbivory. The direct effects of climate and fire on vegetation are not considered, and none of the criteria can be applied without removing their confounding effects. More specifically, changes in browse species abundance due to climate or fire, changes in range plant abundance and composition, and resultant soil erosion due to drought are presumed to be accounted for. Whether these affects have been disentangled in Yellowstone is beyond the scope of this paper.

1. *Reductions of vegetation biomass* by grazing would inevitably be accepted by the YNRH and all other models over intraseasonal time periods. Over longer time periods, a range manager would try to maintain maximum sustainable yield, which is achieved at a higher vegetation biomass than under food limitation.

2. *Decreased vigor of preferred grasses* induced by grazing would have to be accepted by the YNRH and all other hypotheses to some degree

because this is the most sensitive indicator of grazing impact and can arise before reductions in basal area or production (Pond 1957; Mueggler 1975), and certainly before species shifts. Thus it may be a stable condition and an unavoidable consequence of light to moderate grazing.

3. *Reduced plant productivity* would be accepted by the YNRH and all others to a limited degree. A range or wildlife manager might find that animal production is maximized with a small reduction in plant growth. Larger decreases in plant production could be acceptable to other hypotheses because stable equilibria between plants and herbivores probably occur significantly below submaximal plant production (Caughley 1979). Browsing that results in some highlining (browse lines) and some reduced tree and shrub growth, though often more apparent than herbaceous responses, would be similarly viewed.

4. *Plant mortality due to heavy browsing* would not be accepted by the YNRH because this would represent a deviation from the assumed pristine plant-herbivore balance. If browse is heavily foraged, but is not the limiting food, then browse survival must depend on some other limitation of herbivore populations. A wildlife manager might reject browsing-induced mortality to maintain other species that depend on browse for food or habitat. The Caughley model would accept some browse mortality if it is an inevitable consequence of equilibration. The persistence model would accept this nonequilibrial mortality if it is not a consequence of human activity. The persistence model would not necessarily require duplication of conditions in the late nineteenth century, because the plant-herbivore equilibrium may have shifted, may have been unstable, or may never have occurred.

Reductions in growth eventually lead to plant death and to replacement by other species that are more tolerant or better able to avoid herbivory. A resultant species composition that has naturally equilibrated with herbivores is a zootic climax (Daubenmire 1968; Cole 1971; Cayot, Prukop, and Smith 1979). If the equilibrium composition is human induced, such as through disruptions of migration patterns, it may be viewed as a zootic disclimax (Beetle 1974).

5. *A zootic climax* would be acceptable to the YNRH and most other models. The concept of a zootic climax has no meaning for a range manager because any equilibrium that is attained is the result of human manipulation. A wildlife manager might find a zootic climax acceptable, but not if it results in submaximal herbivore production or nondesired habitat quality.

6. *A zootic disclimax* would be rejected by the YNRH because it is

Table 15.1 Comparison of Yellowstone's natural-regulation experiment with other concepts of overgrazing

Ecological Observation	Range Manager	Wildlife Manager	Natural Regulation	Caughley Model	Persistence Model
			Concept Employed to Determine Overgrazing		
Effects on plant (standing crop and production)					
Reduced vegetation biomass	accept	accept	accept	accept	accept
Reduced vigor of preferred species (flower no., stem ht.)	accept	accept	accept	accept	accept
Reduced primary production	limited	limited	limited	limited	limited
Heavy browsing, severely reduced growth of shrubs and plant death	cond.	reject	reject	cond.	cond.
Plant species shifts (death of some individuals of some species)					
Zootic climax	rej.–n.c.p.	cond.	accept	accept	accept
Zootic disclimax					
(a) herbivore production maximal	accept	cond.	reject	accept	reject
(b) herbivore production submaximal	reject	reject	reject	accept	reject
Trend of declining range condition					
(a) irreversible	reject	reject	reject	reject	reject
(b) transient, anthropogenic	reject	reject	reject	cond.	reject
(c) transient, natural	rej.–n.c.p.	accept	rej.–n.c.p.	accept	accept
Extinction of a plant species	cond.	reject	reject	reject	reject

Effects on ungulates

Eruption and re-equilibration after release from artificial control					
(a) predators can control herbivores but they are absent	rej.–n.c.p.	reject	rej.–n.c.p.	accept	reject
(b) predators cannot control herbivores	rej.–n.c.p.	accept	accept	accept	accept
Immigration or reduced emigration					
(a) anthropogenic	rej.–n.c.p.	cond.	rej.–n.c.p.	accept	reject
(b) nonanthropogenic	rej.–n.c.p.	cond.	rej.–n.c.p.	accept	cond.
Competitive displacement of other ungulates	accept	reject	reject	cond.	cond.
Submaximal size, health, and fertility of individual herbivores	reject	reject	accept	accept	accept

Effects on soils

Increased runoff, reduced infiltration	reject	reject	reject	limited	limited
Increased erosion	reject	reject	reject	reject	rare cond.

Note: Specific responses to changes in herbivory level or pattern may either be accepted or rejected relative to goals and assumptions that underlie each definition of overgrazing. Responses may also be accepted under certain conditions (cond.), accepted to a limited degree, or rejected because the model does not consider the event possible (rej.–n.c.p.).

unnatural. A disclimax would be accepted by a range manager, provided the new equilibrium does not decrease herbivore production. The wildlife manager would likely reject a disclimax if it conflicted with other management objectives, and he or she would clearly reject it if it reduced game productivity. The Caughley model would find a disclimax tolerable because it does result in re-equilibration. The persistence model would reject disclimax in the spirit of natural-process preservation.

7. *An irreversible trend* toward vegetal denudation due to grazing would be unacceptable to all the models, including the YNRH (Houston 1976). *A human-induced, transient (reversible) trend* in species composition would be rejected by all the models except the Caughley model, which might accept this if the trend was actually reversed or stabilized. *A natural transient change* in species composition brought about by herbivory is not considered possible by the YNRH because there should be no natural grazing-induced departures from equilibrium. Transient trends are acceptable to the Caughley model, if they are part of re-equilibration. The Caughley model also allows for minor ungulate suberuptions that must produce transient vegetation trends. A natural transient decline might be accepted by the persistence model, if an equilibrium is ruled out.

8. *Plant species extinction* would be unacceptable to any management trying to sustain the integrity of natural systems. This might exclude some strictly production oriented range managers. Even this criterion may be deemed arbitrary in very rare cases, however, because species extinction is also a natural process. Species disappearance from local areas may also be a rare natural process, as range shifts have certainly been documented over paleoecological time.

9. *Herbivore population eruption.* The YNRH assumes no predator control of herbivores, so an eruption attributed to lack of predation would be considered impossible. The YNRH also assumes that eruptions should not occur in populations that are at a stable equilibrium with an ecologically complete habitat (Houston 1976). Range managers would not consider release from artificial control. Wildlife management would probably view an eruption as a sign of ineffective management for a stable system. The Caughley model would accept an eruption followed by re-equilibration. The persistence model would not accept an eruption due to lack of predation because the new equilibrium would be unnatural. If, however, predator control is unlikely, then the persistence model would allow that an eruption could be a form of natural instability.

10. *Herbivore immigration or reduced emigration.* Acceptance would depend on whether these changes in movement were human-induced. The

YNRH does not consider natural variability in movement patterns. The YNRH also assumes that movement patterns are not affected by humans, so there should be no artificial concentrations along park boundaries (Houston 1976). Range managers, of course, would not accept any uncontrolled animal (livestock) movement in or out of the system. Acceptance by wildlife managers would depend on effects on plants and other game. The Caughley model would accept a change in herbivore movement if it is accompanied by gradual system re-equilibration. The persistence hypothesis accepts altered movement only if it can be explained in terms of natural variability. The persistence model might accept, for instance, an immigration due to natural vegetation decline in another grazing area.

11. *Competitive displacement of sympatric ungulate species* would be unacceptable to equilibrial views, including the YNRH (Houston 1976), because concepts of equilibrial community structuring through competition and niche differentiation would be violated. Communities may also be structured by predation (Sinclair 1984), but this would not be considered by the YNRH. A range manager might find competitive displacement acceptable provided the displaced animals were of no potential use. The wildlife manger might reject competitive displacement because he or she is probably trying to maximize diversity and minimize fluctuation. The Caughley model would accept a community restructuring if it is part of re-equilibration. The persistence hypothesis would accept competitive displacement if it results from natural nonequilibrial processes.

12. *Smaller, thinner, and less healthy ungulates* would be accepted by the YNRH and the Caughley hypotheses as an inevitable result of food limitation. These two would also recognize that this may be the effect of climate on carrying capacity. The persistence model would also allow that this may result from climatically induced disequilibrium. The persistence model, however, also allows for the possibility of predator control, in which case food stress would be unacceptable. Reduced herbivore production clearly would be unacceptable to wildlife and range managers.

13. *An increase in runoff* would reflect change and constitute departure from equilibrium. This would have to be determined by establishing the level of runoff that occurs at plant-herbivore equilibrium, which might include some grazing-induced runoff. Increased runoff would be unacceptable to all but the Caughley and the persistence model. These two would accept transient changes during re-equilibration and natural disequilibration, respectively.

14. *Accelerated erosion* due to grazing would represent departure from equilibrium and would be rejected by all equilibrial hypotheses. The

Caughley hypothesis would probably find increased erosion unacceptable because this would be evidence that feedback mechanisms were unsuccessful in preventing system degradation. A very limited increase in grazing-induced erosion would be accepted by the persistence model if rare and extreme climatic events increased susceptibility to grazing.

The possibility that man has disrupted a persistence mechanism (migration) at a larger spatial scale than Yellowstone has been a concern since the inception of overgrazing concepts in Yellowstone and long before the natural-regulation experiment. To establish this as a valid cause of overgrazing would require firm support of the hypotheses that emigration has been inhibited, that immigration has increased, that nondisrupted movements once enhanced persistence, and that disrupted movements now endanger ecosystem persistence. Arguments that some or all wintering grounds were formerly outside the park only shift the location, not the fact that populations are somehow naturally controlled. Whether animals winter in or out of the park, some natural mechanisms that limit population size must be advanced. It is conceivable, however, that the overall ratio of winter to summer range has been altered by human activities outside of Yellowstone Park, as has been shown for the Jackson Hole herd (Cole 1969). In this situation, large elk population sizes may be supported by large summer range, but the limits are set by the size of the winter range. It has been suggested that there should be a balance between summer and winter range in an ecologically complete habitat (Cole 1971). The probability of perfectly stable winter-summer range ratio has not been calculated, however. The role of this ratio for plant-herbivore balance, the degree of its disruption, and the potential effects of such a disruption also have not been established in a quantitative fashion for the northern range.

If natural conditions have changed because of climate shift, long-term cycles of vegetation or fire, or nonequilibrial dynamics, then it may prove impossible to conclude that elk are either a natural or an unnatural part of the system based solely on their abundance just prior to human settlement. The assumption that the presettlement state (1800–1875) was static and thus represents an appropriate experimental control cannot be accepted at face value; steady states are not necessarily expected in climatically variable environments or where biotic interactions are intrinsically unstable. If climate, fire, herbivores, and large predators, or interactions among them, are changing, then there may be no control treatment for either a natural-regulation or an artificial-regulation experiment. Similar problems arise in control of confounding variables at large spatial scales and in comparisons with other land areas, even those abutting the park. To address overgrazing criteria that involve herbivore population responses or movements would require experimentation on a scale that is larger than the Yellowstone northern range. A single control treatment, much less replicate treatments, would be very difficult to find. Other methods of strong inference (Platt 1964) may be necessary to attempt falsification of hypotheses of natural regulation.

A number of steps can be taken, nevertheless, to improve understanding of the northern range grazing ecosystem:

1. Falsifiable hypotheses should be added to the list proposed by Houston (1976). Some of the 1976 hypotheses may need refinement. It is important to define nonambiguous evidence for falsification. Hypotheses that can be falsified through manipulative experimentation on plants and soils are the least likely to be ambiguous. Paleobotanical records of plant species composition, paleoecological evidence of predator abundance, and long-term changes in climate and fire can be used to attempt falsification of hypotheses of past ecosystem dynamics. Such nonmanipulative analyses should rely, however, upon established understanding of ecosystem processes rather than correlative relations.

2. Hypothesized mechanisms of interaction between predators, prey, and plants should be quantitatively formulated (for example, through numerical simulation) so they are clearly stated and related to other ecological processes. This formulation should consider (a) consistency with observed historical changes in range condition, (b) spatial effects and heterogeneity, particularly herbivore movements, effects of landscape heterogeneity on plants, and significance of balance between summer and winter range areas, (c) food quality and quantity distributions in time and in space, (d) ability of herbivores to endure periods of little or no food, (e) effects of food supply on herbivore mortality and natality, (f) effects of predation, (g) direct effects of climate on herbivores, (h) mechanisms of plant responses to herbivory, fire, and climate and interactions between these effects over both short and long temporal scales, and (i) effects of herbivory, fire, and climate on nutrient cycling among plants, soil, and herbivores. Multiple approaches and sets of working hypotheses would be desirable (Platt 1964) and would provide an opportunity for corroboration among models.

3. Concepts of natural regulation should be refined to be consistent with current ecological knowledge. Formulation of a natural-regulation hypothesis generally appears to be an appropriate framework for detecting departures from natural processes that may be occurring on the northern range.

The strict comparability to pristine conditions demanded by Cole (1971) and Houston (1976) is rigorous. However, certain of their assumptions about natural conditions need to be reexamined.

(a) Although it has yet to be verified theoretically or experimentally, the possibility that wolves, combined with other predators including native Americans, may have reduced herbivore numbers needs to be seriously considered rather than dismissed as unimportant. A newer appreciation of potential predation effects has emerged since 1971.

(b) Natural regulation should not be predicated on an assumption that the upper winter range is a self-contained system (Houston 1976, 1982). Migratory elk from the northern herd apparently do not clearly separate into an upper and lower herd (Singer, unpubl.), although an elevational gradient of hunting pressure probably occurs.

(c) Natural regulation should not assume that density-independent effects occur only in unusually severe winters, or especially, that density-dependent mortality is necessarily more consistent, and therefore important (Cole 1971). Density-independent effects of winter severity on both mortality and reproduction should be considered. Hypothesized effects of variability in forage due to climatic fluctuation should be stated much more explicitly and precisely.

(d) The possibility that natural systems are not precisely regulated through homeostasis and therefore do not attain static equilibrium should be considered. Although the existence of an equilibrium would make it far easier to specify a management goal, this may be unrealistic.

4. There should be a short-term evaluation of current understanding of population dynamics, the role of predation, and responses of plants to herbivory in recent and ongoing studies in Yellowstone. Conclusions should be related to historical claims of overgrazing.

REFERENCES

Andrewartha, H. G., and L. C. Birch. 1954. The distribution and abundance of animals. Univ. of Chicago Press, Chicago.

Barmore, W. J. 1968. Aspen ecology in Yellowstone National Park. Pages 146–155 in Annual report. Office of Natural Science Studies, National Park Service, Washington, D.C.

———. 1980. Population characteristics, distribution, and habitat relationships of six ungulate species on winter range in Yellowstone National Park. Final report. Research office, Yellowstone National Park.

Barnes, W. C. 1913. Western grazing grounds and forest ranges. Sander, Chicago.

Beetle, A. A. 1974. The zootic disclimax concept. J. Range Mgmt. 27:30–32.

Bergerud, A. T. 1988. Caribou, wolves and man. Trends Ecol. Evol. 3:68–72.

Bergerud, A. T., W. Wyett, and B. Snider. 1983. The role of wolf predation in limiting a moose population. J. Wildl. Mgmt. 47:977–988.

Bobek, B. 1977. Summer food as the factor limiting roe deer population size. Nature 268:47–49.

Borner, M., C. D. Fitzgibbon, M. Borner, T. M. Caro, W. K. Lindsay, D. A. Collins, and M. E. Holt. 1987. The decline of the Serengeti Thompson's gazelle population. Oecologia 73:32–40.

Brown, B. J., and T. F. H. Allen. 1989. The importance of scale in evaluating herbivory impacts. Oikos 54:189–194.

Cahalane, V. H. 1943. Elk management and herd regulation—Yellowstone National Park. Trans. N. Am. Wildl. Conf. 8:95–101.

Caughley, G. 1970. Eruption of ungulate populations with emphasis on Himalayan thar in New Zealand. Ecology 51:53–72.

———. 1976. Wildlife management and the dynamics of ungulate populations. Pages 183–246 in T. H. Coaker, ed. Applied biology, vol. 1. Academic Press, New York.

———. 1979. What is this thing called carrying capacity? Pages 2–8 in M. S. Boyce and L. D. Hayden-Wing, eds. North American elk: Ecology, behavior, and management. Univ. of Wyoming, Laramie.

———. 1981. Overpopulation. Pages 7–19 in P. A. Jewell and S. Holt, eds. Problems in management of locally abundant wild animals. Academic Press, New York.

Cayot, L. J., J. Prukop, and D. R. Smith. 1979. Zootic climax vegetation and natural regulation. Wildl. Soc. Bull. 7:162–169.

Clements, F. E. 1916. Plant succession: An analysis of the development of vegetation. Carnegie Inst. Publ. 242:1–512.

Cole, G. C. 1969. The elk of Grand Teton and southern Yellowstone national parks. Nat'l Park Serv. Res. Rep. GRTE-N-1. GPO, Washington, D.C.

———. 1971. An ecological rationale for the natural and artificial regulation of native ungulates in parks. Trans. N. Am. Wildl. Conf. 36:417–425.

Connell, J. H., and W. P. Sousa. 1983. On evidence needed to judge ecological stability or persistence. Am. Nat. 121:789–824.

Daubenmire, R. F. 1968. Plant communities: A textbook of plant synecology. Harper and Row, New York.

DeAngelis, D. L., and J. C. Waterhouse. 1987. Equilibrium and non-equilibrium concepts in ecological models. Ecol. Monogr. 57:1–21.

Dyksterhius, E. J. 1949. Condition and management of rangeland based upon quantitative ecology. J. Range Mgmt. 2:104–115.

Edwards, G. 1931. Memorandum to director (from the acting superintendent), March 11, 1931, Yellowstone National Park.

Ellis, J. E., and D. M. Swift. 1988. Stability of African pastoral ecosystems: Alternate paradigms and implications for development. J. Range Mgmt. 41:450–459.

Franzmann, A. W., C. G. Schwartz, and R. O. Peterson. 1989. Moose calf mortality on the Kenai Peninsula, Alaska. J. Wildl. Mgmt. 44:764–768.

Fryxell, J. M. 1987. Food limitation and demography of a migratory antelope, the white eared kob. Oecologia 72:83–91.

Fryxell, J. M., J. Greever, and A. R. E. Sinclair. 1988. Why are migratory ungulates so abundant? Am. Nat. 131:781–798.

Gammill, W. H. 1939–1941. Yellowstone National Park range studies. Yellowstone National Park files.

Gasaway, W. C., R. O. Stephenson, J. L. Davis, P. E. K. Shepard, and O. E. Burris. 1983. Interrelationships of wolves, prey, and man in interior Alaska. Wildl. Monogr. 84:1–50.

Gleick, J. 1987. Chaos: Making of a new science. Penguin, New York.

Graves, H. S., and E. W. Nelson. 1919. Our national elk herds. U.S. Dep't Agric. Circular 51. GPO, Washington, D.C..

Grimm, R. L. 1935–1938. Yellowstone National Park range studies. Yellowstone National Park files.

———. 1943–1947. Yellowstone National Park range studies. Yellowstone National Park files.

Holling, C. S. 1973. Resilience and stability of ecological systems. Ann. Rev. Ecol. Syst. 4:1–23.

Houston, D. B. 1971. Ecosystems of national parks. Science 172:648–651.

———. 1976. The status of research on ungulates in northern Yellowstone Park. Pages 11–27 in Research in the parks. Transactions of the National Parks Centennial Symposium, December 1971. Nat'l Park Serv. Symp. Ser. no. 1.

———. 1982. The northern Yellowstone elk: Ecology and management. Macmillan, New York.

Jonas, R. J. 1955. A population and ecological study of the beaver (*Castor canadensis*) of Yellowstone National Park. M.S. thesis, Univ. of Idaho.

Kay, C. E. 1984. Aspen reproduction in the Yellowstone Park–Jackson Hole area and its relationship to the natural regulation of ungulates. Pages 131–160 in G. W. Workman, ed. Western elk management: A symposium. Utah State Univ. Press, Logan.

———. 1987. Too many elk in Yellowstone. Review of Wildlife in transition, by D. Despain et al. W. Wildlands 13:39–44.

Kittams, W. H. 1948–1958. Northern winter range studies. Yellowstone National Park files.

Krebs, C. J. 1972. Ecology: The experimental analysis of distribution and abundance. Harper and Row, New York.

Lahren, L. A. 1976. The Myers-Hindmann site: An exploratory study of human occupation patterns in the upper Yellowstone valley from 7000 BC to AD 1200. Anthropologos Researches International.

Lotka, A. J. [1924] 1956. Elements of physical biology. Reprint. Dover, New York.

May, R. M. 1977. Thresholds and breakpoints in ecosystems with a multiplicity of stable states. Nature 269:471–477.

Meagher, M. 1973. The bison of Yellowstone National Park. Nat'l Park Serv. Sci. Monogr. Ser. no. 1. Washington, D.C.

———. 1976. Winter weather as a population regulating influence on free-ranging bison in Yellowstone National Park. Pages 29–38 in Research in the parks. Transactions of the National Parks Centennial Symposium, December 1971. Nat'l Park Serv. Symp. Ser. no. 1.

———. 1989. Range expansion by bison of Yellowstone National Park. J. Mammal. 70:670–675.

Messier, F., and M. Crete. 1985. Moose-wolf dynamics and the natural regulation of moose populations. Oecologia 65:503–512.

Mills, H. B. 1935. A preliminary study of the mountain sheep of Yellowstone National Park. Yellowstone National Park files.

Mueggler, W. F. 1975. Rate and pattern of vigor recovery in Idaho fescue and bluebunch wheatgrass. J. Range Mgmt. 28:198–204.

Nicholson, A. J. 1933. The balance of animal populations. J. Anim. Ecol. 2:132–178.

Noy-Meir, I. 1975. Stability of grazing systems: An application of predator-prey graphs. J. Ecol. 63:459–481.

Peek, J. M. 1980. Natural regulation of ungulates. Wildl. Soc. Bull. 8:217–227.

Peterson, R. M., W. C. Clark, and C. S. Holling. 1979. The dynamics of resilience: Shifting stability domains in fish and insect systems. Chap. 15 in R. M. Anderson, B. D. Turner, and L. R. Taylor, eds. Population dynamics. Twentieth Symposium of the British Ecological Society. Blackwell Scientific, Oxford.

Picton, H. D. 1984. Climate and the prediction of reproduction of three ungulate species. J. Appl. Ecol. 21:869–879.

Platt, J. R. 1964. Strong inference. Science 16:347–353.

Pond, F. W. 1957. Vigor of Idaho fescue in relation to different grazing intensities. J. Range Mgmt. 10:28–20.

Rosensweig, M. I., and R. H. MacArthur. 1963. Graphical representation and stability analysis of predator-prey interactions. Am. Nat. 97:209–223.

Rush, W. M. 1933. Northern Yellowstone elk study. Missoulian Publishing, Missoula, Mont.

Sampson, A. W. 1914. Natural revegetation of rangelands based upon growth requirements and life history of the vegetation. J. Agric. Res. 3:93–148.

Sauer, J. R., and M. S. Boyce. 1983. Density dependence and survival of elk in northwestern Wyoming. J. Wildl. Mgmt. 47:31–37.

Schaffer, W. M., and M. Kot. 1985. Do strange attractors govern ecological systems? BioScience 35:342–350.

Schlegal, M. 1976. Factors affecting elk calf survival in north-central Idaho: A progress report. Proc. W. Ass'n State Fish Game Comm'ns 56:342–355.

Sinclair, A. R. E. 1977. The African buffalo. Univ. of Chicago Press, Chicago.

————. 1984. Does interspecific competition or predation shape the African ungulate community? J. Anim. Ecol. 54:899–918.

————. The regulation of animal populations. Jubilee Symposium I. British Ecological Society. In press.

Sinclair, A. R. E., H. Dublin, and M. Borner. 1985. Population regulation of Serengeti wildebeest: A test of the food hypothesis. Oecologia 65:266–268.

Sinclair, A. R. E., and M. Norton-Griffiths. 1982. Does competition or predation regulate migratory ungulate populations in the Serengeti? A test of hypothesis. Oecologia 53:364–349.

Singer, F. J. 1986. Dynamics of caribou and wolves in Denali National Park. Conf. Sci. Nat'l Parks 5:117–157.

Skinner, M. P. 1928. The elk situation. J. Mammal. 9:309–317.

Smuts, G. L. 1978. Interrelationships between predators, prey and their environment. BioScience 28:316–320.

Stoddart, L. A., and A. D. Smith. 1955. Range management. 2d ed. McGraw-Hill, New York.

U.S. Department of the Interior. 1988. Management policies. Washington, D.C.

Uvarov, B. P. 1931. Insects and climate. Trans. Entom. Soc. (London) 79:1–247.

Volterra, V. 1926. Fluctuations in the abundance of species considered mathematically. Nature 118:558–560.

Walker, B. H., D. Ludwig, C. S. Holling, and R. M. Peterman. 1981. Stability of semi-arid savanna grazing systems. J. Ecol. 69:473–498.

Walker, B. H., and I. Noy-Meir. 1982. Aspects of the stability and resilience of savanna ecosystems. Pages 556–590 in B. J. Huntley and B. H. Walker, eds. Ecology of tropical savannas. Springer-Verlag, Berlin.

Weaver, J. 1978. The wolves of Yellowstone. Nat. Resources Rep. 14. National Park Service, Washington, D.C.

Weaver, J. E., and F. E. Clements. 1938. Plant ecology. McGraw-Hill, New York.

Weins, J. A. 1977. On competition and variable environments. Am. Sci. 65:590–597.

————. 1984. On understanding a non-equilibrial world: Myth and reality in community patterns and processes. Pages 439–459 in D. R. Strong, Jr., D. Simberloff, L. G. Abele, and A. B. Thistle, eds. Ecological communities: Conceptual issues and the evidence. Princeton Univ. Press, Princeton, N.J.

Westoby, M., B. Walker, and I. Noy-Meir. 1989. Opportunistic management for rangelands not at equilibrium. J. Range Mgmt. 42:265–273.

Wright, G. M. 1934. Winter range of the northern Yellowstone elk herd and suggested program for its restoration. Report to the director. Office of National Parks, Buildings and Reservations, Washington, D.C.

CHAPTER 16   **Tall-Willow Communities on**
Yellowstone's Northern Range:
A Test of the
"Natural-Regulation" Paradigm

Steve W. Chadde and

Charles E. Kay

Prior to 1968, Park Service personnel contended
that an "unnaturally" large elk (*Cervus elaphus*) population which had
built up in Yellowstone during the late 1800s and early 1900s had severely
"damaged" the park's northern winter range, including willow (*Salix* spp.)
communities (Skinner 1928; Rush 1932; Grimm 1939; Cahalane 1941,
1943; Kittams 1959; Pengelly 1963; Tyers 1981; Kay 1985, 1990; Chase
1986). Later biologists questioned the reality of any significant population
buildup (Houston 1982:11–17) and hypothesized that the northern range
population was "naturally regulated," its general level not having changed
significantly in the 1800s and early 1900s except for short-term fluctuations
associated with variations in winter weather (Cole 1971).

Terms such as *over grazing, range damage,* and *unnatural* elk population were
used in nearly all early government reports about the northern range. Since these
terms are value laden, they are used here only in their historical context.

    Chadde's research was funded by the Montana Riparian Association and Yel-
lowstone National Park. Kay's research was funded by the Rob and Bessie Welder
Wildlife Foundation, Sinton, Texas, and is Contribution no. 362. We are grateful to
Frederic Wagner, William Platts, Mark Boyce, and Richard Prodgers for helpful
comments on the chapter and to Gary Rogers for help with interpretations of repeat
photographs. Robert Pfister, Paul Hansen, Steve Cooper, and John Pierce provided
field assistance and helpful comments during the early stages of this project.
Yellowstone National Park provided permits to conduct this research, and Frank
Singer provided access to park files.

The "natural-regulation" hypothesis, first announced in 1967 as the "natural-control" management policy, has been difficult to test because there is no single succinct and comprehensive publication of the concept and its assumptions, supporting evidence, and implications. Except for brief discussion in Houston (1982:67–68), various aspects of the hypothesis have been presented by different authors in overview publications that make general reference to unpublished research reports, but do not explicitly cite scientific data from which generalizations are inferred (see Cole 1971, 1974, 1983; Houston 1976; Despain et al. 1986). Hence any definition of the model's specifications, assumptions, hypotheses, predictions, and a priori criteria for acceptance is subject to interpretation. The account that follows is our understanding of the model based on careful consideration and synthesis of the above publications.

If human influence is removed from the system, elk populations in Yellowstone will "naturally regulate" their numbers through density-dependent reduction in recruitment and survivorship resulting from intraspecific competition for food, primarily winter forage (Cole 1971). There may be some density-independent mortality associated with winter weather of varying severity. Although predation was invoked in the "natural-control" version of the model, under "natural-regulation" predation is considered to be an assisting but nonessential adjunct to the regulation of ungulate populations through density-dependent homeostatic mechanisms (Cole 1971; Houston 1976). If wolves or other predators were present, they would kill only animals slated to die of other causes, and hence would not limit or lower ungulate populations (see Cole 1971).

Although the elk population is essentially food limited, the park biologists reasoned on evolutionary grounds that the ungulates could not have "progressively reduced food sources that limit their own densities" (Cole 1971). Thus ungulate populations and vegetation must have been in rough equilibrium (Despain et al. 1986), and the vegetation conditions prevailing at the time of the park's formation must have reflected that equilibrium. Houston (1982:129) did observe that willows on the northern range may have declined by roughly 50 percent since the park was established, but that was attributed to primary succession, suppression of fire, and climate change, not to ungulate browsing.

In a 1971 American Association for the Advancement of Science symposium on research in national parks, Houston (1976) proposed a set of bases for rejecting the "natural-regulation" hypothesis. One was evidence that ungulates caused retrogressive plant succession. If willow communities had actually declined on the northern range because of ungulate browsing, this would be a basis for rejecting the hypothesis. Because the "natural-regulation" concept is based on an equilibrium model, grazing-induced changes in vegetation stature (height) would also indicate that the herbivores were not in equilibrium with their food resources.

A second basis for rejection would be competitive exclusion of sympatric herbivores (Houston 1976). According to the "natural-regulation" hypothesis, sympatric herbivores in the park have been over time, and are, in interspecific equilibrium through resource partitioning (Houston 1982:169–178; Despain et al. 1986). Any change in their abundance resulting from ungulate competition would question the existence of a "natural-regulation" equilibrium at the time of park formation.

The preceding is our interpretation of the "natural-regulation" model which was proposed in the early 1970s and is in essence held by park biologists up to the present (see Despain et al. 1986). This chapter examines historical changes in willow communities on the northern range and evaluates the factor or factors responsible for the evident, extensive changes which have occurred in the riparian habitats. It further considers evidence of change in sympatric herbivores and collectively presents this evidence as a test of the "natural-regulation" model based on the criteria for rejection proposed by Houston (1976).

METHODS

Study Area

The study area in this chapter encompasses the northern range of Yellowstone National Park, which is essentially the winter range of the northern elk herd (Despain et al. 1986). Houston (1982) provides a description of its climate, physiography, and vegetation.

In 1957 the Park Service constructed 2.1-ha ungulate-proof exclosures at Mammoth and Lamar-East that enclosed willow communities. Two additional 2.1-ha willow-containing exclosures at Lamar-West and Junction Butte were built in 1962. A fifth willow exclosure was erected at Tower Junction in 1957, but was removed in the early 1970s. Houston (1982:415–420) and Barmore (1981:453–459) provide background information on these exclosures.

Houston (1982) and Despain et al. (1986) should be consulted for Park Service interpretations regarding the northern Yellowstone elk herd. Chase (1986), Kay (1985, 1987, 1990), and Tyers (1981) provide alternative views.

Repeat Photography

Archival photographic collections at Yellowstone National Park, the Montana Historical Society, the University of Montana, Montana State University, the Museum of the Rockies, the University of Wyoming, the Colorado Historical Society, the Library of Congress, the National Archives, and the U.S. Geological Survey's Denver Photographic Library were searched for historical photos of willow communities on the northern range. Nearly fifty thousand images taken in the park were reviewed. However, only a small number were taken on the northern range and fewer still contained views of wetland communities. Other historical photographs were obtained from Warren (1926) and Jonas (1955). Seton (1909) provided several drawings of willow communities and beaver dams near Tower Junction in 1897.

The locations in these historical pictures were rephotographed during 1986–1989 to form sets of comparative photos, a process called repeat photography (Rogers, Malde, and Turner 1984). The photosets were visually evaluated to determine changes in the abundance and distribution of tall-willow communities (G. Rogers, personal communication 1987). Houston (1982) and Gruell (1980a, 1980b) also used comparative photography to study vegetation changes in the Greater Yellowstone Ecosystem.

Field Measurements

Willow communities and their environments were sampled and classified as part of a recent study of wetlands on the northern range (Chadde, Hansen, and Pfister 1988). Sample plots were located within relatively homogeneous stands of willows, based on species composition and dominance within the stand. The canopy-coverage (Daubenmire 1959) and height of all species occurring with 50-m^2 sample plots were estimated.

Soils were sampled and described using standard pedon description methods and terms (Soil Survey Staff 1975; Brichta 1987). Soils associated with willow communities were described to the family level. Water levels associated with representative willow stands were monitored from May to September of 1986 and 1987 using 1-m-long PVC tubes and a portable ceramic-tipped tensiometer. Other soil-water characteristics (conductivity, pH, dissolved-oxygen content) and physical features (elevation, aspect, topographic position) were recorded for each willow plot.

To develop a classification, sample plots were grouped into sets based on floristic similarities in both overstory and undergrowth layers (Chadde, Hansen, and Pfister 1988). Information on soil and site characteristics allowed the placement of community groupings along environmental and successional gradients. Associations or stable communities in equilibrium with environmental conditions were defined, as were seral community types. Grazing relationships for each community were inferred from field observations of browsing levels and from previously published studies on palatability and browsing response.

When the exclosures were constructed, the Park Service established one permanent willow belt transect inside and another outside each exclosure except at Lamar-West (Barmore 1981:453–459; Houston 1982:415–420; Singer 1987). At Lamar-West, a willow transect was established inside the exclosure but not outside. Instead, the agency used the Lamar-East outside willow belt as a control for both the Lamar-East and Lamar-West exclosures. Thus seven permanent willow belt transects are associated with these exclosures, three outside and four inside. The belt transects at Mammoth, Lamar-East, and Lamar-West are all 1.5 × 30.5 m (5 × 100 ft.). Those at Junction Butte are 1.5 × 22.9 m (5 × 75 ft.).

Data on willow canopy-coverage, plant height, and number of individual plants have been collected by the Park Service at intervals since the exclosures were constructed (Singer 1987). They plotted each willow clump within the transect on graph paper and then determined canopy-coverage by using a grid method. However, these belt transects have inherent inadequacies limiting their usefulness in long-term willow trend studies. First, the single canopy-coverage value inside and outside each exclosure precludes statistical testing of mean differences. Second, the plotting technique is subject to a wide degree of observer variability and error. Third, each belt transect includes significant portions of nonwillow communities. Fourth, rare species and other undergrowth shrubs are underestimated or not recorded. Park Service counts of individual willow plants have also been highly variable.

For this study, a series of line intercepts (Hanley 1978) within the existing belt transects were established so that willow canopy-coverage within and outside each exclosure could be compared statistically. Each belt transect was subdivided into six 30.5-m line intercepts, except at Junction Butte, where there were six 22.9-m line intercepts. The length of each line intercepted by various willow species, as well as other shrub species, was recorded to the nearest centimeter. The maximum height of each plant was recorded. These transects were sampled in August 1988.

According to Hurlbert (1984), comparison inside and outside of a single exclosure represents pseudo-replication. However, the transects and the individual plants are not homogeneous and some measure of variance is necessary to evaluate the adequacy of sampling procedures. Statistical tests on data collected inside and outside one exclosure indicate only that the vegetation is different at that site. Statistical tests using each exclosure as a sample point are true replicates, and those results are more conclusive. Our statistical results should be viewed with these concepts in mind.

RESULTS

Historical Perspective

Forty-four repeat photosets were made of willow communities on Yellowstone's northern range. The earliest date from 1871. Some photosets contain four photographs, taken in 1893, 1921, 1954, and 1986–1988. Several contain three photos, taken in 1921, 1954, and 1986–1988. Forty-one out of forty-four comparative photosets show that tall willow communities have totally disappeared (figures 16.1–16.3). In the three other photosets, visual estimates indicate that only 5–10 percent of the original tall willows remain.

In 1871 Captains John W. Barlow and David P. Heap (1872:40) toured Yellowstone Park. On the northern range, they reported "thickets of willows along the river banks." Philetus W. Norris (1880:613), Yellowstone's second superintendent, noted that the park was "well supplied with rivulets *invariably* bordered with willows" (emphasis added). Norris (1880:617) further stated that there were "innumerable dense thickets of willow" in Yellowstone. Based on an analysis of pollen in the sediments from lakes and ponds on the northern range, Barnosky (1988) reported that willow pollen had declined since the early 1900s. All available evidence indicates that tall-willow communities were once common on the northern range but are now almost completely absent.

Four additional photosets were made of willow communities on Yellowstone's Gallatin winter range. Three contained four pictures, taken in 1924, 1949, 1961, and 1986, and the other photoset included 1937, 1961, and 1989 photos. Historically, the Gallatin has had an elk situation similar to that on the northern range (Packer 1963; Patten 1963, 1969; Streeter 1965; Peek, Lovaas, and Rouse 1967; Lovaas 1970). Patten (1968) reported that the vegetation along the Gallatin River changed rapidly from an area nearly devoid of willows near the park's boundary to extensive willow thickets a few kilometers upstream in the park. He noted, "between these areas lies a transition zone of stunted and dead willows." The area with the fewest willows had the largest concentrations of wintering elk (Peek, Lovaas, and Rouse 1967; Lovaas 1970). Where deep snow to the south or hunters north of the park limit elk use, tall willows occur.

Based on visual evaluation of the photographic evidence, tall willows decreased almost completely along this section of the Gallatin River and lower Daly Creek between 1924 and 1961. Since the 1970s, the Montana Department of Fish, Wildlife, and Parks has made a concentrated effort to reduce this elk herd when it migrates from Yellowstone Park. By instituting

Figure 16.1 a. Tall-willow communities in Yancy's Hole on Yellowstone's northern range. 1893 photo by F. Jay Haynes (H-3080) viewed east. Photo courtesy Haynes Foundation Collection, Montana Historical Society, Helena.

b. That same area in 1988. Note the disappearance of tall-willow communities, less than one hundred years later. Other photos of this area show that the tall willows had been heavily browsed and were declining by 1921. Tall willows were absent in 1954 photos. Photo by Charles E. Kay (no. 3051-12 and 3051-13), August 20.

Figure 16.2 a. Close-up of a tall-willow community in Yancy's Hole on Yellowstone's northern range. 1915 photo by Bailey (1930:57) viewed north. Note the dead willow in the right foreground and the hedged appearance of other willows due to "winter browsing by elk." Bailey (1930:55–57) stated that in the early 1910s, "willows of many species are an abundant source of food supply along the streams and meadows. They are often trimmed to mere stumps during winter and in some places they are actually killed out by close browsing." From Vernon Bailey, *Animal Life of Yellowstone National Park* (1930); courtesy of Charles C. Thomas, Publisher, Springfield, Ill.

late-season hunts, the department has reduced the Gallatin elk population by at least 50 percent in recent years (L. Ellig, pers. comm. 1988). In apparent response to this decline in elk numbers, willows have increased in height and canopy-coverage, as shown in repeat photos from 1986 and 1989 (Kay 1990).

Willow Communities on the Northern Range

Willow communities on the northern range occur in a wide range of environments, elevations, and topographical settings. Brichta (1987) identified four general settings that support willow communities: (1) adjacent to stream and river channels, in overflow channels, and on floodplains; (2) in depressions and around kettle lakes formed by blocks of glacial ice; (3) adjacent to springs and seeps on foothill slopes; and (4) in abandoned beaver channels and ponds.

b. That same area in 1987; note the disappearance of tall willows since the 1915 photograph. Photo by Charles E. Kay (no. 2895-25), August 11.

Eight unique willow associations and community types were identified on the northern range (Chadde, Hansen, and Pfister 1988), ranging from low-willow carrs (shrub-dominated wetlands on wet organic soils) to tall-willow types on seasonally dry mineral soils:

1. *Salix candida/Carex rostrata* association. These are infrequent at higher elevations of the northern range. They are restricted to anchored organic mats along pond and lake margins. In addition to *Salix candida* and *Carex rostrata*, *Carex aquatilis* and *Calamagrostis canadensis* may also be present. The low stature of *Salix candida* (maximum height of about 1 m) and its higher-elevation location preclude much ungulate winter use of this species. However, utilization during snow-free periods and the inability of this species to produce vigorous basal sprouts following repeated browsing may result in a conversion to dominance by *Carex rostrata*.

2. *Salix wolfii/Carex aquatilis* association. These common low-willow communities are found at mid-to-high elevations, where they occupy extensive areas of valley bottoms and basins. Soils are typically wet with organic surface horizons. Major species include *Salix wolfii, Salix planifolia, Potentilla fruticosa, Carex aquatilis, Carex rostrata*, and *Deschampsia cespitosa*. Ungulate use of these willows is typically heavy, with

Figure 16.3 a. A tall-willow community in the lower Soda Butte Valley on Yellowstone's northern range. Photo taken in 1896 or 1897 by A. E. Bradley; viewed northeast. Photo courtesy A. E. Bradley Collection (72-158), Mansfield Library, University of Montana, Missoula.

b. That same area in 1988; note the disappearance of tall willows since the earlier photograph. Photo by Charles E. Kay (no. 2976-15A), June 21.

willows maintained at heights of 60 cm or less. A conversion to sedge-dominated communities is likely as willow clumps die and are not re-placed.

3. *Salix wolfii/Deschampsia cespitosa* association. This low-willow association is a minor type of stream-side terraces and seeps. It typically occupies drier environments than the *Salix wolfii/Carex aquatilis* associa-tion. Major shrubs include *Salix wolfii, Salix planifolia,* and *Potentilla fruticosa.* Important herbaceous plants include *Deschampsia cespitosa, Juncus balticus,* and *Poa pratensis.* Ungulates frequently graze these com-munities and browse on the short-statured willows.

4. *Salix lutea/Carex rostrata* association. These minor tall-willow com-munities are found on slopes adjacent to springs and seeps. Soils are wet and range from organic to mineral. *Salix lutea* and *Salix pseudomonticola* are often codominant. Other tall willows, such as *Salix bebbiana* and *S. geyeriana,* are common. Undergrowths are dominated by *Carex rostrata, C. aquatilis,* and *Poa palustris.* These communities could potentially form dense thickets 3–4 m tall. Current levels of ungulate browsing typically limit heights to 1 m or less. Canopy-coverages are also greatly reduced by repeated browsing.

5. *Salix geyeriana/Carex rostrata* association. These widely distributed communities are found on fine-textured mineral soils of alluvial terraces, broad valley bottoms, and adjacent to former beaver ponds. Common tall-willow species include *Salix geyeriana, S. bebbiana, S. drummondiana,* and *S. planifolia.* Herbaceous species include *Carex rostrata, Calamagros-tis canadensis,* and *Poa palustris.* Elk and moose use is high and results in willows of low stature and reduced canopy cover.

6. *Salix geyeriana/Deschampsia cespitosa* association. These com-mon tall-willow communities occur on loamy soils adjacent to seeps and streams. *Salix geyeriana, S. boothii,* and *S. bebbiana* are the dominant willows. *Deschampsia cespitosa, Juncus balticus,* and *Poa pratensis* are common herbaceous species. These communities are potentially highly productive of both browse and forage. However, ungulate browsing main-tains willows at heights of 1 m or less versus potential heights of 3–4 m.

7. *Salix bebbiana/Agrostis stolonifera* community type. This tall-willow community type occupies small areas adjacent to seeps and streams. Soils are mineral but may have surface organic matter accumulations. *Salix bebbiana, Rosa woodsii,* and *Betula occidentalis* are common. The intro-duced species *Agrostis stolonifera, Poa palustris, P. pratensis,* and *Phleum pratense* typically dominate undergrowths and probably are the result of repeated grazing. Browsing has produced open, short-statured stands, in contrast to potential growth of 3–4 m.

8. *Salix exigua/Agrostis stolonifera* community type. This tall-willow community type is typically restricted to low-elevation stream banks and cobble bars, often below high-water levels. *Rosa woodsii* is common. Other tall-growing willows may be present, indicating successional trends toward other willow types. Heavy browsing, however, often reduces or eliminates stands of this community type, leading to replacement by such herbaceous species as *Agrostis stolonifera* and *Poa palustris*.

In general, all willow stands are affected by ungulate browsing, higher-elevation stands being less affected than lower-elevation stands because of greater snow depths. Repeated browsing has resulted in sharp reductions in willow heights and canopy-coverage when contrasted with potential community structure.

Willow Exclosures

Willows inside exclosures are taller and have greater canopy-coverage than those outside (tables 16.1–16.3). Other less palatable shrubs, such as rose (*Rosa woodsii*) and river birch (*Betula occidentalis*) (Nelson and Leege 1982), exhibit this same pattern. When pooled, these differences are statistically significant across all exclosures (tables 16.4 and 16.5). Outside these exclosures, the mean height of all willow species was 34 cm whereas inside it was 274 cm. On average, willows had 10 percent canopy-coverage outside the exclosures, but 74 percent canopy-coverage where ungulates are excluded. However, all belt transects contained some nonwillow communities (table 16.6). When the nonwillow portions of the belt transects were excluded, willow canopy-coverage averaged 14 percent outside the exclosures and 95 percent inside, also a statistically significant difference (table 16.4). Thus willow canopy closure was nearly complete inside the exclosures.

When our line-intercept canopy-coverage data were compared with the Park Service's grid measurements, no significant difference existed for the transects outside the exclosures. However, the agency's method significantly underestimated the amount of willow canopy-coverage inside the exclosures (table 16.7). We believe our line-intercept data more accurately represent the true conditions within the exclosures because aerial photos (Kay 1990) show nearly complete willow canopy closure.

At another willow exclosure on Slough Creek just north of the park, Chadde and Kay (1988) reported that willows increased in height and canopy-coverage when protected from ungulate browsing. At the Slough Creek exclosure, snow accumulation normally precludes that area's utilization as elk winter range, and winter use is generally limited to moose (*Alces*

Table 16.1 Average canopy-cover and plant height of woody species inside and outside the Junction Butte exclosure on Yellowstone's northern range, August 1988

Species	Canopy-Coverage (%)		Plant Height (cm)	
	Outside	Inside	Outside	Inside
Salix lutea	6.7	22.8*	27.5	167.0*
Salix bebbiana	6.7	55.8*	32.5	272.0*
Salix geyeriana	1.5	2.0	43.5	192.2*
Rosa woodsii	1.0	10.7*	31.0	70.5*
Potentilla fruticosa	14.7	19.5	32.8	57.0*
Ribes spp.	0.3	2.3	38.2	113.0*
Populus tremuloides	1.0	—	30.8	—
Total willows	14.7	80.6*		
Total shrubs	32.5	112.8*		

*$p < .01$.

Table 16.2 Average canopy-coverage and plant height of woody species inside and outside the Lamar-West and Lamar-East exclosures on Yellowstone's northern range, August 1988

Species	Canopy-Coverage (%)			Plant Height (cm)		
	Lamar-East Outside	Lamar-East Inside	Lamar-West Inside	Lamar-East Outside	Lamar-East Inside	Lamar-West Inside
Salix bebbiana	3.0	40.3*	40.8*	49.5	357.0*	317.0*
Salix geyeriana	3.7	15.7*	—	40.8	330.5*	—
Salix boothii	—	4.0	36.2*	—	160.0	257.0
Rosa woodsii	3.2	2.8	0.7	29.0	71.0*	62.0*
Potentilla fruticosa	13.3	3.5	0.3	39.0	43.0	65.0
Ribes spp.	0.5	0.5	—	53.5	82.5	—
Populus tremuloides	—	3.2	2.8	—	161.0	375.8
Lonicera involucrata	2.0	4.2	—	34.0	91.8*	—
Symphoricarpos albus	—	—	T	—	—	37.5
Total willows	6.7	60.0*	77.0*			
Total shrubs	25.7	74.2*	81.2*			

*$p < .01$.

Table 16.3 Average canopy-coverage and plant height of woody species inside and outside the Mammoth exclosure on Yellowstone's northern range, August 1988

Species	Canopy-Coverage (%)		Plant Height (cm)	
	Outside	Inside	Outside	Inside
Salix lutea	3.2	0.2	21.5	180.0*
Salix bebbiana	6.8	53.3*	23.8	403.2*
Salix geyeriana	—	12.0*	—	328.0
Salix boothii	—	13.2*	—	353.8
Betula occidentalis	4.7	5.0	82.5	481.8*
Rosa woodsii	0.8	12.0*	19.8	77.8*
Potentilla fruticosa	0.7	—	45.5	—
Total willows	10.0	78.7*		
Total shrubs	16.2	95.7*		

*$p < .01$.

alces). Elk occasionally use the Slough Creek area in late fall and early spring or during winters of low snowfall.

Inside three exclosures in the Gallatin River drainage willows attained heights of 3–4 m with near-complete canopy closure, whereas unprotected plants were all less than 1 m tall (Kay 1990). In Rocky Mountain National Park, Gysel (1960) and Stevens (1980) noted that willows increased in canopy-coverage and height inside exclosures that excluded elk. On elk and moose winter range in Canada's Banff National Park, Trottier and Fehr (1982) reported that willows inside an exclosure were significantly taller than those exposed to ungulate browsing.

In addition to the measurements of plant height and cover that the Park Service has made over the years, they also photographed the willow belt transects each time they were sampled. Those photographs were repeated by Kay (1990) in 1987–1988. The resulting multiple-image photosets confirm that willows inside the exclosures have increased in height and canopy-coverage since they were protected, whereas willow communities outside the exclosures have not.

These comparative photos were also used to evaluate changes in willow communities observed in other repeat photosets because visual estimates from the exclosure photographs could be compared with actual plant measurements. This served to refine or calibrate the visual estimation technique used in this study. It also demonstrated that willows inside the exclosures

Table 16.4 Average willow canopy-coverage inside and outside Yellowstone exclosures. Entire belt transects compared with only the portion of those transects which contain willow communities, August 1988

	Willow Canopy-Coverage (%)	
Exclosure	Entire Belt Transect	Willow Type Only
Mammoth		
Outside	10.0	12.3
Inside	78.5	109.2
Junction Butte		
Outside	14.7	21.0
Inside	80.7	93.2
Lamar-East		
Outside	6.7	9.7
Inside	60.0	86.5
Lamar-West		
Inside	77.0	92.0
Total		
Outside	10.5	14.3
Inside	74.0	95.2
t	9.20	10.77
p	$< .01$	$< .01$

now have the same stature as willows on the northern range did between 1870 and 1900. Thus the conditions inside the exclosures more closely approximate the level of ungulate use which existed when Yellowstone was created than do conditions in the park today.

WILLOW TRENDS

The observed decline in tall-willow communities has been attributed to (1) normal plant succession, (2) climatic change, (3) fire suppression, and (4) ungulate browsing (Houston 1982; Despain et al. 1986). According to Houston (1982:129–134), the willow decline may have been due in part to the lack of new substrates for willows to colonize. He presented a 1974 photo of a newly formed gravel bar in the Gardner River and a 1978 retake, which showed that willows had colonized that area.

Table 16.5 Average height of all willow species and
rose inside and outside Yellowstone exclosures

Exclosure	Average Height (cm)	
	All Willow Species	Rosa woodsii
Mammoth		
Outside	22	20
Inside	316	78
Junction Butte		
Outside	35	31
Inside	210	70
Lamar-East		
Outside	45	29
Inside	282	71
Lamar-West		
Inside	287	62
Total		
Outside	34	27
Inside	274	70
t	7.67	9.62
p	< .01	< .01

Kay (1990) rephotographed that site in 1983, 1986, 1987, and 1988.
Chadde, Hansen, and Pfister (1988) also established plots at that site as part
of their riparian classification study. By 1983, willows were almost entirely
absent from the gravel bar and had been replaced by grasses and other
herbaceous plants. Thus this area changed from bare gravel to willows to
grass in only nine years. Not only is this much faster than normal plant
succession, but it is also contrary to expected successional directions. By
the usual successional sequence, colonizing willows would have been
replaced by other willow species and perhaps cottonwoods (*Populus* spp.)
or eventually Engelmann spruce (*Picea engelmannii*), but not grasses,
sedges, or forbs. Some willow communities on the northern range are
seral, but on many sites willows normally form stable or climax communities (Chadde, Hansen, and Pfister 1988). In nearly all instances, willows
are not seral to grasslands unless there has been a change in hydrology
(Chadde, Hansen, and Pfister 1988). That has not occurred at this site along
the Gardner River.

Houston (1982:276–277) also suggested that willows were seral to
conifers. In some instances this is true, but not for most willow commu

Table 16.6 Associations and community types found on permanent willow belt transects inside and outside exclosures on Yellowstone's northern range

Exclosure/ Willow belt	Year Established	Association or Community Type with Transect Percentage
Junction Butte–In	1962	*Salix geyeriana/Carex rostrata* (87)
		Potentilla fruticosa/Deschampsia cespitosa (13)
Junction Butte–Out	1962	*Salix geyeriana/Deschampsia cespitosa* (80)
		Populus tremuloides/Poa pratensis (20)
Lamar-East–In	1957	*Salix geyeriana/Carex rostrata* (65)
		Phleum pratense (29)
		Populus tremuloides/Phleum pratense (6)
Lamar-West–In	1962	*Salix geyeriana/Carex rostrata* (85)
		Carex rostrata (15)
Lamar-East–Out	1957	*Salix geyeriana/Poa pratensis* (70)
		Potentilla fruticosa/Poa pratensis (30)
Mammoth–In	1957	*Salix geyeriana/Carex rostrata* (69)
		Juncus balticus (16)
		Carex nebraskensis (15)
Mammoth–Out	1957	*Salix bebbiana/Agrostis stolonifera* (80)
		Poa pratensis (20)

Note: Types follow Chadde et al. 1988.

nities. Of the forty-eight repeat photosets of willow communities made for this study, only two show complete replacement by conifers (mainly Engelmann spruce). In three others, approximately 20 to 60 percent of the willow communities in the original photos have now been replaced by conifers. Thus only five of forty-eight photosets (10 percent) show conifer invasion of what were once willow communities. If beaver had not been virtually eliminated from the northern range due to interspecific competition with elk (see discussion below), they might have flooded several of these sites and thereby prevented conifer establishment.

As mentioned above, previous studies recorded the number of individual willow plants on the belt transects inside and outside the exclosures. Those data (Houston 1982:419; Singer 1987) generally show more plants outside the exclosures than inside and have been used to infer the relative ecological health of these communities, independent of plant height or canopy-coverage (Houston 1982:99).

Outside the exclosures, a few stems shorter than 1 m were counted as an individual plant as were another small group of similar-sized stems a short distance from the first "individual." However, unless the roots are exca-

Table 16.7 Willow canopy-coverage inside and outside exclosures on
Yellowstone's northern range, 1958–1988

	Willow Canopy-Coverage (%)							
							This Study	
Exclosure-	Park Service Measurements						*Entire Transects*	*Willow Type Only*
Transect	*1958*	*1962*	*1965*	*1974*	*1981*	*1986*	*1988*	*1988*
Junction Butte								
Outside	—	6.6	6.9	10.6	11.2	13.2	14.7	21.0
Inside	—	16.1	13.2	25.8	33.0	49.1	80.7	93.2
Lamar-East								
Outside	6.0	5.4	6.5	9.5	9.3	9.0	6.7	9.7
Inside	8.2	14.2	23.3	28.4	18.9	37.2	60.0	86.5
Lamar-West								
Inside	—	1.7	5.6	16.6	18.7	43.1	77.0	92.0
Mammoth								
Outside	7.5	8.6	6.2	9.3	8.8	12.9	10.0	12.3
Inside	4.5	10.3	25.2	31.2	26.9	31.2	78.5	109.2
Total								
Outside						11.7	10.5*	
Inside						40.2	74.0**	

Source: National Park Service data, 1958–1986, from Singer (1987).
  *$t = 0.45$, ns.
**$t = 6.77$, $p < .01$.

vated or genetic tests performed, it is impossible to determine whether
neighboring stems are really part of the same plant or different individuals.
Some willow clumps may have been broken into "separate plants" by
repeated browsing. Moreover, Park Service investigators contend that a
plant outside an exclosure with a few short stems is equivalent to a plant
inside the exclosure with several hundred 3-m-tall stems. In our opinion,
the enumeration of supposed individual willow plants inside and outside
exclosures is not an appropriate measure upon which to base ecological
interpretations.

The decline of willows on the northern range has also been attributed
to climatic change, especially the drought during the 1930s (Houston
1982:129–134). This suggestion is not supported by data from the exclosures, since the climate is the same on both sides of the fence. The
microclimate inside the exclosures is certainly different today, but that is an

incorporated variable caused by the plants' response to elimination of ungulate browsing, not the cause of the vegetation's response. Inside a small exclosure near Tower Junction, willows grew vigorously during and after the 1930s drought whereas those outside did not (see NPS photos 15078-4, 1935; 51–21, 1951). Moreover, it is not climate that prevents the plants from growing to their full biological potential outside the exclosures. Measurements of subsurface water levels inside and outside the exclosures throughout the summer failed to show any less water available to the plants on the outside (Brichta 1987; Chadde, Hansen, and Pfister 1988).

The climate-change hypothesis is also not supported by photographic evidence or firsthand accounts. Willows started declining before the 1930s drought (figure 16.2; Kay 1990), and they have continued to decline in recent years. Willows in the western portion of Round Valley, for example, were severely hedged in 1949 but still alive. By 1988, a major decline had occurred in that community (figure 16.4) even though precipitation had been near normal during the 1949–1988 period (Houston 1982:104). Further, there still are abundant springs and seeps at the site (Kay, 1990).

Yellowstone's Tower Junction willow exclosure was constructed in 1957, and by the late 1960s the protected willows had significantly increased in height and canopy-coverage (Singer 1987; Kay 1990). That exclosure was removed in the early 1970s and the protected plants exposed to ungulates. By the late 1970s and early 1980s those willows were extensively hedged and were reverting to lower-statured plants (Kay 1990). These changes certainly cannot be attributed to the 1930s drought. In addition, recent climatic variation appears to be unimportant since this area has abundant subsurface soil moisture (Brichta 1987; Chadde, Hansen, and Pfister 1988).

Houston (1982:101–107) noted that since the late 1890s the mean annual temperature on the northern range at Mammoth had increased 0.5–1.0°C, whereas the mean annual precipitation had declined 1–2 cm. However, to the best of our knowledge, no one has demonstrated that a climatic shift of that size will have any long-term impact on tall willows, especially since nearly all willow communities are subirrigated (Brichta 1987). Most perennial woody floras have so much biological or vegetational inertia that large-scale climatic changes of long duration are required before major shifts in plant species composition or stature occur (Cole 1985; Neilson 1986).

It has also been suggested that willow communities need to burn at frequent intervals if they are to persist on the northern range (Houston

Figure 16.4 a. Heavily browsed willows along the west edge of Round Prairie, Pebble Creek Valley, Yellowstone National Park, in 1949. National Park Service photo no. 49-331.

1982) or grow beyond the reach of browsing ungulates. Based on a sample of fire-scarred trees, Houston (1973, 1982:107) calculated mean intervals of twenty to twenty-five years between fires on the northern range during the three to four centuries before Yellowstone Park was established and the agency began to suppress fires. Although a policy to let many lightning-caused fires burn has been in effect since the early 1970s, 1988 was the first year fires burned more than a small area on the northern range.

In spite of what were considered the worst burning conditions in the park's history, riparian communities were not overly susceptible to the 1988 fires. Some willow communities did burn, but the fires frequently skipped over them (Kay and Chadde, personal observation). Riparian areas and willows are generally too wet to burn. Furthermore, cottonwoods (*Populus trichocarpa* and *P. angustifolia*) have also declined and failed to regenerate successfully on the northern range (Chadde, Hansen, and Pfister 1988). These species are extremely susceptible to fire and are easily killed by even a light burn. Frequent fires certainly would not enhance cottonwood regeneration in the park. Finally, there is no evidence to support the idea, postulated by park personnel (D. Despain, pers. comm. 1988), that burning will cause resprouting willows to grow so fast or become so chemically defended that they can grow beyond the reach of elk and reform

b. That same area in 1988. Note the near-complete decline of willows that has occurred in the past four decades. Numerous springs and seeps still can be found in this area, which suggests that climatic change or lack of water is not primarily responsible for the observed change in plant communities. In all probability, the willows were killed by repeated ungulate browsing. Photo by Charles E. Kay (no. 2976-19A), June 21.

tall-willow communities. Observations of experimental willow burns conducted by the Park Service on the northern range indicate that elk browsed all of the new sprouts; none were able to grow taller than 1 m except where physical barriers prevented elk use (Kay 1990).

Based on a process of elimination and the data we have presented, we conclude that frequent, repeated ungulate browsing is primarily responsible for the decline of tall-willow communities on the northern range. Browsing by elk and moose presently prevents the willows which do exist on the northern range from expressing their full biological height and canopy-coverage. From 1970 through 1978, willow utilization on the northern range averaged over 91 percent (Houston 1982:149) and has not decreased in recent years (Chadde unpubl. data; F. Singer, pers. comm. 1989). Barmore (1981:358) likewise concluded that willows had declined on the northern range due to repeated ungulate browsing, not climatic change.

During the late 1950s and early 1960s, when the Park Service believed that an "unnaturally" high population of elk was causing "range damage" in Yellowstone, they reduced the herd by trapping, transplanting, and killing elk in the park. Barmore (1981:357) noted, "By the late 1960's, the growth form and condition of *Salix* spp. on most of the winter range began to more closely resemble the less heavily browsed conditions of the late 1800's and early 1900's. This change was associated with major reduction of the northern Yellowstone elk herd suggesting that the decline in the distribution and condition of *Salix* spp. from the 1920's to the early 1960's was at least partly due to heavy browsing by elk."

On the Gallatin River, willows have declined only where wintering elk concentrated most heavily (Patten 1968). The willows upstream and downstream from the main elk wintering area have not declined and commonly exceed 3 m. Thus, climatic or hydrologic conditions could not be primarily responsible for the decline near the park boundary since all sections of the river were subjected to the same physical factors. Patten (1968) found that willows farthest from the river had the highest grazing-induced mortality rates. He concluded that plants subjected to physiological stress were less able to withstand grazing pressure. However, it was ungulate browsing which actually caused most of the mortality and reduction in plant growth. Neilson (1986), who worked on a similar climatic change versus grazing problem, concluded that the vegetation would have persisted despite drought had the additional stress of grazing not completely altered the flora.

Houston (1982:131) argued that ungulates were not primarily responsible for the decline of willows on the northern range because willows had also declined outside Yellowstone, as well as on the park's summer range. Willows have in fact declined throughout the West since European settlement, but that has been primarily due to such agricultural practices as irrigation, dewatering, channelization, and livestock grazing, not climatic change (Meehan and Platts 1978; Dobyns 1981; Myers 1981; Marcuson 1983; Platts et al. 1983; U.S. General Accounting Office 1988). A recent study of 262 miles of streams in southwestern Wyoming found that since the 1850s 83 percent of the streams and their associated riparian areas had been severely altered by livestock grazing (Shute 1981). Furthermore, moose and elk also feed upon willows on the park's summer range (McMillan 1950, 1953). Until exclosures are built there, the impact of summer ungulate utilization on those communities cannot be determined.

Morgantini and Hudson (1989) reported that elk in western Canada shifted their diet to willows on summer ranges. In Rocky Mountain National Park, according to Stevens (1980:145), "willow forms a major part of the summer diet for elk, about 21%." Stevens (1980:139) also reported that on the park's summer range "53% of the elk were observed on willow types." Moreover, he found that elk grazing caused willows to decline on the park's summer range. "*Salix brachycarpa* decreased an average of 55% on three of the four transects, with an overall decline from 20% cover to 9%. *Salix planifolia* declined from 37% to 29% cover" (Stevens 1980:135). These declines occurred in only eight years as the elk herd built up in the park (Stevens 1980:136).

IMPACT ON OTHER SPECIES

Beaver. The decline of tall-willow communities on the northern range has in all probability had a negative impact on animals which are usually associated with that habitat, such as beaver. Houston (1982:182–183) implied that beaver were not widespread in Yellowstone until around 1900 and suggests that "ephemeral colonies may be characteristic of most of the park." However, in 1835, 1836, and 1837, Osborne Russell (1965) trapped beaver in Yellowstone Park, where he found a great many on the northern range. For instance, he and his companions trapped beaver from August 3 to 20, 1835, on the upper Gardner River. In 1836 Russell and his party spent several days trapping beaver on the streams which flow into Lamar Valley. The next year he and his associates spent nearly three weeks trapping beaver on Slough and Hellroaring creeks.

Norris (1880:613) reported that beaver were common in the park during the 1870s and 1880s. He stated that trappers took "hundreds, if not thousands" of beaver skins from the park each year during his tenure as superintendent. Seton (1909) found beaver abundant near Tower Junction on the northern range in 1897. Skinner (1927:176) noted that "beaver have always been quite common in Yellowstone National Park, and although fluctuations are noticed at times, the actual number present remains about the same throughout a course of years." Skinner added, "beaver occur in practically every stream and pond (where there is suitable food) in the park." He estimated that there were "about 10,000" beaver in the park.

Bailey (1930:112–114) observed, "beavers are found along almost every stream in Yellowstone Park." He also noted that "the extensive herds of elk" on the northern range kept down the growth of the beavers' food supply, young aspen and willows. Wright and Thompson (1935:72) concluded that beaver in Yellowstone were "endangered through the destruction of aspen and willow on the overbrowsed elk winter ranges." Thus, the available evidence strongly suggests that beaver were common in the Yellowstone area and on the northern range from before park establishment

Figure 16.5 a. Beaver dam on the north fork of Elk Creek on Yellowstone's northern range near Tower Junction in 1921. Note aspen in upper left and willows to the right of the dam. Photo by Edward Warren (1926:84) courtesy College of Environmental Science and Forestry, State University of New York, Syracuse. Photo no. 5145, August 10.

in 1872 through the early 1900s. Warren (1926:183) suggested that beaver had increased during the early 1900s, but he attributed it to "the protection from molestation by trappers" and the "killing of predatory animals" by the Park Service.

In the early 1920s, Warren (1926) conducted a detailed beaver study around Tower Junction on the northern range. He reported 232 beaver and extensive beaver dams. Jonas (1955) repeated Warren's study in the early 1950s and found no beaver or recent dams. Jonas (1955, 1956, 1959, pers. comm. 1987) attributed the decline in beaver to three factors: (1) lack of preferred food plants, (2) poor water conditions, and (3) the rapid silting in of beaver ponds. Jonas concluded that the beavers' "unfortunate food situation . . . was a result more from the overpopulation of elk than from any other single cause." He also concluded that the poor water conditions and the siltation of beaver ponds were caused by overgrazing. In 1986, Kay (1987, 1990) repeated Warren's and Jonas's surveys. He found no beaver and no indication of beaver activity since the 1950s (figure 16.5).

b. That same area in 1954. Note the decline of aspen and willows. The stream has downcut approximately 2 m through the old beaver dam. Photo courtesy Robert Jonas (1955:37), June 12.

Beaver need tall willows or aspen—which have also declined in the park (Kay 1985, 1987, 1990)—as food and dam-building materials. Aspen and willows cut by beaver normally resprout (Kindschy 1989) and in turn provide additional beaver food. However, once the mature aspen trees or tall willows are cut, the new suckers are entirely within reach of browsing elk (McMillan 1950). By preventing aspen and willows from growing into sizable plants, elk and moose eliminate beaver foods, and thus beaver. Flook (1964) reported that high elk numbers negatively affected beaver through interspecific competition for willows and aspen in Banff and Jasper national parks. Bergerud and Manuel (1968) noted that high moose densities had a similar negative effect on beaver in Newfoundland. In South Dakota, heavy grazing by domestic livestock not only reduced woody vegetation, but also negatively impacted beaver populations (Smith and Flake 1983; Dieter 1987; Dieter and McCabe 1989). Though a few beaver persist in Yellowstone, for all practical purposes that species is ecologically absent from the northern range.

Recent studies by Bureau of Land Management and Forest Service

c. That same area in 1986. Note the continued absence of aspen and willows as well as the browse line on the conifers. Most of the area in the original photo has reverted to a dry grassland type. The stream has continued to downcut and is severely eroding its banks. Photo by Charles E. Kay (no. 3081-33), July 15.

researchers have shown that beaver create and maintain riparian areas which are critical to other wildlife. In fact, both agencies have transplanted beaver to restore livestock-damaged riparian areas (Munther 1981, 1983; Smith 1980, 1983a, 1983b). Moreover, other researchers have demonstrated that beaver is a keystone species that completely alters the hydrology, energy flow, and nutrient cycling of aquatic systems (Parker et al. 1985; Naiman, Melillo, and Hobbie 1986; Platts and Onishuk 1988).

Beaver dams impound water and trap sediments which raise the water table, increase the wetted perimeter, and allow the extension of riparian communities into what were once upland sites (Smith 1980; Apple 1983). In addition, beaver dams regulate stream flow by storing water, reducing peak or flood flow, and augmenting low flows during summer (Smith 1983b). During dry periods, 30–60 percent of the water in a stream system can be held in beaver ponds (Smith 1983a). By trapping silt over thousands of years, beaver dams created many of the West's fertile valley floors (Apple 1983).

Munther (1981, 1983) reported that a typical creek without beaver furnishes only about one to two hectares of riparian habitat per stream kilometer on the northern Rockies. With beaver activity, that area can be expanded to ten hectares per kilometer (Munther 1981, 1983). Hence, the elimination of beaver over most of the northern range may have significantly altered the ecology of areas that formerly supported the species.

According to the "natural-regulation" hypothesis, competitive exclusion of sympatric herbivores will not occur. Since elk and moose have apparently acted to competitively exclude beaver, this is another basis for rejecting the "natural-regulation" paradigm. Moreover, in the absence of beaver, several streams on the northern range have downcut 1–2 m (figure 16.5; Kay 1990), lowering the water table and reducing the wetted perimeter. In our opinion, the virtual elimination of beaver has had a greater long term adverse effect on water resources available to willow communities than any drought or hypothesized climatic change. In all probability, many riparian communities on the northern range have become drier over the years due to the competitive exclusion of beaver by elk.

White-tailed Deer. A small population of white-tailed deer (*Odocoileus virginianus*) inhabited Yellowstone's northern range during the late 1800s and early 1900s (Skinner 1929). That population declined during the 1920s and was essentially extinct by 1930 (Houston 1982:182). These whitetails were associated with thickets of riparian vegetation (Skinner 1929:102), as is the case throughout their range north of the park. In recent years whitetail populations have increased outside the park, and a few have been observed in Yellowstone (Singer 1989). However, whitetails have not become reestablished in the park. In our opinion, the absence of tall-willow communities and other tall deciduous shrub habitats on the northern range due to repeated browsing makes it highly unlikely that whitetails will regain a permanent foothold in the park.

Other Species. Judging from other studies (Page et al. 1978; Casey and Hein 1983; Marcuson 1983; Platts et al. 1983; Taylor 1986; Knopf, Sedgwick, and Cannon 1988; Putman et al. 1989), the decline of tall-willow communities on Yellowstone's northern range may also adversely affect birds, small mammals, and even grizzly bears (*Ursus arctos*) (Kay 1990). The elimination of beaver and willow bank cover probably has also caused decreases in the distribution and numbers of native trout species (W. Platts, pers. comm. 1989). Entire plant and animal communities, not just tall willows, may have been altered by ungulate use in the park. Clearly, the physical stature of the vegetation is important in determining the composition of animal communities which use that habitat. The grazing-induced short-willow communities which presently exist in the park are not ecologically equivalent to the tall-willow communities that once occupied those same areas.

Our findings appear to reject the criteria proposed by Houston (1976) for evaluating the "natural-regulation" hypothesis.

REFERENCES

Apple, L. L. 1983. The use of beavers in riparian/aquatic habitat restoration in a cold desert gully-cut stream system: A case history. Proc. Am. Fish. Soc. 18: 29–35.

Bailey, V. 1930. Animal life of Yellowstone National Park. Charles C. Thomas, Springfield, Ill.

Barlow, J. W., and D. P. Heap. 1872. Report of a reconnaissance of the basin of the upper Yellowstone in 1871. 42d Cong., 2d Sess. S. Doc. 66.

Barmore, W. J. 1981. Population characteristics, distribution, and habitat relationships of six ungulate species on winter range in Yellowstone National Park. Final report. Research Office, Yellowstone National Park.

Barnosky, C. W. 1988. The relationship of climate to sedimentation rates in lakes and ponds. Page 4 in F. Singer, ed. First annual meeting of research and monitoring on Yellowstone's northern range. USDI, Nat. Park Ser., Yellowstone Nat. Park.

Bergerud, A. T., and F. Manuel. 1968. Moose damage to balsam fir–white birch forests in central Newfoundland. J. Wildl. Mgmt. 32:729–746.

Brichta, P. H. 1987. Environmental relationships among wetland community types on the northern range, Yellowstone National Park. M.S. thesis, Univ. of Montana, Missoula.

Cahalane, V. H. 1941. Wildlife surpluses in the national parks. Trans. N. Am. Wildl. Conf. 6:355–361.

———. 1943. Elk management and herd regulation: Yellowstone National Park. Trans. N. Am. Wildl. Conf. 8:95–101.

Casey, D., and D. Hein. 1983. Effects of heavy browsing on a bird community in deciduous forest. J. Wildl. Mgmt. 47:829–836.

Chadde, S., and C. E. Kay. 1988. Willows and moose: A study of grazing pressure, Slough Creek exclosure, Montana, 1961–1986. Mont. For. Conserv. Exper. Sta. Res. Note 24:1–5. Univ. of Montana, Missoula.

Chadde, S. W., P. L. Hansen, and R. D. Pfister. 1988. Wetland plant communities on the northern range of Yellowstone National Park. Final report. School of Forestry, Univ. of Montana, Missoula.

Chase, A. 1986. Playing God in Yellowstone: The destruction of America's first national park. Atlantic Monthly Press, Boston.

Cole, G. F. 1971. An ecological rationale for the natural or artificial regulation of native ungulates in parks. Trans. N. Am. Wildl. Conf. 36:417–425.

———. 1974. Population regulation in relation to K. Paper presented at the annual meeting of the Montana chapter of the Wildlife Society, Bozeman, Mont., Feb. 22, 1974.

————. 1983. A naturally regulated elk population. Pages 62–92 in F. L. Bunnell, D. S. Eastman, and J. M. Peek, eds. Symposium on natural regulation of wildlife populations. Univ. Idaho For. Wildl. Range Exper. Sta. Proc. 14.

Cole, K. 1985. Past rates of change, species richness, and a model of vegetational inertia in the Grand Canyon, Arizona. Am. Nat. 125:289–303.

Daubenmire, R. 1959. A canopy-coverage method of vegetational analysis. NW Sci. 33:43–64.

Despain, D., D. Houston, M. Meagher, and P. Schullery. 1986. Wildlife in transition: Man and nature on Yellowstone's northern range. Roberts Rinehart, Boulder, Colo.

Dieter, C. D. 1987. Habitat use by beaver along the Big Sioux River. M.S. thesis, South Dakota State Univ., Brookings.

Dieter, C. D., and T. R. McCabe. 1989. Factors influencing beaver lodge-site selection on a prairie river. Am. Midl. Nat. 122:408–411.

Dobyns, H. F. 1981. From fire to flood: Historic human destruction of Sonoran Desert riverine oases. Anthropological Pap. no. 20. Ballena Press, Socorro, N.M.

Flook, D. R. 1964. Range relationships of some ungulates native to Banff and Jasper national parks, Alberta. Pages 119–128 in D. J. Crisp, ed. Grazing in terrestrial and marine environments. Blackwell, Oxford.

Grimm, R. L. 1939. North Yellowstone winter range studies. J. Wildl. Mgmt. 3:295–306.

Gruell, G. E. 1980a. Fire's influence on wildlife habitat on the Bridger-Teton National Forest, Wyoming, vol. 1. Photographic record and analysis. U.S. For. Serv. Rcs. Pap. INT-235.

————. 1980b. Fire's influence on wildlife habitat on the Bridger-Teton National Forest, Wyoming, vol. 2. Changes and causes, management implications. U.S. For. Serv. Res. Pap. INT-252.

Gysel, L. W. 1960. An ecological study of the winter range of elk and mule deer in the Rocky Mountain National Park. J. For. 58:696–703.

Hanley, T. A. 1978. A comparison of the line-interception and quadrat estimation methods of determining shrub canopy coverage. J. Range Mgmt. 31:60–62.

Houston, D. B. 1973. Wild fires in northern Yellowstone National Park. Ecology 54:1111–1117.

————. 1976. Research on ungulates in northern Yellowstone National Park. Pages 11–27 in Research in the parks. Transactions of the National Parks Centennial Symposium, December 1971. Nat'l. Park Serv. Symp. Ser. no. 1.

————. 1982. The northern Yellowstone elk: Ecology and management. Macmillan, New York.

Hurlbert, S. H. 1984. Pseudo-replication and the design of ecological field experiments. Ecol. Monogr. 54:187–211.

Jonas, R. J. 1955. A population and ecological study of the beaver (Castor canadensis) of Yellowstone National Park. M.S. thesis, Univ. of Idaho, Moscow.

————. 1956. Northern Yellowstone's changing water conditions and their effect upon beaver. Yellowstone Nature Notes 30(1):6–9.

————. 1959. Beaver. Naturalist 10(2):60–61.

Kay, C. E. 1985. Aspen reproduction in the Yellowstone Park–Jackson Hole area and its relationship to the natural regulation of ungulates. Pages 131–160 in G. W. Workman, ed. Western elk management: A symposium. Utah State Univ., Logan.

————. 1987. Too many elk in Yellowstone? W. Wildlands 13(3):39–41, 44.

————. 1990. Yellowstone's northern elk herd: A critical evaluation of the "natural-regulation" paradigm. Ph.D. dissertation, Utah State Univ., Logan.

Kindschy, R. R. 1989. Regrowth of willow following simulated beaver cutting. Wildl. Soc. Bull. 17:290–294.

Kittams, W. H. 1959. Future of the Yellowstone wapiti. Naturalist 10(2):30–39.

Knopf, F. L., J. A. Sedgwick, and R. W. Cannon. 1988. Guild structure of a riparian avifauna relative to seasonal cattle grazing. J. Wildl. Mgmt. 52:280–290.

Lovaas, A. L. 1970. People and the Gallatin elk herd. Montana Fish and Game Department, Helena.

McMillan, J. F. 1950. Summer food habits of moose (*Alces americana shirasi* Nelson) and effects on various factors on food supply in Yellowstone Park. Ph.D. diss., Univ. of Michigan, Ann Arbor.

————. 1953. Some feeding habits of moose in Yellowstone National Park. Ecology 34:102–110.

Marcuson, P. E. 1983. Overgrazed streambanks depress fishery production in Rock Creek, Montana. Pages 143–157 in J. W. Menke, ed. Proceedings of the workshop on livestock and wildlife-fisheries relationships in the Great Basin, May 3–5, 1977. Univ. Calif. Special Publ. 3301.

Meehan, W. R., and W. S. Platts. 1978. Livestock grazing and the aquatic environment. J. Soil and Water Conserv. 33:274–278.

Morgantini, L. E., and R. J. Hudson. 1989. Nutritional significance of wapiti (*Cervus elaphus*) in migrations to alpine ranges in western Alberta, Canada. Arctic and alpine res. 21:288–295.

Munther, G. L. 1981. Beaver management in grazed riparian ecosystems. Pages 234–241 in Proceedings of the wildlife-livestock relationships symposium. Univ. Idaho For. Wildl. Range Exper. Sta., Moscow.

————. 1983. Integration of beaver into forest management. Paper presented to Colorado-Wyoming chapter of American Fisheries Society, Laramie, Wyo.

Myers, L. H. 1981. Grazing on stream riparian habitats in southwestern Montana. Paper presented at meeting of the Society of Range Management, Tulsa, Okla.

Naiman, R. J., J. M. Melillo, and J. E. Hobbie. 1986. Ecosystem alteration of boreal forest streams by beaver (*Castor canadensis*). Ecology 67:1254–1269.

Nellsun, R. P. 1986. High-resolution climatic analysis and southwest biogeography. Science 232:27–32.

Nelson, J. R., and T. A. Leege. 1982. Nutritional requirements and food habits.

Pages 323–367 in J. W. Thomas and D. E. Toweill, eds. Elk of North America: Ecology and management. Stackpole Books, Harrisburg, Pa.

Norris, P. W. 1880. Annual report of the superintendent of Yellowstone National Park. Pages 573–631 in Annual report of the secretary of the interior for the year ended June 30, 1880.

Packer, P. E. 1963. Soil stability requirements for the Gallatin elk winter range. J. Wildl. Mgmt. 27:401–410.

Page, J. L., N. Dodd, T. O. Osborne, and J. A. Carson. 1978. The influence of livestock grazing on non-game wildlife. Calif.-Nev. Wildl. 1978:159–173.

Parker, M., F. J. Wood, Jr., B. H. Smith, and R. G. Elder. 1985. Erosional downcutting in lower order ecosystems: Have historical changes been caused by removal of beaver? Pages 35–38 in R. R. Johnson, C. D. Ziebell, D. R. Patton, P. F. Ffolliott, and R. H. Hamre, eds. Riparian ecosystems and their management: Reconciling conflicting uses. U.S. For. Serv. Gen. Tech. Rep. RM-120.

Patten, D. T. 1963. Vegetational pattern in relation to environments in the Madison range, Montana. Ecol. Monogr. 33:375–406.

———. 1968. Dynamics of the shrub continuum along the Gallatin River in Yellowstone National Park. Ecology 49:1107–1112.

———. 1969. Succession from sagebrush to mixed conifer forest in the northern Rocky Mountains. Am. Midl. Nat. 82:229–240.

Peek, J. M., A. L. Lovaas, and R. A. Rouse. 1967. Population changes within the Gallatin elk herd, 1932–65. J. Wildl. Mgmt. 31:304–316.

Pengelly, W. L. 1963. Thunder on the Yellowstone. Naturalist 14(2):18–25.

Platts, B., and M. Onishuk. 1988. "Good" beavers, "bad" beavers. Idaho Wildl. (March–April):23–27.

Platts, W. S., R. L. Nelson, O. Casey, and V. Crispin. 1983. Riparian-stream habitat conditions on Tabor Creek, Nevada, under grazed and ungrazed conditions. W. Ass'n Fish Wildl. Agencies 63:162–174.

Putman, R. J., P. J. Edwards, J. C. E. Mann, R. C. How, and S. D. Hill. 1989. Vegetational and faunal changes in an area of heavily grazed woodland following relief of grazing. Biol. Conserv. 47:13–32.

Rogers, G. F., H. E. Malde, and R. M. Turner. 1984. Bibliography of repeat photography for evaluating landscape change. Univ. of Utah Press, Salt Lake City.

Rush, W. M. 1932. Northern Yellowstone elk study. Montana Fish and Game Commission, Helena.

Russell, O. 1965. Journal of a trapper, 1834–1843. Edited by A. L. Haines. Univ. of Nebraska Press, Lincoln.

Seton, E. T. 1909. Canadian beaver. Pages 447–479 in Life-histories of northern animals: An account of the mammals of Manitoba, vol. 1, Grass-eaters. Charles Scribner's Sons, New York.

Shute, D. A. 1981. Decline of riparian communities in a portion of southwestern Wyoming. Report on file. Bureau of Land Management, Rock Springs, Wyo.

Singer, F. J. 1987. Range impacts of the northern Yellowstone elk twenty years after cessation of controls. Research Office, Yellowstone National Park.

————. 1989. The ungulate prey base for large predators in Yellowstone National Park. Res./Resources Mgmt. Rep. no. 1. Yellowstone National Park.

Skinner, M. P. 1927. The predatory and fur-bearing animals of the Yellowstone National Park. Roosevelt Wildl. Bull. 4:163–281.

————. 1928. The elk situation. J. Mammal. 9:309–317.

————. 1929. White-tailed deer formerly in the Yellowstone Park. J. Mammal. 10:101–115.

Smith, B. H. 1980. Not all beaver are bad: Or, an ecosystem approach to stream habitat management, with possible software applications. Pages 32–36 in Proceedings of the fifteenth annual meeting of the Colorado-Wyoming chapter of the American Fisheries Society.

————. 1983a. Riparian willow management: Its problems and potentials, within scope of multiple use on public lands. Pages 15–20 in H. G. Fisser and K. L. Johnson, eds. Proceedings of the Ninth Wyoming Shrub Ecology Workshop. Wyoming Section, Society of Range Management, Lander.

————. 1983b. Restoration of riparian habitats within the BLM-Rock Springs District. Paper presented at Wildlife Habitat Rehabilitation and Reclamation Symposium, Jan. 10–11, 1983, Salt Lake City, Utah.

Smith, R. L., and L. D. Flake. 1983. The effects of grazing on forest regeneration along a prairie river. Prairie Nat. 15:41–44.

Soil Survey Staff. 1975. Soil taxonomy. Soil Conserv. Serv. Agric. Handbook 436. U.S. Department of the Interior, Washington, D.C.

Stevens, D. R. 1980. The deer and elk of Rocky Mountain National Park: A ten-year study. National Park Service, Rocky Mountain National Park, Estes Park, Colo. ROMO-N-13.

Streeter, R. G. 1965. Environmental factors affecting vegetational patterns in the Daly Creek basin of northwestern Yellowstone National Park. M.S. thesis, Virginia Polytechnic Institute.

Taylor, D. M. 1986. Effects of cattle grazing on passerine birds nesting in riparian habitat. J. Range Mgmt. 39:254–258.

Trottier, G. C., and A. Fehr. 1982. Re-evaluation of four range exclosures in Banff National Park, 1981. Canadian Wildlife Service, Edmonton, Alta.

Tyers, D. B. 1981. The condition of the northern Yellowstone winter range in Yellowstone National Park: A discussion of the controversy. M.S. thesis, Montana State Univ., Bozeman.

U.S. General Accounting Office. 1988. Public rangelands: Some riparian areas restored but widespread improvement will be slow. GAO Rep. RCED-88-105. GPO, Washington, D.C.

Warren, E. R. 1926. A study of the beaver in the Yancey region of Yellowstone National Park. Roosevelt Wildl. Annals 1:1–191.

Wright, G. H., and G. H. Thompson. 1935. Fauna of the national parks of the United States. Nat'l Park Serv. Fauna Ser. no. 2. U.S. Department of the Interior, Washington, D.C.

CHAPTER 17   **Summer Range and Elk**
               Population Dynamics in
               Yellowstone National Park
               Evelyn H. Merrill
               and Mark S. Boyce

The limitation of food resources in winter is often pointed out as the mechanism that creates density-dependent effects in ungulate populations. Nutrition during winter and spring particularly influences female reproductive performance and juvenile survival. Poor nutrition of females during gestation increases weight loss, depressing calf birth weight and delaying birth date (Sadlier 1969; Thorne, Dean, and Hepworth 1976; Robinson 1977; Hamilton and Blaxter 1980). In turn, low birth weight and late birth decrease neonatal survival (Sadlier 1969; Guinness, Clutton-Brock, and Albon 1978; Clutton-Brock, Major, Albon, and Guinness 1987). As a population increases, winter survival decreases among light-born calves and the number of late-born calves increases (Clutton-Brock et al. 1987; Clutton-Brock, Albon, and Guinness 1988).

Winter weather can modify density-dependent effects or act independently. In red deer (*Cervus elaphus*), birth weight is closely related to temperatures during the latter stages of gestation but is not correlated with population density (Albon, Guinness, and Clutton-Brock 1983). Picton (1984), however, found in Montana that weather can have significant

Our thanks to Ron Marrs, Mary Bramble-Brodahl, Tammy Willette, Daryl Lutz, Kurt Alt, Claire Simmons, Brad Sauer, Don Despain, Linda Wallace, and John Varley. We are indebted to Mary Meagher for the 1982 elk counts, and to Francis Singer for collecting elk population data for the past three years. Our research was funded through the University of Wyoming–National Park Service Research Center under the directorship of Kenneth Diem.

effects on calf recruitment in elk, but only when populations are high. Survival of elk calves in northwestern Wyoming depends on both climate and population size, whereas cow survival is mediated by climate (Sauer and Boyce 1979, 1983; Boyce 1989). In Yellowstone National Park, population size and winter weather affect calf recruitment in elk (Houston 1982).

Little research has focused on the consequences of summer forage dynamics to ungulate population dynamics, primarily because high-quality forage is usually abundant and the extensive summer ranges of most ungulates are not easily surveyed. Klein (1970) argued, however, that even though winter population size and weather may regulate population numbers, summer-forage quality is responsible for decreases in body size of deer at high population levels. Indeed, experimental evidence indicates that mule deer fawns on marginal or low nutritional diets after weaning are lighter in body weight and smaller in most skeletal parameters by mid-December (Verme and Ozoga 1980b). Because survival and age of maturity are related to body weight (Hamilton and Blaxter 1980; Saether and Haagenrud 1983; Lindstedt and Boyce 1985; Albon et al. 1986), limited growth during summer due to poor nutrition may reduce recruitment and reproductive performance.

We have suggested elsewhere that annual variation in summer-forage quality in Yellowstone National Park is primarily related to phenological development (Merrill et al. 1988). During winters of heavy snow accumulation, plant phenology on summer ranges is delayed, providing high-quality forage through late summer, whereas in low-snowfall years greenup occurs early, providing high-quality forage early in the season. We showed that annual variation in plant phenology can be detected on summer ranges in Yellowstone National Park using remote sensing.

In this chapter we test the hypothesis that food resources on summer ranges explain a significant portion of the variation in population growth and calf recruitment of elk in Yellowstone National Park beyond that attributable to population size and winter weather. We predict increased calf recruitment and population growth in years when high-quality forage is available early in the spring and late into the fall.

STUDY AREA

We studied data from elk populations that winter on the northern range of Yellowstone National Park. The geology of this region has been described by Keefer (1972), and general descriptions of soils and vegetation in the park are given by Despain (1973), Meagher (1973), and Barmore (1985). Elevations range from approximately 1,500 to 3,300 m. The climate of the park is characterized by long, cold winters and short, dry summers. Climatic patterns vary considerably within the park (see Houston 1982). Mean annual precipitation is 41.5 cm and 67.0 cm at Mammoth, Wyoming, and Cooke City, Montana, respectively. Mean daily temperature at Mammoth is $-7.3°C$ in January and $18.3°C$ in July; at Cooke City temperatures are $-10.3°C$ and $13.9°C$ for January and July, respectively.

Winter range used by the northern elk herd is generally a steppe or shrub steppe with interspersions of conifers. High-elevation summer ranges include more continuous coniferous forests, sagebrush-grasslands, wet meadows, herb lands, and alpine tundra.

We focused our study on the portion of elk summer range along the northeastern boundary of the park from Mount Norris to the north, southeast to Miller Creek, and southwest to the Mirror Plateau. Some elk that summer in this area also winter in the Sunlight and Crandall drainages east of the park (Rudd 1982), but most winter along 80 km of the Lamar, Yellowstone, and Gardner River drainages (Houston 1982).

METHODS

Population Characteristics

Population numbers, sex and age classification, and harvest information for elk were obtained from Houston (1982), Meagher (unpubl. data), Singer (1988b), and the Montana Department of Fish, Wildlife, and Parks (1987). Because annual population surveys were made from December to late January, we assumed that survey numbers did not include the majority of mortality that occurred that winter.

Hunting eliminates elk from the northern herd when animals move out of the park into Montana. Harvest from Unit 316 north of the park in Montana, which occurs in September and October, includes a relatively small number of animals (80–146 elk) that would winter within the park. Elk harvest from the late Gardiner hunt (Unit 313) generally occurs in January and February. Harvest levels have been variable in this unit, peaking at 1,462 animals killed in 1984. Early harvests from Unit 313 probably include both resident and park elk (K. Alt and F. Singer, personal communication).

Climatic Data

Our selection of climate variables was based on observations offered by Houston (1982), who indicated that Cooke City has a cooler, wetter climate than Mammoth and best represents conditions on elk summer range (Houston 1982), whereas Mammoth best represents winter range. Mean temperature and total precipitation were obtained from weather stations at Cooke City, Montana, and Mammoth, Wyoming, for the months November through August (U.S. Department of Commerce and National Oceanic Atmospheric Administration 1970–1988). When possible, missing weather data for these stations were obtained from regressions from either Yellowstone Lake, Tower, or Mammoth weather stations.

A winter-severity index was calculated from December through March precipitation and temperature measurements from Mammoth. This index provides a single numerical estimate of relative severity of winter by summing inverse signs (+ or −) of deviations from average monthly precipitation and temperature. Our index was similar, but negative to the index as described by Houston (1982). Signs for precipitation were reversed, because snow impedes feeding and increases locomotive costs, that is, below-average temperature contributes to a positive winter-severity index and above-average precipitation contributes to negative winter severity. Consistent with Houston (1982), we used winter weather data from Mammoth, Wyoming.

Summer Range Phytomass

Vegetation was sampled in 1,300 plots at twenty-five sites scattered across the study area (figure 17.1). Vegetation data and spectral values taken from Landsat Multi-Spectral Scanners for the same field sites on August 6, 1987, were used to derive an algorithm which predicted green herbaceous phytomass from spectral values. This algorithm was used in conjunction with Landsat imagery from previous years to calculate annual green herbaceous phytomass (kg/ha) in summer for eleven years between 1972 and 1987 on a 330-km^2 portion of the summer range. Only nonforested areas were included in our calculations. Based on the among-site variation for 1987 we then estimated green herbaceous phytomass for Landsat images from 1972 to 1987. Details of these methods are given by Merrill et al. (1988).

Estimates of green herbaceous phytomass exhibited a strong pattern dependent on the date of the satellite pass, which we suspect is largely attributable to annual variations in phenology. To correct for this effect, we calculated the average seasonal decline in green phytomass during 1972–1987 using a maxima function. Throughout this chapter, summer phytomass will refer to the difference between the average green herbaceous phytomass for a particular date and our estimate of green herbaceous phytomass.

Use of these estimates as forage available to elk on summer range assumes (1) that our estimates of herbaceous green biomass paralleled growth patterns of plants actually used by elk, and (2) that nonforested

Figure 17.1 Capacitance meter used for sampling green herbaceous phytomass on Mount Norris, northeastern Yellowstone National Park.

communities contributed most to nutrient acquisition by elk, because these are the only communities for which herbaceous phytomass estimates can be made using remote sensing.

Since a strong quadratic correlation was found between yearly estimates of summer pytomass and winter precipitation ($r^2 = .81, p < .01, n = 11$: Merrill et al. 1988), we used this relationship to estimate summer phytomass for three years for which we had elk population data (1971, 1977, and 1985).

Data Analysis

The relations among ungulate population characteristics, winter severity, and summer phytomass, X_is, were evaluated using multiple regression (Kleinbaum and Kupper 1978) of the general form

$$y(t) = b_0 + b_1 N(t) + b_2 X_2 + \ldots \tag{Eq. 1}$$

where b_i is the regression coefficient for each independent variable and $N(t)$ is the total winter count at t. Here, per capita population growth rates are defined

$$r(t) = 1n\{[N(t + 1) + H(t + 1)]/[N(t) - LGH(t)]\} \tag{Eq. 2}$$

where $N(t)$ is the winter population count minus adult males in year t (see Houston 1982), $LGH(t)$ is kill of elk during the late Gardiner hunt (Unit 313) in year t, and H($t + 1$) is the harvest from Unit 316 in year $t + 1$.

Proportion of cow elk with calves (approximately eight months) or year-lings (approximately twenty months) "at heel" was transformed using an arcsine–square root transformation (Zar 1974) prior to data analysis.

Multiple-regression models of per capita growth rates were rewritten as difference equations. These equations were used for predicting the dynamics of elk populations based on population size, summer phytomass, and winter climate in the form

$$N(t + 1) = N(t)\exp[b_0 + b_1 N(t) + b_i X_i(t) + \ldots] \quad \text{(Eq. 3)}$$

with b_i defined to be the regression coefficient and X_is to be the independent variables, as in table 17.1. By using mean values of climate and summer phytomass (X_i), this model collapses to a different equation approximation of the logistic model, with N ultimately converging on carrying capacity, K, that is, where $r(t) = 0$. We also used this model to calculate predicted values of $N(t)$ for each year where $X_i(t)$ was assigned observed values for year t.

RESULTS

Summer phytomass and winter weather had significant effects on per capita growth rate of elk and bison after accounting for the effects of population size (table 17.1). Summer phytomass explained 77 percent of the variation in elk population growth rates after accounting for population size and weather effects (figure 17.2). The proportion of cow elk with calves at heel was significantly correlated with summer phytomass ($r^2 = .61, p = .05, n = 9$) as was the proportion of cow elk with yearlings at heel ($r^2 = .74, p < .05, n = 9$) after the effects of population size were removed. Winter severity contributed significantly to variation in yearling recruitment ($p < .05$), but not calf recruitment ($p > .10$).

Using equation 2 and coefficients from table 17.1, and solving for N where $r = 0$, we predict a K of approximately 14,522 elk, assuming long-term average winters and summer phytomass. The logistic curve associated with this carrying capacity is illustrated by the solid line plotted in figure 17.3. If average winter weather and summer phytomass are similar to those during 1985–1988, however, a K of 17,819 elk would prevail. This value compares favorably with a mean count of 17,445 for 1985–1988. Furthermore, using equation 3 with coefficients from the first model in table 17.1, the mild winters in recent years predict almost precisely the large count of 19,043 elk observed in 1988 (figure 17.3).

Our results indicate that summer phytomass has a significant effect on the population dynamics of elk in Yellowstone Park, although its expres-

Table 17.1 Multiple-regression models for elk population parameters as a function of environmental variables during 1971–1988, Yellowstone National Park

Dependent Variable	Coefficients b_i	Variables X_i	r	p	n
$r(t)$	0.43		.936	< .03	8
	−0.0003	$N(t)$			
	−0.0230	Winter(t)			
	−0.00036	Phyto(t)			
$C(t + 1)$	0.8		.890	< .01	9
	−0.000022	$N(t)$			
	−0.00018	Phyto(t)			
$YR(t + 1)$	0.514		.880	< .05	9
	−0.000019	$N(t)$			
	−0.005	Winter(t)			
	−0.0002	Phyto(t)			

Notes: N = winter count of elk conducted by the National Park Service.

Winter = Winter-severity index based on Mammoth weather data for December–March.

Phyto = average herbaceous green phytomass (kg/ha) on summer range estimated for over 330 km² and corrected for date.

C = arcsine–square root of the proportion of cow elk with calves at heel.

YR = arcsine–square root of the proportion of cow elk with yearlings at heel.

$r(t)$ = per capita growth rate for elk defined at equation 2.

sion is complicated by density and weather effects. Density-dependence effects on pregnancy rates, number of cows with calves at heel, and calf survival during a period when park removals kept population levels below carrying capacity have already been reported (Fowler and Barmore 1979; Houston 1982). Population numbers are currently at or above carrying capacity where we would expect density-dependent effects to be fully expressed (Fowler 1987).

Winter weather explained a significant amount of variation in two of the three population parameters for which we had data. Because winter weather effects on elk calf survival to the first winter (autumn cow:calf ratios) have been well documented (Fowler and Barmore 1979; Houston 1982; Clutton-Brock et al. 1987), especially at high population levels (Picton 1984), we suspect that with a larger data set we would have detected such an effect.

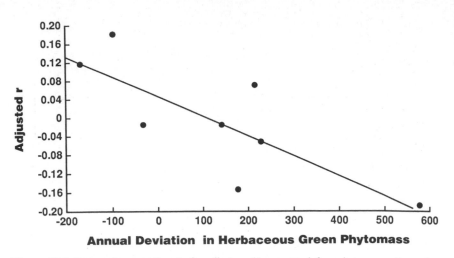

Figure 17.2 Per capita growth rate for elk (eq. 1) corrected for winter severity and population size, as a function of herbaceous green phytomass on summer range corrected for date.

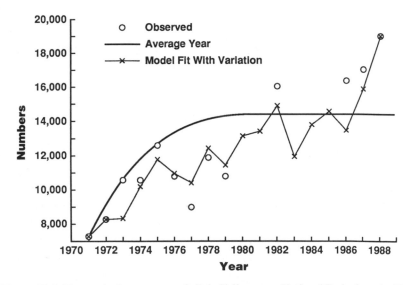

Figure 17.3 Observed winter census of elk in Yellowstone National Park plotted with a logistic fit to the data (solid line). The line with Xs indicates the counts predicted from equation 3 using observed values of winter severity and summer phytomass.

Data used in estimating number of cows with calves at heel was highly variable, representing both ground and helicopter surveys from various observers. Also, different investigators sampled in different areas, potentially creating bias and inflating the among-year variance in population parameters. For example, more calves are usually seen near roads, where counts concentrated in early years (Singer 1988b). Singer (1988a) reviews variation in distribution that may influence sampling, but we are not aware of any systematic biases that would affect our results.

After the effects of population size were removed, summer phytomass explained a significant amount of variation in all the population parameters we examined. Elsewhere we have described that less green phytomass is available in middle to late summer in years when green-up (1) occurs early in spring on ungulate summer ranges and a large proportion of the available ungulate forage is cured by early summer, or (2) is delayed so that green biomass does not reach average levels by midsummer (Merrill et al. 1988). This conclusion was based on a quadratic correlation between green summer phytomass in midsummer and December–March precipitation ($r^2 = .81, p < .01, n = 11$) and suggests that snow accumulation and melt exert an important influence on summer plant phenology.

We suggest that early spring green-up results in high nutrition during the latter stages of gestation, which increases birth weight and juvenile survival (Thorne, Dean, and Hepworth 1976; Clutton-Brock et al. 1987) and is reflected in high male yearling:cow ratios. High nutritional levels at these stages also decrease maternal weight loss, allow cows both to obtain a threshold body weight necessary for conception and to enter the winter with large fat reserves.

In years of high snow accumulation, delayed phenology may provide a higher quality diet for a longer period in late summer and fall than in years of early or average phenological development. Clutton-Brock and Albon (1989) found that when September was dry or rainfall was high, a smaller proportion of red deer milk hinds conceived and overwinter survival of calves and yearlings was lower than in average years. They concluded that drought and heavy rainfall was associated with early decline in food availability and high rains with increased heat loss.

We have focused our attention on summer ranges used by the northern elk herd. Without further investigation, we cannot rule out the possibility that production on summer range is correlated with influences on winter range. For example, delayed phenology may retard the timing of the growth cycle in plants on the winter range so that nutrients normally translocated to roots are fixed in the aerial portions during summer senescence and therefore available (Anderson and Scherzinger 1975).

REFERENCES

Albon, S. D., F. E. Guinness, and T. H. Clutton-Brock. 1983. The influence of climatic variation on the birth weights of red deer (*Cervus elaphus*). J. Zool. (London) 200:295–298.

Albon, S. D., B. Mitchell, B. J. Huby, and D. Brown. 1986. Fertility in female red deer (*Cervus elaphus*): The effects of body composition, age, and reproductive status. J. Zool. (London) 209:447–460.

Anderson, E. W., and R. J. Scherzinger. 1975. Improving quality of winter forage for elk by grazing cattle. J. Range Mgmt. 28:120–125.

Barmore, W. J. 1985. Population characteristics, distribution and habitat relationships of six ungulate species on winter range, Yellowstone National Park. Final report. Research Office, Yellowstone National Park.

Boyce, M. S. 1989. The Jackson elk herd: Intensive wildlife management in North America. Cambridge Univ. Press, Cambridge.

Clutton-Brock, T. H., and S. D. Albon. 1989. Red deer in the Scottish Highlands. Blackwell Scientific, Oxford.

Clutton-Brock, T. H., S. D. Albon, and F. E. Guinness. 1988. Reproductive success in male and female red deer. Pages 325–343 in T. H. Clutton-Brock, ed. Reproductive success: Studies of individual variation in contrasting breeding systems. Univ. of Chicago Press, Chicago.

Clutton-Brock, T. H., M. Major, S. D. Albon, and F. E. Guinness. 1987. Early development and population dynamics in red deer. I. Density dependent effects on juvenile survival. J. Anim. Ecol. 56:53–67.

Despain, D. G. 1973. Major vegetation zones of Yellowstone National Park. Info. Pap. 19. Mimeo.

Fowler, C. W. 1987. A review of density dependence in populations of large mammals. Pages 401–441 in H. H. Genoways, ed. Current mammalogy, vol. 1. Plenum, New York.

Fowler, C. W., and W. J. Barmore. 1979. A population model of the northern Yellowstone elk herd. Pages 427–434 in R. M. Linn, ed. Proc. First Conf. Sci. Res. Nat'l Parks, vol. 1. GPO, Washington, D.C.

Guinness, F. E., T. H. Clutton-Brock, and S. D. Albon. 1978. Factors affecting calf mortality in red deer (*Cervus elaphus*). J. Anim. Ecol. 47:817–832.

Hamilton, W. J., and K. L. Blaxter. 1980. Reproduction in farmed red deer. I. Hind and stag fertility. J. Agric. Sci. (Camb.) 95:261–273.

Houston, D. B. 1982. The northern Yellowstone elk. Macmillan, New York.

Keefer, W. R. 1972. Geologic story of Yellowstone National Park. U.S. Geol. Serv. Bull. 1347. GPO, Washington, D.C.

Klein, D. R. 1970. Food selection by North American deer and their response to over-utilization of preferred plant species. Pages 25–46 in A. Watson, ed. Animal populations in relation to their food resources. Blackwell, Oxford.

Kleinbaum, D. G., and L. L. Kupper. 1978. Applied regression analysis and other multivariable methods. Duxbury Press, North Scituate, Mass.

Lindstedt, S. L., and M. S. Boyce. 1985. Seasonality, fasting endurance and body size in mammals. Am. Nat. 125:873–878.

Meagher, M. M. 1973. The bison of Yellowstone National Park. Nat'l Park Serv. Sci. Monogr. Ser. 1. GPO, Washington, D.C.

Merrill, E. H., M. S. Boyce, R. W. Marrs, and M. K. Bramble-Brodahl. 1988. Grassland phytomass, climatic variation and ungulate population dynamics in Yellowstone National Park. Final report. Yellowstone National Park.

Montana Department of Fish, Wildlife, and Parks. 1987. Big game survey and inventory, Region 3. W-130-R-18. Mimeo.

Picton, H. D. 1984. Climate and the prediction of reproduction of three ungulate species. J. Appl. Ecol. 21:869–879.

Robinson, J. J. 1977. The influence of maternal nutrition on bovine foetal growth. Proc. Nutr. Soc. 36:9–16.

Rudd, W. J. 1982. Elk migrations and movements in relation to weather and hunting in the Absaroka Mountains, Wyoming. M.S. thesis, Univ. of Wyoming, Laramie.

Sadlier, R. M. F. S. 1969. The ecology of reproduction in wild and domestic animals. Methuen, London.

Saether, B. E., and H. Haagenrud. 1983. Life history of moose (*Alces alces*): Reproduction rates in relation to age and carcass weight. J. Mammal. 64:226–232.

Sauer, J. R., and M. S. Boyce. 1979. Time series analysis of the National Elk Refuge census. Pages 9–12 in M. S. Boyce and L. D. Hayden-Wing, eds. North American elk: Ecology, behavior and management. Univ. of Wyoming, Laramie.

———. 1983. Density dependence and survival of elk in northwestern Wyoming. J. Wildl. Mgmt. 47:31–37.

Singer, F. J. 1988a. Elk ecology studies: 1987 annual report. Yellowstone Nat'l Park Rep. National Park Service, Mammoth, Wyo.

———. 1988b. Population summaries of ungulates in Yellowstone National Park. Yellowstone National Park. Mimeo.

Thorne, E. T., R. E. Dean, and W. G. Hepworth. 1976. Nutrition during gestation in relation to successful reproduction in elk. J. Wildl. Mgmt. 40:330–335.

U.S. Department of Commerce and National Oceanic Atmospheric Administration. 1970–1988. Climatological data, Wyoming, Montana: Annual summaries. GPO, Washington, D.C.

Verme, L. J., and J. J. Ozoga. 1980a. Effects of diet on growth and lipogenesis in deer fawns. J. Wildl. Mgmt. 44:315–324.

———. 1980b. Influence of protein-energy intake on deer fawns in autumn. J. Wildl. Mgmt. 44:305–314.

Zar, J. H. 1974. Biostatistical analysis. Prentice-Hall, Englewood Cliffs, N.J.

CHAPTER 18 **Brucellosis in Free-Ranging Bison: Three Perspectives**

E. Tom Thorne, Mary Meagher,
and Robert Hillman

Brucellosis is a bacterial disease of biological, economic, and political importance. Although generally regarded as a bovine
disease, in the Greater Yellowstone Ecosystem brucellosis receives more
notoriety in wildlife than it does in cattle. Brucellosis is biologically
important to wildlife of the GYE, but its significance as a bovine disease
gives it great economic and political importance. As an example, 562 bison
from Yellowstone National Park were taken during the winter of 1988–
1989 in a Montana harvest that was necessary because of concern about
brucellosis transmission to cattle; brucellosis also played a role in the
March 1989 agency reduction of 16 bison from the Jackson herd in Wyoming. Brucellosis in bison of the GYE cannot be discussed without also
considering brucellosis in cattle and elk.

BRUCELLOSIS IN BISON, ELK, AND CATTLE

Bovine brucellosis exists in 120 countries of the world (Bellver-Gallent
1986). It has been eradicated from some countries, but others have not yet
determined if it is present. The disease has existed in all fifty of the United
States, where it was first detected in wildlife in 1917 when diagnosed in
bison in YNP (Tunnicliff and Marsh 1935). During the winter of 1988–1989
brucellosis was detected in 54 percent of the 562 bison shot just north of
YNP (D. Ferlicka, personal communication 1989). In late March 1989,
brucellosis was detected in 11 of 16 bison of the Jackson population.

Brucellosis was first detected in elk in Wyoming in 1930 on the National Elk Refuge (Murie 1951). It was first detected by blood test in elk in YNP in 1933 (Tunnicliff and Marsh 1935). In 1988 brucellosis was detected in 5 of 126 wintering elk from Wall Creek and Ennis Creek, northwest of YNP in Montana (D. Ferlicka, pers. comm. 1989). In Wyoming, where an average of 22,000 elk are fed on winter feedgrounds, both within the GYE and farther south, brucellosis has been detected by blood test and culture in elk from 18 of the twenty-three feedgrounds; this represents approximately 18,000 elk (Thorne, Morton, and Thomas 1978; Thorne, Morton, and Ray 1979; Herriges and Thorne 1988). Brucellosis in elk in Wyoming is believed to be limited to those animals of the feedground complex in the western part of the state. Between 1985 and 1989, nearly 200 elk trapped in southeastern Idaho near Wyoming's Alpine feedground were seronegative for brucellosis. Elk and bison harbor *Brucella abortus* biotypes 1, 2, and 4, the same organisms and biotypes responsible for most bovine brucellosis.

The effects of brucellosis in elk have been thoroughly studied by the Wyoming Game and Fish Department in controlled studies at the department's Sybille Wildlife Research Unit (Thorne, Morton, and Thomas 1978; Thorne, Morton, and Ray 1979; Morton, Thorne, and Thomas 1981). The effects of brucellosis in bison recently were examined in controlled studies at Texas A&M University. There is very little difference between bison, elk, and cattle in their response to brucellosis; abortion is the most common and important sign observed (Thorne, Morton, and Thomas 1978; D. Davis, pers. comm. 1988). In a newly infected herd of cattle, 25 to 85 percent of the cows abort during the third trimester of pregnancy (Bellver-Gallent 1986). In elk, the abortion rate is approximately 50 percent in naturally infected and 50 to 70 percent in artificially inoculated females (Thorne, Morton, and Thomas 1978); in artificially inoculated bison, 100 percent abort (Davis, pers. comm. 1988). Although it cannot be documented, highly infected feedground elk herds may lose as much as 12 percent of their reproductive potential because of brucellosis.

The mode of transmission by bison and elk is the same as with cattle, that is, by contact with reproductive products. Exposure occurs at the time of abortion or birth of a normal calf to an infected female through ingestion or licking of fetal fluids, placentae, fetuses, or recently born calves by a susceptible animal. Concentration of elk during pregnancy on winter feedgrounds has led to the high rate of infection among feedground elk. Bison apparently have a stronger herding instinct than elk, which results in close association during pregnancy, abortion, and calving. Consequently, brucellosis is readily transmitted among bison, and they maintain the disease without exposure to other infected species and in the absence of artificial management practices.

Transmission of brucellosis to cattle confined with infected elk (Thorne, Morton, and Ray 1979) and bison (D. Davis, pers. comm. 1988) during the latter half of pregnancy has been demonstrated under experimental conditions of close contact. Because transmission requires contact with reproductive products, there is little likelihood of transmission from several weeks after parturition until late in the next pregnancy cycle. In elk, therefore, the period of possible transmission is February through mid-June. The breeding season and subsequent calving period of bison in the GYE seems to be somewhat longer than in elk; the period of potential transmission by bison therefore may be longer. Under most circumstances in the GYE, there is no close association of pregnant bison and elk with cattle.

Transmission of brucellosis from free-ranging bison or elk to cattle has not been confirmed under field conditions. Elk to cattle transmission is suspected to have occurred in Wyoming where epidemiologic evaluations failed to detect bovine sources of infection. There is one confirmed case of bison to cattle transmission of brucellosis where ranched, or domestic, bison were pastured with cattle in North Dakota (R. Velure, pers. comm. 1989; U.S. Animal Health Association 1983).

Transmission of brucellosis from bison and elk to cattle is unlikely to occur in the GYE. The states of Montana and Wyoming achieved and have maintained brucellosis-free status regardless of brucellosis in bison and elk. However, the recent large movements of bison in winter to the north boundary area of YNP and in summer in western Wyoming increase the possibility of transmission to cattle. Over time cases would probably occur. Even a single incident of transmission to cattle could have serious consequences for an individual producer and, perhaps, for the livestock industry.

An outbreak of brucellosis detected in November 1988 in cattle near Dubois in Fremont County, Wyoming, is currently under litigation. These cattle graze during summer months in the Union Pass area of the GYE. No bovine source was detected, elk or bison or both were blamed as the source. These cattle pastured during spring and summer with elk, and in 1988 bison were present.

BRUCELLOSIS ERADICATION

Since 1935 the federal government has expended approximately $1.3 billion on brucellosis (J. Huber, pers. comm. 1989). This does not include dollars expended by states to aid in eradication efforts, nor does it include losses by the cattle industry. Available figures for 1952–1981 estimate that losses to the beef and dairy industries exceeded $1.6 billion (Huber, pers. comm. 1989). A 1947 study estimated that the annual losses to the cattle industry in the late 1940s exceeded $90 million (Huber, pers. comm.). Eradication efforts by the industry and by state and federal governments reduce these losses each year.

Since 1940, the U.S. Department of Agriculture has conducted a nation-wide cooperative brucellosis eradication program involving the department, state departments of agriculture, and livestock producers. At the present time, in order to be classified as free of brucellosis a state must have no new cases for at least one year (U.S. Department of Agriculture 1986). It was estimated in 1935 that 11 percent of the cattle herds in the United States were infected with brucellosis. The present infection rate is 0.17 percent. In October 1988, twenty-seven states and the Virgin Islands were free of brucellosis, and there were only thirty-eight infected herds in the western United States (U.S. Department of Agriculture 1988). Of the three states bordering YNP, Montana and Wyoming were considered free of brucellosis in 1985 and Idaho in 1990.

The brucellosis program consists of surveillance to detect infected herds, vaccination to enhance immunity, a test and slaughter system to eliminate infection in herds, and epidemiological testing to trace exposed animals from or to infected herds.

The surveillance program consists of (1) the Brucella Ring Test (BRT), which is performed quarterly on milk from all dairy herds, (2) the Market Cattle Identification (MCI), which tests most adult cattle at slaughter, and (3) change of ownership testing, which is required by many states; animals must have a negative test prior to sale.

The vaccination program consists of calfhood vaccination (female calves vaccinated at four to twelve months of age; mandatory in approximately twenty-five states) and whole herd vaccination (vaccination of all females over four months of age in the herd; used in many states to enhance immunity in the face of great exposure potential).

Herds that have suspicious BRT tests or reactors on the MCI or change of ownership test must undergo a herd test. When infection is found, the herd is quarantined. Adult vaccination may be used. Calves are vaccinated, and the herd is tested every thirty days. Reactors are removed and sent to slaughter. The herd will be tested until no more reactors are found, after which it must undergo two negative tests, the second of which must be at least six months after removal of the last reactor. The quarantine can be released after the second negative test. All herds or animals that are exposed to the infected herd are traced epidemiologically and tested for infection.

Once a state becomes free of brucellosis, requirements for moving cattle within and from that state are relaxed, and the cost of doing business is reduced. Livestock can be moved from free areas without testing, because other states accept free status as a guarantee that the cattle are free of the disease.

An infected herd becomes a threat not only to neighboring producers but also to the status of the entire state and other states in the marketing area, because infection is often present and has opportunity to spread to other herds for several months before it is discovered. If a state becomes reinfected, surveillance techniques and testing must be amplified, marketing costs will increase, and the reputation of the state's livestock industry is lost. For the individual rancher, infection would most likely result in the loss of his entire herd. Two of the three states adjacent to YNP have laws that provide authority to require newly infected herds under certain circumstances to be depopulated in an effort to maintain free status. An example of an appropriate circumstance for depopulation is imminent danger of spread to other cattle herds.

The Wyoming Game and Fish Department initiated studies in 1977 to determine if brucellosis in feedground elk could be controlled by vaccination (Thorne, Walthall, and Dawson 1981). Control by vaccination was chosen rather than eradication because testing and slaughter of seroreactive animals would be logistically and politically impossible and biologically unacceptable. The rationale behind control of brucellosis in elk is to obtain a 90 percent or greater vaccination rate. Once this is accomplished, abortion and concomitant transmission will decline and resistance in exposed animals will increase. The combination of less exposure and enhanced resistance will result in fewer infections. The course of existing infections will not be altered by vaccination, but the infection rate will significantly decline as infected animals cycle out of the population through attrition. Control by vaccination will take many years and may never result in eradication of the disease; control by vaccination thus should be viewed as a long-term endeavor. The results will be increased elk calf production in previously infected feedground herds and great reduction, if not elimination, of elk sources of transmission to cattle.

Elk vaccinated with *B. abortus* strain 19 vaccine have about 70 percent calving success following challenge, whereas unvaccinated elk experience only about 30 percent calving success following similar challenge (Thorne,

Walthall, and Dawson 1981; Herriges, Thorne, and Anderson 1988). High doses of vaccine cause abortion when administered to pregnant cow elk, but this can be prevented by using low doses. Strain 19 vaccine can be lyophilized and placed in bioabsorbable lightweight biobullets shot from an air gun manufactured by BallistiVet, Inc.

In 1983 field studies were initiated to test the biobullet system on free-ranging feedground elk (Herriges, Thorne, and Anderson 1988). Depending on the feedground, one to several weeks are required to acclimate elk to the report of the air gun. On a few feedgrounds elk must first be accustomed to human activity, which may require a couple of years. Once acclimated, most elk, especially calves, can be vaccinated within a few weeks; it is not necessary to vaccinate bulls. Whole-herd vaccination can be achieved within one or two years by vaccinating calves and cows; if only calves are vaccinated, it will take five to seven years. After completion of whole-herd vaccination, only calves need to be vaccinated. Results to date have been very encouraging; approximately 15,000 elk have been vaccinated on nine feedgrounds. About 1,600 elk were vaccinated on the National Elk Refuge during the winters of 1988–1989 and 1989–1990.

Brucellosis has been eradicated from bison on many commercial ranches and among refuge and park herds using traditional bovine techniques—calfhood vaccination with strain 19 and test and slaughter of reactor animals. This approach, however, has never been applied to bison as numerous and as widely ranging as those of the GYE.

Studies currently in progress at Texas A&M University are examining the efficacy of strain 19 vaccination in bison, and the results have not been as encouraging as expected (D. Davis, pers. comm. 1989). Vaccination of pregnant bison with strain 19 caused 69 percent of them to abort. Of the vaccinated adult cows, 48 percent raised calves following challenge one year after vaccination, whereas no unvaccinated cows raised calves following challenge. Postvaccination challenge trials with bison vaccinated as calves two years previously are in progress. Protection, in terms of calving rate, does not appear to be good.

BISON IN THE GREATER YELLOWSTONE ECOSYSTEM

There are two free-ranging bison herds within the GYE. The large herd in YNP has three subpopulations: the Mary Mountain, Northern Range, and Pelican herds. The second herd, known as the Jackson herd, resides in Jackson Hole, Wyoming, and is much smaller.

Bison numbers in Yellowstone National Park were at a historic high during the winter of 1988–1989, with the annual midwinter aerial count totaling 2,707. Major influences on increases in all three subpopulations appeared to be climatic, generated by a series of wet summers and mild winters. The largest subpopulation, the Mary Mountain herd, increased from an estimated 1,200 in the early 1980s to about 1,600 in 1989, and the Northern Range bison increased from an estimated 250 to about 700 in 1988. Increases among the Northern Range herd probably also reflected recent winter-range expansion and perhaps some prewinter emigration from the Pelican subpopulation.

Mixed groups of bison were seen in August and September 1988 in locations where they had not previously been recorded at that time of year. This suggests that high-equilibrium numbers that have fully utilized available habitat with very favorable conditions were on a collision course with the combined influences of drought, fire, and winter. Winter conditions were average to slightly more, severe than average on the several bison winter ranges during 1988–1989. Severe drought the summer of 1988 affected all summer and winter ranges. In addition, the fires of 1988 burned extensive areas of summer range used by the Pelican and Northern Range bison, perhaps 40 percent of the bison-use area of the northern winter range, and 10 percent of the Firehole range (M. Meagher, unpublished data 1988). Winterkill is expected to be similar in pattern to that of 1982, when field surveys showed considerable mortality among calves and among the oldest animals.

A complex of influences contributed to the present Northern Range situation (Meagher 1989b). Beginning with stress dispersal during the winter of 1975-1976, the bison learned new foraging areas and traveled the energy-efficient plowed road. Management attempts to deter movements by blocking natural travel routes probably increased use of the road (Meagher 1989a). Population increases and changes in winter severity contributed, but the gregariousness of bison appears to have been the most important factor.

The Northern Range subpopulation moves regardless of winter severity, apparently in an attempt to recolonize historical habitat. Rather than gradually expanding winter range as their numbers increased, the bison escalated their movements abruptly. By winter 1985–1986, several hundred bison were using the boundary area in spite of mild winters and little snow (Meagher 1989b). During the more usual winter of 1988–1989 nearly the entire herd eventually moved. Roughly 200 were located in the boundary area by December 1. By March 3 only 29 bison were east of Tower where at least 200 bison had wintered in the past.

After cessation of bison population reductions in the 1960s the Park Service implemented a boundary control program to prevent contact between wandering bison and cattle. A few bison were shot in specified boundary areas of the park; state authorities removed some outside the park. This appeared to work well for a time. When larger movements began on the northern range in 1976, the park began testing methods to deter or block movements (Meagher 1989a). These attempts were sometimes successful at a given time and place, but they ultimately were unsuccessful and movements escalated. The entire subpopulation learned new ranges and travel routes. Temporary success sometimes just moved the problem to another site. Operations became difficult as bison developed conditioned avoidance behavior and hazard to personnel increased. The experimental efforts can be summarized by noting that bison can be hazed or herded where they want to go. Removal of a large number, as occurred during winter 1988–1989, will lessen the conflict, but it appears unlikely that movements will stop.

Due to concern about transmission of brucellosis from bison to cattle, the state of Montana implemented public hunting by permit in 1985 to remove bison that left the park. During the winter of 1988–1989 removals from the Northern Range subpopulation totaled 286 bulls, 234 cows, and 53 calves (M. Meagher, unpubl. data 1989). The hunt was carefully regulated by warden personnel; the necessary intensity of hunting pressure, however, apparently forced some bison into side areas and farther north than would otherwise have occurred. As the hunt progressed, observers could readily distinguish newly arrived naive groups of animals from those that had previously been hunted; the latter were much more wary.

In early March 1989, when nearly all the Northern Range subpopulation was in the boundary area, Montana officials requested from the Park a minimum number of bison to be left. After considering the known history of the herd, their demonstrated ability to recover from low numbers, ecological relationships, public viewing opportunities, and aesthetics, park officials requested 200 bison be left after the hunt. Air observations indicated that at least 300 bison remained in the Northern Range subpopulation after the hunt (M. Meagher, unpubl. data 1989).

From the perspective of the Montana Department of Fish, Wildlife, and Parks, recreational hunting managed by permit is an appropriate tool to deal with conflicts between private land uses and wildlife. This perspective applies to elk. The 1989 bison permit hunt, however, served to further define the politics, complexity, and problems associated with the hunt and the presence of bison and brucellosis. The hunt served as a workable tool, but not as a panacea for the issues the bison represent.

The Jackson herd in Wyoming originated from animals accumulated by the National Park Service for display in the old Jackson Hole Wildlife Park. Landownership and jurisdictional authority over the Jackson herd make the presence of free-ranging bison in Jackson Hole a complex question. In 1969 the herd consisted of 8 bison, which were released to roam freely in Grand Teton National Park; they were believed to be free of brucellosis at that time. During the ensuing years the rate of increase was very slow; numbers were probably controlled by severe winter conditions. Beginning in 1978 these bison discovered the feedlines and artificial feed provided for elk on the National Elk Refuge. Winter mortalities apparently declined considerably, and the Jackson herd rapidly increased in size. At this point, control of the herd became an economic and political matter rather than a biological one. Once the herd reached 50 to 60 animals, it began breaking up into smaller subunits and damage to private property and injury of domestic livestock began to occur. Simultaneously, the consumption of natural forage and feed purchased for elk began to increase on the National Elk Refuge.

The Jackson bison herd currently numbers just over 100 animals. They spend the summer months in Grand Teton National Park and migrate to the National Elk Refuge feedlines for the winter. At times during these movements, they cross private land and mingle with cattle. More than ever before in recent history, bison were observed, and in many cases shot, throughout the Wind River Mountains and in other parts of western Wyoming during the summer of 1988. The origin of these bison, approximately 8 to 19 animals, is not known, but the Jackson herd is the most likely source. Those that were shot were likely killed because of concern about brucellosis transmission.

During the past several years the subject of the Jackson bison as a wild free-ranging herd has been studied and discussed by the Wyoming Game and Fish Department, the U.S. Fish and Wildlife Service, the National Park Service, the U.S. Forest Service, and private individuals and groups within the Jackson Hole region. Draft plans were prepared, and the National Elk Refuge and Grand Teton National Park completed a draft environmental assessment in February 1988. The public response was varied and without a general consensus for any one of the proposed alternatives. Concerns were expressed over proposed reductions and size of the Jackson herd and methods used to control herd size. It was assumed, because of their winter association with brucellosis-infected elk, that the bison were also infected; it was assumed also that brucellosis placed constraints upon how the herd could be controlled (N. Swanson, pers. comm. 1988). Transfer from a brucellosis infected or exposed herd is not permitted unless the animals are spayed or castrated. Otherwise, bison could be removed from the herd only if sent to slaughter. There was no strong agreement between the agencies and the public regarding the desired size of the Jackson bison herd. The Wyoming state veterinarian, however, speaking for the Wyoming Livestock Board and stockgrowers, expressed a strong belief that the herd should be reduced to and held at 50 animals in order to decrease the opportunity of transmission of brucellosis from bison to cattle; he recommended also that a brucellosis-control program should be created (Swanson, pers. comm. 1989).

An interim management plan for the Jackson bison herd was adopted and implemented in March 1989 (Nat'l. Park Service et al. 1988). Under the interim plan, the herd is to be held between 90 and 110 animals. Consequently, 16 bison were shot in an agency reduction in late March 1989, and a public hunting season occurred in the fall and winter of 1989–1990.

THE BISON-BRUCELLOSIS CONFLICT

Federal and state governments and livestock producers in the states adjoining the GYE are concerned about the apparent lack of progress in solving the brucellosis problem, and they are concerned about the threat of reintroduction of brucellosis to neighboring cattle populations. The potential loss of brucellosis-free status because of the reservoir in the GYE is a constant worry to stockmen. The threat of introduction of brucellosis infection from bison to cattle is very real. The livestock industry and the government feel they have expended far too much money, time, and effort to allow the brucellosis threat in the GYE to continue unabated (N. Swanson, pers. comm. 1989; G. Nelson, pers. comm. 1989; D. Ferlicka, pers. comm. 1989). They believe that the technology and expertise are available to resolve the problem without destroying the bison population or other wildlife. However, the management objective of YNP as a natural area allows natural regulatory processes to operate to the maximum extent possible within the park, an objective that probably can be tested only in a large national park. The origin of *Brucella abortus* is important to park managers.

Boundary control, whether by attempts to block movements or by permit-hunt removal addresses the problem of transmission from YNP bison indirectly. Direct methods to reduce the incidence of brucellosis must address appropriate technology. Past experience with procedures applicable to livestock demonstrated that such a program would be devastating to the bison and to the ecological relationships dependent on them. Consideration of any direct brucellosis program must include the logistics of application, its biological effectiveness, and the behavior and biology of bison.

Wyoming is currently investigating the possibility of controlling brucellosis in elk. Although strain 19 vaccine in elk is not perfect, it does produce adequate immunity to reduce abortion and to afford protection against infection. The biobullet delivery system appears to provide a safe and effective means of administration of vaccine to feedground elk. Thus it appears that a brucellosis-control program for feedground elk is feasible. If such a program is fully implemented, it will likely require vaccinating elk on all feedgrounds, possibly as far into the future as elk are artificially fed during winter. This will require a strong commitment from the Wyoming Game and Fish Department, the U.S. Fish and Wildlife Service, and the U.S. Department of Agriculture.

Because of the concentration of bison and elk on feedgrounds of the National Elk Refuge in winter and their occasional association on winter, spring, and summer ranges, brucellosis can never be fully controlled in elk unless it is also controlled in bison of the GYE. This is especially true of the Jackson herd.

As we examine brucellosis in bison of the GYE from three perspectives— (1) that of the livestock industry and officials responsible for brucellosis eradication, (2) that of elk and a wildlife management agency, and (3) that of ecosystem maintenance and the National Park Service—it is clear the disease presents a serious and complex problem to managers and administrators responsible for bison, elk, and cattle of the ecosystem. The bovine brucellosis outbreak in Fremont County, Wyoming, provides an example of the continuing threat brucellosis in bison and elk poses to the livestock industry. The outbreak may have had a bovine source; but in the absence of a clear-cut bovine origin wildlife have been blamed. Determining whether a bison or an elk was the source is impossible. The ill will on the part of the livestock industry toward wildlife, especially those harboring brucellosis, in any case has been strengthened. Even if the outbreak is determined not to have originated from wildlife, its occurrence will strengthen the belief that the question is not whether, but when brucellosis will be transmitted from wildlife to cattle. Whereas most people regard the GYE and its wildlife as a world treasure, because of its reservoir of brucellosis, others regard the GYE as a threat to an important international industry and economy and a black eye to their efforts.

The livestock industry is proceeding at great cost with the brucellosis eradication program and will fight to maintain its free status. Wyoming is implementing a brucellosis-control program for elk. Both programs could be confounded by brucellosis in bison. Yet bison are an integral component of the GYE, and eradication of brucellosis in bison by traditional means would eliminate bison as a part of the ecosystem. This would be contrary to National Park Service policy and contrary to the will of the vast majority of the public.

Progress toward resolving the problem without destroying a wildlife resource of the GYE is being made, albeit slowly. A technique has been developed recently that should control brucellosis in elk, some officials responsible for brucellosis eradication have softened their demand for a traditional test and slaughter approach to brucellosis in bison, and National Park Service representatives have conducted research on boundary control and participated in informative meetings to address the problem. The Wildlife Diseases Committee of the U.S. Animal Health Association discussed the problem in a nonpolitical manner at its 1987 and 1988 meetings (Thorne et al. 1987, 1988), representatives of most of the agencies and industries involved have participated in two tristate brucellosis meetings, and an ad hoc technical committee on bison and brucellosis in Yellowstone has been formed. That committee, which was created to discuss and resolve technical questions regarding brucellosis in bison of YNP, met in Little Rock, Arkansas, in 1988, in May 1989 in Yellowstone National Park, and again in Denver in 1990; it has expanded in scope to include elk and cattle and the GYE.

There is no easy solution to the problem of brucellosis in the GYE that is satisfactory to all concerned parties. Additional research on strain 19 and other vaccines should be conducted with bison, and field trials with the biobullet and strain 19 system should be conducted. The question of whether *Brucella abortus* is native to bison should be resolved. Efforts should be made by wildlife and land management agencies and by cattlemen to reduce contact between bison and cattle. Acquiring winter range for wildlife is one possible avenue; delaying movement of cattle to forest grazing allotments until after bison and elk calving periods may be another. Cattle in and around the GYE should be vaccinated against brucellosis, and surveillance for brucellosis in cattle may have to be continued indefinitely. Harvest of bison that could come into contact with cattle will undoubtedly continue to be necessary; but it is hoped that ways can be found to reduce this measure. Finally, compromise and dialogue must be continued and increased, and the matter of brucellosis in bison of the GYE addressed in a sound manner with a minimum of disruption to the ecosystem.

REFERENCES

Armstrong, J. B. et al. 1983. Report of the Committee on Brucellosis: A case history of a brucellosis outbreak in a brucellosis free state which originated in bison. Proc. U.S. Anim. Health Ass'n. 87:171–172.

Bellver-Gallent, M., ed. 1986. Animal health yearbook. FAO-WHO-0IE. Page 34.

Herriges, J. D., and E. T. Thorne. 1988. The incidence and importance of brucellosis in elk in northwestern Wyoming. Pages 38–40b in Job Perf. Rep. BDGACAB551. Wyoming Game and Fish Department, Cheyenne.

Herriges, J. D., E. T. Thorne, and S. L. Anderson. 1988. Immune response of elk vaccinated with a reduced dose of strain 19 *Brucella* vaccine. Pages 42–54 in Job Perf. Rep. BDSWCBF551. Wyoming Game and Fish Department, Cheyenne.

Meagher, M. 1989a. Evaluation of boundary control for bison of Yellowstone National Park. Wildl. Soc. Bull. 17:15–19.

———. 1989b. Range expansion by bison of Yellowstone National Park. J. Mammal. 70:670–675.

Morton, J. K., E. T. Thorne, and G. M. Thomas. 1981. Brucellosis in elk. III. Serologic evaluation. J. Wildl. Dis. 17:23–31.

Murie, O. 1951. The elk of North America. Stackpole Books, Harrisburg, Pa.

National Park Service, U.S. Fish and Wildlife Service, U.S. Forest Service, and Wyoming Game and Fish Dept. 1988. Interim agreement management plan of the Jackson bison herd. Period of agreement–September 1, 1988 to December 31, 1994.

Thorne, E. T., et al. 1988. Report of the committee on wildlife diseases. Proc. U.S. Anim. Health Ass'n. 92:514–523.

———. 1987. Report of the committee on wildlife diseases. Proc. U.S. Anim. Health Ass'n. 91:97–103.

Thorne, E. T., J. K. Morton, and W. C. Ray. 1979. Brucellosis: Its effect and impact on elk in western Wyoming. Pages 212–220 in M. S. Boyce and L. D. Hayden-Wing, eds. North American elk: Ecology, behavior, and management. Univ. of Wyoming, Laramie.

Thorne, E. T., J. K. Morton, and G. M. Thomas. 1978. Brucellosis in elk. I. Serologic and bacteriologic survey in Wyoming. J. Wildl. Dis. 14:74–81.

Thorne, E. T., T. J. Walthall, and H. A. Dawson. 1981. Vaccination of elk with strain 19 *Brucella abortus*. Proc. U.S. Anim. Health Ass'n. 85:359–374.

Tunnicliff, E. A., and H. Marsh. 1935. Bang's disease in bison and elk in Yellowstone National Park and the National Bison Range. J. Am. Vet. Medic Ass'n. 86:745–752.

U.S. Department of Agriculture. 1986. Class free states: brucellosis eradication uniform methods and rules. USDA/APHIS/Veterinary Services. APHIS 91–1.

U.S. Department of Agriculture. 1988. Herds quarantined because of brucellosis. USDA/APHIS/Veterinary Services/Cattle Diseases and Surveillance Staff. Monthly report.

CHAPTER 19   **A Prehistoric Perspective**
on the Northern Range
Cathy Whitlock,
Sherilyn C. Fritz, and
Daniel R. Engstrom

In 1963 the Advisory Board on Wildlife Manage-
ment, chaired by A. Starker Leopold, submitted a report to Secretary of the
Interior Stewart Udall. The document, now known as the Leopold report,
provided an independent evaluation of wildlife management policy for the
National Park Service. The recommendations of the report formulated a
general philosophy for ecosystem management in Yellowstone National
Park, which has been subject to a wide variety of interpretation and criticism. At the heart of some of the controversy is the importance of understanding and reconstructing a prehistoric condition. The report stated that

> as a primary goal we would recommend that the biotic associations within each
> park be maintained, or where necessary recreated, as nearly as possible in the
> condition that prevailed when the area was first visited by the white man. A
> national park should represent a vignette of primitive America. . . . A reason-
> able illusion of primitive America could be recreated, using the utmost in skill,
> judgment, and ecological sensitivity. (Leopold et al. 1963:32)

At issue is whether such a goal is attainable, but more fundamental is
whether the prehistoric condition can be known in sufficient detail to guide
management policies.

This research was funded by grants from the University of Wyoming–National Park
Service Research Center (to C. Whitlock Barnosky and H. E. Wright) and the National
Science Foundation (ATM-8815170 to C. Whitlock). Our thanks to Robert Gress-
well, Mary Meagher, and Brian Sherrod for their helpful comments on the chapter.

Critics of the Park Service point to the management of Yellowstone's northern range as a case where the Leopold report has led to ill-advised decisions. The debate focuses on the current policy of "natural regulation," in which the northern range is left alone to function as a natural ecosystem. The policy was adopted only after earlier practices were shown to be unsuccessful; from 1886 to 1930 park policy promoted the expansion of ungulate herds through winter feeding and the elimination of predators by hunting. Concern for the long-term viability of winter rangelands, however, led to a new policy of direct reduction of elk populations by trapping and shooting from 1935 to 1968 (Houston 1982). By 1969 political and scientific criticism was so great that elk removals were curtailed, and the natural-regulation policy was adopted and tested. In ungulate populations, natural regulation is determined by the carrying capacity of the winter range, rather than by human manipulation, even though—as critics are quick to note—key elements of the pristine ecosystem are missing, for example, predators, native Americans, and contiguous range outside the park (Chase 1986; Kay 1985).

Central to the natural-regulation concept is the premise that it provides the closest approximation of a prehistoric condition. To test this hypothesis requires ultimately that the environmental history be known and that conditions after park establishment in 1872 be compared with those that prevailed before. Fortunately, the fossil record offers windows on the past that disclose past environmental conditions through a set of paleoecologic indicators. Each indicator has specialized resolving powers (and assumptions) in reconstructing the past; the best approach is always multidisciplinary.

In this chapter, we review some of the research that has been undertaken on the prehistoric northern range, particularly with respect to possible deterioration of the landscape from overutilization of food resources and increased erosion. Two time periods are of interest: the past 14,000 years (referred to as the postglacial record), beginning with the retreat of late-Pleistocene glaciers and including climatic and vegetational changes since then. The time resolution for this interval is fairly coarse, based on radiocarbon dating with a precision of plus or minus a hundred years or more. The second period of interest is the past 100–150 years, which can be examined on a yearly or decadal scale by lead-210 dating.

THE PALEOECOLOGIC RECORD

Paleoecologic data are complex, consisting of many types of indicators obtained from samples scattered through space and time (Birks and Birks

1980). To interpret these data sets, the principle of uniformitarianism—that the present is key to understanding the past—is assumed. The reconstruction of past conditions thus reflects how much is known of the relationship between environmental indicators and the modern environment. Because the data sets that are used as paleoecologic tools have responded to a combination of environmental forcings, it is often not possible to identify a single agent of change in the past; one must select the most plausible of multiple working hypotheses. When several types of data vary synchronously over a wide area, however, the cause is probably a large-scale force operating on the region, such as climate change or dramatic shifts in land usage.

Lakes and their sedimentary constituents are important repositories of paleoecologic information. The data sources include both biotic and abiotic components that enter the system through airborne fallout, slope movement, stream transport, and internal biologic production (figure 19.1). Fossil pollen provides an integrated picture of vegetation change. The assemblage of pollen types records changes in local riparian communities as well as in upland vegetation around the site. The scale of the pollen-recruitment area varies primarily with the size of the basin; large lakes collect pollen from a bigger region than small wetland hollows (Jacobson and Bradshaw 1981). The vegetational reconstruction rests on a knowledge of the modern pollen "rain" and its relation to modern vegetation. It also depends on the taxonomic level to which pollen can be identified; species of grass, for example, cannot usually be distinguished by their pollen, whereas members of the rose family often can. When pollen data are examined from several sites in different ecological settings, it is possible to infer past climatic changes affecting an entire region. Such paleoclimate scenarios can be tested against other proxy data and also against simulations produced by general circulation models (Cooperative Holocene-Mapping Project members 1988).

Sedimentary charcoal, another source of paleoecologic information, provides a means of recognizing past fires and determining their frequency. Charcoal data can be compared with both the vegetation and the paleo-climatic reconstructions to determine how changes in the disturbance regime affect long-term community composition. Fossil diatoms and other algae are excellent indicators of limnologic conditions, including changes in nutrient status, water depth, littoral to benthic area, and salinity. The chemical constituents of the sediments themselves provide information on erosion rates, sources of clastic input, nutrient enrichment, and lake productivity (Engstrom and Wright 1984).

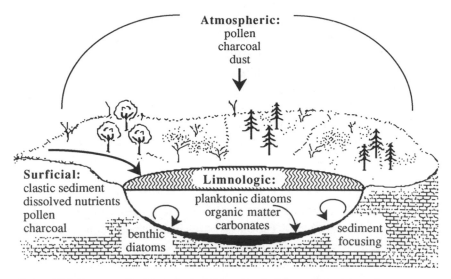

Figure 19.1 Sources of paleoecologic information in lake-sediment records.

In Yellowstone Park the paleoecologic record will register the episodes of heavy use by elk, bison, antelope, and deer in predictable ways. If ungulates had been the sole agent of environmental change since the park's formation, the following changes would have been expected during periods of intense use: (1) an increase in silt derived from eroded hill slopes or from trampled lake margins; (2) a decrease in the pollen of browse species favored by ungulates, namely aspen, willow, alder, and birch; (3) an increase in the pollen of weedy plants associated with soil disturbance, including ragweed and various chenopods; and (4) an increase in indicators of eutrophic conditions in the lake, caused by increased manuring near the lake shore. In reality, of course, the model is by no means so simple, because other environmental changes have occurred. Most notably, climate has fluctuated, fire frequency has varied, and beaver populations and their utilization of riparian plants have changed. Any landscape reconstruction has to consider the synergistic effect of all factors.

THE POSTGLACIAL RECORD

Several pollen records are available from the Yellowstone region (figure 19.2; Baker 1976, 1983; Waddington and Wright 1974; Barnosky 1987). Two from the northern range span the past 14,000 years and thus have direct bearing on its long-term history. Records from Blacktail Pond (Gennett and Baker 1986) and Gardners Hole (Baker 1983) suggest that tundra-

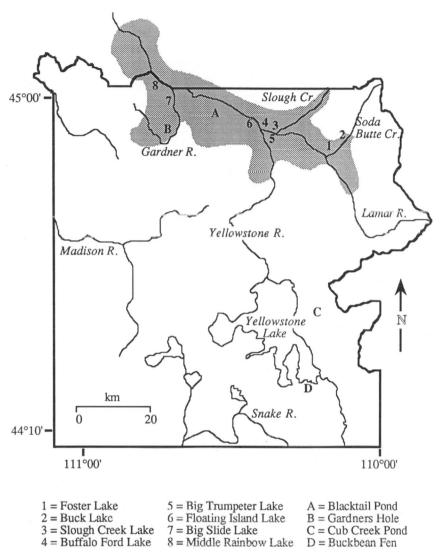

1 = Foster Lake	5 = Big Trumpeter Lake	A = Blacktail Pond
2 = Buck Lake	6 = Floating Island Lake	B = Gardners Hole
3 = Slough Creek Lake	7 = Big Slide Lake	C = Cub Creek Pond
4 = Buffalo Ford Lake	8 = Middle Rainbow Lake	D = Buckbean Fen

Figure 19.2 Locality map of paleoecologic site. Shaded area is the northern range.

like communities were present from the earliest stages of ice retreat to ca.
12,800 years ago (figure 19.3). Birch (*Betula glandulosa* and *B. occidentalis*), aspen (*Populus tremuloides*), and willow (*Salix* spp.) were not major
components of tundra vegetation on the northern range, although their
pollen is found in sites in the southern part of the park and in the Jackson
Hole region (Baker 1976; Waddington and Wright 1974; Barnosky 1987).

BLACKTAIL POND, YELLOWSTONE N.P.
Gennett and Baker, 1986

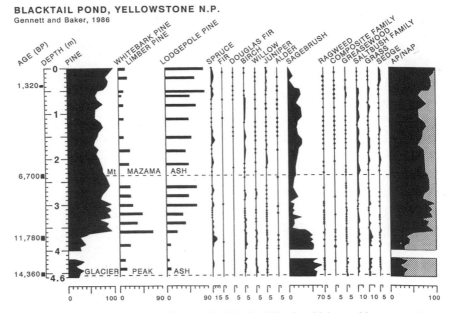

Figure 19.3 Pollen percentage diagram for Blacktail Pond, which provides a record of vegetational and climate change for the past ca. 14,000 years.

Spruce (*Picea engelmannii*) invaded the area ca. 12,800 years ago, leading to the formation of parkland communities. After ca. 11,800 years ago, whitebark pine (*Pinus albicaulis*), subalpine fir (*Abies lasiocarpa*), and lodgepole pine (*Pinus contorta*) moved into the region, and forest was established. The inference from the pollen data is that growing-season temperature increased, permitting tundra and spruce parkland to be replaced by closed conifer forest.

Between 9,300 and 6,700 years ago, a forest composed almost exclusively of lodgepole pine developed on the northern range. This period apparently was a heyday for lodgepole pine everywhere, inasmuch as it grew beyond its present range throughout the western United States. Conditions warmer and drier than today seem to explain the northern range vegetation at this time. Regional climate reconstructions for the northwestern United States suggest that solar radiation between 9,000 and 6,000 years ago was 8 percent higher in summer than it is today. The effect was to increase July temperature and evapotranspiration rates and to decrease precipitation. Drought conditions favored more frequent fires, as evidenced by the elevated levels of charcoal in the sediment (Barnosky, Anderson, and Bartlein 1987).

Lodgepole pine forest on the northern range was replaced by Douglas fir parkland ca. 6,700 years ago, but in the past 1,600 years percentages of lodgepole pine again increased, reflecting its present role in the vegetation. The Blacktail Pond record suggests that the present-day parkland formed ca. 6,700 years ago, when percentages of *Artemisia* (probably bigleaf sagebrush) and Chenopodiineae (saltbush and amaranth families) became high.

Two important points are raised from these long-term records. The first is that in the past 14,000 years the northern range sustained modern taxa in communities different from those of today. Tundra, spruce-fir-pine forest, pine forest, and Douglas fir parkland have all been present in postglacial time. These shifts in vegetation were greater than any vegetational perturbation in historical times, and they were driven by large-scale changes in the climate system. In response, vegetation throughout the northwestern United States changed relatively synchronously and in a comparable way climatically.

A second consideration is the role of aspen and willow in the past 14,000 years. The northern range records show no history of these taxa, although pollen data elsewhere imply that they grew in Yellowstone early on. Pollen records from Cub Creek Pond (Waddington and Wright 1974) and Buckbean Fen (Baker 1976) show increases in aspen and willow pollen in the early stages of deglaciation. These shrubs were apparently well suited to colonize areas of minerogenic soil and stagnant ice in the absence of competitors. In Jackson Hole, aspen experienced a resurgence during the warm, dry period between 9,000 and 6,700 years ago. Whether this was caused by drought conditions, more frequent fires, or some related factor cannot be determined. On the northern range, however, their poor fossil record suggests that aspen and willow have always been minor parts of the vegetation and not likely to have greatly exceeded their present-day coverage of 3 percent (Houston 1982).

THE PAST 200 YEARS

A study of the sedimentary record of eight small lakes reveals the environmental changes of the past two centuries (figure 19.2; Engstrom et al. 1991). Concentrations of major metals and nutrient elements were analyzed to determine shifts in sediment input and nutrient supply, and the lead-210 method was used to date changes of the past 150 years. Pollen was examined to determine changes in local and regional vegetation, and diatoms were studied at five sites to identify changes in lake trophic state and water depth (see Engstrom et al. 1991 for details of methodology). Study lakes were chosen in largely unforested areas known to receive heavy winter use by elk, bison, and antelope. The lakes were small, with small catchments and a minimal fringe of littoral vegetation, which might otherwise screen out sediment washed in from hill slopes. With one exception, the sites were far enough from a road so that erosion during road construction and subsequent maintenance would not be a significant constituent of the sediment. Major stratigraphic events and their interpretation are summarized in figure 19.4.

Vegetational Change

Compared to changes encountered during the past 14,000 years, the vegetation of the past 150 years has changed little. There is also no synchroneity in the timing of pollen changes that would suggest a regional response to a widespread environmental perturbation. The pollen records are dominated by pine, most of which is identified as lodgepole. Spruce, fir, Douglas fir, and juniper produce less pollen, and small fluctuations in their abundance may imply modest changes in forest composition. Small increases in pollen percentages of various conifers and sagebrush may be related to the absence of major fires in the study area during the past 150 years. Perceptible decreases in pollen of willow, aspen, alder, and birch at different times may reflect local ungulate browsing, although slightly drier climatic conditions may have been a factor as well.

Aspen and willow, perhaps the taxa most critical to the issue of overbrowsing, are notoriously poor pollen producers. Both plants reproduce sexually and asexually, depending on the age of the plant and the environmental conditions. Questions have been raised in particular about the preservability of aspen pollen in lake sediments, although it is abundant in late-glacial sediments (Lichti-Federovich and Ritchie 1965; Cushing 1967). The aspen parkland of Canada, which is dominated by quaking aspen (*Populus tremuloides*) and black cottonwood (*P. trichocarpa*), produces 1–5 percent aspen and cottonwood pollen. By comparison, pine pollen, with a source in the boreal forest, accounts for 20–45 percent of the pollen. In northwestern Wyoming sites aspen pollen accounts for 0–3 percent of the present-day pollen rain, with its highest values in samples collected near aspen groves. The presence of aspen pollen thus implies that flowering stands of aspen grew near the site, although the extent of aspen cannot be inferred with assurance. It is important to remember, however, that the pollen-recruitment area is larger than a single stand. Changes in aspen-pollen abundance reflect changes in pollen production related to some combination of climate, stand age, and areal extent of aspen groves.

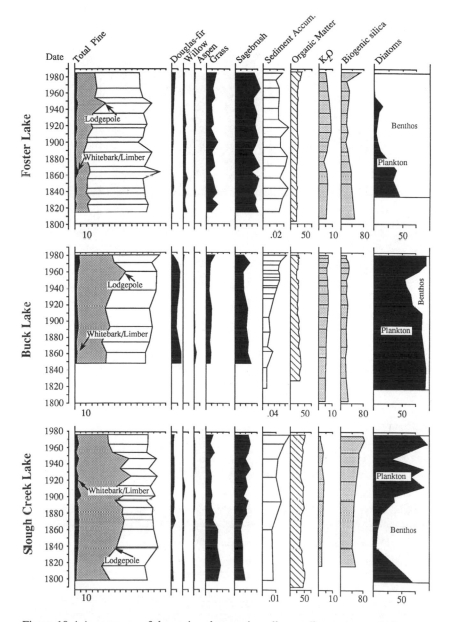

Figure 19.4 A summary of the major changes in pollen, sediment accumulation rates, chemistry, and diatoms during the past ca. 150 years at eight lakes in the northern range. Pollen, organic matter, and diatom curves represent percentage of composition. Sediment accumulation is measured as g/cm²/yr. Note that the horizontal scale for sediment accumulation differs from lake to lake. K₂O and biogenic silica are measured in mg/g sediment.

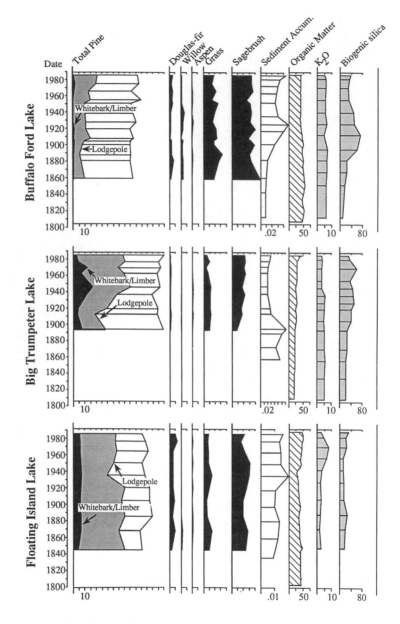

Figure 19.4 (*continued*)

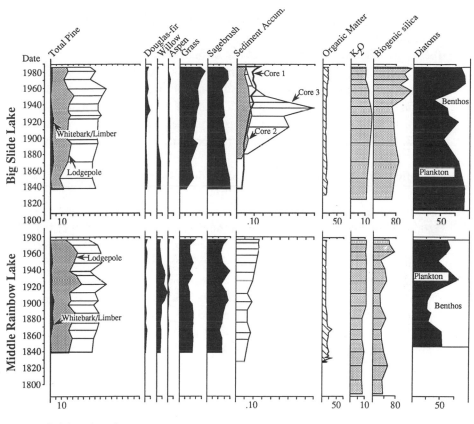

Figure 19.4 (*continued*)

Erosional History

Sediment accumulation rates (grams of sediment/cm²/yr) in a lake provide one means of measuring erosion on adjacent slopes. The sediment-
accumulation rate profiles show considerable variability among the lakes
during the past century. Many of the lakes show higher rates of sediment
accumulation immediately after the park was established. All sites except
Foster Lake show accelerated rates of sediment accumulation after 1920,
although the onset and magnitude of the increases differ from site to site.
Care must be taken in interpreting these trends, however, because changes
in sedimentation at a single coring site in the lake can have several causes.
First and most obviously, change in sedimentation may signify changes in
erosion rate and sediment input to the system. Changes in the erosion
pattern within the catchment will alter the proportion of clastic materials in
the sediment and the concentration of associated elements, illustrated here
by the profiles for K_2O (figure 19.4).

Second, the movement of sediment within a lake can also change rates of sediment accumulation at a coring site, in a process called sediment focusing. Changes in water level, wind-induced currents, and thermal stratification all influence focusing. This process can be distinguished from changes in erosion or biological production, however, in that sediment focusing does not typically alter the chemical composition of the sediments. In the stratigraphic record, it is registered as a change in sediment accumulation without any change in the proportion of chemical constituents.

Third, in many small lakes a large fraction of the accumulating sediment is a product of biological activity within the lake. This fraction includes organic matter, calcium carbonate precipitated during algal photosynthesis, and biogenic silica, which represents the remains of diatoms and chrysophytes. When nutrient inputs from the catchment are altered, the concentration of these components in the sediment will change, affecting biological production within the lake.

The sediment accumulation rates in combination with the geochemical profiles show clear evidence for increased erosion at two sites: Floating Island Lake and Big Slide Lake. At Floating Island Lake an increase in sediment accumulation occurred between 1930 and 1940 and was accompanied by an increase in the clastic fraction of the sediment (revealed by the K_2O profile). The sedimentary record no doubt reflects the 1932–1934 construction of the road that runs along the north shore of the lake, which introduced dust and eroded clastic material. After construction ceased, sediment accumulation rates declined, as might be expected, although the rates remained elevated above pre-park levels. It is possible, of course, that such factors as ungulate grazing and climatic change contributed to the changes in erosion rate at Floating Island Lake. But it is unlikely that these more subtle changes could be differentiated against the strength of the signal generated from road construction.

At Big Slide Lake clastic input and sediment accumulation rates increased between 1880 and 1940. The cause of increased erosion, however, is not clear. The Gardner River valley has been the scene of active mass-wasting, which continually plagues efforts to keep the highway open. Episodes of slope movement may have been directly responsible for the increase of silicate-rich clastics in the lake. More specifically, dust from the Old Gardner Road, which lies within the Slide Lake drainage, may be the source of increased sediment accumulation rates. The decline in sediment accumulation rates and clastic input after 1940 accords well with the opening of a paved road in the Gardner River valley and the decreased use of the dirt Old Gardner Road. Just as at Floating Island Lake, however, alternative explanations alone or in concert may account for the erosion signal. Water levels may have been altered by climate and beaver activity; ungulate usage of the area may have changed; landslides within the catchment may have been reactivated.

Other lakes show some evidence of higher erosion rates in the past (Foster Lake, 1800–1850, Buck Lake, 1860–1870, and Middle Rainbow Lake, 1880–1900). In these cases, the changes in accumulation rate were modest and short in duration. Given the variability in timing, climatic change seems an unlikely cause. Changes in ungulate usage within the catchment may have been responsible, but the size of elk populations during the early years of the park are too poorly known to examine changes in size. Furthermore, if erosion rates in these catchment were sensitive to ungulate use, one might expect evidence of greater erosion in the past two decades, when populations reached record numbers (Houston 1982); such is not the case.

Periods of increased sediment focusing characterize several sites (Buck Lake, 1920–1960, Buffalo Ford Lake, 1920–present, Middle Rainbow Lake, 1940–present, and Big Trumpeter Lake, 1890–1920). During these intervals sediment accumulation rates increased with no attendant change in the chemical composition of the sediment.

Limnological Change

Increased concentrations of sedimentary organic matter, biogenic silica (diatoms and chrysophytes), and carbonates indicate greater lake productivity driven by elevated nutrient flux to the lake. This type of signal accompanied high sediment accumulation rates at four of the eight sites. Buck, Slough Creek, and Middle Rainbow lakes show higher production after 1960, and Buffalo Ford Lake was more productive between ca. 1880 and 1920. Changes in sediment composition without a concurrent increase in sediment accumulation rate are seen in Slough Creek Lake from 1890 to 1920 and in Big Trumpeter Lake after 1945. Sedimentological evidence suggests higher productivity after 1940 in Floating Island Lake and Big Slide Lake, but the increase in erosion at that same time confounds clear interpretation of the signal.

The geochemical evidence for limnological change is supported by the sedimentary diatom record. The pre-park diatom assemblages were dominated by mesotrophic and eutrophic planktonic species, primarily from the genera *Stephanodiscus* and *Cyclostephanos*. The dominance of taxa characteristic of nutrient rich waters implies that catchment nutrient yields are naturally quite high in the northern range. The lakes show considerable variability in the pattern of limnological change over time, primarily in fluctuations between the proportion of benthic taxa (living on rocks, aquatic plants, and the sediment surface) and planktonic taxa (floating types) (figure 19.4). Shifts in the proportion of benthic to planktonic diatoms commonly reflect changes in water chemistry, particularly phosphorus or silica inputs, or changes in lake level.

The variability in timing, magnitude, and duration of limnological change suggested by the diatoms indicates that the lakes in the northern range were not responding to large-scale environmental fluctuations but rather to local site-specific factors. At all sites, benthic diatoms, including *Fragilaria* spp., *Amphora ovalis, Cocconeis placentula,* and several *Navicula* spp., increased relative to planktonic types in the latter half of the nineteenth century. Their increase was quite small in Buck, Big Slide, and Middle Rainbow lakes and more pronounced in Foster and Slough Creek lakes. It is not clear whether this shift in the diatom composition was caused by changes in nutrient input or by increased littoral area resulting from lowered lake levels. The asynchroneity of the changes, however, indicates that a regionwide change in water level driven by climate was not likely and that nutrient inputs declined site by site, perhaps as a result of a lower fire frequency driven by climatic change.

The diatom records show considerable variation during the first half of the twentieth century. These fluctuations indicate different and asynchronous use of lake catchments by grazing ungulates, although corresponding changes in the pollen data that might be attributed to ungulate activity do not occur. From the early 1960s to the present all sites except Foster Lake show an increase in eutrophic diatom plankton. This trend coincides with the time when elk populations are known to have increased, and the diatom flora could well reflect elevated nutrient inputs from manuring near the lake shores. However, these changes must be viewed from the longer-term perspective provided by the overall sedimentary record. The post-1960 diatom flora is quite similar to that which existed in the lakes prior to park establishment. Thus, regardless of the cause, these lakes have not been recently perturbed outside their normal range, and none have been enriched in recent decades beyond their "natural" condition.

MANAGEMENT IMPLICATIONS OF THE PREHISTORIC RECORD

The paleoecologic record usually lacks the temporal or spatial resolution to reconstruct a snapshot of environmental conditions at an exact time or place. Rather, prehistoric data are best considered in terms of how far they depart from the present state, and how variable they are over time. In the case of Yellowstone's northern range, we have the opportunity to study aspects of the environment over thousands of years as well as over decades. The long-term pollen record suggests that over the past 14,000 years the magnitude of vegetation change has been quite great. For the first millennium after glacier retreat, the region was covered by tundra. As the climate warmed, spruce, then fir and pine, formed a subalpine forest, which was maintained for more than 2,000 years. Subsequently, with warmer, drier conditions and frequent fires, lodgepole pine forest predominated. The present-day parkland developed in the past 6,700 years, and more directly in the last 1,600 years. From this record, we can infer that climate changes do ultimately drive the ecosystem. The history of aspen, willow, and other browse species is imprecisely known, but clearly these were never abundant species in the northern range. The history of particular stands of aspen or willow cannot be resolved from the paleoecologic record.

Study of the past 150 years provides a different picture of environmental variability in the northern range. The present state of the range does not seem to lie outside the spectrum of conditions evident in the past two centuries. Climatic changes, such as the end of the Little Ice Age ca. 1890 and the drought years of the 1930s, perturbed the system subtly, but not in ways that register as regionwide changes in vegetation or limnology. Climate and fire frequency affect the vigor and distribution of certain trees and shrubs. The pollen record shows an increase in conifer pollen in the past century that can be related to a closing of the forest in the absence of fires. The aspen and willow record indicates that these species were present as minor elements on the landscape, pollinating near some lakes and not others.

Erosion within the catchment is influenced by vegetation type and density, animal trampling, human activity, and climate. Increased rates of erosion occurred around two sites, one that lies next to a road and one that lies in an area of landslides. The erosion signal coincides with the time of road construction in the first case and periods of slope movement in the second. The argument for accelerated erosion on the northern range resulting from ungulate grazing is not supported by stratigraphic studies.

Lake productivity and biota are affected by nutrient influx, water clarity, and water depth. The diatom record shows great variability over time, but the patterns are not uniform among the five lakes studied. Changes in the proportion of benthic and planktonic diatoms indicate a decrease in nutrients or lowered water levels in the latter half of the nineteenth century and early twentieth century. The signal is metasynchronous across the region, which suggests that climatic change is not the forcing factor. Lower fire frequency may have changed nutrient inputs to the system. Most of the lakes show an increase in lake productivity in the past 20 years, but the trophic conditions today do not differ much from what they were before the park was established.

The fossil record gives credence to a policy of natural regulation and to the ability of the present-day ecosystem to function in most ways as it did in prehistoric times. On a millennial time scale, regional climatic changes cause the greatest perturbations in the ecosystem. Our knowledge of climate and vegetation interactions, however, allows us to predict the direction of such changes. On a shorter time scale, the modern parkland vegetation of the northern range developed during the past 1,600 years, when the present-day climate was introduced. Data on the prehistoric fauna indicate that most of the mammals of the northern range today have been there for at least the past 1,000 years (Hadly 1990). In Hadly's study a notable exception is wolf, which is absent today but was present in prehistoric times. Elk, bighorn, bison, and pronghorn became part of the ecosystem as modern vegetation developed, and their influence on those communities is inextricable. The lake-sediment records from the northern range do not convincingly show direct or indirect effects of ungulate grazing during the history of the park.

REFERENCES

Baker, R. G. 1976. Late Quaternary vegetation history of the Yellowstone Basin, Wyoming. U.S. Geol. Surv. Prof. Pap. 729-E.

Baker, R. G. 1983. Holocene vegetation history of the western United States. Pages 109–127 in H. E. Wright, Jr., ed. Late Quaternary environments of the United States, vol. 2. University of Minnesota Press, Minneapolis.

Barnosky, C. W. 1987. Late-glacial and postglacial vegetation and climate of Jackson Hole and the Pinyon Peak Highlands, Wyoming. Final report. University of Wyoming National Park Service Research Center, Laramie.

Barnosky, C. W., P. M. Anderson, and P. J. Bartlein. 1987. The northwestern U.S. during deglaciation: Vegetational history and paleoclimatic implications. Pages 289–321 in W. F. Ruddiman and H. E. Wright, Jr., eds. North America and adjacent oceans during the last deglaciation. Vol. K-3 of The Geology of North America. Geological Society of America, Boulder, Colo.

Birks, H. J. B., and H. H. Birks. 1980. Quaternary paleoecology. Edward Arnold Press, London.

Chase, A. 1986. Playing God in Yellowstone. Atlantic Monthly Press, New York.

Cooperative Holocene Mapping Project members. 1988. Climatic changes of the last 18,000 years: Observations and model simulations. Science 241:1043–1052.

Cushing, E. J. 1967. Evidence for differential pollen preservation in late Quaternary sediments in Minnesota. Rev. Palaeobotan. Palynol. 4:87–101.

Engstrom, D. R., C. Whitlock, S. C. Fritz, and H. E. Wright, Jr. 1991. Recent environmental changes inferred from the sediments of small lakes in Yellowstone's northern range. J. Paleolimnology 5:139–174.

Engstrom, D. R., and H. E. Wright, Jr. 1984. Chemical stratigraphy of lake sediments as a record of environmental change. Pages 11–67 in E. Y. Haworth and J. W. G. Lund, eds. Lake sediments and environmental history. Leicester Univ. Press, Leicester.

Gennett, J. A., and R. G. Baker. 1986. A late Quaternary pollen sequence from Blacktail Pond, Yellowstone National Park, Wyoming. Palynology 10:61–71.

Hadly, E. A. 1990. Late Holocene mammalian fauna of Lamar Cave and its implications for ecosystem dynamics in Yellowstone National Park, Wyo. M.S. thesis, Northern Arizona Univ.

Houston, D. B. 1982. The northern Yellowstone elk: Ecology and management. Macmillan, New York.

Jacobson, G. L., Jr., and R. H. W. Bradshaw. 1981. The selection of sites for paleovegetational studies. Quaternary Res. 16:80–96.

Kay, C. 1985. Aspen reproduction in the Yellowstone Park–Jackson Hole area and its relationship to the natural regulation of ungulates. Pages 131–160 in G. W. Workman, ed. Western elk management: A symposium. Utah State Univ., Logan.

Leopold, A. S., S. A. Cain, C. M. Cottam, I. N. Gabrielson, and T. L. Kimball. 1963. Wildlife management in the national parks. Trans. N. Am. Wildl. Conf. 28:28–45.

Lichti-Federovich, S., and J. C. Ritchie. 1965. Recent pollen assemblages from the western interior of Canada. Rev. Palaeobotan. Palynol. 7:297–344.

Waddington, J. C. B., and H. E. Wright, Jr. 1974. Late Quaternary vegetation changes on the east of Yellowstone Park, Wyoming. Quaternary Res. 4:174–184.

PART IV   WOLF RECOVERY

Predators are now protected in the parks of the United States, although unfortunately they were not in the early years and the wolf, grizzly bear, and mountain lion became extinct in many of the national parks. Even today populations of large predators, where they still occur in the parks, are kept below optimal level by programs of predator control applied outside the park boundaries.

A. S. Leopold et al., *"Study of Wildlife Problems in the National Parks," in* Report of the Special Advisory Board on Wildlife Management for the Secretary of the Interior. *Washington, D.C.: Government Printing Office, 1963.*

The Secretary of the Interior shall . . . appoint a 10 member Wolf Management Committee. The Committee's task shall be to develop a wolf reintroduction and management plan for Yellowstone National Park.

United States Congress, Amendment No. 218, Department of the Interior, Fiscal Year 1991 Appropriations Bill.

Overleaf. *Wolf nursing her pups. Photo courtesy of Wyoming State Museum, Cheyenne, Wyoming.*

CHAPTER 20 **Returning the Wolf to Yellowstone**

L. David Mech

Only seventy-five years ago, the howl of the wolf reverberated across the Lamar Valley, along the Yellowstone River, and among the hot springs, hills, valleys, and forests of Yellowstone National Park. A few decades later, everything remained the same except that the wolves were missing, snuffed out by the hand of man, who had decreed that they did not belong in this natural system. There were good animals and bad animals in those days, and the wolf was clearly bad. By 1926 the last wolf had been trapped in Yellowstone National Park, although a few held on into the mid-thirties (Weaver 1978). Ever since, the park has remained without its major predator. Although there have been tracks reported, pseudo-sightings, and even rumored transplants, Yellowstone exists today without the wolf.

What happened to the wolves in Yellowstone was similar to their fate throughout the West. Like elsewhere in Montana, Wyoming, and Idaho, from the plains through the mountains they were trapped, shot, and poisoned as official government policy (Weaver 1978). And that is the paradox. As a national park, Yellowstone was supposed to preserve its natural complement of flora and fauna. One of the mandates of the national parks is to preserve complete natural systems. Somehow Yellowstone was shorted. For more than sixty years it has preserved an incomplete system.

It can be argued that no ecosystem is complete anymore, and that other national parks have lost various components of their natural systems. Such

Thanks to S. H. Fritts, T. Kaminski, J. D. Varley, and J. Weaver for many helpful suggestions for improving this chapter. The opinions expressed in this chapter are those of the author and do not necessarily reflect those of the U.S. Fish and Wildlife Service.

situations do not compare with Yellowstone's lack of wolves. Wolves are integral parts of predator-prey systems that include our largest and most appealing wildlife. The wolf is the preeminent predator on northern hoofed animals. Yellowstone's incomplete system is a conspicuous and ecologically influential one with a strong public constituency. Thus it is not surprising that conservationists and wildlife enthusiasts have long suggested restoring wolves to Yellowstone.

The attitude that fostered such a suggestion reflected the general feelings of the time about wildlife. In the early 1900s, wolves were regarded much the same as the rat is today—only with more vehemence. This led to the official wolf extermination program of that era. By the late 1930s and early 1940s, however, predators were being seen in a new light. Stanley Young (1944), who chronicled the wolf's depredations throughout the development of the United States and detailed the many methods used by the government and the public to exterminate wolves, wrote in 1942 that "where not in conflict with human interests, wolves may well be left alone. They form one of the most interesting groups of all mammals, and should be permitted to have a place in North American fauna" (Young 1942:574).

Several scientific studies of wolves followed, and a clearer, more objective view of the animal emerged. The subspecies of wolf that originally inhabited Yellowstone was the northern Rocky Mountain wolf, of which I will have more to say below. Murie (1944) showed that wolves in Alaska's Mount McKinley National Park (now Denali National Park and Preserve) tended to take primarily inferior members of the Dall sheep population. Cowan (1947) found indications that wolves had little numerical effect on their prey in the Rocky Mountain national parks of Canada. Stenlund (1955:47) concluded, referring to Minnesota's Superior National Forest, "at present, figures show that in areas which sustain both wolf predation and hunting pressure, only the annual increment is removed from the deer herd." I learned that wolves in Isle Royale National Park (Lake Superior) succeed less than 10 percent of the time in hunting moose, their main prey, and they take primarily inferior members of the herd (Mech 1966).

With the publication of several other pertinent wolf studies, the plot began to thicken. We learned that when such factors as a series of severe winters or overhunting drastically affected prey populations, wolves could contribute to the reduction of prey numbers (Mech and Karns 1977; Gasaway et al. 1983; Bergerud, Wyett, and Snider, 1983, but compare Thompson and Peterson 1988; Bergerud and Ballard 1988, 1989, but compare Van Ballenberghe 1985, 1989). Nevertheless, it is abundantly clear after decades of study that in national parks where hunting is forbidden, wolves do not wipe out their prey (Murie 1944; Mech 1970; Carbyn 1974; Haber 1977; Allen 1979; Peterson and Page 1988).

As scientific data about wolves and wolf predation began to replace myth, legend, folklore, and frontier thinking, the eminent Canadian conservationist Douglas H. Pimlott (1967) approvingly foresaw the day when wolves would be reintroduced into Yellowstone. The next year the U.S. National Park Service (1968) confirmed its role to preserve natural environments and to compensate for significant missing components (Cole 1969). I later echoed Pimlott's and others' sentiments about restoring wolves to Yellowstone (Mech 1970, 1971).

None of this represented profound thinking, but was merely pure and simple logic. If we cannot preserve natural integrity in national parks, where can we? If we do not have a place for the wolf—or the grizzly, the cougar, and the wolverine—in national parks, where else do we? If India can find room—nay, make room—for the tiger in special preserves (Saharia 1982), why cannot the United States find room for the wolf in its first and foremost national park?

The seeds of logic found fertile ground in the thinking of many conservationists. Among them, then Assistant Secretary of the Interior for National Parks and Wildlife Nathaniel H. Reed decided to examine the suggestion more closely. In the early 1970s he called a meeting in Yellowstone to discuss the subject. At that time there were unexamined rumors of recent wolf sightings, so we recommended that a thorough survey and investigation be conducted of the possible existence of wolves in the park; if no breeding wolf pack was found, then wolves should be reintroduced.

After extensive ground and aerial searches, as well as investigation of numerous reports, biologist John Weaver concluded that "resident wolf packs . . . were eliminated from Yellowstone National Park by the 1940's." He recommended "a transplant of wolves from British Columbia or Alberta, or perhaps Minnesota, to restore a viable population of this native predator to Yellowstone National Park" (Weaver 1978).

This formal recommendation, however, was then caught up in the bureaucratic process of recovery-plan preparation. Because the wolf is on the federal endangered species list, a special recovery team was appointed to develop a plan for promoting recovery of the subspecies. The team included wolf biologists, administrators, an environmentalist, and a member of the livestock industry. The plan had to consider not only Yellowstone National Park, but also the remainder of the subspecies's range, which originally covered much of Wyoming, Idaho, and Montana as well as parts of neighboring states. Developing the recovery plan thus took considerable time, several drafts, and extensive outside review. The original plan was approved on May 28, 1980, and the revised version was signed by the deputy regional director of the U.S. Fish and Wildlife Service, John L. Spinks, on August 3, 1987.

The revised plan stated that "natural recolonization of the Yellowstone area remains an extremely remote possibility. From a wolf recovery perspective, translocating wolves to the Yellowstone area is appropriate now" (U.S. Fish and Wildlife Service 1987:24). The plan also designated the U.S. Fish and Wildlife Service and the National Park Service as lead agencies to develop a reestablishment plan and an environmental impact statement for the project.

No EIS has yet been conducted. The seeds of logic, sprouting on fertile ground, have encountered inclement weather in the form of opposition by ranchers and other people living around the park and throughout the West. These folks, too, have a logic: (1) they currently have no problems attributable to wolves, (2) if wolves are reintroduced, their problems due to wolves will increase, and (3) they therefore oppose wolf reintroduction.

Wolf restoration opponents foresee two types of problems from wolf reestablishment in Yellowstone. First, they believe that wolves dispersing from an established population in Yellowstone might kill livestock. Second, they believe that their own activities could be further restricted by government regulations seeking to protect wolves. One frequently asked question, for example, is whether certain roads will be closed to protect wolves on public lands. The assumption seems to be that wolf management around Yellowstone would be as restrictive as grizzly bear management.

Presumably such local opposition has delayed the EIS covering wolf reintroduction in Yellowstone (Shabecoff 1987). However, one of the region's most influential politicians, former U.S. senator James McClure of Idaho, supports wolf reestablishment in Yellowstone. In a 1988 interview Senator McClure stated, "We already have wolves in the Glacier Park area, and I think they're also appropriate in Yellowstone. I see no reason not to have them in some of the designated wilderness in Idaho—for example, along the Idaho-Montana border where there's no livestock grazing. Yes, wolves have an appropriate place. But the only way we'll achieve wolf recovery is if we do it in a way that doesn't threaten people who live near the recovery area" (Cutler 1988:9).

The need to minimize threats to local residents may seem to be the ill breeze that still blows on wolf restoration in Yellowstone. But is it really an ill breeze? Or could it be instead a pruning, trimming, shaping wind, which will ensure that when the plant does grow and mature, it will be strong and viable? Once wolves are restored to Yellowstone, it will probably be forever. Prudence dictates that the residents of the region should be protected from possible ill effects.

Several specific objections to restoring wolves to Yellowstone have been voiced by various people speaking both officially and unofficially for opponents of restoration. These objections merit a response.

1. *Wolves are dangerous to humans.* There is no documented case of an unprovoked nonrabid wolf killing or seriously injuring a human being in North America; rabies does not seem to be a problem in wolves south of midlatitude Canada (Mech 1990).

2. *Wolves will be serious predators on livestock surrounding Yellowstone.* Wolves no doubt will kill some livestock outside the park, but if appropriate wolf management is allowed outside the park, the incidence of such behavior will be minimal. In Minnesota and Alberta, for example, most wolves prey primarily on natural prey, and those that do kill livestock are subject to destruction by official control programs (Fritts and Mech 1981; Fritts 1982; Bjorge and Gunson 1983; Gunson 1983a, 1983b). In addition, a fund to compensate ranchers for livestock losses from wolves has been established by Defenders of Wildlife (Fischer 1989).

3. *Wolf management around Yellowstone will be prohibited by the Endangered Species Act.* This is a common misconception. Based on a 1982 amendment to the ESA, a reintroduced population can be managed as an officially designated "experimental/non-essential population," which would allow killing, removal, or other practices necessary to protect local residents from undue hardship. The usual "Section 7 (ESA)" consultation on land uses does not apply stringently (except in national wildlife refuges and national parks); it would not preclude land uses that might "jeopardize" the wolf. In northeastern North Carolina, where red wolves have been reintroduced, such a designation has been very successful (Parker 1989). Furthermore, even without the experimental designation, the "endangered" Montana wolf population has been subjected to control of individual wolves killing livestock.

4. *Once wolves are translocated to Yellowstone, they will get out and cannot be caught again.* If proper reintroduction techniques are used, such as those employed with the red wolf (Phillips and Parker 1988), chances are good that most released wolves would remain primarily in the reestablishment area. With the availability of the new radio capture collar, however, there is a high probability that released wolves wearing such a collar and emigrating from the area can be retrieved (Mech et al. 1984, 1990).

5. *Unreasonable regulations inside Yellowstone will restrict visitors in*

order to protect wolves. Few new regulations would be needed to protect restored wolves in Yellowstone since wolves tend to den in secluded areas before the park's peak period of human visitation. For one month each spring a relatively small area around each den conceivably might have to be closed to human travel (compare Chapman 1979). Such closures should affect visitors little. Bear management areas have been used in the park since 1983 to reduce bear-human conflicts.

6. *Wolves will eliminate or seriously reduce prey herds in Yellowstone.* As discussed above, this has not happened in other national parks (Mech 1970). In fact, in Isle Royale National Park, both wolves and their main prey, moose, have reached the highest densities reported anywhere (Peterson and Page 1988). Fifteen wolf experts and several wolf/prey modelers agree that if wolves are restored to Yellowstone they will not eliminate their prey (National Park Service 1990). Singer (chapter 21 in this volume) reaches the same conclusion.

7. *Wolves will ruin hunting outside Yellowstone of such animals as elk, deer, and bison, some of which migrate annually out of the park.* Wolves could reduce some of these prey herds under certain conditions, but given the reservoir of animals in the park not subject to hunting, the effect of Yellowstone wolves outside the park should be minimal and manageable (National Park Service 1990).

8. *Wolves will kill or compete with grizzly bears.* No grizzly biologist or anyone concerned with grizzly recovery has raised this issue, and for good reason. In Glacier Park, Denali Park, and other areas cohabited by wolves and grizzlies, the two live together with little direct competition, and what little there is usually favors the grizzly (Weaver 1986). Five wolf and brown bear experts from across the Soviet Union confirmed that no serious competition exists between the two species there either (National Park Service 1990). This issue should be considered a smoke screen raised by folks who want neither the wolf nor the grizzly.

9. *Once wolves are restored to Yellowstone, they will spread throughout the rest of the West and cannot be controlled.* It is true that an established wolf population in Yellowstone will generate dispersers that can travel long distances (Fritts 1983; Mech 1987; Ream et al. chapter 22 in this volume) and that they will try to establish new populations (Rothman and Mech 1979; Fritts and Mech 1981). With adequate management, however, wolves can be kept out of areas where they may be unwanted. Such management must be agreed upon before any wolves are released and wolf advocates must not challenge such management when it is implemented. In fact, if necessary to restore wolves to Yellowstone, I favor a program

allowing wolves to be killed everywhere outside of the designated re-establishment area (Mech 1979). Everyone must understand that when wolves are restored to Yellowstone, wolf management outside the park will become a fact of life.

10. *Wolves never really inhabited Yellowstone.* Few people seriously believe this. Weaver (1978) adequately documented their presence (and demise) in Yellowstone from the mid-1800s through the late 1930s. Furthermore, there is good reason to believe that wolves were there long before that (Hadly 1990). Wherever wolves have not been wiped out, for example, throughout Alaska and most of Canada, they occupy every available habitat where there are large ungulates to feed on.

11. *The subspecies of wolf that originally inhabited Yellowstone, the northern Rocky Mountain wolf (Canis lupus irremotus), is now extinct, so it would be wrong to reintroduce another subspecies.* The layperson cannot really be blamed for making this argument, for wolf taxonomy is confusing. It does appear that the so-called northern Rocky Mountain wolf is extinct, although one might argue that the wolves currently inhabiting the Glacier Park area (Ream et al. chapter 22 in this volume) are of this race.

The major reason why this contention should not be an issue is that most currently recognized wolf races were arbitrarily assigned and are most likely invalid. The New World taxonomists were overly liberal in assigning wolf subspecies. In all of Europe and Asia only eight wolf subspecies are recognized, whereas in North America some twenty-four were named (Mech 1970). In reexamining wolf taxonomy, Nowak (1983) concluded that a thorough analysis may well show that North American wolves could all be lumped into five subspecies. The race inhabiting Yellowstone would be the same as that currently occupying southwestern Canada. Even if this were not the case, most of the twenty-four so-called subspecies are so similar that they cannot be distinguished from one another without measuring great numbers of skulls. For most practical purposes they are basically alike.

12. *Once wolves are restored to Yellowstone and dispersers travel outside the park, the government will force unreasonable restrictions on the public, such as closing forest roads (Thiel 1985; Jensen, Fuller, and Robinson 1986; Mech et al. 1988 but compare Mech 1989a), to protect the wolf.* This possible problem could be overcome, under the 1982 amendment to the ESA, by designating the reintroduced Yellowstone population as "experimental/non-essential" over a broad area centered around Yellowstone, or by "delisting" (removing from the endangered species list) the wolf population within a certain distance of the park. Federal agencies

would then not be legally mandated to take extra measures to protect wolves, and wolf protection and management could become state based.

Congress appropriated $200,000 in fiscal year 1989 to obtain definitive answers to several of these concerns (National Park Service 1990). Sponsors of the appropriation feel that such answers are needed before any further progress can be made on the restoration issue. Proponents of wolf restoration, however, consider this to be another stalling action and are concerned that the planning of restoration is proceeding too slowly.

Congressman Wayne Owens (D-Utah) introduced a bill in 1988 that would require the agencies to begin the EIS process. At hearings on the bill (U.S. House of Representatives Subcommittee on National Parks and Public Lands, July 20, 1989), Sen. Alan Simpson (R-Wyoming) indicated a willingness to consider the issue, given adequate safeguards. There is no question about the popular support for wolf reestablishment in Yellowstone. A survey of Yellowstone visitors showed them overwhelmingly favoring wolf restoration (McNaught 1987). Just as significant was a survey of Wyoming residents indicating that almost half were favorable to wolves, a third were neutral, and only 16 percent were negative (Bath and Buchanan 1990; Bath chapter 23 in this volume).

In May 1990 the National Park Service released a congressionally mandated report concluding that wolves would not adversely impact wildlife populations in Yellowstone National Park (National Park Service 1990). A week later, Sen. James McClure introduced legislation in the U.S. Senate providing for wolf reintroduction in Yellowstone National Park as well as central Idaho. Senator McClure's legislation called for introducing three breeding pairs of wolves into Yellowstone and three breeding pairs into the central Idaho wilderness and treating them as an endangered species under the Endangered Species Act, so long as they remain in the park and Idaho recovery area. Outside these areas, however, wolves would be "delisted" from the ESA and subject to management by state wildlife officials.

Biologically, there is no reason Yellowstone cannot support wolves. As of 1988, the following numbers of ungulates were reported present in the park: more than 30,000 elk in summer and 22,000 in winter; 3,000 mule deer (Singer 1988; Singer chapter 21 in this volume); 2,700 bison (Bishop 1989); and smaller numbers of moose, pronghorn, bighorn, and mountain goats (Singer 1988; Bishop 1989). To give some perspective on this potential wolf-prey system, one can look at Denali National Park, where 2,600 caribou, 2,000 moose, and 2,000 Dall sheep support 110 to 150 wolves (Mech 1989b and unpublished data). With 100 wolves, wolf-prey ratios of 1:260 in winter and 1:380 in summer are possible in Yellowstone.

As for size of the area, Yellowstone Park itself is large enough for quite an adequate wolf population. The park encompasses some 8,888 sq km (3,472 sq mi). Compare that with Isle Royale National Park, which covers only 538 sq km (210 sq mi), where wolf numbers have ranged between 12 and 50 (Peterson and Page 1988; R. O. Peterson, personal communication). Anyone who believes that Yellowstone Park alone does not have enough room for genetic diversity (compare Theberge 1983 and Shields 1983) should consider that Isle Royale, which almost certainly was colonized by not more than two wolves (Mech 1966) with little or no outbreeding, has supported a wolf population for forty years. Although in 1988 and 1989 there was some concern about possible inbreeding depression at Isle Royale, by late 1989 the population clearly was still breeding and apparently increasing (R. O. Peterson, pers. comm.).

Finally, no more research is necessary to restore the Yellowstone wolf. Methods of live trapping, anesthetizing, transporting, feeding, holding, releasing, and studying wolves were all worked out long ago (Kolenosky and Johnston 1967; Mech 1974; Weise et al. 1975; Fritts, Paul, and Mech 1984, 1985; Phillips and Parker 1988). Methods of controlling wolves are well documented (Young 1944) and are practiced routinely in Minnesota (Fritts 1982) and Canada (Banville 1983; Gunson 1983a; Heard 1983; Smith 1983; Kolenosky 1983; Stardom 1983; Tompa 1983).

So what more needs to be done to restore wolves to Yellowstone? According to the approved northern Rocky Mountain wolf recovery plan, a specific reestablishment plan and an EIS are still the first steps (see above). But because the question is currently in the political arena, the political process must first proceed, and there is evidence of gathering momentum for wolf recovery.

In October 1990, during the waning hours of the 101st Congress, Senator McClure successfully amended the Department of the Interior's 1991 appropriations bill to provide $375,000 to fund a Wolf Management Committee to develop a wolf reintroduction and management plan for Yellowstone National Park and central Idaho wilderness areas. The ten-member committee is to be appointed by the secretary of the interior and will include one representative from the fish and game departments of Idaho, Montana, and Wyoming, one each from the National Park Service, the Forest Service, and the U.S. Fish and Wildlife Service, two from conservation groups, and two from the livestock-sportsmen community. The committee has until May 15, 1991, to submit a report to the secretary. This report, then, will provide the basis for an administratively implemented wolf recovery effort under the Endangered Species Act, or it might provide the basis for further congressional legislation on the matter. If Congress forces the federal agencies into preparing an EIS, there no doubt will be deadlines, and they will be adhered to. Assuming that the preferred alternative agreed upon through the EIS process is to reintroduce wolves to the park, then preparations for that alternative will probably proceed.

Additional roadblocks could still be thrown in front of the process. However, both the political process and the EIS process will force negotiation and safeguarding through compromises to solve the quandary faced by the government. The ESA requires the government to promote recovery of endangered species, and the government's own approved plan indicates that restoration of the wolf to Yellowstone is one of the necessary steps (U.S. Fish and Wildlife Service 1987). But the specific actions necessary for reintroduction require public funding, and that means congressional approval.

It is heartening to note that progress toward compromise has been made. In the political arena, two key local senators, McClure and Simpson, have given their support to wolf restoration so long as safeguards are adequate. Congressman Owens has drafted amendments to his bill that attempt to address the necessary safeguards. Furthermore, the Defenders of Wildlife livestock-loss compensation fund mentioned above has been started. These are symbolic and meaningful contributions toward getting the job done.

If the political process and the attempt to restore the wolf to Yellowstone via an EIS procedure should fail, quite conceivably a suit would be filed to do the same thing. Or, given the overwhelming public support, additional pressure on elected officials might increase until a bill is passed.

One thing is certain. Compared with Pimlott's lone voice in 1967, the current expression and support for restoring wolves to Yellowstone is the clamor of a whole culture that echoes constantly. I cannot believe that it will stop until finally replaced by the clamor of wolf packs in the park.

REFERENCES

Allen, D. L. 1979. The wolves of Minong: Their vital role in a wild community. Houghton Mifflin, Boston.

Banville, D. 1983. Status and management of wolves in Quebec. Pages 41–43 in L. Carbyn, ed. Proceedings of the Canadian wolf workshop. Canadian Wildlife Service, Ottawa.

Bath, A. J., and T. Buchanan. 1990. Attitudes of interest groups in Wyoming toward wolf restoration in Yellowstone National Park. Wildl. Soc. Bull. 17:519–525.

Bergerud, A. T., and W. B. Ballard. 1988. Wolf predation on caribou: The Nelchina herd case history, a different interpretation. J. Wildl. Mgmt. 52:344–357.

————. 1989. Wolf predation on the Nelchina caribou herd: A reply. J. Wildl. Mgmt. 53:251–259.

Bergerud, A. T., W. Wyett, and B. Snider. 1983. The role of wolf predation in limiting a moose population. J. Wildl. Mgmt. 47:977–988.

Bishop, N. A. 1989. Population status of large mammals in Yellowstone National Park. Yell-270 Leaflet. Yellowstone National Park.

Bjorge, R. R., and J. R. Gunson. 1983. Wolf predation of cattle on the Simonette River pastures in northwestern Alberta. Pages 106–111 in L. Carbyn, ed. Proceedings of the Canadian wolf workshop. Canadian Wildlife Service, Ottawa.

Carbyn, L. N. 1974. Wolf predation and behavioural interactions with elk and other ungulates in an area of high prey diversity. Ph.D. thesis, Univ. of Toronto. Can. Wildl. Serv. Rep., Edmonton, Alta.

Chapman, R. C. 1979. Human disturbance at wolf dens: A management problem. Pages 323–328 in R. M. Linn, ed. Proceedings of the first Conference on Scientific Research in the National Parks. Nat'l Park Serv. Trans. Proc. Ser. 5, vol. 1. Department of the Interior, Washington, D.C.

Cole, G. F. 1969. Mission-oriented research in the natural areas of the National Park Service. Res. Note 6. Yellowstone National Park.

Cowan, I. M. 1947. The timber wolf in the Rocky Mountain national parks of Canada. Can. J. Res. 25:139–174.

Cutler, M. R. 1988. Welcome the wolf? Defenders 63:8–9, 29–30.

Fischer, H. 1989. Restoring the wolf. Defenders 64:9, 36.

Fritts, S. H. 1982. Wolf depredation on livestock in Minnesota. U.S. Fish Wildl. Serv. Resource Publ. 145. Washington, D.C.

————. 1983. Record dispersal by a wolf from Minnesota. J. Mammal. 64:166–167.

Fritts, S. H., and L. D. Mech. 1981. Dynamics, movements, and feeding ecology of a newly protected wolf population in northwestern Minnesota. Wildl. Monogr. 80:1–79.

Fritts, S. H., W. J. Paul, and L. D. Mech. 1984. Movements of translocated wolves in Minnesota. J. Wildl. Mgmt. 48:709–721.

————. 1985. Can relocated wolves survive? Wildl. Soc. Bull. 13:459–463.

Gasaway, W. C., R. O. Stephenson, J. L. David, P. E. K. Shepherd, and O. E. Burris. 1983. Interrelationships of wolves, prey, and man in interior Alaska. Wildl. Monogr. 84:1–50.

Gunson, J. R. 1983a. Status and management of wolves in Alberta. Pages 25–29 in L. Carbyn, ed. Proceedings of the Canadian wolf workshop. Canadian Wildlife Service, Ottawa.

————. 1983b. Wolf predation of livestock in western Canada. Pages 102–105 in L. Carbyn, ed. Proceedings of the Canadian wolf workshop. Canadian Wildlife Service, Ottawa.

Haber, G. C. 1977. Socio-ecological dynamics of wolves and prey in a subarctic ecosystem. Ph.D. thesis, Univ. of British Columbia. Published by the Joint Federal-State Land Use Planning Commission for Alaska, Anchorage.

Hadly, E. A. 1990. Late Holocene mammalian fauna of Lamar Cave and its implications for ecosystem dynamics in Yellowstone National Park, Wyo. M.S. thesis, Northern Arizona Univ.

Heard, D. C. 1983. Historical and present status of wolves in the Northwest Territories. Pages 44–47 in L. Carbyn, ed. Proceedings of the Canadian wolf workshop. Canadian Wildlife Service, Ottawa.

Jensen, W. F., T. K. Fuller, and W. L. Robinson. 1986. Wolf (Canis lupus) distribution on the Ontario-Michigan border near Sault Ste. Marie. Can. Field-Nat. 100:363–366.

Kolenosky, G. B. 1983. Status and management of wolves in Ontario. Pages 35–40 in L. Carbyn, ed. Proceedings of the Canadian wolf workshop. Canadian Wildlife Service, Ottawa.

Kolenosky, G. B., and D. H. Johnston. 1967. Radio-tracking timber wolves in Ontario. Am. Zool. 7:289–303.

McNaught, D. 1987. Wolves in Yellowstone Park? Park visitors respond. Wildl. Soc. Bull. 15:518–521.

Mech, L. D. 1966. The wolves of Isle Royale. Nat'l Park Serv. Fauna Ser. 7. GPO, Washington, D.C.

———. 1970. The wolf: The ecology and behavior of an endangered species. Natural History Press/Doubleday, Garden City, N.Y.

———. 1971. Where wolves are and how they stand. Natural History 80:26–29.

———. 1974. Current techniques in the study of elusive wilderness carnivores. Proc. Int'l Cong. Game Biol. 11:315–322.

———. 1979. Some considerations in re-establishing wolves in the wild. Pages 445–457 in E. Klinghammer, ed. The behavior and ecology of wolves. Garland STPM, New York.

———. 1987. Age, season, distance, direction, and social aspects of wolf dispersal from a Minnesota pack. Pages 55–74 in B. D. Chepko-Sade and Z. Halpin, eds. Mammalian dispersal patterns. Univ. of Chicago Press, Chicago.

———. 1989a. Wolf mortality in an area of high road density. Am. Midl. Nat. 121:387–389.

———. 1989b. Stubborn hunter in a harsh land. Nat'l Wildl. 27(5):19–24.

———. 1990. Who's afraid of the big bad wolf? Audubon 92(2):82–85.

Mech, L. D., R. C. Chapman, W. W. Cochran, L. Simmons, and U. S. Seal. 1984. A radio-triggered anesthetic-dart collar for recapturing large mammals. Wildl. Soc. Bull. 12:69–74.

Mech, L. D., S. H. Fritts, G. Radde, and W. J. Paul. 1988. Wolf distribution in Minnesota relative to road density. Wildl. Soc. Bull. 16:85–88.

Mech, L. D., and P. D. Karns. 1977. Role of the wolf in a deer decline in the Superior National Forest. U.S. For. Serv. Res. Rep. NC-148. North Central Forest Experiment Station, St. Paul, Minn.

Mech, L. D., K. E. Kunkel, R. C. Chapman, and T. J. Kreeger. 1990. Field testing of commercially manufactured capture collars on wild deer. J. Wildl. Mgmt. 54:297–299.

Murie, A. 1944. The wolves of Mt. McKinley. Nat'l Park Serv. Fauna Ser. 5. GPO, Washington, D.C.

National Park Service. 1968. Administrative policies for natural areas of the national park system. GPO, Washington, D.C.

———. 1990. Wolves for Yellowstone? A report to the United States Congress. Yellowstone National Park, Mammoth, Wyo.

Nowak, R. M. 1983. A perspective on the taxonomy of wolves in North America. Pages 10–19 in L. Carbyn, ed. Proceedings of the Canadian wolf workshop. Canadian Wildlife Service, Ottawa.

Parker, W. T. 1989. An overview and guide for experimental population designations. Red Wolf Mgmt. Ser. Tech. Rep. no. 4. U.S. Fish and Wildlife Service, Atlanta.

Peterson, R. O., and R. E. Page. 1988. The rise and fall of Isle Royale wolves, 1975–1986. J. Mamm. 69:89–99.

Phillips, M. K., and W. T. Parker. 1988 Red wolf recovery: A progress report. Conserv. Biol. 2:139–141.

Pimlott, D. H. 1967. Wolves and men in North America. Defenders of Wildlife News 42:36–53.

Rothman, R. J., and L. D. Mech. 1979. Scent-marking in lone wolves and newly formed pairs. Anim. Behav. 27:750–760.

Saharia, V. B. 1982. Wildlife in India. Natraj, Dehra Dun, India.

Shabecoff, P. 1987. The wolf, long gone, returns to the U.S. New York Times, Oct. 27, 1987, 15.

Shields, W. M. 1983. Genetic considerations in the management of the wolf and other large vertebrates: An alternative view. Pages 90–92 in L. Carbyn, ed. Proceedings of the Canadian wolf workshop. Canadian Wildlife Service, Ottawa.

Singer, F. J. 1988. The ungulate prey base for large predators in Yellowstone National Park. Res./Resources Mgmt. Rep. No. 1. National Park Service, Washington, D.C.

Smith, B. L. 1983. The status and management of the wolf in the Yukon Territory. Pages 48–50 in L. Carbyn, ed. Proceedings of the Canadian wolf workshop. Canadian Wildlife Service, Ottawa

Stardom, R. R. P. 1983. Status and management of wolves in Manitoba. Pages 30–34 in L. Carbyn, ed. Proceedings of the Canadian wolf workshop. Canadian Wildlife Service, Ottawa.

Stenlund, M. H. 1955. A field study of the timber wolf (Canis lupus) on the Superior National Forest, Minnesota. Minn. Dep't Conserv. Tech. Bull. 4.

Theberge, J. B. 1983. Considerations in wolf management related to genetic variability and adaptive change. Pages 86–89 in L. Carbyn, ed. Proceedings of the Canadian wolf workshop. Canadian Wildlife Service, Ottawa.

Thiel, R. P. 1985. The relationship between road densities and wolf habitat suitability in Wisconsin. Am. Midl. Nat. 113:404–407.

Thompson, I. D., and R. O. Peterson. 1988. Does wolf predation alone limit the moose population in Pukaskwa Park? A comment. J. Wildl. Mgmt. 52:556–559.

Tompa, F. S. 1983. Problem wolf management in British Columbia: Conflict and program evaluation. Pages 112–119 in L. Carbyn, ed. Proceedings of the Canadian wolf workshop. Canadian Wildlife Service, Ottawa.

U.S. Fish and Wildlife Service. 1987. Northern Rocky Mountain wolf recovery plan. Department of the Interior, Washington, D.C.

Van Ballenberghe, V. 1985. Wolf predation on caribou: The Nelchina herd case history. J. Wildl. Mgmt. 49:711–720.

———. 1989. Wolf predation on the Nelchina caribou herd: A comment. J. Wildl. Mgmt. 53:243–250.

Weaver, J. L. 1978. The wolves of Yellowstone. Nat'l Park Serv. Nat. Resources Rep. 14. GPO, Washington, D.C.

———. 1986. Of wolves and grizzly bears. W. Wildlands 12:27–29.

Weise, T. F., W. L. Robinson, R. A. Hook, and L. D. Mech. 1975. An experimental translocation of the eastern timber wolf. Audubon Conserv. Rep. 5. U.S. Fish and Wildlife Service, Twin Cities, Minn.

Young, S. J. 1942. The war on the wolf. Am. Forests 48:552–555, 572–574.

———. 1944. The wolves of North America. Part I. Dover, New York.

CHAPTER 21 **The Ungulate Prey Base for Wolves in Yellowstone National Park**

Francis J. Singer

Yellowstone National Park has been identified as one of three potential recovery sites for the gray wolf, *Canis lupus* (U.S. Fish and Wildlife Service 1987). Many questions have arisen regarding the choice of Yellowstone National Park and surrounding areas as a proposed recovery site, including a recovered wolf population's impact on big game numbers. Large generally unhunted populations of elk (*Cervus elaphus*) and bison (*Bison bison*) exist in the area, the size of remote national park and forest wilderness areas exceeds 2 million hectares (5 million acres), and the wolf is the only missing element of Yellowstone's fauna. Yet big game hunting is a major industry in Greater Yellowstone, and the extent to which wolves will populate areas outside the park and compete with hunters for elk and other ungulates is unknown. How much effect wolves will have on big game is debatable—the predictions range from none at all, to minor (Fischer 1986), to significant (Zumbo 1987).

Ungulates constitute the bulk of the wolf's diet across North America (Mech 1970). A first step in determining the potential success of wolf

Thanks to John Varley and Robert Barbee for their strong support and encouragement of this work. Graham Taylor, Ruth Gale, Garvis Roby, and James Yorgason graciously provided data from their surveys and field notes on elk herds that summer in Yellowstone National Park. Cathy Wilson, Dave Albert, Karl Biastoch, and Peggy Tufts assisted with the data collection and map work. Tom France and Norman Bishop graciously allowed access to their literature on wolves. Norman Bishop, Mark Boyce, Wayne Brewster, Sue Consolo, Steve Fritts, Douglas Houston, Mary Meagher, Kerry Murphy, and Doug Scott reviewed this chapter.

reintroduction to the Yellowstone area is to gather and consolidate information on the park's ungulate herds. Eight elk herds summer within Yellowstone National Park (Houston 1982:33), but only four winter wholly or partially within the park. Three bison herds exist within the park (Meagher 1973). Two of these bison herds, the Pelican Valley and Mary Mountain herds, occupy areas with deep winter snows on the park's Central Plateau (Meagher 1971). Mule deer (*Odocoileus hemionus*) summer throughout the park, but most leave in winter because of deep snows. Bighorn (*Ovis canadensis*) winter in eight locales on the northern range (Houston 1982:161). Moose (*Alces alces*) are found in low numbers throughout the park in summer and winter. Pronghorn (*Antilocapra americana*) winter in a restricted area of the northern range near Gardiner, Montana. Some pronghorn migrate each summer to the Lamar Valley, Tower Falls, and Gardners Hole areas of the northern range. A few white-tailed deer (*Odocoileus virginianus*) are observed throughout the park each summer.

This chapter primarily discusses the five ungulate species inhabiting the northern winter range. This area holds the greatest prospects for year-round wolf occupation, since it is the winter range for the Greater Yellowstone Area's largest ungulate prey base. Parkwide data on elk numbers and demography are also presented, since elk are by far the most numerous ungulate in the area. Greater detail on bison and bighorn is presented elsewhere (Meagher 1973, 1989; M. Meagher, personal communication).

STUDY AREAS

Nearly the entire area of Yellowstone National Park provides summer range for elk and to some extent other ungulates. The park is 79 percent forested; about 81 percent of the forest is dominated by lodgepole pine (*Pinus contorta*) at elevations between 2,300 m and 2,600 m (Houston 1982). In summer, elk are concentrated near wet meadows, herblands on the higher plateaus, alpine tundra, and a wide variety of forest openings (Meagher 1973; Houston 1982).

Winter snowfalls force elk and other ungulates to leave most of the park area. Annual precipitation on the Pitchstone Plateau, for example, is 190 cm, most of which falls as snow, and other high plateaus and ridges (Two Ocean Plateau, Big Game Ridge, Chicken Ridge) receive nearly as much.

Houston (1982) described Yellowstone's northern winter range as the approximately 100,000 ha between Silver Gate and Dome Mountain, Montana, where the northern Yellowstone elk herd spend their winters. About 82 percent of the northern winter range lies within Yellowstone

National Park, and the remaining 18 percent lies north of the park boundary on Gallatin National Forest and private lands. Northern range elevations are lower (1,500–2,400 m) and somewhat warmer, receiving less precipitation than the rest of the park (Houston 1982); thus more ungulates are able to winter there than on the park interior's higher plateaus (Meagher 1973; Houston 1982). Most of the northern range averages 75 cm or less total precipitation (Houston 1982; P. Farnes, unpublished data). Precipitation, however, varies greatly due to the considerable range in elevation. For example, mean annual precipitation is 30 cm near Gardiner, Montana, but 55 cm near the Lamar Ranger Station, 35 km farther uprange.

About 41 percent of the northern winter range is forested, largely Douglas fir (*Pseudotsuga menziesii*) stands with a grass understory (Cooper 1975; Houston 1982; Despain 1990). About 55 percent of the area is grassland, especially Idaho fescue (*Festuca idahoensis*) and big sagebrush (*Artemisia tridentata*) habitat types (Mueggler and Stewart 1980), about 2 percent aspen (*Populus tremuloides*) stands, and about 4 percent willow (*Salix* spp.) and riparian shrub stands. Most of the arable bottom land north of the park boundary consists of seeded and irrigated hay fields. These fields attract pronghorn, mule deer, and bison and are used to a lesser extent by elk during severe winter weather.

METHODS

State agencies from Idaho, Montana, and Wyoming were contacted for data on elk herd counts, elk movements into the park, and elk harvest statistics from areas bordering the park. The relative proportion of elk migrating into Yellowstone National Park each summer was estimated from the proportion of animals who were radio collared on winter ranges and then migrated to Yellowstone (Cada 1975; Rudd 1982; Taylor 1986; B. Smith unpubl. data) combined with aerial summer range estimates (Brown 1985). Park files and survey reports for ungulate counts between 1980 and 1984 were reviewed. Counts and classifications of elk, mule deer, and moose were conducted from 1985 to 1988 in the park, and pronghorn monitoring was conducted from 1985 to 1987.

Pronghorn. Aerial counts indicating minimum size of the pronghorn population were made from 1969 to 1989 using a small fixed-wing aircraft (Piper Super Cub). The counts were made at initial green-up, usually in March or early April, when pronghorn were still concentrated on winter range (for 1979–1989 counts, see table 21.1). Two to three ground classi-

Table 21.1 Highest aerial counts of pronghorn on Yellowstone's northern range, 1979–1989

Year	Number of Pronghorn	Pronghorn per Square km	Date of Count	Observer/Pilot
1979	152	3	4/16	M. Meagher/D. Stradley
1980	157	3	4/08	M. Meagher/D. Stradley
1981	102	2	3/21	M. Meagher/D. Stradley
1982	131	3	4/17	M. Meagher/D. Stradley
1983	310	6	3/08	M. Meagher/D. Stradley
1984	365	8	3/23	T. Black/D. Stradley
1985	364	8	4/09	A. Mitchell/D. Stradley
1986	363	8	2/28	F. Singer/B. Ferguson
1987	478	10	3/17	C. McClure/D. Stradley
1988	495	10	4/16	K. Buechner/B. Ferguson
1989	372	8	4/13	D. Trofka/B. Chapman

fications of pronghorn sex and age groups were made during the same years. The counts and classifications through 1979 are provided in Houston (1982).

Moose. Moose were counted from Piper Super Cubs incidental to elk surveys by both Barmore (1980) and Houston (1982) for the period 1968–1978. Both researchers tallied moose over the entire northern range. The areas flown, flight patterns, and pilot were consistent during all these years. Moose were not surveyed over the entire northern range after 1979. During the winters of 1985–1988, only the upper ends of five drainages (Soda Butte, Pebble, Slough, Buffalo Fork, and Hellroaring creeks) on the northern range were flown. Five or six aerial surveys were flown during each winter-spring period. No sightability correction was available for moose.

Horseback surveys of moose were conducted in the upper ends of the same five drainages on the northern range outside the park. These surveys were conducted during two periods, 1942–1949 and 1985–1987 (Swenson 1985; Puchlerz 1986). The same trails were ridden each year during mid-September. About 11–15 km were ridden each day, and the average number of moose seen per rider-day was tabulated.

Mule deer. Mule deer were counted by one observer from a small helicopter in 1979, 1986, 1988, and 1989. In 1987, a Jet Ranger II helicopter and two observers were employed. Fawn to adult ratios were recorded during the helicopter surveys. These surveys were conducted during the period of spring green-up, usually from late February to late March. Areas surveyed, sequence of areas surveyed, and one observer (Singer) were consistent. No sightability correction was available for mule deer.

Elk.   Elk were counted from a Piper Super Cub during a one- to three-day period in early winter during 1952–1979. Data from these and more variable aerial and ground counts are summarized through the year 1979 in Houston (1982). Two aircraft with pilot-observer teams were used to count elk in the winter of 1981–1982, but no more counts were made until 1985. During the next three winters, 1985–1988, elk counts were completed in a single day using four aircraft simultaneously to eliminate errors from elk movements between count days. No sightability correction was available for elk prior to 1986.

The elk counts after 1986 were subjected to sightability corrections according to the method of Samuel et al. (1987). A total of 47 elk were radio collared on the northern range between 1986 and 1988. The northern range was divided into sixty-six count units (figure 21.1). Each count unit was flown in sequence by a pilot-observer team, and the search time was recorded. From the air, each group of elk was counted, radio collars were noted, the group location was plotted on a 1:24,000-scale map, and the percentages of snow cover and tree cover were estimated. Immediately before or after the survey flight, a separate aircraft was used to locate all radio-collared elk. A sightability model (stepwise logistic regression) employing the variables of pilot, observer, search time per square mile, percentage of tree cover, percentage of snow cover, and group size was developed from the numbers of radio-collared elk observed or not observed. The model was then applied to the conditions of tree cover, snow cover, and group size observed in each count unit during each survey (Samuel et al. 1987). All sixty-six count units were flown during each aircraft survey.

Classifications of elk sex and age groups were made from the park road with the aid of a 15–45 power spotting scope during 1964–1986 (Barmore 1980; Houston 1982, J. Swenson unpubl. data). During late winter in 1987, 1988, and 1989, classifications of elk sex and age were conducted from a helicopter.

RESULTS

Pronghorn.   Between 1930 and 1947, pronghorn numbers on the northern winter range varied from 500 to 800 (Houston 1982). Concern about declines in big sagebrush on the pronghorn winter range motivated park staff to artificially reduce pronghorn numbers during the 1947–1967 period

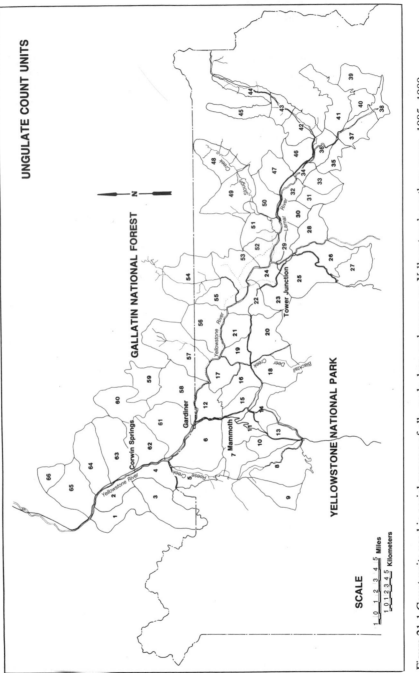

Figure 21.1 Count units used in aerial surveys of elk, mule deer, and moose on Yellowstone's northern range, 1985–1989.

(Houston 1982:168). As a result of the reductions, counts were below 200 during the 1969–1980 period (Scott 1987; Houston 1982). Fawn ratios remained low at 38 ± 15 ($\bar{x}$ + SD) fawns per 100 does from 1967 to 1979 (Houston 1982). During the 1980s, however, pronghorn increased three-fold to nearly 500 animals (table 21.1). Fawn ratios were not determined from 1980 to 1984, but ratios after 1984 were higher than for the 1967–1979 period. A total of 80 fawns per 100 does were observed in November 1986, the highest recorded ratio since 1963 (Houston 1982). Pronghorn density on the 48-km area of winter use increased from 3 per km² in 1979 to 10 per km² in 1988. Pronghorn declined about 27 percent following the drought of 1988 and the severe winter of 1988–1989.

In 1983, two fields on the Royal Teton Ranch near Spring Creek, about .5 km north of the park, were plowed and reseeded, which attracted 20–25 pronghorn. After complaints from the landowner, a damage-control hunt was instituted on the ranch from 1985 to 1988 (table 21.2). Of the total herd, 2–10 percent was harvested each year on private lands.

Mule deer.   Mule deer have increased from 1,007 in 1979 (Erickson 1979) to 2,217 (a 120 percent increase) in 1988 (table 21.3). Surveys using helicopters proved 43–62 percent more effective than Piper Super Cubs in spotting mule deer (table 21.3). Time devoted to the count increased 75 percent between the 1979–1986 period and 1987–1988. The increase in search effort was largely a product of counting more mule deer and counting to higher snow lines. The winters of 1986–1987 and 1987–1988 were mild. Snowpacks averaged 70–80 percent and 50–70 percent of the average, respectively. The snow line was 480–800 m higher during the 1987 count than during the 1986 count, and 300–800 m higher during the 1988 count than during the 1987 count. Aircraft typically flew only up to snow line since all the deer were concentrated below snow line on green-up. As a result of higher snow lines, the size of the area counted increased in 1987 and 1988. Helicopter surveys of mule deer in the Bridger Mountains, where terrain and vegetation are similar, yielded about a 66 percent sightability (Mackie et al. 1980), suggesting that the herd on the northern range might number at least 3,000 mule deer.

Highest densities of mule deer were in count units 2 and 4 west of the Yellowstone River and north of Yellowstone National Park (figures 21.1 and 21.2). These count units include most of the irrigated hay fields of the Royal Teton Ranch, which provides additional mule deer habitat. Spring ratios of fawns per 100 adult mule deer have been very high ($\bar{x}$ = 45) in most years, except for 1983 and 1989, corresponding to the dramatic

Table 21.2 Pronghorn damage control hunt statistics on Yellowstone's northern range, 1985–1989

Year	No. Permits Issued	No. Animals Killed	Approximate Percentage of Herd
1985–1986	15	10–12	3
1986–1987	50	12–15	2
1987–1988	39	16	3
1988–1989	100	49	10

Source: Data obtained from K. Alt, Montana Department of Fish, Wildlife, and Parks files.

Table 21.3 Aerial counts of mule deer on Yellowstone's northern range, 1979–1989

Year	Date of Count	Deer Counted	Pilot	Observer(s)	Aircraft
1979	—	572	D. Stradley	Houston	Super Cub
1979	4/3	1,007	M. Duffy	Erickson	Jet Ranger II
1986	3/4	706	B. Ferguson	Singer	Super Cub
1986	3/14–15	1,863	C. Rogers	Singer	Bell-206
1987	3/31–4/1	2,134	M. Duffy	Alt/Hoppe/Singer	Jet Ranger II
1988	4/11–12	2,217	G. Ewen	Singer/McClure	Helier 12-E
1989	4/30–5/2	1,796	R. Hawkins	Lemke/Singer	Helier 12-E

Sources: Erickson 1979; Houston 1982; Singer 1986; Alt, Hoppe, and Singer 1987; Singer et al. 1988; Lemke and Singer 1989.

increase in mule deer numbers since 1979 (table 21.4). The mule deer count declined about 19 percent after the severe winter of 1988–1989. Fawn mortality was apparently high, and late winter 1988–1989 fawn ratios were the lowest for the decade (table 21.4).

Harvests of mule deer in the area steadily increased during the 1980s; 1983 had the highest reported harvest on record for the area (Foss 1985; table 21.4).

White-tailed deer.   White-tailed deer were probably never common anywhere in Yellowstone National Park, and they were rare on the northern range (Skinner 1929). The area lacks the extensive riverine deciduous shrubs and forests that typify white-tailed deer habitat in Montana (Allen 1968; Martinka 1968; Dusek 1981). Snow depths south of the Mammoth-

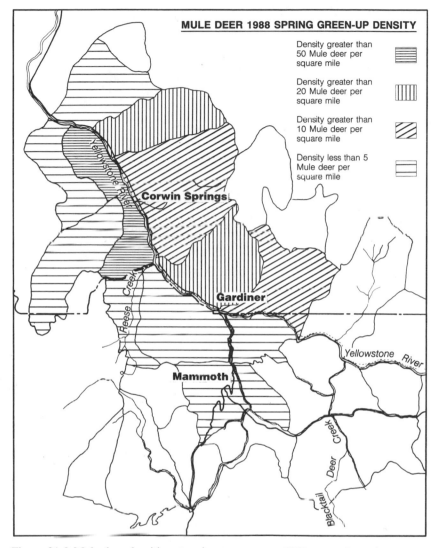

Figure 21.2 Mule deer densities at spring green-up on Yellowstone's northern range (count units correspond to those in figure 21.1).

Gardiner area are excessive for white-tailed deer, although the animals have been observed to winter in thickets along the lower Gardner and Yellowstone rivers at the park boundary. Yellowstone Park represents the very fringe of white-tailed deer habitat. Skinner (1927) reported about 100 white-tailed deer on the northern range prior to 1916. Between 1914 and 1921 the population declined, and by 1924 white-tailed deer were gone

Table 21.4 Deer harvest and classification data for Yellowstone's northern range north of the park boundary and east of the Yellowstone River (Hunting District 313)

	Posthunting Season (Dec.) Ratios				Spring Ratios				Harvests	
Year	Bucks: 100 Does	Fawns: 100 Does	Fawns: 100 Adults	Sample Size	Fawns: 100 Adults	Sample Size	Fawn Mortality (%)	Recruitment	Mule Deer	Whitetails
1979	17	67	52	345	32	1,108	23	29	234	9
1980	—	—	61	286	—	—	—	—	256	11
1981	15	65	56	97	40	300	29	29	504	27
1982	—	—	55	381	48	727	13	32	571	44
1983	7	65	60	303	29	420	52	23	746	11
1984	21	88	73	159	47	508	36	32	580	12
1985	0	42	42	68	44	562	0	31	404	33
1986	—	—	—	—	50	624	—	—	488	31
1987	—	—	—	—	47	2,134	—	—	358	17
1988	—	—	—	—	52	1,936	—	—	503	33
1989	4	41	38	745	14	1,796	—	—	—	—

Sources: Foss 1985; Alt, Hoppe, and Singer 1987; Singer et al. 1988; Lemke 1990.

altogether from the northern range (Skinner 1929). Supplemental feeding at Gardiner and Mammoth likely influenced white-tailed deer presence in the park during the early 1920s. Harvests suggest that white-tailed deer increased substantially on the northern range just north of Yellowstone (Hunting Districts 313 and 314) during the 1980s (table 21.4). Wildlife report cards from Yellowstone National Park files include eighteen summer sightings of white-tailed deer within the boundaries of Yellowstone during the 1980s.

Moose.   Moose reportedly had colonized the area south of Yellowstone Lake and the Jackson Hole region by the 1870s (Houston 1982:158). Moose did not appear on the northern range or in adjacent south-central Montana until around 1913 (Stevens 1971; Walcheck 1976; Houston 1982). These reports may describe either an increase of moose, which were considered rare at the time, or moose that were returning after a period of absence.

By the 1930s and 1940s moose had increased on the northern range and were abundant around Slough Creek (McDowell and Moy 1942). The subsequent status of moose on the northern range is unclear. Chadde and Kay (1988), citing unpublished Gallatin National Forest files, reported that moose sightings by U.S. Forest Service personnel declined between 1940 and the early 1960s. Erickson (1979) reported that moose numbers were relatively stable from 1961 to the late 1970s. Moose seen on elk-observation flights in 1969–1973 (figure 21.3) averaged 32 ± 16 ($\bar{x} \pm SD$) in December and 45 ± 20 in May, but these counts declined to 17 ± 9 in December and 27 ± 10 in May for the years 1974 to 1977. Mean declines for December and May were 47 percent and 40 percent, respectively ($t = 3.68$, $df = 4$, $p < .05$ for December; $t = 1.67$, $df = 7$, $p < .15$ for May). Counts in upper Slough Creek suggested a decline of moose in the mid-1970s with a recovery of population numbers by the late 1980s (table 21.5). However, twice as many moose were seen in the 1940s during horseback surveys as in the 1980s (table 21.6).

Houston (1982:169) conservatively estimated that there were 200 moose on the northern range in 1979. Moose harvests increased from 35 in 1979 to 47 in 1986 on bordering areas. If Houston's estimate was correct, then these harvests corresponded to 18 percent and 24 percent of the population, respectively. If moose did increase in the 1980s (table 21.4), then the relative harvest rates would be decreased. Montana hunting districts were realigned in 1986 to better distribute the harvest, and beginning in 1986 the number of permits was increased. Decreasing the moose population was a corrective to reduced carrying capacity and low calf ratios (Swenson 1985).

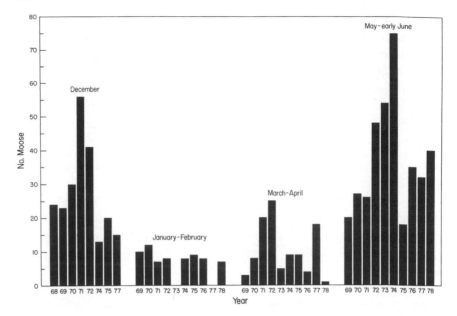

Figure 21.3 Number of moose observed incidentally during elk distribution flights on Yellowstone's northern range from December to early June of each year, 1968–1978 (Barmore 1980; Houston 1982). Upper Soda Butte and upper Hellroaring drainages were not surveyed.

Northern Yellowstone elk herd.   From 1970 to 1988, as the northern elk herd recovered from the population reduction period, it was characterized by population growth and further migrations north of the park by more of the herd. The herd had been reduced to fewer than 5,000 animals by 1968 because of artificial removals by park staff since 1935. By the late 1970s counts had increased to about 12,000 (Houston 1982). Population size averaged 9,026 between 1970 and 1974 (Houston 1982:17) and 11,906 from 1975 to 1980 (table 21.7).

In the 1980s, the northern elk herd steadily increased to a population of 18,913 in 1988. Population size averaged 16,488 from 1981 to 1988 (table 21.7). Sightability of elk was about 86 percent during the winter of 1986–1987, and about 91 percent the following winter (1987–1988). Bull to cow ratios in the northern herd averaged 30:100 and calf to cow ratios averaged 20:100 from 1986 to 1988.

The percentage of the northern elk herd migrating from the park averaged 7 between 1970 and 1974 (Houston 1982:29) and 17 from 1975 to 1988. Elk became more available to hunters north of the park beginning in 1975. Harvest of the prehunt population averaged less than 1 percent in

Table 21.5 Highest winter counts of moose, 1968–1978, seen in specific locales incidental to elk counts on Yellowstone's northern range

Year	Below Mammoth	Gardner River–Mount Everts	Above Mammoth–Gardners Hole	Blacktail Plateau	Tower Area	Lower Slough Creek	Upper Slough Creek	Lamar Valley
1968–1969	4	3	4	1	4	1	14	6
1969–1970	5	2	11	2	5	3	10	3
1970–1971	2	1	5	7	9	10	13	5
1971–1972	3	1	16	8	14	25	27	6
1972–1973	1	3	6	0	13	14	14	1
1973–1974	3	3	4	3	14	14	23	11
1974–1975	3	3	7	1	4	7	6	2
1975–1976	5	4	6	2	13	15	3	2
1976–1977	1	1	3	3	12	6	9	3
1977–1978	1	3	4	2	8	2	11	7
1985–1986	—	—	—	—	—	—	4	—
1986–1987	—	—	—	—	—	—	14	—
1987–1988	—	—	—	—	—	—	28	—
1988–1989	—	—	—	—	—	—	29	—

Source: Data from Barmore (1980) and Houston (1982).

Note: Locales other than upper Slough Creek were not available for comparison in 1985–1989.

Table 21.6 Autumn horseback counts of moose on the northeastern northern range (upper Hellroaring, Buffalo Fork, and Slough Creek drainages), Gallatin National Forest

Year	Period	No. Days[a]	Moose Seen	Moose Observed per Day
1942	June–Oct.	100	194	1.94
1947	9/5–10/3	29	78	2.69
1948	9/4–9/29	26	53	2.04
1949	9/8–9/27	20	24	1.20
1985	9/11–9/20	23	12	0.52
1986	9/11–9/17	16	13	0.81
1987	9/9–9/14	22	20	0.90
1988	9/11–10/15	22	59	2.70
1989	9/11–9/17	34	36	1.06

[a]Several parties surveyed each day.
Sources: Swenson 1985; Puchlerz 1986.

1970–1974 (Houston 1982:17), 8 percent from 1975 to 1980, and 9 percent from 1981 to 1988 (table 21.7). Bulls represented the majority of the late season harvest until 1981–1982 and the majority of the general season harvest until 1986–1987 (table 21.7). Harvest prior to 1981, therefore, had proportionally less effect (if any) upon population growth.

Seven of the first eight winters in the 1980s received lower than average precipitation. The 1988 drought caused a decline in forage production, the 1988 fires burned 39 percent of the northern winter range, hunters took an estimated 14–16 percent of the herd, and another 24–27 percent were winter-killed during 1988–1989 (table 21.7). The elk count declined to 10,908 in the late winter (table 21.7). Elk sightability declined to 60 percent, apparently due to deep-crusted snow, smaller groups of elk, and their greater tendency to use tree cover.

Bulls and calves died at a higher rate during the severe winter of 1988–1989. By late winter bull to cow ratios were 18:100 and calf to cow ratios were 7:100 (Singer et al. 1989). The typically low calf ratios for the northern elk herd (Houston 1982; Singer 1990) imply the potential for a strong compensatory reproduction response if wolves are restored to Yellowstone.

Elk in the remainder of Yellowstone National Park. In 1987–1988 an estimated 31,000 elk summered, and approximately 20,000 elk wintered, within the park boundaries (table 21.8). Significant portions of seven different elk herds and a few animals from an eighth herd, the Carter Mountain herd, summer within Yellowstone National Park (figure 21.4). Radio-collared elk were representative of all sex groups, age groups, and capture sites on winter ranges; thus these figures are probably useful as tenuous but preliminary estimates.

Elk from more than one herd share several summer ranges in Yellowstone National Park. Two summer ranges are shared by three herds: the Madison Plateau (occupied by the Madison-Firehole, Sand Creek, and northern herds); and the Madison-Firehole area (occupied by the Madison-Firehole, Gallatin, and northern herds) (figure 21.4). In the upper Yellowstone River–Thorofare area, southeast of Yellowstone Lake, as many as four elk herds (the Jackson, North Fork Shoshone, northern, and possibly a few elk from the Carter Mountain herd) share a summer range. Summer ranges in the central and north-central portions of the park are occupied only by the northern herd.

Elk summer distributions have changed somewhat in the 1980s. About 800 elk from the Jackson herd once migrated northeast of Jackson Lake to summer on the Pitchstone Plateau in the 1960s (J. Yorgason, pers. comm.; B. Smith, unpubl. data). This segment may have been eliminated due to extensive hunting on Uhl Hill of elk that traveled across Burned Ridge and Antelope Flats toward the National Elk Refuge. Alternatively, there may have been a natural shift in migration patterns (M. Boyce, pers. comm.). In either case, the Pitchstone Plateau is now occupied in summer primarily by the Sand Creek herd (Brown 1985).

A small number of elk wintered in scattered thermal areas. A survey on April 16, 1988, counted 31 elk in small thermal areas, including 11 elk in the Bechler Meadows area, 11 elk in the Heart Lake Geyser basin, 5 elk at Hot Springs Geyser basin, and 4 elk near West Thumb Geyser basin.

Population trends have varied considerably among the herds. The Sand Creek herd increased fivefold from 1959 to 1983, but was relatively stable or increasing slowly between 1983 and 1988 (Chu, Naderman, and Gale 1988). Present management goals in the *Sands Management Plan* (Bureau of Land Management 1978) call for no further growth of the Sand Creek herd due to potential conflicts with livestock grazing (Trent, Parker, and Naderman 1985) and aim to keep the herd to a count of 2,000 posthunt on the winter range (J. Naderman, pers. comm.). The Madison portion of the Gallatin herd, however, grew to about 650 elk in the 1980s (Taylor 1984). Counts of the Madison-Firehole elk herd declined 21 percent during the 1980s (F. Singer and G. Bowser, unpubl. data). Six aerial counts conducted

Table 21.7 Aerial counts, harvests, and sightability estimates of elk on Yellowstone's northern range, 1978–1989

Year	Actual Early Winter Count	Actual Count In Park	Actual Count North of Park	Estimated Prehunt Population Count Size[a]	Sightability Corrected Prehunt Population[b]	Total Harvest	% of Prehunt Count (or of Corrected Count) Harvested	% Bulls in Harvest General	% Bulls in Harvest Late	% Total Harvest in Late Hunt
1974–1975	12,607	9,821	2,786[d]	12,607	—	147	1	48	no hunt	0
1975–1976	12,014	10,314	1,700[d]	13,218	—	1,401	11	74	68	86
1976–1977	8,980[eg]	8,480	500	8,980	—	88	1	82	no hunt	0
1977–1978	12,680	10,480	2,200[d]	13,483	—	952	7	81	56	84
1978–1979	10,838	9,338	1,500	10,908	—	268	3	78	86	26
1979–1980[f]	—	—	—	—	—	605	6	79	61	80
1980–1981[f]	—	—	—	—	—	247	—	84	56	54
1981–1982	16,019	14,922	1,097	16,462	—	1,234	7	90	48	82
1982–1983[f]	—	—	—	—	—	1,804	—	95	33	81
1983–1984[f]	—	—	—	—	—	1,955	—	78	24	85
1984–1985[f]	—	—	—	—	—	1,419	—	75	14	75
1985–1986	16,286	13,288	2,998	16,599	—	1,371	8	80	12	77
1986–1987	17,007	15,284	1,723	17,773	—	1,595	9	52	8	52
1987–1988	18,913	18,430	483	19,000	21,075–22,961	215	1 (0.9)	—	5	77
1988–1989	10,908[g]	5,618	5,290	12,608	17,207–19,059	2,773	22 (15)	—	2	—

Note: These figures were extended to 1976–1977, the approximate year when elk began to recolonize the area north of Yellowstone Park following the 1960s reductions. Also, 1976–1977 marked the resumption of significant harvests north of the park and an increase in the elk herd's carrying capacity as a consequence of the resumed migration.

[a] Most early winter counts were conducted December to January following the general hunt (approximately October 19 to November 30) and either preceded the late hunt (usually December 15 to February 15) or took place during the early part of the late hunt. The total elk taken during hunts on the date of the count were added back into the actual early winter count to estimate the prehunt size.

[b] The sightability correction is further described in Singer et al. (1989).

[c] Both the general (October to November) and special late (December to February) hunts were combined.

[d] Maximum counts of elk outside Yellowstone Park occurred later during the winter than the early winter counts on April 12–13, 1975, December 17–18, 1976, and January 30, 1978.

[e] Houston (1982:16,23) subtracted elk harvested by the date of the aerial count, 1976–1980, in order to report a late winter population size. To be consistent, we added those removals back in.

[f] No counts were made these winters.

[g] The 1976–1977 and 1988–1989 early winter counts were poor counts that were conducted after elk had dispersed into forests.

Table 21.8 Estimates of elk from eight herds summering and wintering in Yellowstone National Park, 1965–1988

Name of Herd	Herd Size	Proportion of Radio-Collared Elk Summering	Sample Size of Collared Elk	Est. No. Summering	Mean No. Wintering	Years of Radio-Location Data	Days Spent on Summer Range	Summer Locations
Gallatin	1,850[c1]	.48	72	900	580[c]	1969–1986	150	Gallatin Range, Specimen Creek
Sand Creek	4,900[e]	.21	84	1,056[e]	0	1981–1987	138	Bechler Meadows, Madison Plateau, Chick Creek
Jackson	11,000[e2]	.28	85	3,080	0	1978–1982	150	Thorofare, Two Ocean Plateau, Big Game and Chicken ridges
Carter Mountain	2,550[e]	—[3]	0[3]	100+	0	1986–1988	—	South Fork Shoshone
North Fork Shoshone	2,600[e]	.78	18	2,020	0–500	1979–1980	160	Signal Hills, Thorofare
Clarks Fork	3,180[e]	.83	18	2,600	0	1979–1980	160	Upper Lamar, Pelican Valley, Mist Creek
Northern	21,000[e]	.98	68	20,580	17,457	1985–1988	140	All of Yellowstone Park
Madison-Firehole	800[c]	1.00	6	800	800	1965–1966	—	Madison drainage, Madison Plateau
Total				31,136	18,380–19,337			

c = count

e = estimate

[1]Vales and Peek (1990) concluded that this number is an underestimation of the herd size.

[2]A 1989 model revises the estimate for the Jackson herd to over 16,000 elk for 1987 and 1988 (Lockman, Roby, and Woolrab 1989).

[3]No radiotelemetry studies were conducted on the Carter Mountain herd. Such a study is scheduled for 1990 (L. Roop, pers. comm.).

Sources: Cada 1970–1975; Craighead et al. 1973; Taylor 1981–1986; Rudd 1982; Brown 1985; Davidson et al. 1985, 1986; Yorgason et al. 1986; Boyce 1989; Vore 1990; B. Smith (in press); D. Vales unpubl. data.

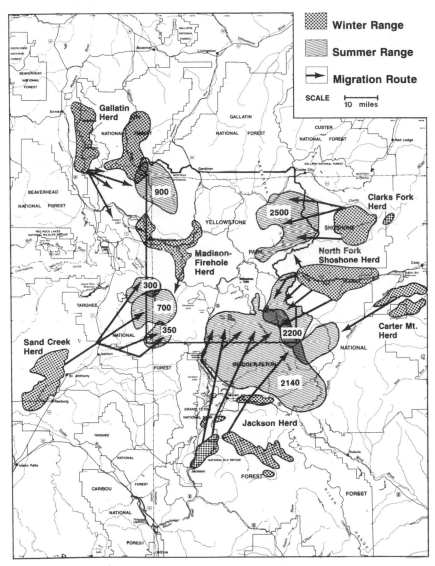

Figure 21.4 The approximate winter ranges and summering areas for seven elk herds other than the northern herd that use Yellowstone National Park.

from 1965 to 1980 averaged 763 elk (range 593–959), whereas eight counts conducted in 1985–1988 averaged only 601 elk (range 487–736). Since no sightability correction is available for these counts, the trends are speculative.

Harvest levels on the eight elk herds also varied considerably (table

21.9). The Jackson, Sand Creek, and Gallatin herds were harvested near, at, or above maximum sustained yield (table 21.9; Boyce 1989). Boyce (1989) calculated that the Jackson herd harvest averaged 86 percent of maximum sustained yield. Harvests of the North Fork Shoshone and Clarks Fork herds were more moderate, and harvests of the northern and Madison-Firehole herds averaged 9 percent and less than 1 percent, respectively (table 21.9).

POTENTIAL PREY BASE FOR WOLVES

An average of 14,491 ungulates on the northern range from 1980 to 1988 and 4,030 ungulates on other park ranges in 1988 were completely available to large predators (table 21.10). Ungulates in the Yellowstone River canyon between Gardiner and Dome Mountain, Montana (average 4,064) were judged to be less available to wolves because of 800 year-round human residents and extensive road access. From 1980 to 1988, about 22,963 ungulates wintered in Yellowstone Park. The total summer in-park ungulate population may have exceeded 37,804 (table 21.10). When considering only ungulates completely available to wolves and a minimally recovered population of 100 wolves, initial wolf to ungulate ratios park-wide would be 1:225 in winter and 1:378 in summer. A minimally recovered wolf population of 100 wolves would correspond to the following mean ratios for the 1980–1988 period: (1) 1 wolf:145 ungulates on the northern range within the park (14,491 ungulates); (2) 1 wolf:231 ungulates for all the northern range and all other winter ranges combined (23,085 ungulates); and (3) 1 wolf:186 ungulates for all of the northern range both inside and outside Yellowstone National Park (18,555 ungulates).

Keith (1983) reported wolf to ungulate ratios of 1:96–328 for wolf-occupied areas of North America. A minimally recovered population of wolves in Yellowstone would be on the high side of these ratios. Theberge (1990) cautioned that wolf to prey ratios be used for preliminary assessments only. He argued that functional responses in wolf predation, lags in numerical responses of wolves, variable rates of prey switching, variable use of nonungulate prey, and the proximity of ungulates to their nutrient-climate ceiling greatly complicated use of wolf to prey ratios. Wolf predation tends to be compensatory with starvation when the ungulate population is near ecological carrying capacity and thus has less population consequence, but wolf predation is additive to other mortality below that level (Theberge and Gauthier 1985).

Recovery of elk populations will take several years. The events of 1988,

Table 21.9 Estimated population sizes and harvests of eight elk herds inhabiting Yellowstone National Park, 1980–1987

Elk Herd	Population Size	Mean Harvest	Period	Sex and Age Classes Harvested				Source
				Spikes	Mature Bulls	Cow	Calves	
Jackson	11,000e	2,913	1950–1987		818[1]	1,043	320	Boyce 1989
Sand Creek	4,900e	966	1981–1987	310	297	359[2]	31	Trent, Parker, and Naderman 1987
Gallatin[3]	2,500c	912	1980–1985	320	342	219	23	Taylor 1981–1986
North Fork Shoshone	2,600e	570	1982–1987	122	245	80	23	Yorgason 1986
Clarks Fork	3,180e	713	1982–1987	103	236	313	61	Yorgason 1986
Carter Mountain	2,550e	658	1982–1986	162	170	262	64	Yorgason 1986
Madison-Firehole	800c	< 20	1980–1988	—	—	—	—	Craighead et al. 1973
Northern	18,986se	1,401	(a) 1980–1986, reg.	87	132	73	106	Foss 1985
			(b) 1980–1987, late	59	198	574	207	

Note: Several harvest rates are likely overestimated since population sizes are likely underestimated.

c = count

e = estimate

se = sightability estimate

[1] Combined total for spikes and older bulls.

[2] The antlerless category includes calves, but the numbers were not available.

[3] In this case, elk numbers and harvests on the southeastern side of the Madison Valley are included (for example, Hunting District 360).

Table 21.10 Ungulates available to large predators in Yellowstone National Park, 1980–1988

| | Winter Counts[1] | | | | | | Summer Estimates |
| | Northern Winter Range | | | | Other Winter Ranges[2] | | (All Yellowstone Park, including Northern Range) |
Species	Completely Available to Wolves (M)	Less Available to Wolves near Gardiner (M)	Total Northern Range, Low and High Counts	All of Northern Range Postfire, 1989–1990	1988	1989	
Elk	15,681	1,776	10,226–19,000	15,000	1,900	600	31,136
Bison	433[3]	0	233–594	457	~2,000	<2,000	>2,500
Pronghorn	100	292	102–495	372	0	0	495
Mule deer[4]	~100	1,714	1,007–2,274	1,796	<30	<30	>3,000
Bighorn[5]	~176	160–180	300–600	—	<30	—	>273
Moose	200e	a few	—	—	>100	>50	>300[6]
White-tailed deer	<10	<100	—	<100	0	0	<100
Total	16,700+	4,062+	—	17,725	4,030+	2,680	37,804+[6]
Ungulates : wolf for 100 wolves	145	41	—	154	—	—	378

e = estimate from Houston 1982.

[1] Actual counts for all species. Average counts are provided for the period 1980–1988 except for pronghorn and bighorn, where only recent counts are provided since pronghorn were still recovering from reductions and bighorn from a disease outbreak (Meagher n.d.). Elk and bison counts were conducted during early winter; mule deer and pronghorn counts were conducted during spring green-up (March–April).

[2] Includes Madison-Firehole, Pelican Valley, upper Yellowstone River–Thorofare.

[3] Means of 1980–1987 counts (Meagher 1989).

[4] Mule deer numbers parkwide are almost totally unknown; however, most of the mule deer from the northern range are suspected to migrate each summer into the park. Summer mule deer numbers for the entire park are likely several times that of the northern herd.

[5] Data from Meagher (pers. comm.) for 1980–1988. Winter ranges north of the park included both Cinnabar Mountain and Spring Creek areas. Also, an unknown number of bighorn occupy the Thorofare Creek–Trident area of the park.

[6] Moose and mule deer parkwide in summer are likely greatly underestimated.

including the reduction of forage due to drought, the burning of winter ranges in the autumn, and a severe winter, resulted in increased harvest and winterkill of ungulates (Singer et al. 1989). Reductions in most ungulate populations were between 10 and 20 percent. The northern Yellowstone elk herd, however, declined about 40 percent, and the Madison-Firehole herd probably declined more than 50 percent (Singer et al. 1989). Elk calf crops were reduced in 1989, apparently as a consequence of the severe winter (Singer et al. 1989).

Research over the next few years will be directed at documenting the effects of the 1988 fires on elk populations and habitat relationships. The carrying capacity of Yellowstone's elk ranges is predicted to increase as a result of the fires. Herbaceous and shrub production (Lyon and Stickney 1976), along with protein content and palatability, will likely increase in forages returning on burned areas (Spalinger, Robbins, and Hanley 1986). Winter-range enhancement may be very brief; the positive effects of burning on grasses and forbs often lasts only one to five years (Hobbs and Spowart 1984; Wood 1988). Summer-range enhancement may be more significant than winter-range effects. Many new forest openings will be created, and herbaceous and shrub vegetation will increase in burned forests. Elk population responses should take just a few years. The recovery of the park's ungulates to levels at least equal to and possibly higher than prefire levels would likely occur before wolves were reintroduced into the park.

REFERENCES

Allen, E. O. 1968. Range use, foods, condition, and productivity of white-tailed deer in Montana. J. Wildl. Mgmt. 32:130–141.

Alt, K., P. Hoppe, and F. Singer. 1987. Northern Yellowstone spring mule deer count. Yellowstone National Park, Gallatin National Forest, and Montana Department of Fish, Wildlife, and Parks files.

Barmore, W. J. 1980. Population characteristics, distribution, and habitat relationships of six ungulate species on winter range in Yellowstone Park. Final report. Research office, Yellowstone National Park.

Boyce, M. S. 1989. The Jackson elk herd: Intensive wildlife management in North America. Cambridge Univ. Press, Cambridge.

Brown, C. 1985. Sand Creek elk. Completion Rep. Proj. W-160-R. Idaho Dep't of Fish and Game, Boise.

Bureau of Land Management. 1978. Sands habitat management plan. Department of the Interior, Idaho Falls District, Idaho Falls.

Cada, J. 1970–1975. Gallatin big game studies. P-R Proj. W-130-R-17. Montana Dep't of Fish and Game, Helena.

Chadde, S., and C. Kay. 1988. Willows and moose: A study of grazing pressure, Slough Creek exclosure, Montana, 1961–1986. Mont. For. Conserv. Exper. Sta. Res. Note 24:1–5. Univ. of Montana, Missoula.

Chu, T., J. Naderman, and R. Gale. 1988. Elk, Region 6. in L. E. Oldenburg, L. J. Nelson, J. Turner, and B. Mulligan, eds. Statewide Surv. and Inven. Proj. W-170-R-12. Idaho Dep't of Fish and Game, Boise.

Cooper, S. V. 1975. Forest habitat types of northwestern Wyoming and contiguous portions of Montana and Idaho. Ph.D. thesis, Washington State Univ., Pullman.

Craighead, F., C. Craighead, Jr., R. L. Ruff, and B. W. O'Gara. 1973. Home ranges and activity patterns of nonmigratory elk of the Madison drainage herd as determined by radiotelemetry. Wildl. Monogr. 33:1–50.

Davidson, D., et al. 1985. Elk. Area 5. Completion Rep. P-R Proj. W-170-R. Idaho Dep't of Fish and Game, Boise.

———. 1986. Elk. Area 5. Completion Rep. P-R Proj. W-17-R. Idaho Dep't of Fish and Game, Boise.

Despain, D. 1990. Yellowstone vegetation: Consequences of environment and history in a natural setting. Roberts Rinehart, Boulder, Colo.

Dusek, G. L. 1981. Population ecology and habitat relationships of white-tailed deer in river bottom habitat in eastern Montana. Pages 75–100 in R. J. Mackie, ed. Montana deer studies. P-R Proj. W-120-R-12. Montana Dep't of Fish, Wildlife, and Parks, Bozeman.

Erickson, G. 1979. Game production count, mule deer, Hunting Dist. 313 and Yellowstone National Park. Montana Dep't of Fish, Wildlife, and Parks files, Bozeman.

Fischer, H. 1986. L. David Mech discusses the wolf. Defenders 61:7–15.

Foss, A. 1985. Montana big game survey and inventory, Region 3. Job Prog. Rep. Job No. I-3 Segment A. P-R Proj. W-130-R-15. Montana Dep't of Fish, Wildlife, and Parks, Helena.

Hobbs, N. T., and R. A. Spowart. 1984. Effects of prescribed fire on nutrition of mountain sheep and mule deer during winter and spring. J. Wildl. Mgmt. 48:551–560.

Houston, D. B. 1982. The northern Yellowstone elk. Macmillan, New York.

Keith, L. B. 1983. Population dynamics of wolves. Pages 66–77 in L. N. Carbyn, ed. Wolves in Canada and Alaska: Their status, biology, and management. Can. Wildl. Serv. Rep. Ser. 45. Ottawa.

Lemke, T. 1990. Northern Yellowstone Cooperative spring mule deer survey. Yellowstone National Park files.

Lemke, T., and F. Singer. 1989. Northern Yellowstone cooperative spring mule deer survey: Interagency count. Yellowstone National Park, Gallatin National Forest, and Montana Department of Fish, Wildlife, and Parks files.

Lockman, D., G. Roby, and L. Woolrab. 1989. Pages 1–20, 59–71, 214–263, 301–313, 354–377, 414–426 in Annual big game herd unit reports, Dis. I. Wyoming Game and Fish Department, Cody.

Lyon, L. J., and P. F. Stickney. 1976. Early vegetal succession following large northern Rocky Mountain wildfires. Proc. Tall Timbers Fire Ecol. Conf. 16:344–375.

McDowell, L., and M. Moy. 1942. Montana moose survey: Hellroaring-Buffalo-Slough Creek Unit. Montana Department of Fish, Wildlife, and Parks, Helena.

Mackie, R. J., et al. 1980. Montana deer studies. P-R Proj. W-120-R-12. Montana Dep't of Fish, Wildlife, and Parks, Bozeman.

Martinka, C. J. 1968. Habitat relationships of white-tailed and mule deer in northern Montana. J. Wildl. Mgmt. 32:558–565.

Meagher, M. M. 1971. Winter weather as a population regulating influence on free-ranging bison in Yellowstone National Park. Pages 29–38 in Research in the parks. Trans. Nat'l Park Serv. Symp. Ser. 1.

———. 1973. The bison of Yellowstone National Park. Nat'l Park Serv. Sci. Monogr. Ser. 1. GPO, Washington, D.C.

———. 1989. Range expansion by bison of Yellowstone National Park. J. Mammal. 70:670–675.

———. In review. Infectious keratoconjunctivitis in bighorn sheep of Yellowstone National Park: Population consequences. J. Wildl. Dis.

Mech, D. L. 1970. The wolf: The ecology and behavior of an endangered species. Natural History Press/Doubleday, New York.

Mueggler, W. F., and W. L. Stewart. 1980. Grassland and shrubland habitat types of western Montana. U.S. For. Serv. Gen. Tech. Rep. INT-66. Ogden, Utah.

Puchlerz, T. 1986. Moose survey. Gardiner Ranger District, Gallatin National Forest, Gardiner, Mont.

Rudd, W. J. 1982. Elk migrations and movements in relation to weather and hunting in the Absaroka Mountains, Wyo. M.S. thesis, Univ. of Wyoming, Laramie.

Samuel, M. D., E. O. Garton, M. W. Schlegel, and R. G. Carson. 1987. Visibility bias during aerial surveys of elk in northcentral Idaho. J. Wildl. Mgmt. 51:622–630.

Scott, D. 1987. Pronghorn antelope in Yellowstone: Life history and management issues. Yellowstone National Park files.

Singer, F. J. 1986. Mule deer helicopter count, northern winter range. Yellowstone National Park files.

———. 1990. Some predicted effects concerning wolf recovery into Yellowstone National Park. Section 4 in National Park Service, Wolves for Yellowstone? A report to the U.S. Congress, vol. 2. Research and analysis. Yellowstone National Park, Mammoth, Wyo.

Singer, F. J., C. McClure, S. Consolo, and K. Alt. 1988. Northern Yellowstone spring green-up mule deer count. Yellowstone National Park files.

Singer, F. J., W. Schreier, E. O. Garton, and J. Oppenheim. 1989. Drought, fires, and large mammals. BioScience 39:716–722.

Skinner, M. P. 1929. White-tailed deer formerly in Yellowstone National Park. J. Mammal. 10:101–115.

Spalinger, D. E., C. T. Robbins, and T. A. Hanley. 1986. The assessment of handling time in ruminants: The effect of plant chemical and physical structure on the rate of breakdown of plant particles in the rumen of mule deer and elk. Can. J. Zool. 64:312–321.

Stevens, D. R. 1971. Shiras moose. Pages 89–95 in T. W. Mussehl and F. W. Howell, eds. Game management in Montana. Montana Department of Fish and Game, Helena.

Swenson, J. 1985. Moose survey in the Absaroka high country. Memo to LeRoy Ellig, Montana Department of Fish, Wildlife, and Parks, Bozeman.

Taylor, G. 1981, 1982, 1983, 1984, 1985, 1986. Montana big game survey and inventory, Region 3. P-R Proj. W-130-R-17. Montana Dep't of Fish, Wildlife, and Parks, Helena.

Theberge, J. B. 1990. Potentials for misinterpreting impacts of wolf predation through prey:predator ratios. Wildl. Soc. Bull. 18:188–192.

Theberge, J. B., and D. A. Gauthier. 1985. Models of wolf-ungulate relationships: When is wolf control justified? Wildl. Soc. Bull. 13:449–458.

Trent, T., T. Parker, and J. Naderman. 1985. Elk. Area 5. Completion Rep. P-R Proj. W-170-R. Idaho Dep't of Fish and Game, Boise.

U.S. Fish and Wildlife Service. 1987. Northern Rocky Mountain wolf recovery plan. Department of the Interior, Washington. D.C.

Vales, D., and J. Peek. 1990. Estimates of the potential interactions between hunter harvest and wolf predation on the Sand Creek, Idaho, and Gallatin, Montana, elk populations. Section 3 in National Park Service, Wolves for Yellowstone? A report to the United States Congress, vol. 2. Research and analysis. Yellowstone National Park, Mammoth, Wyo.

Vore, J. 1990. Movements and distribution of some northern Yellowstone elk. M.S. thesis, Montana State Univ., Bozeman.

Walcheck, K. 1976. Montana wildlife 170 years ago. Mont. Outdoors 7:15–30.

Wood, G. W. 1988. Effects of prescribed fire on deer forage and nutrients. Wildl. Soc. Bull. 16:180–186.

Yorgason, J., et al. 1986. Elk. Big game herd unit reports, Dist. II. Wyoming Game and Fish Department, Casper.

Zumbo, J. 1987. Should we cry wolf? Outdoor Life (December):50–53.

CHAPTER 22   **Population Dynamics and Home Range Changes in a Colonizing Wolf Population**

Robert R. Ream,
Michael W. Fairchild,
Diane K. Boyd, and
Daniel H. Pletscher

During the late 1800s and early 1900s, wolves were extirpated throughout most of their historical range in the United States (Mech 1970). They apparently were eliminated from Montana by 1936, though occasional wolves—probably dispersers from Canada—have been killed in recent years (Singer 1979; Day 1981; Ream and Mattson 1982). In the early 1980s wolves began to recolonize the North Fork of the Flathead River drainage in British Columbia, adjoining Glacier National Park and the Flathead National Forest in Montana (Ream and Mattson 1982).

The Northern Rocky Mountain Wolf Recovery Plan (U.S. Fish and Wildlife Service 1987) identified three potential wolf recovery areas: north-

We gratefully acknowledge funding provided by the Montana Department of Fish, Wildlife, and Parks through section 6 of the Endangered Species Act, the University of Montana Forestry School, the U.S. Fish and Wildlife Service, Glacier National Park, and Flathead National Forest. Personnel from these agencies and the British Columbia Wildlife Branch provided invaluable assistance. Thanks to Len and Sandy Sargent of the Cinnabar Foundation, Lucy Dayton and Mark O'Keefe, Brad Lindner, and Cynthia Wayburn for financial assistance. Jerry DeSanto, Bruce McLellan, Dick Thiel, Project Lighthawk, and numerous volunteers made valuable contributions to the field work.

western Montana, including GNP, Yellowstone, centered around Yellowstone National Park, and central Idaho.

We believe that results from our studies in northwestern Montana will provide insights into what may occur in YNP. Although the habitats of the two areas are different and wolf recovery in YNP is to be effected through reintroduction, the areas are similar. Both recovery areas have high-density and diverse prey populations for wolves, provide protection through their national park status, and are surrounded by lands likely to be population sinks for wolves.

This chapter reviews the status of wolves within the study area from 1979 to 1983 and describes wolf population dynamics and home range changes during wolf recolonization of the GNP area from 1984 through 1988.

STUDY AREA

The study was conducted primarily along the North Fork and the adjacent Wigwam River drainage (figure 22.1). The North Fork is a 4–10-km-wide valley surrounded by steeper foothills and rugged mountains. The valley is approximately 1,200 m in elevation and is mostly forested with lodgepole pine (*Pinus contorta*), interspersed with meadows, marshes, and riparian habitats (Habeck 1967). The Wigwam River valley is bordered by steep mountains and is less than 1 km wide in most places. It is also dominated by lodgepole pine forests, but meadows and marshes are not as common as along the North Fork.

Ungulates were abundant in the study area and were the most important items in the wolf diet (Boyd et al. n.d.). The most common species killed by wolves were white-tailed deer (*Odocoileus virginianus*), elk (*Cervus elaphus*), and moose (*Alces alces*). Only four permanent residents lived in the British Columbia portion of the study area, compared with several hundred permanent and seasonal residents along the North Fork in Montana.

The history of wolf recolonization in the study area is illustrated in figure 22.2. A 36-kg gray female wolf (W114) was captured and radio collared on April 8, 1979, 10 km north of GNP in British Columbia (Ream and Mattson 1982). There was no evidence of denning by this or any other wolf in 1979, 1980, or 1981 in the North Fork. The closest known breeding population of wolves in 1981 was at least 100 km north of GNP and perhaps as far as Banff National Park, 250 km north of GNP (Ream and Harris 1986). W114 did not den, and no other wolf appeared to be present during the sixteen months she

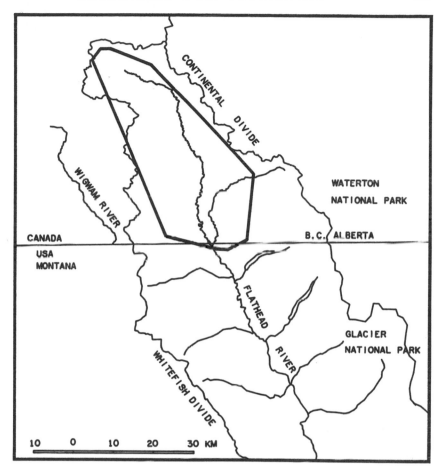

Figure 22.1 Study area and W114 home range (from Ream et al. 1985).

was radio tracked from April 1979 to July 1980 (Ream et al. 1985). Only tracks of a lone wolf were observed until autumn 1981, when a large black three-toed wolf was observed north of GNP, within the home range of W114 (Ream et al. 1985). In late February 1982, tracks of a male and a female wolf (ascertained by urination postures and proestral bleeding) were observed together in the northwestern corner of GNP. W114's radio ceased transmitting in July 1980, leaving no way to determine whether she was the female of this pair. Four gray and three black pups were observed 7 km north of GNP in July 1982, presumably belonging to the pair described above. The following winter, tracks of six or seven wolves were observed, and in summer 1983, pack howling was heard on several occasions. We

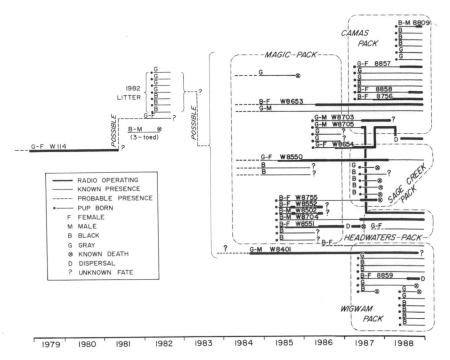

Figure 22.2 Wolf population and pack affiliations in study area following recoloniza-tion.

believe that the present population originated from the successful litter of 1982.

METHODS

Wolves were captured and radio collared as described by Mech (1974). We used modified Newhouse No. 4 (equivalent to offset No. 14s) and Braun (Wayne's Oddjobs, Ltd.) leg-hold traps to capture wolves. An injection of 11 mg/kg ketamine HCl and 2.2 mg/kg promazine HCl was administered with a jab stick to immobilize wolves. A detailed description of injuries and old scars on each animal was recorded. After processing, personnel re-mained nearby to observe the wolf until it could leave the site on its own.

Radio-collared wolves in accessible areas were usually located three times per week from the ground. Locations were determined by triangula-tion of at least three azimuths and described by Universal Transverse Mercator coordinates to the nearest 0.1 km. Radio-collared wolves in remote areas were aerially located, weather permitting. Long-distance dispersers were located aerially and with the assistance of Canadian wild-life authorities. Minimum convex polygon home ranges (Mohr 1947) were calculated and plotted using the home-range analysis program of Samuel et al. (1985).

Pack sizes and pup production were determined from aerial observations. The first pup observations were made while aerially locating radio-collared adults in mid-June, when the pups began spending more time in the open. Because we could not determine if any pup mortality occurred before the first pup counts, those counts represent a minimum reproductive effort. Visually distinguishing between pups and adults was easy through September because of obvious size differences. By October, however, size distinction was difficult to discern from the air. Telemetry and differences in pelage color allowed visual identification of some pack members.

RESULTS

Trapping

Trapping during the study resulted in twenty-six captures of eighteen wolves (table 22.1). W8550 was captured in an Aldrich cable foot snare by bear researchers and fitted with a radio collar. W8401 was inadvertently captured on December 31, 1987, by a British Columbia fur trapper; we replaced the wolf's collar and released him with the permission of the British Columbia Wildlife Branch. All other captures were made by project personnel.

Trap injuries (Van Ballenberghe 1984; Kuehn et al. 1986) in this study were minimal. The most serious injury occurred when W8653 was captured on May 28, 1986, and two middle toes were broken. No significant toe damage was noted when she was recaptured a year later. Examination of eight recaptured wolves and aerial observations of all radio-collared wolves revealed no evidence of disabling injuries from trapping.

Formation of Packs and Dispersal

A pack of six wolves (Magic Pack) was snow tracked in the study area in winter 1984–1985, but no member was radio-collared until May 1985, when the lactating alpha female (W8550) was captured. There is strong evidence that the Magic Pack was directly descended from or contained some of the same individuals that had used the area previously. The Magic Pack used essentially the same home range that W114 had used in 1979–1980 (see below), the rendezvous site where the 1982 litter was observed

Table 22.1 Wolves captured in and near Glacier National Park, 1984–1987

| | | *Date* | | | *Weight* | *Capture·* | |
Wolf	*Sex*	*Captured*	*Color*	*Age*[a]	*(kg)*	*Site*	*Fate and Comments*
8401	M	08-26-84	gray	adult	48	B.C.	transmitting
8401	M	10-25-85	gray	adult	46	B.C.	new collar; transmitting
8401	M	12-31-87	gray	adult	—	B.C.	new collar; transmitting
8550	F	05-18-85	lt gr	adult	37[b]	B.C.	transmitting
8502	M	09-07-85	black	5 mos	30	B.C.	lost collar 09-08-85 died 09-86
8551	F	09-09-85	black	5 mos	22	B.C.	transmitting
8551	F	05-22-86	black	13 mos	34	B.C.	dispersed; died 07-11-87
8552	F	09-09-85	black	5 mos	28	B.C.	lost collar 09-10-85
8653	F	05-28-86	black	adult	44	B.C.	transmitting
8653	F	05-15-87	black	adult	41	GNP	new collar; transmitting
8653	F	06-12-88	black	adult	38	?	new collar; transmitting
8654	F	10-09-86	gray	6 mos	32	GNP	signal quit 05-12-87
8654	F	06-08-87	gray	14 mos	42	B.C.	new collar; transmitting
8703	M	05-16-87	gray	adult	46[b]	GNP	transmitting
8755	F	05-19-87	black	adult	36	GNP	transmitting
8755	F	06-24-87	black	adult	—	B.C.	died 09-18-87
8704	M	06-12-87	black	adult	51	B.C.	transmitting
8705	M	06-19-87	gray	adult	51	B.C.	transmitting
8756	F	10-04-87	black	5 mos	23	B.C.	transmitting
8756	F	06-08-88	black	14 mos	35	?	new collar; transmitting
8857	F	06-05-88	gray	14 mos	34	B.C.	transmitting
8858	F	06-18-88	black	14 mos	33	?	transmitting
8859	F	07-21-88	black	14 mos	39	B.C.	transmitting
8860	F	07-29-88	gray	3 mos	13	B.C.	not collared
8808	M	07-29-88	gray	3 mos	14	B.C.	not collared
8809	M	09-04-88	black	5 mos	27	B.C.	transmitting

[a]adult is yearling or older
[b]estimated weight

was near the center of the Magic Pack home range in 1985, and the colors of the pups observed in 1982 matched those of the Magic Pack in 1984 (figure 22.2).

W8550 produced seven pups in 1985 and five pups in 1986, but was displaced from the alpha position in the Magic Pack by packmate W8653

W8550 left the Magic Pack in January 1987 and moved to the northern portion of the Magic Pack home range. Snow tracking indicated that she was alone through most of February and March. In April and May she was joined by Magic Pack males W8704 and W8705 and females W8654 and W8755. W8550 apparently bred about a month later than the previous year and denned in late May. Her pack was called the Sage Creek Pack. The three remaining Magic Pack wolves in GNP were designated the Camas Pack, and W8653 produced a 1987 litter during the normal denning season in mid- to late April (figure 22.2).

Further pack splitting occurred in June 1987 when two males from the Sage Creek Pack, W8704 and W8705, departed and established an adjacent home range. By September 1987 they were joined by a third wolf of unknown origin and were named the Headwaters Pack.

Lone male W8401, captured in August 1984, was probably also a former member of the Magic Pack. W8401 was captured in and used the same home range as the Magic Pack, but he remained temporally separate from them. His summer home range was much larger than the Magic Pack's until mid-1986, when he was frequently seen with a black wolf. He was observed with a black wolf throughout the 1986–1987 winter, and in June 1987 they were observed with pups and designated the Wigwam Pack.

Long-distance movements were also observed. Female W8551 was captured as a pup in September 1985. She was last located with the Magic Pack on December 19, 1986, 12 km north of GNP. Three days later the pack was 35 km south in GNP, but W8551 was not with them and was not radio located again. The British Columbia Wildlife Branch notified us that W8551 had been killed on July 11, 1987, while crossing private land with another wolf about 18 km southeast of Pouce Coupe, British Columbia. Her radio was returned and was still operating, so she must have quickly left our study area. This dispersal distance (840 km from her last radio location) nearly equals the record dispersal reported by Fritts (1983) for a young male from Minnesota and may be a record for a female wolf.

Male W8502 was a pup when captured in September 1985 in the Magic Pack's home range in British Columbia. His collar fell off several days later. He was identified by his ear tags after being shot in September 1986, approximately 60 km south of Calgary, Alberta. This represents a dispersal distance of approximately 160 km.

Female W8654 was initially captured as a pup in GNP in October 1986. She remained within her natal home range until January, 1988, when she began making short exploratory movements to the west through mid-March. By mid-June 1988 she had established a home range near the junction of the Montana, Idaho, and British Columbia borders, approximately 95 km west of her former range. In late 1988 she was seen with two to three other wolves but was illegally killed in Montana less than two months after this study ended.

To be successful, movements from natal home ranges must result in the establishment of a new home range with suitable prey and a mate (Rothman and Mech 1979). Mech (1987) described three dispersal strategies used by wolves: appropriating a portion of the natal home range; establishing a home range adjacent to the natal home range; and long-distance dispersal.

Our results indicate that all of these strategies were used by wolves in this colonizing situation. W8550 and her Sage Creek packmates essentially carved out a portion of the Magic Pack home range. W8704 and W8705 later moved to an adjacent home range, as did W8401. Long-distance dispersal was observed with three wolves in this area of abundant, available habitat. These movements, which may be adaptations to reduce inbreeding, occur in most wolf populations.

Home Range Shifts

When food resources are scarce, packs may expand their territories into other established territories, displacing or killing members of other packs (Mech 1977; Fritts and Mech 1981). Food was not scarce at the time of this study, however, and in November 1985 only the Magic Pack and W8401 were present. On November 11, 1985, the pack left its home range, mostly north of the international border, and traveled 50 km south over the next week; they remained south of the border for the remainder of the winter (figure 22.3). This shift may have occurred because one member of the Magic Pack was killed by hunters on October 20. Hunting and other human activity may have pushed the pack south into GNP; the abundant prey base of white-tailed deer south of the border in winter may have provided sufficient prey for them to stay. The area the pack shifted to had been pioneered by W8401 during the previous year. Scent markings by wolves leave signs that an area has been used before (Peters and Mech 1975; Rothman and Mech 1979). Evidence from this study suggests that exploratory movements into unoccupied wolf range by lone wolves may pave the way for later settlement of a new area.

After the Magic Pack split in winter 1987, W8550 returned to her former home range north of the border, and her new Sage Creek Pack used essentially the same home range that the Magic Pack had used previously and that W114 used in 1979–1980. When W114 was radio tracked in 1979–1980, her home range covered an area from the international border

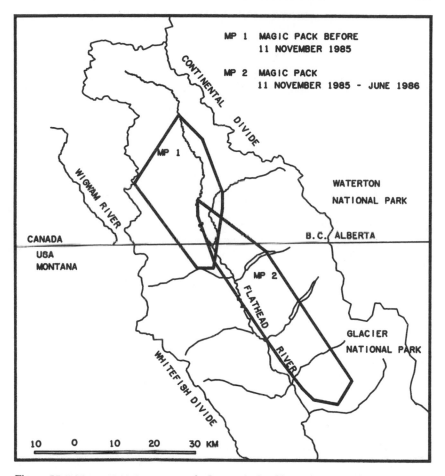

Figure 22.3 Magic Pack home range before and after November 11, 1985.

to the headwaters of the Flathead River (figure 22.1), with the headwaters used only periodically in summer (Ream et al. 1985). When the Magic Pack was tracked in the snow during winter 1984–1985 and radio tracked (W8550) from May 18 to November 10, 1985, its home range appeared very similar to W114's (figure 22.3).

W8401 used the area near the border in late 1984 but moved 40–50 km south into GNP in the autumn and settled there for the winter, moving north and south along the North Fork valley (figure 22.4). The following winter the Magic Pack moved south into GNP, using the same areas that W8401 had the previous year (figure 22.3).

It appears that use of new areas by lone wolves may open the way for

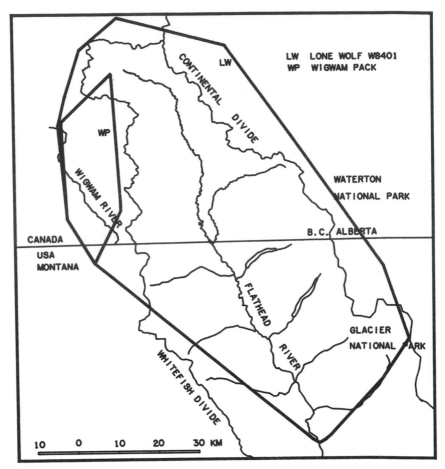

Figure 22.4 W8401 home range as loner and as alpha male of Wigwam Pack in 1987.

settlement of those areas by other pairs or packs, or by that lone wolf when it finds a mate.

Home Range Sizes

Minimum convex polygons (MCP) were used to estimate home-range sizes of wolves in the study area (Mohr 1947). The wolf with the largest total home range, 5,964 km², was W8401, a lone wolf during the first two years of this study (figure 22.4). His home range was more than twice as large as any of the other radio-collared wolves, and larger than home ranges of lone wolves reported elsewhere (Carbyn 1980; Fritts and Mech 1981; Ballard, Whitman, and Gardner 1987). After Autumn 1986, when W8401 was with a mate, he settled into an area less than 10 percent of the size of his previous home range.

The Magic Pack, based on the movements of W8550, had a total home range of 1,795 km² from 1985 through 1987, considerably larger than reported by Carbyn (1980) in Manitoba, or Fritts and Mech (1981) in Minnesota, but comparable to those reported by Peterson, Woolington, and Bailey (1984), and Ballard, Whitman, and Gardner (1987) in Alaska. The 1,795 km² total included the period before November 11, 1985, when W8550 and the Magic Pack shifted their home range south into GNP (figure 22.3). From denning season 1987 through denning season 1988, total home ranges for the Camas, Sage Creek, Headwaters, and Wigwam packs were 1,087, 343, 1,186, and 537 km², respectively. W8550, representing the Sage Creek Pack, became a lone wolf late in 1987 when most of her pack were killed; her radio failed in early 1988. Home ranges of the packs present in 1987 (figure 22.5) and 1988 (figure 22.6) suggest that both the Headwaters and Camas packs expanded their home ranges into the area formerly occupied by the Sage Creek Pack after that pack failed.

The size of total home ranges reported here may be larger than those reported in some other studies, for several reasons. The population we studied was a newly colonizing population with few established wolf territories. Also important may be the rugged topography of the study area compared with that of other studies; wolves in this study used the valley bottoms almost exclusively, but the MCP method of calculating home range does not take this into account. Hence high ridges and mountains that were never recorded as being used by the animals are included within the calculated home range. These larger home ranges are probably not representative of the sizes necessary for wolves except in areas with mountainous terrain as rugged as that of our study area. They also may not represent the required home-range sizes once wolves become fully established in the ecosystem.

Pack Cohesion and Interpack Associations

Unlike most other wolf populations studied, all the wolves in our study were believed to be related (figure 22.2). With time, more immigration may occur. The twelve-to-thirteen-member Magic Pack exhibited strong cohesion throughout 1985 and 1986, even though available space was abundant around its home range. A member of the pack was killed in fall 1985, and the remaining twelve stayed together until four disappeared in March 1986. Alpha female W8550 had five pups in 1986, and the pack of thirteen stayed together through most of that year.

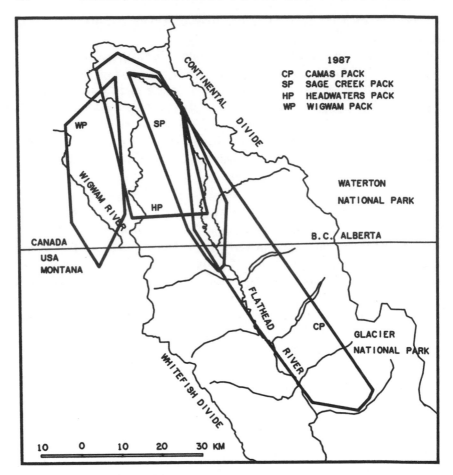

Figure 22.5 Camas, Sage Creek, Headwaters, and Wigwam packs in 1987.

In late April 1987 yearling female W8654, a Camas Pack member, moved 40 km north of the pack, and on April 27 was within 1 km of the Sage Creek Pack. On May 11 she was 50 km north of the international border, again within 1 km of the Sage Creek Pack. Her radio failed, but she was recaptured and recollared on June 8 near the Sage Creek Pack den about 10 km north of GNP. W8654 remained with the Sage Creek Pack until October 1, when she again began traveling with the Camas Pack.

On July 31, 1987, both alpha female W8653 and male W8703 of the Camas Pack were located near the Sage Creek Pack den. The two packs had inhabited separate ranges since mid-April 1987. W8703 remained with the Sage Creek Pack for the next four days and returned to the Camas Pack by

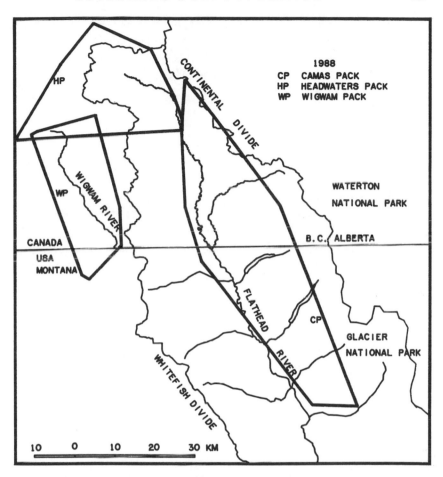

Figure 22.6 Camas, Headwaters, and Wigwam packs in 1988.

August 7, whereas W8653 remained there only one day. Conversely, adult female W8755 of the Sage Creek Pack was found with the Camas Pack's pups and W8653 on August 10–11 and 28. The Camas Pack moved north in late September, and from September 28–30 the packs appeared to be together on several occasions. W8654, W8703, and W8755 were pups of W8550.

Fritts and Mech (1981) found that territories of related groups of wolves did not overlap any more than those of other groups. Murie (1944) and Mech (1966) documented temporary pack splitting. Van Ballenberghe (1983) described a female that spent time in two packs. All these records are from established wolf populations. We found considerable interpack associations between closely related wolves, but for relatively short periods of time. We studied a recolonizing, relatively disjunct population, so all the wolves were quite closely related and bonds between individuals in different packs may still have been strong. There was also little need for competition for food resources.

POPULATION DYNAMICS

Characteristics of this wolf population reflected the apparent abundance of, and lack of competition for, prey in their newly occupied habitat. Eight litter sizes ranged from five to seven, averaging six (table 22.2). This reproductive rate is higher than that reported by most other studies (table 22.3). Van Ballenberghe and Mech (1975) constructed a standard weight table from which they compared age-specific weights with survivorship of wolf pups in Minnesota. Pups attaining at least 80 percent of standard weight had "high survivability" in their study. Weights of all eight pups captured in this study exceeded 100 percent of standard weight. Thirty-three of forty-one pups (81 percent) observed in June were also observed the following December. Six of the eight missing pups were killed by humans, and the fate of the other two is unknown.

A total of twelve wolf mortalities were documented during this study, all human caused. One wolf was illegally shot in British Columbia in October 1985. In September 1987 wolves became legal big game animals in the Flathead and Wigwam areas of British Columbia. Adult female W8755 and four pups from the Sage Creek Pack, and one pup from the Wigwam Pack,

Table 22.2 Production and survival of wolf pups in the study area

Year	Pack	Adults in May	Pups in Late June	Pups Surviving > 9 months	Location	Alpha Female
1982		2	7	unknown	B.C.	?
1985	Magic	6	7	7	B.C.	8550
1986	Magic	8	5	3	GNP	8550
1987	Sage Creek	5	5	1	B.C.	8550
1987	Camas	3	6	6	GNP	8653
1987	Wigwam	2	6	5	B.C.	?
1988	Camas	5–8	6	6	B.C.	8653
1988	Wigwam	5	6	6	B.C.	?
Averages			6.0	4.9 (81%)		

Table 22.3 Mean number of wolf pups produced per litter reported in early summer from selected studies

Study	Area	No. Pups/Litter (M)	No. Litters
Present study	se B.C. and nw Mont.	6.0	8
Carbyn 1975	Jasper Nat'l Park, Alta.	4.4	5
Ballard, Whitman, and Gardner 1987	s central Alaska	5.5–5.6	28
Fritts and Mech 1981	n central Minn.	4.7	18
Cowan 1947	se B.C. and sw Alta.	5.0	4
Kelsall 1968	N.W.T.	4.0	5
Stenlund 1955	n Minn.	6.4	8
Peterson, Wollington, and Bailey 1984	Kenai, Alaska	4.1	14

Table 22.4 Annual pup production, mortality, and survival of wolves in study area

	1984	1985	1986	1987	1988	Total
Pups observed in July	—	7	5	17	12	41
Known mortality	—	1	0	6	2	9
Dispersal (all died)	—	0	1	1	1	3
Dispersal (unknown mortality)	—	0	3	2	4	9
Total wolves in December	7	13	14	22	27	

were legally killed. In 1988 only the Wigwam area was open to wolf hunting, and one female pup and a yearling male were killed there. All three wolves that dispersed out of the study area were killed by humans.

In spite of these mortalities our study area population increased from seven wolves to twenty-seven between December 1984 and December 1988 (table 22.4), an average annual increase of 40 percent. Keith (1983) calculated finite rates of increase from successive population estimates in seven different wolf studies and found a high of 1.46 in the Peace River District of Alberta, a low of 1.15 on Isle Royale, and a mean of 1.29.

IMPLICATIONS FOR WOLF RECOVERY

The United States portion of the study area is part of the northwestern Montana recovery area identified in the Northern Rocky Mountain Wolf Recovery Plan (U.S. Fish and Wildlife Service 1987). This plan has a goal of ten breeding pairs in each of the three recovery areas. Two of the three packs at the end of the study spent most of their time in southeastern British Columbia, and the third, the Camas Pack, spent most of its time in the United States. Thus only one of the ten breeding pairs called for in the recovery plan is in the United States recovery area.

A considerable amount of unoccupied potential wolf range exists north of the international border. If our suggestion that wolves are more likely to move into areas "pioneered" by other wolves is true, then dispersers may be more likely to colonize areas in British Columbia than in Montana. Recovery of the wolf population within the northwestern Montana recovery area may therefore be a distant goal even after the current population in the study area grows to ten breeding pairs.

Colonizing populations of wolves can be expected to exercise a variety of dispersal patterns, including long-distance movement. Survival of all these dispersers is not necessary for population growth. Managers should be prepared for dispersal into areas where wolves are not wanted.

Wolf recovery appears to be proceeding rapidly; at the end of this study there were a number of breeding-age wolves that could initiate new packs. Similar rates of recovery could presumably be achieved in the other two recovery areas once an initial breeding pair is established. Dispersal distances indicate that recovery could be achieved in the other two areas in the future with dispersers from the study area. This would require dispersals to the southeast or southwest. Dispersers would face no barriers greater than those crossed by the first wolves that moved into our study area from farther north.

REFERENCES

Ballard, W. B., J. S. Whitman, and C. L. Gardner. 1987. Ecology of an exploited wolf population in south-central Alaska. Wildl. Monogr. 98:1–54.

Boyd, D., R. Ream, M. Fairchild, and D. Pletscher. Manuscript in preparation. Prey characteristics of colonizing wolves in the Glacier National Park area.

Carbyn, L. N. 1975. Wolf predation and behavioural interactions with elk and other ungulates in an area of high prey diversity. Ph.D. thesis. Univ. of Toronto.

————. 1980. Ecology and management of wolves in Riding Mountain National Park, Manitoba, 1977–1979. Large Mammal System Studies Rep. no. 10. Canadian Wildlife Service, Edmonton, Alta.

Cowan, I. M. 1947. The timber wolf in the Rocky Mountain national parks of Canada. Can. J. Res. 25:139–174.

Day, G. L. 1981. Status and distribution of wolves in the northern Rocky Mountains of the United States. M.S. thesis, Univ. of Montana, Missoula.

Fritts, S. H. 1983. Record dispersal of a wolf from Minnesota. J. Mammal. 64:166–167.

Fritts, S. H., and L. D. Mech. 1981. Dynamics, movements, and feeding ecology of a newly protected wolf population in northwestern Minnesota. Wildl. Monogr. 80:1–79.

Habeck, J. R. 1967. The vegetation of northwestern Montana: A preliminary report. Department of Botany, Univ. of Montana, Missoula.

Keith, L. B. 1983. Population dynamics of wolves. Pages 66–77 in L. N. Carbyn, ed. Wolves in Canada and Alaska: Their status, biology, and management. Can. Wildl. Serv. Rep. Ser. 45. Ottawa.

Kelsall, J. P. 1968. The migratory barren ground caribou of Canada. Canadian Wildlife Service, Ottawa.

Kuehn, D. W., T. K. Fuller, L. D. Mech, W. J. Paul, S. H. Fritts, and W. E. Berg. 1986. Trap-related injuries to gray wolves in Minnesota. J. Wildl. Mgmt. 50:90–91.

Mech, L. D. 1966. The wolves of Isle Royale. Nat'l Park Serv. Fauna Ser. 7. GPO, Washington, D.C.

———. 1970. The wolf: The ecology and behavior of an endangered species. Natural History Press, Garden City, New York.

———. 1974. Current techniques in the study of elusive wilderness carnivores. Proc. Int'l Cong. Game Biol. 11:315–322.

———. 1977. Productivity, mortality, and population trends of wolves in northeastern Minnesota. J. Mammal. 58:559–574.

———. 1987. Age, season, distance, direction, and social aspects of wolf dispersal from a Minnesota pack. Pages 55–74 in B. Chepko-Sade and Z. Halpin, eds. Mammalian dispersal patterns. Univ. of Chicago Press, Chicago.

Mohr, C. O. 1947. Table of equivalent populations of North American small mammals. Am. Midl. Nat. 37:223–249.

Murie, A. 1944. The wolves of Mt. McKinley. Nat'l Park Serv. Fauna Ser. 5. GPO, Washington, D.C.

Peters, R. P., and L. D. Mech. 1975. Scent-marking in wolves. Am. Sci. 63:628 637.

Peterson, R. O., J. D. Woolington, and T. N. Bailey. 1984. Wolves of the Kenai Peninsula, Alaska. Wildl. Monogr. 88:1–52.

Ream, R., and R. Harris. 1986. Wolf movements in southern Alberta. Nat'l Geog. Res. Rep. 21:405–409.

Ream, R., R. Harris, J. Smith, and D. Boyd. 1985. Movement patterns of a lone wolf (Canis lupus) in unoccupied wolf range, southeastern British Columbia. Can. Field-Nat. 99:234–239.

Ream, R., and U. Mattson. 1982. Wolf status in the northern Rockies. Pages 362–381 in F. H. Harrington and P. C. Pacquet, eds. Wolves of the world. Noyes, Park Ridge, N.J.

Rothman, R. J., and L. D. Mech. 1979. Scent-marking in lone wolves and newly formed pairs. Anim. Behav. 27:750–760.

Samuel, M. D., D. J. Pierce, E. O. Garton, L. J. Nelson, and K. R. Dixon. 1985. User's manual for program home range (revised January 1985). For. Wildl. Range Exper. Sta. Contribution no. 259. Univ. of Idaho, Moscow.

Singer, F. J. 1979. Status and history of timber wolves in Glacier National Park, Montana. Pages 19–42 in E. Klinghammer, ed. The behavior and ecology of wolves. Garland STPM, New York.

Stenlund, M. H. 1955. A field study of the timber wolf (*Canis lupus*) on the Superior National Forest, Minnesota. Minn. Dep't Conserv. Tech. Bull. 4.

U.S. Fish and Wildlife Service. 1987. Northern Rocky Mountain wolf recovery plan. Department of the Interior, Washington, D.C.

Van Ballenberghe, V. 1983. Extraterritorial movements and dispersal of wolves in southcentral Alaska. J. Mammal. 64:168–171.

———. 1984. Injuries to wolves sustained during live-capture. J. Wildl. Mgmt. 48:1425–1429.

Van Ballenberghe, V., and L. D. Mech. 1975. Weights, growth, and survival of timber wolf pups in Minnesota. J. Mammal. 56:44–63.

CHAPTER 23   **Public Attitudes about**
Wolf Restoration in
Yellowstone National Park
Alistair J. Bath

Discussions of the possibility of restoring wolves to Yellowstone National Park have captured the attention of many interest groups and the general public nationwide. The issue has become polarized with the emergence of two distinct camps, those strongly in favor of wolf restoration and those strongly against. As is typical of many wildlife management issues, the proposed wolf recovery in Yellowstone National Park is not as much a biological issue as a sociopolitical one. Resource managers involved in the complex decision-making process concerning wolf restoration need to base their decisions not only on sound biological data but also on an understanding of the human component of the wildlife management equation. Information on public attitudes toward wolves and willingness to reintroduce the animal needs to be identified and documented. This chapter uses the issue of wolf restoration in Yellowstone National Park to focus on human dimensions in wildlife resources management.

Human dimensions in wildlife resources (HDWR) research has been defined as research that "focuses on the public's knowledge levels, expectations, attitudes and activities concerning fish and wildlife resources and associated habitats. There is a close tie between human dimensions and conservation education research" (Adams 1988:4). The importance of such research in wildlife issues has only recently been acknowledged. Wildlife management has been defined as "the science and art of changing the characteristics and interactions of habitat, wildlife animal populations, and people to achieve specific human goals by means of managing wildlife resources. . . . In one form or another, everything done in wildlife management is done for people" (Anderson, Beiswenger, and Purdom 1987:234). This definition explicitly outlines the importance of the human component in wildlife management. Much as a business must understand its customers, so must wildlife managers know their wildlife constituency (Duda 1986).

Research in HDWR can have many applications for the resource manager. The results can be used to better assess the species people prefer to hunt, observe, and photograph (Duda 1986). Thus human dimensions research can rank species and direct management to emphasize particular species. The public's knowledge of an issue or species can be identified, thus allowing managers to specifically address any weaknesses in knowledge with educational programs. The effectiveness of educational programs in changing attitudes and knowledge can be assessed with HDWR research, and changes can be monitored over time. Public support is essential for successful implementation of wildlife projects and management plans, whether the plan is wolf reintroduction or wolf control. Public support for specific programs and specific policies can be identified using HDWR research, thus allowing effective implementation of projects as well as allowing resource managers to market their decisions once made (Duda 1986).

METHODS

Data were collected through a mail-out survey with 1,026 respondents, representing the Wyoming general public, Wyoming members of the Defenders of Wildlife, members of the Wyoming Wildlife Federation, and members of the Wyoming Stock Growers Association. The general public sample consisted of randomly selected residents of Wyoming statewide (N = 371) and countywide (N = 201). The latter sample represented residents who lived in the counties (Bighorn, Fremont, Hot Springs, Lincoln, Park, Sublette, Teton, and Washakie) surrounding Yellowstone National Park. Samples of the general public were randomly chosen proportional to county population from telephone directories. Members of the Wyoming Stock Growers Association attending their annual meeting in Casper, Wyoming, were handed surveys and asked to return them to a box at the end of the meeting. The respondents (N = 80) resided in twenty-one of twenty-three counties in Wyoming. Samples of Wyoming members of the Defenders of Wildlife (N = 130) and members of the Wyoming Wildlife Federation (N = 244) were randomly chosen from lists provided by the respective groups. No respondent appeared in more than one sample group.

Survey procedures outlined by Dillman (1978) were followed. The survey included a cover letter that briefly explained the study and the participating organizations. A return self-addressed stamped envelope was also enclosed. A postcard follow-up and an additional mailing of the survey were required to increase the response rate. The overall completion rate was 63 percent, ranging from 48 percent for the Wyoming general public statewide to 82 percent among members of the Defenders of Wildlife.

The survey consisted of questions covering attitudes toward and knowledge about the wolf and the wolf restoration issue, as well as respondent demographic characteristics. This chapter discusses specifically the attitudinal items and the differences in attitude toward the wolf among the five groups. Attitude scores were computed by adding and averaging responses to the eight attitudinal items. A five-point Likert format of response options ranging from "strongly agree" to "strongly disagree" was used. Scale reliability was assessed with Cronbach's alpha (Carmine and Zeller 1979) for the ordinally scaled attitudinal items, which revealed a reliability estimate of .928. A reliability coefficient of 1.00 indicates that the scale items are perfectly consistent in terms of participant responses. A reliability estimate equaling .60 was established as acceptable (Nunnally 1970). Cronbach's alpha is a measure of internal consistency reliability. It yields the mean sum for all possible split-half reliability coefficients. If high internal consistency exists, then test items measure the same thing (Carmine and Zeller 1979). In this case, an attitude score was being measured. Attitude toward the wolf scores, composed of eight items, were computed and compared using analysis of variance across the five groups. Univariate statistics were used to present a description of frequency distribution of responses for each attitudinal item. Willingness to restore the wolf to Yellowstone National Park was assessed and also compared across the five groups using analysis of variance. Factors were identified to suggest why individuals were in favor of or against wolf restoration in Yellowstone National Park.

RESULTS

Contrary to the belief that attitudes toward the wolf seem to fall into two categories, a love 'em group and a hate 'em group, table 23.1 indicates that a large percentage of general public respondents neither liked nor disliked the animal. Most (93.1 percent) Defenders of Wildlife members "liked" or "strongly liked" the wolf, whereas most (67.5 percent) Wyoming Stock Grower members "disliked" or "strongly disliked" the animal. The majority (67.2 percent) of Wyoming Wildlife Federation members liked the wolf.

Table 23.1 Responses (in percents) to selected statements about wolf restoration in Yellowstone National Park from a survey of Wyoming residents and interest groups, 1987

Survey Group	Strongly Agree	Agree	Neither	Disagree	Strongly Disagree
"Which answer best describes your attitude toward the wolf?" [a]					
Stock growers	0.0	5.0	22.5	17.5	50.0
Defenders of Wildlife	56.2	36.9	6.2	0.8	0.0
Wildlife Federation	25.0	42.2	21.3	5.7	3.3
Countywide public	19.9	17.4	38.3	5.5	15.9
Statewide public	18.1	29.1	33.2	7.5	8.1
"The monetary costs of reintroducing the wolf will exceed any benefits gained by having the wolf in the park."					
Stock growers	73.7	15.0	2.5	3.7	3.7
Defenders of Wildlife	2.3	4.6	8.5	41.5	41.5
Wildlife Federation	12.3	13.9	16.4	41.4	13.9
Countywide public	30.8	19.9	17.9	17.9	10.9
Statewide public	18.1	18.6	27.8	23.7	9.4
"Wolves would have a significant impact on big game hunting opportunities near Yellowstone National Park."					
Stock growers	45.0	36.2	10.0	6.3	0.0
Defenders of Wildlife	0.0	6.2	8.5	48.5	36.2
Wildlife Federation	5.3	16.8	12.3	52.9	11.9
Countywide public	14.4	20.9	20.4	31.8	10.0
Statewide public	10.0	17.3	17.0	41.2	11.6
"Wolves would deplete elk numbers to unacceptable levels in Yellowstone National Park."					
Stock growers	31.3	27.5	23.8	13.7	1.2
Defenders of Wildlife	0.0	2.3	7.7	40.0	50.0
Wildlife Federation	4.1	11.9	11.1	50.8	20.9
Countywide public	11.4	17.9	19.4	35.8	13.9
Statewide public	9.7	13.7	16.4	40.4	17.5
"If reintroduced wolves killed livestock, the problem wolf should be killed."					
Stock growers	67.5	20.0	1.2	1.2	7.5
Defenders of Wildlife	3.8	23.8	6.9	43.1	20.8
Wildlife Federation	12.7	32.8	11.5	34.0	8.2
Countywide public	27.9	29.9	13.4	14.4	10.9
Statewide public	20.2	38.3	9.4	21.6	8.1

Table 23.1 (*Continued*)

Survey Group	Strongly Agree	Agree	Neither	Disagree	Strongly Disagree
"Wolves reintroduced into Yellowstone National Park would cause more damage to livestock than wolves presently do in Minnesota livestock range."					
Stock growers	35.0	30.0	21.2	8.8	0.0
Defenders of Wildlife	2.3	2.3	10.8	36.2	47.7
Wildlife Federation	2.0	11.9	25.4	45.1	14.8
Countywide public	13.9	15.4	30.8	27.9	10.4
Statewide public	6.7	12.7	32.3	34.8	11.6
"Wolves would be a significant predator on the livestock industry around Yellowstone National Park."					
Stock growers	70.0	21.2	5.0	2.5	0.0
Defenders of Wildlife	0.8	6.2	10.8	46.9	34.6
Wildlife Federation	4.9	22.1	19.7	42.2	10.7
Countywide public	20.4	27.4	18.9	23.4	7.0
Statewide public	13.2	25.9	16.4	34.2	7.8
"Because healthy populations of wolves exist in Canada and Alaska, there is no need to have wolves in Yellowstone National Park."					
Stock growers	72.5	20.0	5.0	1.2	1.2
Defenders of Wildlife	0.8	6.9	0.8	38.5	53.1
Wildlife Federation	9.0	11.5	10.2	48.4	20.5
Countywide public	28.4	17.9	10.0	29.4	12.4
Statewide public	15.4	16.7	14.0	35.3	16.2

Source: Bath and Buchanan 1989:521.

[a]This question is measured on a strongly like to strongly dislike scale.

The ends of the emotional wolf spectrum became more evident when analyzing further attitudinal items. In response to the statement, "The monetary costs of reintroducing the wolf will exceed any benefits gained by having the wolf in the park," the stock growers adamantly agreed (88.7 percent), whereas the Defenders of Wildlife almost as adamantly disagreed (83.0 percent). The majority of both general public samples agreed, but most Wildlife Federation members disagreed.

Concern has been voiced over the impact of wolves on big game populations in Yellowstone and the surrounding area. Results of this re search suggest that all groups, except the stock growers, felt that wolves would not have a significant impact on big game hunting opportunities near

Yellowstone National Park. Most (64.8 percent) of the hunter-oriented Wyoming Wildlife Federation members did not believe that big game opportunities would be significantly affected. In response to a specific item concerning impacts on elk numbers, all groups except the stock growers indicated even more strongly that wolves would not deplete elk numbers to unacceptable levels in the park. There was also a significant increase among the stock grower respondents in agreement with the other four groups.

The northern Rocky Mountain wolf recovery plan recommends that wolves restored to the park be considered an "experimental population," thus allowing problem wolves to be killed (U.S. Fish and Wildlife Service 1986). Public support seems to exist for the destruction of wolves that kill livestock. All groups, except the Defenders of Wildlife, supported the statement: "If reintroduced wolves killed livestock, the problem wolf should be killed." Approximately 28 percent of the Defenders members did agree with the above statement, indicating some willingness to compromise by this pro-wolf group. The Wildlife Federation members were almost equally divided (45.5 percent agreed and 42.2 percent disagreed) on this attitudinal item.

Wolves do not currently exist in Yellowstone, and there has been no pack activity in the park since the early 1930s (Weaver 1978). Little is known of the possible effects of wolves on livestock near Yellowstone. Wolves do occasionally prey on livestock, but evidence from Minnesota, where there are approximately 1,200 wolves (Mech 1977), suggests that losses are less than 1 percent (Fritts 1982). No group, except the stock growers, believed that wolves restored to Yellowstone would cause more damage to livestock than wolves presently do in Minnesota. A similar statement, however, produced dramatically different results. Most (47.8 percent) of the countywide general public group agreed that wolves would be a significant predator on the livestock industry around Yellowstone National Park. The statewide general public was equally divided on this issue, with 39.1 percent agreeing and 42.0 percent disagreeing. A large percentage (70.0) of the stock growers strongly agreed, and most (91.2 percent) agreed in general.

Many opponents to wolf restoration in Yellowstone National Park have stated that because healthy populations of wolves exist in Canada and Alaska, there is no need to have wolves in Yellowstone National Park. Such a statement was posed to the public surveyed in this study. Approximately 52 percent of the statewide general public disagreed. The Defenders of Wildlife and Wildlife Federation members also disagreed, 91.6 percent and 68.9 percent, respectively. The stock growers agreed with the statement

Table 23.2 Results of the analysis of variance of attitude toward the wolf score by various groups

Source	df	Sum of Squares	Mean Squares	F-Ratio	F-Prob.
Between	4	317.2489	79.3122	93.724	< .001
Within Groups	949	803.0706	0.8462		

Note: Attitude toward the wolf score.

Mean	Group
1.6964a	Wyoming Stock Growers Association
2.9019b	Countywide Wyoming general public
3.1492c	Statewide Wyoming general public
3.4935d	Wyoming Wildlife Federation
4.1835e	Wyoming members of the Defenders of Wildlife

1.0 = strongly dislike, 2.0 = dislike, 3.0 = neither, 4.0 = like, 5.0 = strongly like
Means with different letters are different at $p < .05$ using Tukey's HSD procedure.

(92.5 percent) as adamantly as the Defenders of Wildlife disagreed. A majority of the countywide general public agreed, but a large percentage (41.8) disagreed with the statement.

A score for each group was computed using the eight items discussed above. A score of 1.0 indicated a strong dislike of the wolf, and a score of 5.0 indicated a strong like of the animal. A score of 3.0 indicated a neutral attitude toward the wolf. Most respondents held a positive attitude toward the predator, with the definite exception of the respondents of the Wyoming Stock Growers Association, who received a mean score of 1.696, indicating an attitude between strong dislike (1.0) and dislike of the wolf (2.0). The respondents of the general public countywide group held a slightly negative attitude (2.902). The statewide general public group received a mean score of 3.149, indicating a slightly positive attitude toward the wolf. The respondents of the Wyoming Wildlife Federation received a mean score of 3.493, indicating an attitude between neither like nor dislike of the wolf (3.0) and like of the wolf (4.0). The Defenders of Wildlife had the most positive attitude toward the wolf, with a mean score of 4.183 indicating an attitude between like (4.0) and strong like of the wolf (5.0). Analysis of variance found at least one significant difference ($p < .001$) between groups, and Tukey's HSD post-hoc procedure (Lutz 1983) was used to identify the groups that were significantly different (table 23.2). The stock growers had a statistically significant difference in score from all other groups, and all groups had statistically significant differences in score from each other. The statewide general public, for example, had a statistically

Table 23.3 Responses to the survey question "Are you in favor
of reintroducing the wolf into Yellowstone National Park?"

Survey Group	Yes	No	No Opinion
Stock growers	6.3	91.2	2.5
Defenders of Wildlife	89.2	6.2	4.6
Wildlife Federation	66.8	22.1	11.1
Countywide public	38.8	51.7	9.5
Statewide public	48.5	34.5	17.0

significant difference in score from the countywide general public. It seems
that respondents closer to potential wolf range have a more negative
attitude toward the animal than those respondents farther away from the
potential wolf recovery area.

Table 23.3 illustrates how each group specifically responded to the
question "Are you in favor of reintroducing the wolf into Yellowstone
National Park?" Most respondents were in favor of restoring the wolf to the
park, stating that wolves occupied the area historically as their primary
reason. The statewide general public and the Defenders of Wildlife and
Wildlife Federation members all supported wolf restoration 48.5 percent,
89.2 percent, and 66.8 percent respectively. The countywide general public
were against wolf restoration (51.7 percent). Most (91.2 percent) stock
growers opposed restoration. Those respondents opposing wolf restoration
in Yellowstone National Park stated that the costs of the program would be
too high as their primary reason.

The fundamental differences in attitude toward the wolf, and in willingness to restore the animal, among the five groups have led to conflict in the
wolf recovery issue. Compromises must be made by all involved in this
complex resource management issue.

This study found some willingness to compromise by the pro-wolf
group, but little from the anti-wolf group. For example, respondents who
indicated their opposition to wolf restoration were asked if their opinion
would change under any of the following conditions: (1) financial compensation for livestock losses attributed to wolves; (2) restriction of livestock
losses to less than 1 percent; (3) containment of wolves within the park and
the surrounding wilderness areas; and (4) destruction of wolves that killed
livestock. Most anti-wolf respondents indicated they would not change
their opinion under any of these conditions. Most respondents in favor of
wolf restoration, though, were willing to pay an increase in taxes to support

the costs of wolf recovery. This is an important point, especially considering that the primary reason stated by respondents against wolf restoration
was the high cost of the program.

The wolf in Yellowstone will be a nonconsumptive wildlife program. As
wolves will probably not be seen, their value may be predominantly
appreciative. Awareness, interest, and financial commitment are increasing
nationwide regarding nonconsumptive wildlife-related recreation. A fund
established for wolf recovery in Yellowstone, to which interested individuals could contribute, might reduce the monetary concerns of anti-wolf
respondents. Livestock losses are another concern, especially by the stock
growers. The Defenders of Wildlife are currently proceeding with a compensation program for verified livestock losses attributed to wolves. Fair
market price for livestock losses needs further discussion. Approximately
28 percent of the Defenders of Wildlife group were in favor of killing
problem wolves. In this respect, they seem to be making an effort to
compromise.

Wolf restoration in Yellowstone National Park is a controversial issue, in
which all sides have legitimate concerns. This research suggests that certain issues are not obstacles to wolf restoration in Yellowstone National
Park. For example, most members of the Wyoming Wildlife Federation do
not believe that wolf recovery would reduce big game hunting opportunities or elk numbers to unacceptable levels. This predominantly hunter-
based group does not see any conflict between humans as predators and
wolves as predators. This is a positive aspect of the issue for resource
managers. Wolf restoration in Yellowstone National Park is supported also
by the majority of Wyoming residents.

Wolf restoration in Yellowstone National Park will continue to be controversial throughout the decision-making process. Continued public involvement is essential in such wildlife management issues as wolf recovery. To truly involve the public, resource managers must move beyond the
traditional realm of public meetings toward a more comprehensive understanding of the public. Public meetings can be used to identify extreme
viewpoints, because those who attend are usually strongly supportive or
strongly opposed to the plan or action proposed by the agency. The vast
majority of the public, who are ultimately affected by the decision, is not a
part of the decision-making process when public meetings alone are used.

If we recall the definition of wildlife management (Anderson et al.
1987), wildlife is managed not for the lobby groups (either "for" or
"against"), but for the public as a whole. At the same time, wildlife
management should not become a popularity contest; instead, the human

component is integrated into the biological, habitat, and people triangle (Duda 1986). Wildlife management has evolved from an initial concentration on big game harvesting, toward an understanding of habitat, and finally to an understanding of the people who use those wildlife resources. The successful resolution of the wolf restoration issue will require much public involvement (human dimensions research) and continued use of this broadening definition of wildlife management.

REFERENCES

Adams, C. E. 1988. Establishing a human dimensions program. Human Dimen. Wildl. Newsl. 7:3–7.

Anderson, S. H., R. E. Beiswenger, and P. W. Purdom. 1987. Environmental science. 3d ed. Merrill, Toronto.

Bath, A. J., and T. Buchanan. 1989. Attitudes of interest groups in Wyoming toward wolf restoration in Yellowstone National Park. Wildl. Soc. Bull. 17:519–525.

Carmine, E. G., and R. A. Zeller. 1979. Reliability and validity assessment. Quantitative Application in the Social Sciences Ser. no. 07-017. Sage, London.

Dillman, D. A. 1978. Mail and telephone surveys: The total design methods. John Wiley and Sons, Toronto.

Duda, M. D. 1986. Wildlife management: The human element. Fla. Wildl. (September–October):15–17.

Fritts, S. H. 1982. Wolf depredation on livestock in Minnesota. U.S. Fish Wildl. Serv. Resource Publ. 145:282–292.

Lutz, G. M. 1983. Understanding social statistics. Macmillan, New York.

Mech, L. D. 1977. Productivity, mortality, and population trend of wolves in northeastern Minnesota. J. Mammal. 58:559–594.

Nunnally, J. C. 1970. Introduction to psychological measurement. McGraw-Hill, New York.

U.S. Fish and Wildlife Service. 1986. Northern Rocky Mountain wolf recovery plan. U.S. Department of the Interior, Washington, D.C.

Weaver, J. 1978. The wolves of Yellowstone. Nat'l Park Serv. Nat. Resources Rep. 14. GPO, Washington, D.C.

PART V   **GREATER YELLOWSTONE'S FUTURE**

Future visitors and residents of the Greater Yellowstone Area will encounter a landscape where natural processes are operating with little hindrance on a grand scale. . . . The overriding mood of the Greater Yellowstone Area will be one of naturalness, a combination of ecological processes operating with little restraint and humans moderating their activities so that they become a reasonable part of, rather than encumbrance upon, those processes.

Greater Yellowstone Coordinating Committee, "Vision for the Future: A Framework for Coordination in the Greater Yellowstone Area" (Draft, 1990).

Overleaf: *Mammoth Hot Springs, lower basins, looking up. Yellowstone National Park, Wyoming, 1878. Photo by W. H. Jackson; courtesy of U.S. Geological Survey, Denver, Colorado.*

CHAPTER 24   **Greater Yellowstone's Future:**
Ecosystem Management in
a Wilderness Environment
Robert B. Keiter
and Mark S. Boyce

One might fairly ask why so much of a book about
Greater Yellowstone focuses on fire, elk, and wolves. The answer should
be evident by now. In significant respects, fire, elk, and wolves epitomize
the transition to ecosystem management that is now occurring in Greater
Yellowstone; how they are handled on the public domain will set the stage
for how other human-nature conflicts are addressed. Transcending the
bureaucratic domain of any single agency, these resources can be managed
effectively only on an ecosystem scale. And ecosystem management policies can be devised only by reaching consensus on how to integrate humans
and nature on America's remaining wildlands. Even a policy permitting
ecological processes to prevail must be implemented on the basis of human
judgments—which in itself highlights the human role in the ecosystem
(Huff 1989). In short, the management philosophy applied to these vital
components of Greater Yellowstone's ecosystem will reveal whether federal officials can define and implement comprehensive ecologically oriented policies for the entire region.

The evolution of elk, fire, and wolf management policies reflects a
profound change in human attitudes toward the natural environment on
western public lands. Ever since Yellowstone was proclaimed the world's
first national park, the elk has been valued as a "good" animal and a useful
commodity (see, for example, Kellert 1986) and thus protected and given

priority over other species. In contrast, fire and wolves historically have been viewed as undesirable, destructive, and "bad" natural entities (Lopez 1978; Knight chapter 8 in this volume). Early on, therefore, the government suppressed wildfires on the Yellowstone public domain (Runte 1987) and systematically eliminated wolves from the Yellowstone ecosystem (Weaver 1978).

This has now changed. In response to the now famous 1963 Leopold report (Leopold et al. 1963), National Park Service management policies have been redesigned to permit ecological processes, including fire and predators, to prevail in the national parks. And under the Wilderness Act of 1964 (16 U.S. C. §§ 1131-1136), which enshrined the wilderness concept as a resource management principle on the public domain, the Forest Service is also committed to a "let nature take its course" philosophy on its wilderness lands. At least within the national parks, elk are now less likely to be given priority over other species and they are being managed as part of the larger ecosystem. Natural fires are no longer regarded as "bad"; rather, fire is seen as an ecological phenomenon necessary to ensure regeneration and evolution in the Yellowstone forests (Knight chapter 8 in this volume). Wolves, though still loathed in many quarters, are also now being viewed as a missing ecological component in the Greater Yellowstone Ecosystem (National Park Service 1990). Paradoxically, therefore, where human interests may have once justified wholesale destruction of natural systems and indigenous species, these same systems and species are now being protected—and even reestablished—as part of a redefinition of our wilderness heritage.

What we are witnessing in Greater Yellowstone is the emergence of a new era in public land management, predicated on a fundamental realignment of the human relationship with nature. The defining characteristic of this new era is a commitment to ecosystem-based management—one reflecting the fact that ecological processes are dynamic and cannot be constrained by artificial jurisdictional boundaries (President's Commission on Americans Outdoors 1987; Gordon et al. 1989; Keiter 1989; Sweeney 1990). In Greater Yellowstone, federal natural resource management policy is evolving toward protecting ecological processes on a large scale (Patten chapter 2 in this volume; Craighead chapter 3 in this volume), restoring disturbed ecological processes (Sax chapter 7 in this volume; Varley and Schullery chapter 9 in this volume; Mech chapter 20 in this volume), and giving priority to amenity values (O'Toole chapter 4 in this volume). Traditional economic interests are giving way—albeit grudgingly—to the ecological imperatives of modern natural resource management (Sax chapter 7 in this volume). The challenge, therefore, is no longer how to control nature, but rather how to integrate human activities with ecological imperatives to ensure the region's natural integrity (Boyce chapter 14 in this volume).

Drawing upon changes occurring in Greater Yellowstone, it is now possible to identify several important dimensions of an emerging ecosystem management policy. First, ecosystem management is built upon cooperative interagency institutional structures, as well as public involvement and support (Agee and Johnson 1988; Clark and Harvey 1988). Second, ecosystem management draws heavily upon scientific principles and research; it requires an improved understanding of ecological systems so that management proposals can be designed to minimize disruption of ecosystem processes (Keiter 1990). Third, ecosystem management is committed to preserving and restoring biological diversity within regional fauna and flora (Boyce chapter 14 in this volume; Keiter 1990). Finally, ecosystem management policies must manifest broadly shared public values. In Greater Yellowstone, where public lands have been set aside as national parks and wilderness areas, this means that ecosystem management policies must take account of aesthetic concerns and amenity values, and thus preserve the natural integrity and appearance of the area (Keiter 1990; Lockhart chapter 5 in this volume).

This evolutionary change in federal natural resource management policy is not coming easily in Greater Yellowstone. Many people still object to the notion of a Greater Yellowstone Ecosystem. They object even more strenuously to the concept of ecosystem-based management (Reynolds 1987; Budd chapter 6 in this volume). Yet local political officials and land managers have long understood that Yellowstone and Grand Teton national parks are tied—as if by an economic umbilical cord—to the surrounding gateway communities of Jackson, Cody, West Yellowstone, and other neighboring towns. These same people have also long recognized that the Yellowstone region national forests are linked directly to the economic welfare of adjacent local communities, which depend on these forests for resource commodities, jobs, and recreational opportunities (Keiter chapter 1 in this volume). Now, it is clear that these same public lands, as well as surrounding private lands, are also linked together ecologically (Patten chapter 2 in this volume; Boyce chapter 14 in this volume). What occurs within the national parks often has environmental ramifications beyond park boundaries, just as what occurs on the national forests and elsewhere may have environmental impacts within the parks and within designated wilderness areas (Craighead chapter 3 in this volume; Congressional Research Service 1986). This calls into question long-standing assumptions about the appropriate role and scale of natural processes, the relation between preserved and multiple-use lands, and the balance between commodity uses and amenity values.

These issues are now being addressed by the National Park Service and the U.S. Forest Service, which are primarily responsible for the Greater Yellowstone public lands. Their ecosystem management initiatives, although still in the formative stage, will not escape intense public scrutiny and congressional review. And given Yellowstone's prominence, these initiatives will undoubtedly also influence resource management practices elsewhere on the public domain and throughout the world. In this concluding chapter, therefore, we try to put these Greater Yellowstone developments in perspective. We begin by identifying the principal conflicts involved in this transition to an ecosystem-based management policy in Greater Yellowstone. Next, we undertake a critical examination of current ecosystem management initiatives, focusing on the existing institutional structures, the role of science, and the influence of public values. Finally, we offer some tentative observations about the future of ecosystem management in Greater Yellowstone and elsewhere.

THE LEGACY OF THE BOUNDARY LINE

Borders to national parks and forests seldom have much relation to meaningful ecosystem boundaries (Newmark 1985; Runte 1987). With Greater Yellowstone facing the transition to an ecosystem-based management policy, the legacy of these conventional boundary lines calls directly into question how management of resources on an ecosystem scale can be squared with human interests. At one level, the question is whether recent efforts to restore natural fire, wolves, and other processes to their original ecological role can be reconciled with historical human uses, including the interests of neighboring landowners and commodity development industries. At a second level, the question is how the environmental integrity of Greater Yellowstone's park and wilderness resources can be protected from the adverse effects of development activities, such as oil and gas exploration, timber harvesting, and livestock grazing, that occur on adjacent lands. At a third level, the question is whether the development that inevitably accompanies an expanding recreation-based economy built on the region's amenity values can occur without jeopardizing its ecological integrity.

Ecological-Process Management

In Greater Yellowstone, recent management initiatives involving fire, elk, and wolves reflect a commitment to maintaining, protecting, and restoring ecological processes that have shaped the natural environment. As we have seen, the Greater Yellowstone Coordinating Committee's draft "Vision" document proposes to conserve the region's sense of naturalness by permitting ecological processes to function on a large scale (Keiter chapter 1 in this volume). Many local citizens and commodity development interests, however, view the National Park Service's current emphasis on ecological-process management with skepticism and alarm. They likewise question the wisdom of the Forest Service's "let nature prevail" wilderness management philosophy. Both agencies, nonetheless, have permitted natural fires to burn on park and wilderness lands, viewing fire as a critical ecological component in forest and range ecosystems. The Park Service is also relying on nature to regulate elk population numbers within Yellowstone National Park, while the Forest Service is working to reestablish historical elk migration routes. And the Park Service is committed to restoring the wolf to its original ecological niche. Significantly, each of these ecological-process policy initiatives seems to enjoy considerable public support, though further refinements will be necessary to accommodate local interests.

The still-evolving natural-fire management policy is aimed toward restoring fire to its historical role in the ecosystem. During the summer 1988 fires, these policies came under attack from local citizens concerned that the magnitude of the fires would destroy the region's aesthetic attractiveness and keep visitors away, as occurred while the fires were burning. Even though tourists returned in record numbers the following two years, many residents are not convinced that nature's forces should be given such free rein. In spite of the political imbroglio accompanying the 1988 fires, the policy's fundamental premises have not been shaken; Greater Yellowstone is today reaping ecological benefits still only partially understood (Knight chapter 8 in this volume; Varley and Schullery chapter 9 in this volume; Minshall and Brock chapter 10 in this volume). That Congress has not legislatively altered the fire management policy suggests a surprising degree of public understanding—or at least tolerance—of the role ecological processes play in Greater Yellowstone, and thus may signal an evolving consensus on the rudiments of an ecological-process management philosophy.

Elk management policies based on ecological processes are also being implemented throughout Greater Yellowstone. Even in the intensively managed Jackson elk herd, the current U.S. Fish and Wildlife Service justification for winter feeding is to replace winter range occupied by human development and thus to emulate historical processes (Boyce 1989).

On Yellowstone's northern range, 7,000 to 8,000 elk from the northern herd perished during the 1988–1989 winter due to high population density, a summer-long drought, and a winter of average severity (Singer et al. 1989). Such elk mortality had been predicted for several years by park scientists (Houston 1982; Despain et al. 1986), as the way that population regulation was bound to occur in the absence of hunting by humans and predation by wolves. Public reaction to the winter mortalities was remarkably mild, again suggesting public acceptance of ecological processes as an important dimension of wilderness management policy.

South of Yellowstone National Park, the Forest Service is seeking to reestablish historical elk migration patterns. For many years, scientists have recommended restoring elk migration routes from southern Yellowstone National Park through the Teton Wilderness to Jackson Hole (Cole 1969; Boyce 1989). More than 30 percent of the Jackson elk herd historically migrated through the Togwottee Pass area east of Moran, Wyoming. During the early 1960s, logging roads built into the Spread Creek area made easier access for hunters, which resulted in heavy elk kills. Consequently, the Togwottee area now supports only 3–5 percent of the autumn migration for the Jackson elk herd (Boyce 1989). Although the Wyoming Game and Fish Department, responding to political pressure from outfitters and hunters, has been unwilling to impose the elk harvest regulations necessary to restore preexisting routes, Bridger-Teton National Forest officials seemingly have committed themselves to restoring these migration patterns (U.S. Forest Service 1989a).

Moreover, wolf recovery now appears likely in Yellowstone National Park. The public supports wolf recovery, notwithstanding the wolf's traditional "bad" image (McNaught 1987; Bath chapter 23 in this volume). Local ranchers, however, are concerned about the impact wolves may have on livestock and on their grazing permits, and they oppose the wolf recovery proposal (Mech chapter 20 in this volume). Some hunters and outfitters are concerned that a resident wolf population could significantly reduce ungulate herd sizes, which might lead state wildlife management officials to limit hunting opportunities (Zumbo 1987). And commodity development interests, drawing on their experience with the "threatened" grizzly bear, fear the legal constraints that may accompany wolves protected under the Endangered Species Act (Keiter and Holscher 1990). Even though wolves undoubtedly will kill park wildlife and some domestic livestock, few people dispute that wolves represent a key component in the wildlife ecology of Greater Yellowstone. That Congress has now appropriated funds to establish a Wolf Management Committee to recommend how wolves should be reintroduced into Yellowstone reveals just how dramatically public attitudes about predators and nature have changed, again reflecting public understanding of the role ecological systems play on the public domain.

Further scientific studies addressing the ecological impact of the summer 1988 fires, as well as elk management options and the effect of wolf reintroduction on ungulate populations, are now under way. Findings from these studies will enable managers to fine tune their policies and to mitigate the effects that such natural processes may have on local interests. But the study results will not satisfy those who consider any policy that permits nature to prevail over human interests fundamentally wrong, regardless of ecological or other justifications. And the study results will not allay the concern that if management priorities are established on an ecologically viable scale, these policies will inevitably conflict with human activities — economic and otherwise—occurring on lands beyond the park and wilderness boundaries. This is a very real concern, and one that the agencies can resolve only by confronting directly the question of priorities.

Ecosystem Integrity and Consumptive Use

As the significance of the boundary line diminishes, a fundamental question confronting Greater Yellowstone is whether intensive consumptive use can coexist with preservation of the region's ecological integrity. Such resource development activities as oil and gas exploration, timber harvesting, and livestock grazing have traditionally taken place on the region's multiple-use forest lands. Although these activities provide important local jobs and tax revenues, they are also heavy on the land, both environmentally and aesthetically. Indeed, the cumulative impact of industrial activity, aggregated throughout the Greater Yellowstone region, has much more significance environmentally than an isolated development; it can potentially fragment and disrupt vital ecological processes and alter the area's natural character (Reese 1984; Harris 1984). Many people, therefore, are now questioning the propriety of intensive industrial activity on the still largely undisturbed national forest lands.

Oil and gas. Oil and gas exploration in the Greater Yellowstone region has generated extensive controversy and litigation. The Overthrust Belt, which has produced several rich discoveries of natural gas in southwestern Wyoming, extends into the region. Anxious to explore promising geologic formations, oil companies have leased nearly half the open lands in Wyoming's Bridger-Teton National Forest, making it the principal battleground over oil and gas development in the national forests (Keiter 1989; compare

Mountain States Legal Found. v. Andrus 1980 with Sierra Club v. Peterson 1983). Environmentalists, joined by the National Park Service, fear that exploratory drilling, which often requires new access roads into remote areas, could adversely affect sensitive wildlife species like the elk and grizzly bear, open roadless lands to human access and additional development, and detract from the region's aesthetic appearance (Sierra Club 1986; Keiter 1989). Nevertheless, the Forest Service has opened nearly 95 percent of the Bridger-Teton's nonwilderness lands for leasing (U.S. Forest Service 1989a).

Faced with conflicting legal precedents under the National Environmental Policy Act (42 U.S.C. § 4321; compare Park County Resource Council v. U.S. Dep't of Agric. 1987 with Conner v. Burford 1988), Bridger-Teton officials have completed a comprehensive environmental analysis of the oil and gas development cycle in the forest plan. They also plan to impose lease restrictions on steep-slope lands and lands located in critical grizzly bear habitat (U.S. Forest Service 1989a). Environmentalists, however, are concerned that leasing stipulations will be waived, and that the Forest Service will not be able to control development in the event of a promising strike. Their concerns are not chimerical. In the Yellowstone region, the federal government has never refused an exploratory drilling permit, and the Forest Service has waived even stringent "no surface occupancy" stipulations to allow drilling on pristine roadless lands in the shadow of Grand Teton National Park (Keiter 1989). In each case, the Forest Service has relied on scientific data to conclude that the environmental effects could be controlled or mitigated.

Even if the environmental impacts can be minimized (which is not certain), is Greater Yellowstone an appropriate setting for the intensive industrial development that would accompany a major strike? Most residents in Jackson, Wyoming, believe the answer is no, and they have vigorously opposed the Forest Service's oil and gas development plans, as have residents in other communities near proposed exploratory drilling operations (U.S. Forest Service 1989b; Associated Press 1989). However, other residents in communities less dependent on a tourism-based economy, as well as state political officials, view oil and gas activity as a vital component of the regional economy (Associated Press 1990; Leal, Black, and Baden 1990). The GYCC, in its recent draft "Vision" document, seeks the middle ground; it imposes no constraints on leasing, while proposing to involve the Park Service in the Forest Service's leasing review process, apparently to ensure that drilling does not adversely impact park resources. But with no local consensus and with such high economic and environmental values at stake, the issue of oil and gas development may now exceed the ability of any single agency to handle and may not be subject to a scientific solution. Instead, Congress may have to decide whether oil and gas development on Greater Yellowstone public lands is compatible with the region's natural values.

Timber. Timber harvesting also has generated intense controversy. Environmentalists complain that extensive logging has diminished important wildlife habitat, fragmented migration routes, opened previously inaccessible forest lands for human use, and otherwise compromised the natural appearance of the area. They also note that every Yellowstone region forest loses money on its timber program, and that logging inhibits recreational opportunities (O'Toole chapter 4 in this volume; Leal 1990). Park Service officials are particularly concerned that extensive clearcutting on Yellowstone's borders, which has occurred in the Targhee National Forest, will alter basic ecological processes and destroy important grizzly habitat (Wilderness Society 1987; Keiter 1989). Yet local communities rely on the timber industry for important jobs and tax revenues. Long dominated by its timber management mission, the Forest Service defends clearcut logging, arguing that it can promote a healthy forest, improve wildlife habitat, minimize destructive wildfires, and enhance local economic stability and diversification (Keiter chapter 1 in this volume).

The Forest Service's emphasis on timber harvesting varies between the Yellowstone region forests. The Bridger-Teton and Shoshone national forests have reduced timber harvest levels in their forest plans in order to promote other resource values (Keiter 1989). In fact, the Bridger-Teton National Forest has even withstood a legal attack on its decision to eliminate commercial logging in the northern portion of the forest—a decision that forced Louisiana-Pacific to close its Dubois, Wyoming, sawmill, putting 125 residents out of work (Intermountain Forest Industries Ass'n v. Lyng 1988; Keiter chapter 1 in this volume). Other Yellowstone region national forests, however, plan to increase timber harvesting levels. This decision is difficult to justify; timber traditionally has been a money-losing proposition and can have significant adverse impacts on wildlife habitat (Greater Yellowstone Coordinating Committee 1987; O'Toole chapter 4 in this volume). The cyclical logging industry is simply not a major factor in the region's economy. And the adverse environmental and aesthetic ramifications of clearcut logging will not only be felt on the ground, but could also negatively affect the region's burgeoning recreation-tourism economy.

Significantly, in its draft "Vision" document, the GYCC appears to contemplate a scaled-down timber program on the national forests. The document provides that "timber management will be performed to meet land management objectives and in such a way as to provide for the integrity of the ecosystem and the natural appearance of the area" (Greater Yellowstone Coordinating Committee 1990). Moreover, the GYCC proposes to assist local communities develop value-added industries, which could not only enhance the economic importance of the local timber industry but also diminish its impact on the region's forests. After the Lyng decision, the Forest Service certainly has the authority to curb timber harvesting levels to protect other resources. If the agencies are serious about limiting harvest levels, this would represent a clear shift in priorities. It would move the Forest Service away from its historical timber bias (Clary 1986), toward a commitment to protecting Greater Yellowstone's environmental integrity and natural appearance, and toward a recognition of the regional economic importance of recreation and tourism.

Livestock grazing. Because more than 44 percent of the Greater Yellowstone public lands are open to cattle and sheep grazing (Amato and Whittemore 1989; Greater Yellowstone Coordinating Committee 1987), livestock and wildlife conflicts are recurrent on the region's public lands. Seldom able to operate economically viable cattle or sheep operations on their own private lands, ranchers lease grazing allotments on public lands, where domestic livestock may compete with native wildlife for forage, degrade riparian habitats, and are subject to predation. Wildlife do not always fare well in this competition. In the Gros Ventre River valley, for example, cattle grazing has reduced winter habitat for elk, necessitating highly artificial winter-feeding programs to maintain the elk herd (Murie and Murie 1966). Although Wyoming Game and Fish Department biologists have expressed interest in purchasing strategic grazing allotments to use for elk winter range along the Gros Ventre River (D. Moody, personal communication), Bridger-Teton forest officials have refused such a solution, thus foreclosing an opportunity to eliminate elk feeding programs (Boyce 1989). In the case of the grizzly bear, one-fifth of the Greater Yellowstone grizzly bear mortalities have been related to conflicts with domestic sheep grazing, leading wildlife officials to designate several grazing allotments as grizzly bear mortality "sinks" (Knight, Blanchard, and Eberhardt 1988; Congressional Research Service 1986). That the grizzly bear is the inevitable loser in this situation is particularly disturbing: the grizzly bear is legally protected as an endangered species and it is perhaps more intensively managed and monitored than any other species.

Wildlife-livestock conflicts also occur on private lands throughout Greater Yellowstone. Wildlife often rely on private ranchlands—usually located at lower elevations—for winter habitat or as migration corridors. Elk and bison, however, can infect domestic cattle with brucellosis, a disease that causes spontaneous abortion (Thorne, Morton, and Ray 1979; Thorne, Meagher, and Hillman chapter 18 in this volume). When this occurs, ranchers in the GYE have no alternative but to destroy their cattle herd, in order to protect their state's brucellosis-free status, which is vital to maintaining access to interstate markets. The threat of brucellosis transmission to cattle has been the principal justification for killing bison that leave the national parks. During the 1988–1989 winter, the Montana Fish, Wildlife, and Parks Department authorized a controversial "hunt" to kill bison that wandered out of Yellowstone National Park in search of feed. The decision drew adverse national publicity, as hunters were photographed in the process of shooting approximately 570 of 900 bison in Yellowstone's northern herd in what can only be described as a slaughter. After consulting with Montana wildlife officials, the Park Service now proposes to have its own rangers participate in the bison hunt by helping to shoot cow bison as they leave the park (National Park Service 1990a). A similar controversy is brewing in the Jackson area, where Wyoming Game and Fish Department officials, in conjunction with the U.S. Fish and Wildlife Service, have authorized a bison hunt on the National Elk Refuge to reduce the population and to minimize contact between bison and domestic cattle.

Unfortunately, there are no effective means of eradicating brucellosis from wild ungulates. Although the Wyoming Game and Fish Department is using biobullets to vaccinate elk at state-owned winter feed lots, this method—at best—can only reduce the risk of transmission to livestock. Neither the vaccine nor biobullets are effective on bison. Despite their commitment to an ecological-process management policy, Park Service officials have thus far condoned the hunting, viewing it as an expedient option for reducing conflicts with agricultural interests. Scientists, however, do not believe that brucellosis can be controlled by hunting or by any other available wildlife management technique (Boyce 1989). In fact, the only plausible means of dealing with the problem is to minimize contact between domestic livestock and wildlife during late winter and spring when the disease is most likely to be transmitted by an aborted fetus. If Greater Yellowstone's wildlife are to remain free roaming, some accommodation must be forthcoming from local agricultural interests. However, recent efforts involving the Park Service, state wildlife officials, and local ranchers have not yielded a satisfactory cooperative solution.

The real problem, of course, is that no one has yet addressed the question of priorities between wildlife and livestock on the Greater Yellowstone public domain. Should the northern Yellowstone bison or elk herd face oblivion upon leaving the park to protect the interests of a handful of ranchers? Without clear priorities and standards, such as those governing grizzly bear management, these conflicts will continue. Other than calling for additional interagency coordination, the GYCC's draft "Vision" document fails to address this issue explicitly, even though federal agencies have had recurrent problems reaching a satisfactory solution with state wildlife officials in Montana and Wyoming. Perhaps this is not surprising since wildlife outside the national parks are under the jurisdiction of the states, where ranching and hunting interests have considerable political power. As a result, however, these issues are being resolved piecemeal on the basis of raw political power, rather than comprehensively on the basis of scientific data and economic realities.

Emphasizing Amenity Values:
A Preview of Future Conflicts?

With commodity development becoming increasingly less important in the Greater Yellowstone economy, recreation and tourism are being promoted as the key to a sustainable economic future. In fact, recent data suggest that recreation contributes far more revenues to the local economy than any other activity and that recreation already is the predominant activity on Greater Yellowstone's public lands (Greater Yellowstone Coordinating Committee 1987). The recreation economy, of course, draws on national park and national forest amenity values, principally scenery and wildlife. Recognizing the importance of recreation in Greater Yellowstone, the GYCC draft "Vision" document proposes to enhance recreational opportunities (Greater Yellowstone Coordinating Committee 1990). The important question, therefore, is how to integrate recreation and tourism with a commitment to the region's ecological integrity.

Neither tourism nor recreation is an environmentally benign activity; each requires infrastructure development and guarantees an increased human presence. Resort developments, such as the proposed Ski Yellowstone complex on forest lands outside West Yellowstone, could negatively affect grizzly bear habitat and otherwise interfere with wildlife, particularly if accompanied by extensive private development (U.S. Forest Service 1987). An emphasis on recreation will inevitably bring more people onto public lands, jeopardizing the wilderness solitude many visitors seek. Popular activities, including Snake River float trips and backpacking in the Teton range, are already overcrowded and no longer afford visitors a true wilderness experience. Outside the parks, the Forest Service is under constant pressure to upgrade roads and campground facilities, which will bring more visitors and further degrade wildlife habitat and other resources.

Moreover, a commitment to a recreation-based economy will have a direct effect on private land-use decisions. Private land development is already escalating throughout the Greater Yellowstone region (Kwong 1990). Long-time ranches, which historically provided open space for wildlife, have been acquired by nonranching interests and are being sub-divided for vacation homes and the like. Statistics reveal that grizzly bear mortalities are much higher near private lands than elsewhere in the region (Congressional Research Service 1986). Federal law generally does not apply to private property (Sax 1976), and the GYCC has pointedly avoided any suggestion that its coordination efforts will result in federal regulation of private land use—a politically charged issue throughout the West. State and local laws governing land-use development vary widely within the region. Most communities have been hesitant to limit development, though some restraint is being shown in places like Teton County, Wyoming, which has developed a comprehensive land-use plan to control local de-velopment (Keiter chapter 1 in this volume).

Excessive visitation is a particularly acute problem in the national parks. During 1989 and 1990, visitation to Yellowstone National Park broke previous records; more than 2.6 million people toured the park each year. These numbers inevitably strain park campgrounds and visitor facilities and affect important wildlife habitat. Yet the gateway communities that depend on park tourists for their economic sustenance have consistently opposed Park Service policies that might limit or discourage visitation. When Yellowstone officials planned to close the Fishing Bridge camp-ground to protect valuable grizzly bear habitat, local businesses in nearby Cody, Wyoming—fearing an adverse impact on their tourist industry—exerted sufficient political pressure to reverse the decision (Keiter 1989). Similar pressures have been directed at Park Service officials who are preparing a long overdue winter-use plan for Yellowstone and Grand Teton national parks. Towns such as West Yellowstone, Montana, have developed a substantial snowmobile business, which has given birth to a booming winter economy. Naturally, local officials and businesses oppose restric-tions on snowmobile access, and they have urged park officials to expand winter facilities to attract additional visitors. In addition, the state of Wyoming, which supports development of a transmountain snowmobile trail to encourage winter tourism, has pressured the National Park Service to provide unlimited access through previously closed terrain.

Cumulatively, these developments portend dramatic environmental, economic, and aesthetic consequences for the Greater Yellowstone region. On the public lands, the GYCC must take a hard look at the quality of the visitor experience, adverse environmental impacts on wildlife and other resources, and the appropriate level of public and private sector development. Beyond the public lands, the states and local communities must begin to consider similar issues. A joint federal-state effort addressing these issues comprehensively would provide a forum for defining an appropriate relation between federal, state, and private lands, and for determining how to integrate local concerns into federal ecosystem management initiatives.

IN TRANSITION TO ECOSYSTEM MANAGEMENT

With the Greater Yellowstone public lands administered by separate federal agencies and with such resources as wildlife and water under the overlapping jurisdictional authority of federal and state officials, establishing comprehensive ecologically sound, yet politically viable, management policies is not an easy task. Environmentalists and industry have both shown that they are willing to litigate to promote their own agendas. Congressional intervention on behalf of powerful local interests has become a way of life. Moreover, in the aftermath of the 1985 oversight hearing, the threat of comprehensive federal legislation looms like the sword of Damocles over the entire Yellowstone region, along with the ever-present threat of general park protection legislation (Keiter 1985).

In this unsettled atmosphere, the Park Service and the Forest Service are taking seriously the need to address issues on an ecosystem-wide basis. They have created institutional structures to address resource management issues comprehensively, and they are undertaking an unprecedented federal coordination effort that will attempt to define future management priorities. They are increasingly relying on scientific data as the basis for management decisions. And they appear intent on defining a new vision or future for Greater Yellowstone—one that takes account of ecological concerns and reflects evolving public values. Although these initiatives represent a significant commitment to bringing an ecosystem-based management policy to fruition, the agencies still must overcome deeply embedded institutional traditions, long-standing interagency rivalries, and considerable local political opposition.

Federal Coordination: Institutions and Processes

Thus far, the Greater Yellowstone Coordinating Committee—now revitalized in response to harsh congressional criticism following the 1985

Greater Yellowstone Oversight Hearing—is relying on a process-based approach to ecosystem management (Keiter 1989). This is evidenced by the GYCC's complex "Vision" document procedure, which will effectively define comprehensive management priorities for the two national parks and six national forests that constitute the Greater Yellowstone Area (Keiter 1989; Keiter chapter 1 in this volume; Budd chapter 6 in this volume). This approach is based on the premise that locally formulated policies are preferable to congressionally mandated ones. Such an approach also assumes that when people have the opportunity to participate in the governmental decisions that shape their lives, they will be more likely to accept the results, even if they disagree with them (Stewart 1975). In the final analysis, an ecosystem management policy is more apt to succeed if it enjoys the tacit support of the nearby citizenry (Gilbert 1975).

The law gives Park Service and Forest Service officials considerable discretionary authority to set management policy on their respective lands. The National Park Service Organic Act contains a strong preservation mandate as well as an obligation to protect park resources from harm that supports the Park Service's commitment to coordinated regional management (16 U.S.C. § 1, § 1a-1; Simon 1988; Lockhart chapter 5 in this volume). The National Forest Management Act, which has modified the Forest Service's multiple-use responsibilities, also reflects a strong commitment to ecologically sound forestry practices and provides for integrated, interdisciplinary forest planning, coordinated with neighboring landowners (Wilkinson and Anderson 1985; Sax and Keiter 1987). These laws, in conjunction with the Endangered Species Act and other preservation-oriented statutes, provide park and forest officials with a firm legal basis for pursuing cooperative interagency initiatives and for developing substantive ecosystem-based resource management policies (Keiter 1989).

Besides the GYCC's coordination process, several other interagency management initiatives have been undertaken, reflecting federal and state recognition of Greater Yellowstone's ecological interconnectedness. Clearly, the most prominent of these initiatives is the grizzly bear recovery program. Acting under the powerful Endangered Species Act, which requires federal agencies to "conserve" and "recover" protected species, federal and state officials have mounted a concerted campaign through an Interagency Grizzly Bear Committee to bring the Yellowstone grizzly back from the brink of extinction (McNamee 1984; Amato and Whetmore 1989). The committee has promulgated interagency grizzly bear guidelines establishing stringent uniform management requirements throughout the Greater Yellowstone Ecosystem (U.S. Fish and Wildlife Service 1982), which have curbed some intensive development activity on critical grizzly bear habitat lands. The committee also has developed a compúterized cumulative effects model to measure the effect that proliferating development proposals might have on the bear's habitat requirements (U.S. Forest Service 1987). With current population estimates suggesting that grizzly numbers are increasing and mortalities decreasing (Legg 1990), this program demonstrates the effectiveness of joint federal-state conservation programs and could serve as a model for even broader cooperative interagency management efforts, including perhaps a Greater Yellowstone Ecosystem management oversight committee. But without the compulsion of the powerful ESA, will federal and state officials relinquish their own managerial prerogatives and autonomy to secure the natural integrity of the Greater Yellowstone region?

Other interagency management programs—usually involving representatives from the Park Service, Forest Service, U.S. Fish and Wildlife Service, and state wildlife management agencies—have been established to address the habitat needs of migratory wildlife that cannot be resolved by a single agency. The first of these was the Jackson Hole Cooperative Elk Studies Group, established in 1958. More recently, a similar cooperative interagency group was created to address ungulate and range management on Yellowstone's northern range. Under the Endangered Species Act, interagency recovery committees have been established to manage the peregrine falcon and bald eagle. The agencies also are developing a cooperative interagency committee for management of the trumpeter swan. And if wolves are reintroduced into Yellowstone National Park, they most likely will be managed on an ecosystem-wide basis through the same type of interagency management program (U.S. Fish and Wildlife Service 1987). In addition, after reassessing federal fire policy in the aftermath of the 1988 fires, the Park Service and the Forest Service are developing an interagency fire management program, designed to define the role of natural fire and to coordinate fire policy in Greater Yellowstone (Schullery 1989).

In sum, these initiatives reflect a serious commitment to devising institutional structures and procedures to coordinate natural resources management policy in Greater Yellowstone on an ecosystem scale. They also make clear that the region cannot be managed effectively without breaching traditional jurisdictional limitations. In an area rife with interagency jealousies and turf confrontations, federal officials can derive some satisfaction from this coordination effort. Conservationists can take some solace from the GYCC's evident commitment to developing a more comprehensive and environmentally sensitive approach to regional issues. But the Park Service and the Forest Service confront strongly entrenched local interests who oppose any significant change (Budd chapter 6 in this volume), and they are still far from translating these nascent ecosystem management initiatives into meaningful policy reforms.

Indeed, coordinated ecosystem-wide management is still more a myth than a reality throughout much of the Greater Yellowstone region. The GYCC membership is composed only of representatives from the Park Service and the Forest Service; it does not include representation from other federal agencies, such as the Bureau of Land Management or the Fish and Wildlife Service, nor does it include state or local representatives. Notwithstanding the GYCC's public involvement process, its limited composition could hamper its ability to forge a mutually shared vision for the region and to garner broad local support for its policy initiatives. Moreover, the GYCC's limited membership seriously undermines its ability to address private land use and development issues—a critically important aspect of ecosystem-based management.

The evidence suggests that the Forest Service is not yet fully committed to coordinated management for the Greater Yellowstone region. Individual forests have taken quite different approaches to controversial resource management issues, ones strikingly inconsistent with ecological imperatives and the rhetoric of interagency coordination. The Targhee National Forest, for instance, continues to harvest timber on Yellowstone's western border at an accelerated rate; its allowable sale quantity exceeds that set for any other Greater Yellowstone forest by a factor of ten (Greater Yellowstone Coordinating Committee 1987). Although the Bridger-Teton and Shoshone forests have reduced their timber harvest levels, other forests have sharply increased their harvest levels in recent forest plans (Keiter 1989). The Shoshone and Custer national forests have placed critical grizzly bear lands off limits for oil and gas leasing, but the Bridger-Teton and other forests permit leasing on theirs (Keiter 1989). On an ecosystem-wide basis, the cumulative environmental consequences of such disparate management decisions threaten the ecological and aesthetic integrity of the wildland resource (Congressional Research Service 1986; Clark and Zaunbrecher 1987). Such decisions also reveal a troubling lack of consistency and an absence of defined priorities within the region's individual forests.

The Park Service, too, has not shown that it is institutionally capable of fully implementing management policies based on preserving ecological processes. It has not consistently withstood the local political repercussions that inevitably accompany management decisions giving precedence to nature over local interests. As we have noted, park officials have retreated from their initial decision to close the Fishing Bridge campground in important grizzly bear country, bowing to political opposition from the Cody business community (Schneebeck 1986). The Park Service has recently agreed to kill bison that wander outside Yellowstone to placate ranchers who fear that migrating bison could infect their cattle herds with brucellosis (National Park Service 1990a). The natural-fire management policy is currently on hold, and Park Service employees have been intermittently reluctant to promote wolf recovery publicly (Melnykovych 1989). In another nod to local economic interests, the Park Service's winter-use plan will open Grand Teton National Park to snowmobiling and thus allow completion of a transmountain snowmobile trail that will traverse the two peaks. Unless the National Park Service can successfully defend its ecological-process management policy on its own domain, there is little reason to believe that management policies giving precedence (or even equal respect) to nature can be successfully introduced on adjacent public lands.

A lack of coordination is also common between state and federal agencies. Bridger-Teton National Forest, for example, recently made a commitment to restore historical elk migration routes in the Jackson elk herd (U.S. Forest Service 1989a), yet the Wyoming Game and Fish Department has thwarted this objective by encouraging greater hunter harvests of elk in eastern portions of the Jackson elk herd unit. Similarly, although large numbers of summer visitors to Grand Teton National Park enjoy viewing the park's free-ranging bison herd, the Wyoming Game and Fish Department and the U.S. Fish and Wildlife Service are intent on reducing the herd size to minimize their winter feeding costs on the National Elk Refuge near Jackson, Wyoming. In these and other related instances, there is no authority such as the Endangered Species Act that compels the agencies to coordinate their priorities, nor is there any requirement that they base management policy on good science. All too often, local political interests are responsible for setting the management agenda.

Additional federal and state conflicts are likely to develop in the near future over sport hunting. State wildlife agencies usually have a strong bias in favor of hunting, generally because a majority of their revenues come from the sale of hunting licenses. At this time, hunting causes few conflicts with ecological-process management policies in Greater Yellowstone, probably because hunting has effectively replaced predation that normally would be caused by wolves. In the future, however, it may be necessary to temper the states' bias toward hunting to ensure that ecological-process management goals can be met. A reintroduced wolf population would compete with hunters for elk and other ungulates (National Park Service

1990b), perhaps precipitating conflicts between federal and state agencies over wolf control to protect game for hunting.

Little progress has been made addressing the complex problems presented by private land development, which is accelerating as the regional economy grows more dependent on revenues from recreation and other amenity values. Private land-use decisions are constrained only by state law, which is notoriously weak throughout the western states, where people have traditionally opposed government-imposed restraints on private property rights (Sax 1976). The problem is illustrated by the Park Service's inability to staunch development on the Royal Teton Ranch, which is located just north of Mammoth Hot Springs. Although the Park Service, as well as local environmental groups, regards this development as a serious threat to Yellowstone's wildlife and geyser system, the religious order that owns the ranch has undertaken a massive construction effort, turning what had been open ranchland into a small city of more than five thousand people, and it proposes to develop geothermal resources by drilling into a local hot spring (Montana Department of Health and Environmental Sciences 1989). A lawsuit based on the Montana Environmental Policy Act (Mont. Code Ann. § 75-1-101 et seq.) challenging this development failed, though development has been temporarily halted in the aftermath of a toxic chemical leak that threatened an important local trout fishery. In the meantime, a private conservation organization recently purchased 1,215 ha (3,000 acres) from the ranch to preserve winter habitat for elk, but the cult still retains control over other key parcels of winter range for the northern Yellowstone elk herd.

The striking fact is that the fate of private lands throughout Greater Yellowstone is outside the authority of the Greater Yellowstone federal land management agencies. Yet the GYCC's coordination effort has thus far not included representatives from state or local governments that are ultimately responsible for regulating private lands. Not only does this leave private lands outside the coordination process, it also has called into question the legitimacy of the GYCC's proposals with important segments of the local community (Budd chapter 6 in this volume). Although acquisitions through the Land and Water Conservation Fund (16 U.S.C. §§ 4601-4 to -11) or other financing devices could alleviate some particularly acute problems, a more comprehensive approach to the private lands problem is necessary. As a beginning, greater state and local involvement in the GYCC's coordination process might reduce some problems while broadening the effectiveness of the federal coordination initiatives. If its ecosystem management initiatives are to succeed, the GYCC must convince private landowners that its vision of protecting Greater Yellowstone's ecological integrity is not only valid but also consistent with these owners' best interests. Then, perhaps, private landowners might begin to show some voluntary restraint in the use and development of their lands.

The Role of Science: Its Promise and Limitations

The science of conservation biology and recent advances in ecology have contributed important scientific insights about Greater Yellowstone's natural systems and ecological dynamics. In significant respects, the scientific data support recent ecosystem management initiatives and should assist managers to frame appropriate policies. Although science alone cannot solve all of Greater Yellowstone's resource management controversies, science can ensure that the difficult value judgments implicit in these controversies are addressed knowledgeably with an understanding of the ecological ramifications. Moreover, scientific data can help shift the balance of power in the political arena and insulate difficult management decisions from legal review.

Several chapters in this volume illustrate how science is contributing to recent management initiatives protecting ecological processes. Yellowstone's 1972 natural-burn fire management policy, for example, was based on fire ecology research, and subsequent research has supported the fundamental soundness of this policy (Varley and Schullery chapter 9 in this volume). Research on fire history and shifting mosaics of vegetation by Knight (chapter 8 in this volume) and his students have established a basis for understanding the role of fire in the region (Romme and Knight 1982). Recent research has also established that planned ignitions cannot mimic natural fires or prevent wildfires from occurring (Brown chapter 11 in this volume). Although park visitors may not be able to perceive differences in larger streams caused by the 1988 fires, Minshall and Brock (chapter 10 in this volume) conclude that fires are essential to the maintenance of biotic diversity and productivity in these aquatic systems. Fire can enhance forage quality and quantity for native ungulates (Van Dyke, Dibenedetto, and Thomas chapter 13 in this volume), and the spatial arrangement of burned and unburned areas can affect ecosystem processes (Knight chapter 8 in this volume). Indeed, it is noteworthy that the Canadian parks are keenly interested in using the Yellowstone fire management policy as a model to develop policies for their parks (Lopoukhine chapter 12 in this volume).

Science has also helped the National Park Service define ungulate management policies for Yellowstone's northern range. Despite recurrent criticism that elk population numbers are too high and that elk are destroying important native vegetation (Craighead chapter 3 in this volume), scientific research suggests that the elk population is consistent with historical patterns and that dynamic interactions with vegetation are to be expected. Over the years, scientists' perceptions of the interactions between herbivores and plant communities on the northern range have changed, and their conclusions have clearly influenced management policies (Coughenour and Singer chapter 15 in this volume). Although certain plants, particularly aspen and willow, may be suppressed by ungulate browsing (Chadde and Kay chapter 16 in this volume), browsing was certainly an important factor in the ecology of these plants during prehistory. Vegetation reconstructions based on pollen deposition suggest that aspen has not been particularly abundant during the past eleven thousand years (Whitlock, Fritz, and Engstrom chapter 19 in this volume). Moreover, elk numbers appear to be stabilizing, albeit at higher densities than previously expected (Merrill and Boyce chapter 17 in this volume). All of these conclusions offer important insights for park managers faced with maintaining ungulate populations and their habitats (Boyce chapter 14 in this volume).

Similarly, scientific studies have provided park and wildlife managers with important information relevant to wolf recovery (National Park Service 1990b; Mech chapter 20 in this volume). These research results should allay residents' concerns that wolves would devastate local fauna (Singer chapter 21 in this volume) or that they would inflict heavy depredation losses on the regional livestock industry (Mech chapter 20 in this volume). Research on recolonizing wolves in northwestern Montana should assist managers in understanding wolf population fluctuations and home range requirements (Ream et al. chapter 22 in this volume). Although the final decision on whether to proceed with reintroduction will evidently be a political one, this scientific information could shift the balance of power in the political arena and contribute to a biologically sound recovery program.

On several occasions, the Forest Service and the Park Service have relied on scientific data to defend controversial policy decisions. In the case of the Bridger-Teton National Forest, well-documented studies on the impact of timber harvesting on elk habitat in the northern end of the forest enabled Forest Service officials to withstand a legal challenge to their decision to curtail logging in that portion of the forest (Keiter chapter 1 in this volume). In another instance, Bridger-Teton officials successfully defended a controversial oil drilling proposal at Sohare Creek just north of Jackson, Wyoming, against legal attack by modifying the exploration proposal in accordance with scientific data and thus minimizing its impact on wildlife (Whipple 1988; Keiter 1989). In the case of Yellowstone National Park, Park Service officials relied on findings from the Interagency Grizzly Bear Committee's cumulative effects model to overcome an Endangered Species Act legal challenge to their decision to retain the controversial Fishing Bridge campground (National Wildlife Federation v. National Park Service 1987). Just as the agencies have used scientific information to insulate these fractious management decisions from challenge, they should also be able to defend current ecological-process management initiatives with reliable scientific data.

Agency officials, however, often appear reluctant to draw on scientific information when formulating management policy. Contingents within the National Park Service still have strong reservations about using science and research in managing the national parks, leaving the role of science ill defined (Chase 1986, 1990). A recent General Accounting Office report concluded that "some parks do not have an approved resource management plan, even though they were required to be completed by the end of 1981, others have not updated their plans, and the plans that have been prepared are not being used in formulating the Park Service's annual budget" (U.S. General Accounting Office 1987). The GAO also noted that the Park Service has not consistently supported resource management initiatives, failing to undertake base-line inventories of important resources and critical research studies (U.S. General Accounting Office 1987). According to another recent review of the Park Service's resource management programs, the agency invests only 2 percent of its operating budget in research (Gordon et al. 1989), despite repeated calls for expanded research programs (Sellers 1989). This is particularly distressing because the Park Service was chastised as early as 1963 about the need to incorporate scientific research into its management decision-making process (Leopold et al. 1963; Craighead chapter 3 in this volume).

In the Forest Service, land managers also are not fully utilizing available scientific information. In the case of the grizzly bear, the cumulative effects model must be constantly revised, updated, and validated as additional scientific information becomes available (Reid and Gehman 1987). Although recent research has demonstrated that security cover is an important habitat component for grizzly bears (McLellan and Shackleton 1989), the negative consequences of clearcutting have yet to be incorporated into the cumulative effects model, and Forest Service officials have authorized timber sales in critical grizzly bear habitat. In another case, Shoshone National Forest officials recently approved a timber salvage sale in the unique Cathedral Cliffs area, partly justifying the sale as a means to reduce pine bark beetle infestations in the fire-damaged timber. In a court proceeding challenging the sale, however, a prominent biologist testified that salvage logging would not reduce the threat of pine bark beetle to trees in adjacent forests. And evidence from hydrological studies suggested that erosion could be severe subsequent to salvage logging in the Cathedral Cliffs area (Marston, Shroder, and Schmitt 1990). The court, nonetheless, deferred to the Forest Service's decision and allowed the logging to proceed, demonstrating the crucial importance of having managers utilize the best available scientific information.

The Park Service could benefit immeasurably from an enhanced emphasis on independent scientific research (Gordon et al. 1989; Chase 1990). The Park Service has not always accorded outside scientists a welcome reception (Craighead 1979; Chase 1986; Gordon et al. 1989; Craighead chapter 3 in this volume). Although academics may sometimes pursue topics of marginal relevance to management, additional scientific data will only improve management decision making. Such data would also provide the Park Service with an independent and objective basis for meeting the persistent complaints of its critics. Moreover, scientific research on ecological processes can provide the Park Service with an objective basis for recommending ecosystem-based resource management policies for public and private lands adjacent to the parks.

Important scientific research remains to be done before Greater Yellowstone officials can knowledgeably establish ecosystem-wide management standards. Some of this research should focus on the complex interactions among plant and animal communities, an important component of any ecosystem. In Yellowstone National Park, for example, ungulate management on the northern range recognizes the existence of a complex plant-herbivore system, but no one has yet attempted to model the system (Boyce chapter 14 in this volume). Additional research on fire ecology and the impact of the 1988 fires is also necessary. This should include the nutritional and structural dynamics of forage plants and the spatial relations between vegetation and ungulate use. In the case of wolf recovery, basic information on moose and mule deer populations in the park is necessary to enable managers to project the likely consequences of recovery on these species (Boyce 1990; Singer chapter 21 in this volume). In addition, still other studies are needed to monitor ecological changes over time (Gordon et al 1989). These should include studies on the impact of global climate change on the Greater Yellowstone Ecosystem, the relation between elk browsing and shrub cover on the northern range (Chadde and Kay chapter 16 in this volume), and changes in the riparian system due to ungulate browsing (Minshall and Brock chapter 10 in this volume)

Another important research priority is the relation between human activities and the natural environment. Studies are needed to determine the effects of intensive development, such as exploratory drilling and timber harvesting, on wildlife, water quality, geothermal systems, and ecosystem function. For example, because clearcutting reduces available cover for grizzly bears (McLellan and Shackleton 1989), research should be undertaken to establish how this relation should be incorporated into the cumulative effects model. Research is also needed to determine elk habitat requirements during migration to evaluate the potential consequences of timber harvesting or exploratory drilling. And with winter recreation burgeoning in the Yellowstone region, research should be conducted to assess the effect these activities may have on wildlife and other resources. Disturbances to wildlife during winter, when the animals are already naturally stressed, may result in increased mortality (Cassirrer and Ables 1990). Yet the physiological consequences of such disturbances and the implications for management have only begun to be explored. Moreover, bison use snowmobile trails in Yellowstone as dispersal corridors, thus gaining access to additional range and apparently increasing their carrying capacity (Meagher 1990). Studies of such effects should be completed before the Park Service commits itself to a long-term winter-use policy.

A Priority for Ecosystem Preservation

Inevitably, Greater Yellowstone's future will be forged in the political arena, which is where federal public lands and natural resource policy has always been crafted. Just as Congress, the courts, and the agencies have jointly participated in defining current management policies in Greater Yellowstone, these same institutions will be involved in shaping the contours of emerging ecosystem-based management policies. As should be evident by now, fundamental value conflicts—rather than disagreement over scientific data or the composition of interagency committees—lie at the root of much of the controversy engulfing the region. Such value conflicts invariably call into question basic social, cultural, economic, political, and philosophical beliefs. At the heart of the conflict is the question of the appropriate relationship between people and the natural environment (Leopold 1949). In our democratic system, such value conflicts are resolved openly through public debate and the political process.

In spite of the looming threat of congressional legislation and the recurrent specter of judicial intervention, the Forest Service and the Park Service still bear the initial responsibility for charting the region's immediate future. They must make the critical threshold value judgments that will determine management priorities and give meaning to the notion of ecosystem management. Significantly, their recent proposals and policies represent the basic rudiments of an ecosystem management policy that gives an evident priority to ensuring the region's ecological integrity and its natural appearance. As primary overarching management goals, the GYCC proposes in its draft "Vision" document to "conserve the sense of natural-ness and maintain ecosystem integrity, encourage opportunities that are biologically and economically sustainable, and improve coordination" (Greater Yellowstone Coordinating Committee 1990). The GYCC envisions "a landscape where natural processes are operating with little hindrance on a grand scale . . . a combination of ecological processes operating with little restraint and humans moderating their activities so they become a reason-able part of, rather than encumbrance upon, those processes" (Greater Yellowstone Coordinating Committee 1990). On a lesser scale, recent elk, fire, and wolf policy initiatives manifest a similar commitment to permit-ting ecological processes to function on park and wilderness lands with minimal human intervention. Although this shift in priorities does not exclude people from the Greater Yellowstone environment, it does suggest a clear value judgment that the Greater Yellowstone public domain is more valuable in its natural state than as a fragmented landscape scarred by industrial development or extensive human settlement.

Congress has effectively endorsed this policy direction. Federal law and policy plainly seek to protect Greater Yellowstone's park and wilderness resources. Congress has designated more than half of the Yellowstone region as park and wilderness areas, thus precluding intensive development and giving priority to nature in what amounts to a de facto Greater Yellow-stone Ecosystem. Congress is still debating wilderness system additions for Idaho and Montana, as well as making wild and scenic river designations that will undoubtedly expand Greater Yellowstone's wildland base. Con-gress's recent amendments to the Geothermal Steam Act (30 U.S.C. §§ 1001-1025) not only recognize that geothermal aquifers do not stop at park boundaries, but they also reflect a national commitment to preserving these unique resource systems from threatening development proposals. The powerful Endangered Species Act, which governs management of the grizzly bear and other imperiled species in Greater Yellowstone, gives species facing extinction priority over human interests and protects their habitats—or ecosystems—from destruction regardless of jurisdictional boundaries. Moreover, the National Forest Management Act (16 U.S.C. §§ 1600-1614) mandates ecologically sound forestry management practices, provides for interdisciplinary forest planning as well as interagency coordi-nation, and elevates environmental considerations to the same level as economic considerations.

This emerging federal commitment to ecosystem-based management mirrors contemporary public views about the relationship between people and the natural environment. Throughout this century, the utilitarian tradition in federal natural resources management policy has gradually been displaced by a commitment to preserving the remnants of our wilderness heritage (Hays 1987; Nash 1989). But where wilderness has traditionally been regarded as a static viewscape within confined boundaries, the developments in Greater Yellowstone reflect a growing public appreciation of wilderness as a dynamic natural environment subject to the forces of nature. Indeed, that Congress has not reversed the natural-burn fire policy suggests public understanding of the role ecological processes play in a wilderness environment, as well as an appreciation of ecological complexities. Similarly, the steady movement toward a congressionally sanctioned Yellowstone wolf recovery program reflects a dramatic reversal in the public perception of predatory wildlife as well as a willingness to accept the consequences of nature. Even locally in Greater Yellowstone, there is clear support for this evolution in priorities between nature and human interests (Bath chapter 23 in this volume).

This transition in federal policy and public values is not without consequence for residents who rely on the Greater Yellowstone public lands for their economic sustenance. Indeed, any meaningful shift in management emphasis toward protection of ecosystem integrity will entail some restructuring in traditional uses on the Greater Yellowstone public lands. On national forests, the Forest Service may impose some additional constraints on intensive development activity on its multiple-use lands, including limitations on timber harvest levels (as has occurred on the Shoshone and Bridger-Teton national forests), more extensive regulation of oil and gas leasing, and perhaps some reduction in livestock grazing on public lands. In the national parks, the Park Service could impose some limitation on human access and visitor accommodations to reduce the impact of visitor facilities and human activity on wildlife and other natural features. And to the extent that these changes occur on the public domain, similar shifts in use and emphasis can be expected on the surrounding private lands.

Probably the most difficult task facing federal officials is to convince still skeptical segments of the local populace that this shift in priorities is compatible with their own long-term interests. Clearly, the agencies must be sensitive to local interests since any effective ecosystem-based management policy in a region as diverse as Greater Yellowstone must rely on local cooperation and assistance to ensure the region's environmental integrity. Economic considerations provide a powerful argument in support of this transition in management priorities. As we have seen, recreation and tourism are a far larger part of the regional economy than the traditional extractive or consumptive industries. In the aftermath of the mill closing in Dubois, Wyoming, the town has not gone into a permanent decline; rather, it has successfully begun to market the area's natural amenities, seasonally attracting retirees who are building vacation homes as well as year-round recreational enthusiasts. But for such an economic transition to occur, the underlying resource base must not be degraded to the point that local communities cannot draw upon the region's natural attractions, as may already have occurred in portions of the Targhee National Forest in Idaho where extensive timber harvesting has severely impacted the appearance and health of the forest. Although this does not mean that traditional consumptive uses should not continue on the region's national forests, it does suggest that these uses must be harmonized with the natural appearance and integrity of the region.

But even the compelling logic of science and economics will not convince everyone that natural processes should be given priority over other human interests throughout the Greater Yellowstone region. It would be a mistake, therefore, to conclude that the transition to ecosystem-based management is proceeding smoothly, or even that the agencies can single-handedly accomplish such a shift in priorities. In fact, the transition has thus far been a piecemeal, halting process. Incremental progress has been made in establishing institutional structures to break down boundary-based management traditions, other progress has been made in defining management policies on the basis of contemporary scientific criteria. Nevertheless, the fire policy is still on hold, federal and state officials have not reached any agreement on wildlife-livestock priorities outside the national parks, and wolf reintroduction is still pending. The ongoing dispute over the appropriateness of oil and gas exploration on national forest lands is not resolved, and timber harvest levels are still quite high on several of the forests. This state of affairs suggests that federal officials have not yet convinced resistant local interests that a primary commitment to maintaining ecological processes on a meaningful scale in Greater Yellowstone can accommodate their concerns.

Nonetheless, Yellowstone's international prominence as the world's first national park and as the preeminent example of this nation's wilderness legacy virtually ensures that evolving national values will define the region's future. The important developments now occurring within the Greater Yellowstone land management agencies, which mirror contemporary human perceptions of nature's role on the Yellowstone public domain, will plainly influence how these value judgments are made. Most important, their policy initiatives effectively legitimize Greater Yellowstone as an ecological entity and thus provide Congress with the basis for defining future priorities at a regional level. Should the agencies, therefore, fail in their ecosystem management initiatives, they will have mapped the trail for Congress to follow in devising governing priorities for the Greater Yellowstone public domain. Whether it is by bold administrative initiatives or by congressional intervention, Greater Yellowstone appears destined to be governed by an ecosystem management policy that gives priority to the region's natural values and recognizes the ecological connections necessary to sustain these values.

KEEPING FAITH WITH NATURE

The transition to ecosystem-based management that is occurring in Greater Yellowstone reflects a profound change in public land management policy. This transition is part of a fundamental realignment of the relationship between people and nature at all levels, but particularly on the nation's public domain. Recognizing the international significance of Greater Yellowstone's natural treasures, the Park Service and the Forest Service are now developing ecosystem management principles that will redefine priorities on their respective lands and also have broad ramifications beyond the federal estate. Their emerging commitment to preserving ecological processes and the dynamic systems that constitute Greater Yellowstone's complex natural environment portends additional restraint on the level and intensity of human use. Rather than operating on the principle of controlling nature for human utilitarian interests, this transition to ecosystem management manifests a willingness to accept nature largely on its own terms and to control incompatible human uses.

With Yellowstone's high visibility and national prominence, these developments will undoubtedly influence public land management policies elsewhere. Already calls for ecosystem-based management are being heard in other locations, notably in the Glacier region of northwestern Montana, throughout the Pacific Northwest to preserve ancient forest ecosystems, and on the Colorado Plateau in the Southwest. In each of these settings, conflict is intense between preservationists determined to minimize human impact on the natural environment and the extractive industries eager to maintain their traditional access rights to public resources. With intermixed park, wilderness, and multiple-use public lands, the ecosystem-based concept of management is as viable in these locations as in Greater Yellowstone. Even though these areas may lack the international stature of a

Yellowstone, the irresistible logic of the ecosystem-based management principle cannot escape the attention of natural resource managers responsible for the welfare of our nation's treasures. Clearly, then, the Greater Yellowstone controversies cannot—and should not—be viewed in isolation.

Significantly, the transition to ecosystem-based management in Greater Yellowstone seems to have acquired a momentum of its own. Though somewhat timidly, park and forest officials are utilizing their discretionary authority under existing law to promote ecosystem-based management policies for the Greater Yellowstone public domain. The interagency coordination process as well as the other interagency management committees already in place have effectively validated the concept of a Greater Yellowstone Ecosystem and thus legitimized the principle of regional management. Science, quite obviously, is assuming an increasingly important role in the formulation of resource management policy, both in the Forest Service and in the Park Service. And public sentiment, which has long supported wilderness preservation for aesthetic reasons, evidently is now prepared to accept the consequences of ecological processes as part of the wilderness environment, thus providing important political support for the transition to ecosystem-based management. Though the agencies still face intense local opposition as well as sometimes strident scientific criticism, the fundamental policy direction in Greater Yellowstone is plainly toward public land management on an ecosystem scale.

Yellowstone is the birthplace of the world's first real experiment with wilderness preservation. It is appropriate, therefore, that Greater Yellowstone is now serving as a laboratory for testing an expanded, enlightened vision of wilderness policy—one that is based on preserving ecological processes and the resource systems that sustain them. How elk, fire, and wolves fare in Greater Yellowstone will undoubtedly influence the immediate direction that natural resource management policy takes on much of the western public domain and perhaps elsewhere in the world. It also will indicate just how much faith we are willing to place in nature and the sometimes unpredictable ecological processes that have shaped the environment our ancestors found worth preserving for future generations.

POSTSCRIPT—1993

Much has happened in Greater Yellowstone since 1991. The issues highlighted here remain unresolved, though it has become clear that coordinated, ecosystem-based policies must be part of the solution. Recent developments involving bison management, wolf recovery, fire policy, multiple-use activities, and federal coordination efforts highlighted the region's ecological connections and the corresponding need for ecosystem management.

Bison management remains mired in controversy. The bison population continues to expand and to extend its winter range beyond Yellowstone National Park boundaries. In March 1991 Montana legislature bowed to national opposition and outlawed bison hunting outside the park. State officials hoped to shift the problem of bison control to the Park Service. Meanwhile, seven lawsuits have challenged bison management policies. An animal rights organization twice unsuccessfully challenged Yellowstone's interim management policies, which allow bison leaving the park to be shot to protect cattle from the threat of brucellosis. In the absence of adequate environmental analysis, however, Grand Teton National Park and National Elk Refuge officials have been prohibited from implementing a bison reduction policy. Two proposals that would have taken bison to Texas for brucellosis studies at experimental facilities have also been enjoined for lack of adequate environmental analysis. In two lawsuits, a Wyoming rancher unsuccessfully sued federal and state agencies, claiming that his cattle were contaminated with brucellosis by bison or elk. The Wyoming Governor's Task Force on Brucellosis has since called for a regionwide approach to the problem. Meanwhile, Yellowstone and Grand Teton park service officials are drafting separate bison management plans.

Wolf recovery in the Greater Yellowstone Ecosystem is moving closer to reality. In July 1993 the U.S. Fish and Wildlife Service issued a draft environmental impact statement supporting the reintroduction of approximately thirty wolves into Yellowstone during 1994. The wolves would enjoy full protection inside the park but could be managed by federal and state officials outside the park. Several recent reliable wolf sightings in the region, however, have led some conservationists to suggest that the proposal is inappropriate. They argue that under the Endangered Species Act any wolves released into the park are entitled to full legal protection wherever they are found. Meanwhile, long-time wolf opponents, asserting that the sightings are proof that wolves are recolonizing the area, oppose any reintroduction. After a public comment period, federal officials will decide whether wolves should be reintroduced. Given the controversy, however, litigation can be expected whatever the recommendation.

A revised fire management plan for Yellowstone National Park allows natural fires to burn in the park backcountry. But the policy does specify numerous considerations—drought indexes, weather forecasts, and determinations of threat to human and animal populations—that must be reviewed and monitored before a fire will be allowed to burn. The plan also supports the use of management-ignited prescribed fires. Similarly, the Forest Service will allow natural fires to burn in Greater Yellowstone wilderness areas under strict monitoring.

Controversy swirls around multiple-use activity levels in the surrounding national forests. The Shoshone National Forest is revising its oil and gas leasing policies and reportedly will allow leasing on critical grizzly bear lands despite environmental opposition. But because of intense local opposition to an exploratory drilling proposal at Brooks Lake, a popular Wyoming recreation area, Shoshone officials have reversed an earlier recommendation to open the area for exploration. Timber harvest levels have declined in the Targhee and Gallatin national forests. One large mill that relied primarily on timber from the Targhee forest recently closed, citing lack of available timber. Yet environmental organizations still challenge individual timber sales throughout the Yellowstone region, objecting to the effects of clearcutting and road construction on wildlife and water quality. A lawsuit alleges that intensive harvesting in the Targhee National Forest has diminished grizzly bear habitat, violating the Endangered Species Act. Attention recently shifted to the proposed Crown Butte gold mine, to be located on Gallatin National Forest lands. Under the General Mining Law of 1872, the company may mine the area, subject to federal and state compliance. Environmentalists assert that a worse location for a mine—at the headwaters of three major drainages—could not be imagined and note a legacy of toxic runoff from previous mining activity. Cooke City, Montana, residents are split, while Wyoming officials are concerned about the potential social impacts of an influx of workers. Although an environmental impact statement is being prepared, litigation is almost certain. In short, there is no consensus on the appropriate level of developmental activity on Greater Yellowstone national forest lands.

The GYCC's much anticipated Vision Document process has concluded disappointingly. After supporting the concept of ecosystem management in its draft document, the GYCC released a dramatically revised final document. Renamed "A Framework for Management," it reads more like a bureaucratic memorandum than a visionary natural resource policy. Evidently succumbing to local political pressures, the GYCC reinforces the separate missions of the Park Service and the Forest Service and contemplates little change in management policies. Although the document articulates the noteworthy goal of maintaining functional ecosystems, it merely acknowledges a need for a better understanding of ecological processes that cross administrative boundaries. Gone is any language about ecosystem management or preserving a sense of naturalness. No new institutional structures or procedures are in place to facilitate interagency coordination. And the agencies do not seem to be relying on the document in such matters as bison management or oil and gas leasing. It remains to be seen whether the GYCC document will influence forest plan revisions or national park planning.

In the wake of this failure, environmental organizations are making the case for fundamental change in federal land and resource management policies. The Greater Yellowstone Coalition, an umbrella organization of national and local environmental groups, has released "A Profile of the Greater Yellowstone Region," which scientifically establishes the region's ecological connections and fragility. The coalition is now preparing a "Blueprint for Greater Yellowstone's Future," which will integrate its ecological findings with concepts of sustainable development. The Wilderness Society has released a comprehensive regional economic study that documents growing dependence on tourism, recreation, and service industries and the decline of extractive and agricultural industries. Several area communities have acknowledged these realities and are exploring alternative development options. In other words, the concept of Greater Yellowstone as an integrated ecological and economic entity has taken hold.

Beyond Greater Yellowstone, the concept of ecosystem management has also taken root. The Forest Service, Bureau of Land Management, National Park Service, and U.S. Fish and Wildlife Service have all endorsed the concept. Agency officials are defining ecosystem management in concrete terms and developing appropriate policies. The lessons of Greater Yellowstone will influence this effort. Likewise, the emerging federal commitment to ecosystem management will influence the resolution of bison, wolf, fire, and multiple-use policies in Greater Yellowstone. Now more than ever Greater Yellowstone's future is moving inexorably toward sustaining natural processes at the ecosystem level.

REFERENCES

Agee, J. K., and D. R. Johnson, eds. 1988. Ecosystem management for parks and wilderness. Univ. of Washington Press, Seattle.

Associated Press. 1989. Jackson chamber fights oil, gas leasing proposal. Casper Star Tribune, Dec. 31, 1989, at B1.

Associated Press. 1990. Sullivan supports Brooks Lake drilling. Casper Star Tribune, Dec. 16, 1990, at B1.

Boyce, M. S. 1989. The Jackson elk herd: Intensive wildlife management in North America. Cambridge Univ. Press, Cambridge.

———. 1990. Wolf recovery for Yellowstone National Park: A simulation model. Pages 3.5–3.58 in National Park Service, ed. Wolves for Yellowstone: A report to the United States Congress, vol. 2. Yellowstone National Park, Mammoth, Wyo.

Cassirrer, E. F., and E. D. Ables. 1990. Effects of disturbance by cross-country skiers on elk in northern Yellowstone National Park. Final report to Yellowstone National Park, Mammoth, Wyo.

Chase, A. 1986. Playing God in Yellowstone: The destruction of America's first national park. Atlantic Monthly Press, Boston.

———. 1990. What Washington doesn't know about the national park system. Pages 139–150 in J. Baden and D. Leal, eds. The Yellowstone primer: Land and resource management in the Greater Yellowstone Ecosystem. Pacific Resources Institute for Public Policy, San Francisco.

Clark, T., and A. Harvey. 1988. Management of the Greater Yellowstone Ecosystem: An annotated bibliography. Northern Rockies Conservation Cooperative, Jackson, Wyo.

Clark, T., and D. Zaunbrecher. 1987. The Greater Yellowstone Ecosystem: The ecosystem concept in natural resource policy and management. Renewable Resources J. (Summer):8–16.

Clary, D. 1986. Timber and the Forest Service. Univ. Press of Kansas, Lawrence.

Cole, G. F. 1969. The elk of Grand Teton and southern Yellowstone national parks. Nat'l Park Serv. Res. Rep. GRTE-N-1. GPO, Washington, D.C.

Congressional Research Service. 1986. Greater Yellowstone Ecosystem: An analysis of data submitted by federal and state agencies. 99th Cong., 2d Sess. Comm. Print 6.

Conner v. Burford, 848 F.2d 1441 (9th Cir. 1988), cert. denied sub nom. Sun Exploration & Prod. Co. v. Lujan, 109 S. Ct. 1121 (1989).

Craighead, F. C., Jr. 1979. The track of the grizzly. Sierra Club Books, San Francisco.

Despain, D., D. Houston, M. Meagher, and P. Schullery. 1986. Wildlife in transition: Man and nature on Yellowstone's northern range. Roberts Rinehart, Boulder, Colo.

Gilbert, D. L. 1975. Natural resources and public relations. 2d ed. Wildlife Society, Washington, D.C.

Gordon, J. C., et al. 1989. National parks: From vignettes to a global view. National Parks and Conservation Association, Washington, D.C.

Greater Yellowstone Coordinating Committee. 1987. The Greater Yellowstone Area: An aggregation of national park and national forest management plans. U.S. National Park Service and U.S. Forest Service, Washington, D.C.

———. 1990. Vision for the future: A framework for coordination in the Greater

Yellowstone Area. Draft. U.S. National Park Service and U.S. Forest Service, Billings, Mont.

Harris, L. 1984. The fragmented forest: Island biogeography theory and the preservation of biological diversity. Univ. of Chicago Press, Chicago.

Hays, S. 1987. Beauty, health, and permanence: Environmental politics in the United States, 1955–1985. Cambridge Univ. Press, New York.

Houston, D. B. 1982. The northern Yellowstone elk: Ecology and management. Macmillan, New York.

Huff, D. E. 1989. Introduction to the role and effect of fire in Greater Yellowstone. George Wright Forum 6(3):12–16.

Intermountain Forest Industries Ass'n v. Lyng, 683 F. Supp. 1330 (D. Wyo. 1988).

Keiter, R. 1985. On protecting the national parks from the external threats dilemma. Land & Water L. Rev. 20:355–420.

———. 1989. Taking account of the ecosystem on the public domain: Law and ecology in the Greater Yellowstone region. U. Colo. L. Rev. 60:923–1007.

———. 1990. NEPA and the emerging concept of ecosystem management on the public lands. Land & Water L. Rev. 25:43–60.

Keiter, R., and P. Holscher. 1990. Wolf recovery under the endangered species act: A study in contemporary federalism. Pub. Lands L. Rev. 11:19–51.

Kellert, S. R. 1986. Social and perceptual factors in the preservation of animal species. Pages 50–73 in B. G. Norton, ed. The preservation of species: The value of biological diversity. Princeton Univ. Press, Princeton, N.J.

Knight, R. R., B. M. Blanchard, and L. L. Eberhardt. 1988. Mortality patterns and population sinks for Yellowstone grizzly bears, 1973–1985. Wildl. Soc. Bull. 16:121–125.

Kwong, J. 1990. A private property rights approach to land use conflicts. Pages 81–93 in J. Baden and D. Leal, eds. The Yellowstone primer: Land and resource management in the Greater Yellowstone Ecosystem. Pacific Resources Institute for Public Policy, San Francisco.

Leal, D. 1990. Saving an ecosystem: From buffer zone to private initiatives. Pages 25–45 in J. Baden and D. Leal, eds. The Yellowstone primer: Land and resource management in the Greater Yellowstone Ecosystem. Pacific Resources Institute for Public Policy, San Francisco.

Leal, D., G. Black, and J. Baden. 1990. Oil and gas development. Pages 117–136 in J. Baden and D. Leal, eds. The Yellowstone primer: Land and resource management in the Greater Yellowstone Ecosystem. Pacific Resources Institute for Public Policy, San Francisco.

Legg, C. 1990. Grizzlies seem on comeback in GYE. Casper Star Tribune, Feb. 19, 1990, at B1.

Leopold, A. 1949. A Sand County almanac. Oxford Univ. Press, New York.

Leopold, A. S., S. A. Cain, C. M. Cottam, I. N. Gabrielson, T. L. Kimball. 1963. Wildlife management in the national parks. Trans. N. Am. Wildl. Nat. Resources Conf. 28:29–44.

Lopez, B. H. 1978. Of wolves and men. Charles Scribner's Sons, New York.

McLellan, B. N., and D. M. Shackleton. 1989. Immediate reactions of grizzly bears to human activities. Wildl. Soc. Bull. 17:269–274.

McNamee, T. 1984. The grizzly bear. Alfred A. Knopf, New York.

McNaught, D. A. 1987. Wolves in Yellowstone? Park visitors respond. Wildl. Soc. Bull. 15:518–521.

Marston, R. A., J. F. Shroder, and J. G. Schmitt. 1990. Changes in geomorphic processes in the Snake River following impoundment of Jackson Lake and potential changes due to 1988 fires in the watershed. Univ. Wyo.–Nat'l Park Serv. Res. Center Ann. Rep. 13:99–105.

Meagher, M. 1990. Changes in bison ecological carrying capacity because of human activities. Paper presented at meeting of the George Wright Society, El Paso, Tex., Nov. 14, 1990.

Melnykovych, A. 1989. Wolf bashers slash Yellowstone education program. Pronghorn 8:4.

Montana Department of Health and Environmental Sciences. 1989. Church Universal and Triumphant, Final Environmental Impact Statement. State of Montana Printing Office, Helena.

Mountain States Legal Found. v. Andrus, 499 F. Supp. 383 (D. Wyo. 1980).

Murie, M., and O. Murie. 1966. Wapiti wilderness. Charles Scribner's Sons, New York.

Nash, R. 1989. The rights of nature: A history of environmental ethics. Univ. of Wisconsin Press, Madison.

National Park Service. 1990a. Environmental assessment of National Park Service involvement in control of Yellowstone bison: A finding of significant impact. Dec. 3, 1990. GPO, Washington, D.C.

———. 1990b. Wolves for Yellowstone? A report to the United States Congress. U.S. Department of the Interior, Yellowstone National Park, and U.S. Fish and Wildlife Service, Mammoth, Wyo.

National Wildlife Federation v. National Park Service, 669 F. Supp. 384 (D. Wyo. 1987).

Newmark, W. 1985. Legal and biotic boundaries of western North American national parks: A problem of congruence. Biol. Cons. 33:197–208.

O'Gara, G. 1990. Conference sees problems with delisting grizzlies. Casper Star Tribune, June 11, 1990, at A1.

Park County Resource Council v. U.S. Dep't of Agric., 817 F.2d 609 (10th Cir. 1987).

President's Commission on Americans Outdoors. 1987. Americans outdoors: The legacy, the challenge. Island Press, Washington, D.C.

Reese, R. 1984. Greater Yellowstone: The national park and adjacent wildlands. Montana Magazine, Helena.

Reid, M., and S. Gehman. 1987. A common sense approach to grizzly bear habitat evaluation. Forest Watch 8:9–15.

Reynolds, G. 1987. Promise or threat? A study of "Greater Yellowstone Eco-system" management. WeCare, Riverton, Wyo.

Romme, W. H., and D. H. Knight. 1982. Landscape diversity: The concept applied to Yellowstone Park. BioScience 32:664–670.

Runte, A. 1987. National parks: The American experience. 2d ed. Univ. of Nebraska Press, Lincoln.

Sax, J. 1976. Helpless giants: National parks and the regulation of private lands. Mich. L. Rev. 75:239–274.

Sax, J., and R. B. Keiter. 1987. Glacier National Park and its neighbors: A study of federal interagency relations. Ecology L. Q. 14:207–263.

Schneebeck, R. 1986. State participation in federal policy making for the Yellow-stone ecosystem: A meaningful solution of business as usual? Land & Water L. Rev. 21:397–416.

Schullery, P. 1989. The fires and fire policy. BioScience 39:686–694.

Sellers, R. W. 1989. The national parks: Not just another pretty facade. Washington Post, Apr. 9, 1989.

Sierra Club. 1986. Yellowstone under siege: Oil and gas leasing in the Greater Yellowstone region. Sierra Club, Washington, D.C.

Sierra Club v. Peterson, 717 F.2d 1409 (D.C. Cir. 1983).

Simon, D. 1988. Our common lands: Defending the national parks. Island Press, Washington, D.C.

Singer, F. J., W. Schreier, J. Oppenheim, and E. O. Garton. 1989. Drought, fires, and large mammals. BioScience 39:716–722.

Stewart, R. 1975. The reformation of American administrative law. Harv. L. Rev. 88:1667–1814.

Sweeney, J. M., ed. 1990. Management of dynamic ecosystems. North Central Section, Wildlife Society, West Lafayette, Ind.

Thorne, E. T., J. K. Morton, and W. C. Ray. 1979. Brucellosis, its effect and impact on elk in western Wyoming. Pages 212–220 in M. S. Boyce and L. D. Hayden-Wing, eds. North American elk: Ecology, behavior and management. Univ. of Wyoming, Laramie.

U.S. Fish and Wildlife Service. 1982. Grizzly bear recovery plan. U.S. Depart-ment of the Interior, Washington, D.C.

———. 1987. Northern Rocky Mountain wolf recovery plan. U.S. Department of the Interior and Northern Rocky Mountain Wolf Recovery Team, Denver, Colo.

U.S. Forest Service. 1987. Ski Yellowstone biological assessment. Appendix 1. U.S. Forest Service, Gallatin National Forest, Bozeman, Mont.

———. 1989a. Final Bridger-Teton land and resource management plan. U.S. Department of Agriculture, Washington, D.C.

———. 1989b. Final Bridger-Teton land and resource management plan environ-mental impact statement. U.S. Department of Agriculture, Washington, D.C.

U.S. General Accounting Office. 1987. Limited progress made in documenting and mitigating threats to the parks. GAO Rep. RCED-87-36. GPO, Washington, D.C.

Weaver, J. L. 1978. The wolves of Yellowstone. Nat'l Park Serv. Nat. Resources Rep. 14.

Whipple, D. 1988. Amoco to begin work on Sohare Creek well. Casper Star Tribune, Oct. 21, 1988, at A1.

Wilderness Society. 1987. Management directions for the national forests of the Greater Yellowstone Ecosystem. Bozeman, Mont.

Wilkinson, C., and M. Anderson. 1985. Land and resource planning in the national forests. Or. L. Rev. 64:1–173.

Zumbo, J. 1987. Should we cry wolf? Outdoor Life (December):50–53.

Contributors

Alistair J. Bath, Department of Geography, Memorial University, St. John's, Newfoundland

Mark S. Boyce, Department of Zoology and Physiology, University of Wyoming, Laramie

Diane K. Boyd, School of Forestry, University of Montana, Missoula

James T. Brock, Department of Biological Sciences, Idaho State University, Pocatello

James K. Brown, Intermountain Fire Sciences Laboratory, U.S. Forest Service, Missoula, Montana

Karen J. Budd, Dray, Madison, and Thomson, Cheyenne, Wyoming

Steve W. Chadde, Arlee, Montana

Michael B. Coughenour, Natural Resources Ecology Lab, College of Forestry and Natural Resources, Colorado State University, Fort Collins

John J. Craighead, Craighead Wildlife–Wildlands Institute, Missoula, Montana

Jeffrey P. Dibenedetto, Beartooth Ranger District, U.S. Forest Service, Red Lodge, Montana

Daniel R. Engstrom, Limnological Research Center, University of Minnesota, Minneapolis

Michael W. Fairchild, School of Forestry, University of Montana, Missoula

Sherilyn C. Fritz, Limnological Research Center, University of Minnesota, Minneapolis

Robert Hillman, Idaho Bureau of Animal Health, Boise

Charles E. Kay, Department of Fisheries and Wildlife, Utah State University, Logan

Robert B. Keiter, College of Law, University of Wyoming, Laramie

Dennis H. Knight, Botany Department, University of Wyoming, Laramie

William J. Lockhart, College of Law, University of Utah, Salt Lake City

Nikita Lopoukhine, Natural Resources Branch, Canadian Parks Service, Ottawa, Ontario

Mary Meagher, Research Biologist, Yellowstone National Park, Mammoth, Wyoming

L. David Mech, Patuxent Wildlife Research Center, U.S. Fish and Wildlife Service, Laurel, Maryland

Evelyn H. Merrill, Department of Zoology and Physiology, University of Wyoming, Laramie

G. Wayne Minshall, Department of Biology, Idaho State University, Pocatello

Randal O'Toole, Cascade Holistic Economic Consultants, Oak Grove, Oregon

Duncan T. Patten, Center for Environmental Studies, Arizona State University, Tempe

Daniel H. Pletscher, School of Forestry, University of Montana, Missoula

Robert R. Ream, School of Forestry, University of Montana, Missoula

Joseph L. Sax, University of California at Berkeley School of Law, Berkeley

Paul Schullery, Research Division, Yellowstone National Park, Mammoth, Wyoming

Francis J. Singer, Research Division, Yellowstone National Park, Mammoth, Wyoming

Steven C. Thomas, Covenant College, Lookout Mountain, Georgia

E. Tom Thorne, Wyoming Game and Fish Department, Research Laboratory, University of Wyoming, Laramie

Fred G. Van Dyke, Montana Department of Fish, Wildlife, and Parks, Red Lodge

John D. Varley, Research Division, Yellowstone National Park, Mammoth, Wyoming

Cathy Whitlock, Department of Geography, University of Oregon, Eugene

Index